Lecture Notes in Computer Science 8650

Commenced Publication in 1973
Founding and Former Series Editors:
Gerhard Goos, Juris Hartmanis, and Jan van Leeuwen

Andrea Kő   Enrico Francesconi (Eds.)

Electronic Government and the Information Systems Perspective

Third International Conference, EGOVIS 2014
Munich, Germany, September 1-3, 2014
Proceedings

 Springer

Volume Editors

Andrea Kő
Corvinus University of Budapest
Fővám tér 13-15
1093 Budapest, Hungary
E-mail: ko@informatika.uni-corvinus.hu

Enrico Francesconi
ITTIG - CNR
Institute of Legal Information Theory and Techniques
Italian National Research Council
Via de' Barucci 20
50127 Florence, Italy
E-mail: francesconi@ittig.cnr.it

ISSN 0302-9743   e-ISSN 1611-3349
ISBN 978-3-319-10177-4   e-ISBN 978-3-319-10178-1
DOI 10.1007/978-3-319-10178-1
Springer Cham Heidelberg New York Dordrecht London

Library of Congress Control Number: 2014945814

LNCS Sublibrary: SL 3 – Information Systems and Application,
incl. Internet/Web and HCI

Typesetting: Camera-ready by author, data conversion by Scientific Publishing Services, Chennai, India

Printed on acid-free paper

Springer is part of Springer Science+Business Media (www.springer.com)

Preface

The third International Conference on Electronic Government and the Information Systems Perspective, EGOVIS 2014, took place in Munich, Germany during September 1–3, 2014. The conference belongs to the 25th DEXA Conference Series.

The international conference cycle EGOVIS focuses on information systems aspects of e-government. Information systems are a core enabler for electronic government/governance in all its dimensions: e-administration, e-democracy, e-participation, and e-voting. EGOVIS brought together experts from academia, public administrations, and industry to discuss e-government and e-democracy from different perspectives and disciplines, i.e. technology, policy and/or governance, and public administration.

The Program Committee accepted 23 papers from recent research fields like open government, open and linked data, government cloud, identity management and e-government architectures, intelligent systems, and semantic technologies applications. Beyond theoretical contributions, papers covered e-government experiences from all over the world; cases were presented from Europe and Asia.

This proceeding is organized into 9 sections, one for invited contributions, 9 for paper sessions.

We are honoured that EGOVIS 2014 keynote speech was given by Prof. Ronald Traunmüller: he is one of the pioneers in e-government studies and has contributed for years to identify limits and opportunities in the field. The new trends of open data and open government have recently fostered the development of applications for electronic government to improve participation and democracy. Prof. Traunmüller's speech discussed the complementary characteristics of such trends, as well as the potential conflicts between open government and e-government for actually promoting transparency in the public administration.

Chairs of the Program Committee wish to thank all the reviewers for their valuable work, the reviews raised several research questions to discuss in the conference. We would like to thank Gabriela Wagner for the administrative support and stimulating us in proper scheduling.

We wish pleasant and beneficial learning experiences for the readers and we hope that the discussion will continue after the conference between the researchers and contribute to building a global community in the field of e-government.

September 2014

Enrico Francesconi
Andrea Kő

Organization

General Chair

Roland Traunmüller   University of Linz, Austria

Program Committee Co-chairs

Enrico Francesconi   Italian National Research Council, Italy
Andrea Kő   Corvinus University Budapest

Honorary Chairpersons

Wichian Chutimaskul   King Mongkut's University of Technology, Thailand
Fernando Galindo   University Zaragoza, Spain

Program Committee

Luis Álvarez Sabucedo	Universidade de Vigo, Spain
Victor Bekkers	Erasmus University Rotterdam, The Netherlands
Jaro Berce	University of Ljubljana, Slovenia
Francesco Buccafurri	Università degli Studi Mediterranea di Reggio Calabria, Italy
Alejandra Cechich	Universidad Nacional del Comahue, Argentina
Wojciech Cellary	Poznan University of Economics, Poland
Wichian Chutimaskul	King Mongkut's University of Technology, Thailand
Flavio Corradini	University of Camerino, Italy
Peter Cruickshank	Edinburgh Napier University, UK
Vytautas Cyras	Vilnius University, Lithuania
Joan Francesc Fondevila Gascón	Universitat Abat Oliba CEU (UAO), Spain
Ivan Futo	National Tax and Customs Administration, Hungary
András Gábor	Corvinus University of Budapest, Hungary
Fernando Galindo	University of Zaragoza, Spain
Johann Gamper	Free University of Bozen, Italy
Matjaz Gams	Jozef Stefan Institute, Slovenia
Francisco Javier García Marco	University of Zaragoza, Spain
Julia Glidden	21consultancy.com, UK

Stefanos Gritzalis	University of the Aegean, Greece
Henning Sten Hansen	Aalborg University, Denmark
Patrik Hitzelberger	Centre de Recherche Public - Gabriel Lippmann, Luxembourg
Zahir Irani	Brunel University, UK
Christos Kalloniatis	University of the Aegean, Greece
Nikos Karacapilidis	University of Patras, Greece
Evangelia Kavakli	University of the Aegean, Greece
Bozidar Klicek	University of Zagreb, Faculty of Organization and Informatics Varazdin, Croatia
Ah Lian Kor	Leeds Metropolitan University, UK
Jaroslav Kral	Charles University of Prague, Czech Republic
Irene Krebs	Brandenburg University of Technology in Cottbus, Germany
Hun-yeong Kwon	Kwangwoon University, South Korea
Christine Leitner	Centre for Economics and Public Administration Ltd. (CEPA), UK
Herbert Leitold	E-Government Innovation Center EGIZ, Austria
Ralf Lindner	ISI Fraunhofer, Germany
Marian Mach	Technical University of Koice, Slovakia
Peter Mambrey	University of Duisburg-Essen, Germany
Rony Medaglia	Copenhagen Business School, Denmark
Francesco Molinari	Italy
Pedro Rafael Muro-Medrano	University of Zaragoza, Spain
Robert Müller-Török	University of Applied Sciences Ludwigsburg, Germany
Sinisa Neskovic	University of Belgrade, Serbia and Montenegro
Mara Nikolaidou	Harokopio University of Athens, Greece
Javier Nogueras	University of Zaragoza, Spain
Monica Palmirani	University of Bologna, Italy
Aljosa Pasic	Atos, Spain
Andrea Polini	ISTI-CNR, Italy
Reinhard Posch	Technical University Graz, Austria
Aires J. Rover	Federal University of Santa Catarina, Brazil
Christian Rupp	Federal Chancellery of Austria/Federal Platform Digital Austria, Austria
Erich Schweighofer	University of Vienna, Austria
Ella Taylor-Smith	Edinburgh Napier University, UK
Daniela Tiscornia	ITTIG Institute for Theory and Techniques for Legal Information, Italy
A Min Tjoa	Vienna University of Technology, Austria
Roland Traunmüller	University Linz, Austria

Julian Valero   iDertec - Innovation, Law & Technology
                                 Research Group. University of Murcia, Spain
Tom M. van Engers   University of Amsterdam, The Netherlands
Costas Vassilakis   University of Peloponnese, Greece
Jorge Viera da Silva   Mobility Ticketing & Applications, Belgium
Gianluigi Viscusi   EPFL - CDM -CSI, Switzerland
Melanie Volkamer   Technical University Darmstadt, Germany
Roland Wagner   University Linz, Austria
Christopher C. Wills   Caris Research Ltd., UK
Frank Wilson   Interaction Design, UK
Radboud Winkels   University of Amsterdam, The Netherlands
Robert Woitsch   BOC Asset Management, Austria
Chien-Chih Yu   National ChengChi University, China

External Reviewers

Miguel Ángel Latre Abadía   Universidad de Zaragoza, Spain
Javier Lacasta Miguel   Universidad de Zaragoza, Spain
Prokopis Drogkaris   University of the Aegean, Greece
Stephan Neumann   Technical University Darmstadt, Germany
Oksana Kulyk   Technical University Darmstadt, Germany
Jurlind Budurushi   Technical University Darmstadt, Germany
Stavros Simou   University of the Aegean, Greece
Evangelos Goggolidis   University of the Aegean, Greece
Agustina Buccella   GIISCo, Universidad Nacional del Comahue,
                                 Argentina
Elmar Kiesling   Vienna University of Technology, Austria

Table of Contents

Semantic Technologies in E-Government

E-Government Cases

Open Government Data and G-Cloud

Privacy and Security in E-Government

Open Government Data and G-Cloud

Social Signature: Signing by Tweeting

Francesco Buccafurri, Lidia Fotia, and Gianluca Lax

DIIES, Università Mediterranea di Reggio Calabria
Via Graziella, Località Feo di Vito
89122 Reggio Calabria, Italy
{bucca,lidia.fotia,lax}@unirc.it

Abstract. In many application contexts, qualified electronic signature appears difficult to be adopted both for the cost of smart cards and qualified certificates and for the complexity of the signing, verification, registration and certificate management. However, the European legislation allows us to use electronic signatures when application scope of the signature is limited. As a consequence, designing new signature protocols that relax the heaviest features of qualified electronic signature in favor of usability and cheapness is a timely and important issue. In this paper, we propose a new lightweight e-signature protocol with a good level of security, not using public key cryptography and dedicated devices. The protocol is conceived for closed domains of users, such as the case of document exchanges between citizens and municipal public offices or private companies and employees. According to the protocol, signature functions are spread out over the popular social network Twitter, without requiring changes of its features, so that the adoption of our solution appears both realistic and effective.

1 Introduction

Qualified electronic signature is certainly the basic tool of any digitalization process, where exchanging documents with full legal validity has a significant role. This is, for example, the case of dematerialization process occurring in the Public Sector, where paper documents should disappear and long-term traditional archives should be digitalized by ensuring authenticity and integrity of documents by means of qualified electronic signature. In general, we expect that in e-government applications, and also in transactions between citizens and companies, the use of qualified electronic signature will always be increasing in the next future. However, there are some aspects that limit the diffusion of electronic signatures. These aspects are of two types: related to the cost and related to the usability of qualified electronic signature. Indeed, the cost of smart cards is certainly not negligible. Moreover, the invasiveness of the operations related to signing, verification, registration and certificate management is relevant. On the other hand, when we limit the application scope to specific cases in which the European legislation allows us to use electronic signatures, designing new signature protocols that relax the heaviest features of qualified electronic signature in favor of usability and cheapness, is a timely and important issue. According

A. Kő and E. Francesconi (Eds.): EGOVIS 2014, LNCS 8650, pp. 1–14, 2014.

to the Italian legislation [3,5], this is the case, for example, of closed domains, where electronic signatures are applied to document exchange between municipal public offices and registered citizens, university and its students, or private company and employees. In these cases, *advanced electronic signature* can be adopted. Advanced electronic signature is technology-neutral, so that it does not refer to any technology. As required by the EU legislation [1], technological constraints of qualified electronic signature can be relaxed, included the presence of qualified certificate, provided that the solution satisfies the following properties: (1) It allows the identification of the signer and the unique connection of her/him to the signed document, (2) such a connection is created using means that the signatory can maintain under her/his exclusive control, and (3) it allows us to detect if the data has been modified after the advanced electronic signature is applied.

In this paper, we propose a new lightweight e-signature protocol with a good level of security, not using public key cryptography and dedicated devices. The protocol is conceived for closed domains of users, and can be configured in such a way that it falls into the scope of the Italian advanced electronic signature because, as properties (1)–(3) are guaranteed. However, it's application can be universal, either with enforceable-against-third-parties legal value in those Countries where the EU directive [1] was transposed such as Italy, or in C2C, B2B and B2C private transactions where all parties agree. According to our protocol, signature functions are spread out over the popular social network Twitter, without requiring changes of its features, so that the adoption of our solution appears both realistic and effective. Observe that the use of social networks in other contexts is diffused. For example, social networks have been used to evaluate resources on the Web [12,13] and to analyze users' preferences [14,15].

The paper is organized as follows. In the next section, we recall some background notions, which are digital signature and Twitter. In Section 3, we define the social signature and describe how it is generated and verified in closed domains of users. In Section 4, we analyze the security of our signature protocol. Section 5 is devoted to the related literature. Finally, in Section 6, we draw our conclusions and sketch possible future work.

2   Background

In this section, first we describe how digital signatures are generated and validated. Then, we briefly recall some specifics of Twitter. The knowledge of these concepts is necessary to understand the technical aspects of our proposal.

2.1   Digital Signature

The digital signature mechanism relies on a public key infrastructure [23], enabling the binding of public keys with user identities by means of a trusted third party, the Certification Authority. Each user owns two keys, a private key and a public one. The private key is kept secret and the public one is made public.

The first step of the signature generation process is the computation, on the document to be signed, of a cryptographic hash function [25,24], such as SHA-256. The result is called *digest* of the document. The properties of the hash function guarantee that the digest can substitute the original document in the signature generation process as the probability of having two distinct documents producing the same digest is negligible. Moreover, the problem of finding a document with digest equal to that of another given document is unfeasible, so that an attacker cannot corrupt a signed document without the digest changes. The digest is computed on the PC by the signature software (typically supplied by the certification authority) and sent to the smart card embedding the private key of an asymmetric cryptographic cipher, typically RSA [37]. The smart card is then enabled by the user (typically by inserting a secret PIN) to encrypt the digest with the private key, thus producing the digital signature. This is sent from the smart card to the signature software running on the PC to produce the cryptographic message, which can be encoded in several formats, such as PKCS#7 [29], CMS [28], CAdES [34], XAdES [22] or pdf [40].

The cryptographic message typically contains at least the document, the signature, and the certificate of the signer. Given a cryptographic message B, the verification of the signature on the document contained in B is done by:

1. computing the digest I of the document D,
2. computing J as the result of the decryption of the signature with the public key of the subscriber (included in the certificate), and
3. checking that the decrypted digest J coincides with the computed digest I.

The verification is completed by checking recursively also validity, trustworthiness, and non-revocation of the certificate.

One of the most significant applications of digital signatures is the certification of public keys in large networks. Certification is a means for a trusted third party to tie up the user's identity to a public key, so that other entities can authenticate a public key without assistance from a trusted third party. There are two general classes of digital signature schemes:

1. Digital signature schemes with appendix, which require the original message as input to the verification algorithm.
2. Digital signature schemes with message recovery, in which the original message is recovered from the signature itself.

The first class of digital signature schemes (based on cryptographic hash functions) is the most commonly used in practice because is less prone to existential forgery attacks. Examples of mechanisms providing digital signatures with appendix are the ElGamal [9], DSA [27] and Schnorr [11] signature schemes. The second class has the feature that the message signed can be recovered from the signature itself. In practice, this feature is of use for short messages. Examples of mechanisms providing digital signatures with message recovery are RSA [37], Rabin [10], and Nyberg-Rueppel [41] public-key signature schemes.

2.2 Twitter Specifics

Twitter is a microblogging services made up of 140-character messages called *tweets*. It is an easy way to discover the latest news coming from other people. It was designed to fit into the character limit of a text message, and Twitter still works on any SMS-ready phone. Brevity keeps Twitter fast-paced and relevant by encouraging people to tweet in the moment and to focus on the essential idea they are trying to communicate. Inside a tweet the user can see photos and videos from people he knows or behind-the-scenes moments from the biggest stars. The user can link to news stories, blogs, websites and apps. Once the user tweet is generated, it is publicly posted on his Twitter profile. The stream of tweets of a user is called *timeline*. A user can *follow* another user and becomes a *follower*. Tweets of a user appear in the timeline of their followers and are called *retweets*. Each Twitter user is identified by a username starting with the symbol @. People use @ to mention a person in tweets. To categorize tweets by keyword, people use the hashtag symbol # before a relevant keyword or phrase (no spaces) in their tweet. Moreover, hashtags are indexed to make it easier to find a conversation about that topic. Applications and websites which use Twitter are built using the Twitter API. There are three kinds of API: (i) The REST API is used to do things like post tweets, follow someone, create lists and more; (ii) the Search API is for performing searches; (iii) the Streaming API is for application developers who want to receive a real-time stream of the public tweets on Twitter. The official guide to Twitter [2] provides more detail on these aspects.

3   Social Signature

In this section, we define the social signature and we describe how it is generated and verified in closed domains of users, such as the case of document exchanges between selected citizens and municipal public offices. Indeed, in these scenarios, it may raise the necessity of a lightweight procedure to guarantee integrity and authenticity of documents created by (selected) people. In our proposal, the lightweight procedure referred above is implemented by social signature.

Like a digital signature, a social signature allows us to be aware of the identity of the person who created an electronic document (a text file, an image, a video, etc.) and to ensure that this document has not been altered since that person created it. Differently from digital signature, a social signature does not rely on a certification authority, asymmetric cryptography, or signature device such as smart card or USB key. As the name suggests, the solution is based on the usage of the famous social network Twitter. Indeed, our signature protocol requires that each entity involved in the procedure have a Twitter profile.

Now, we describe how social signature procedure works by referring, as a concrete scenario and w.l.o.g., to the closed domain of a company and its employees, which adopt social signature to exchange documents relating to their work.

The social signature process involves the following two entities:

1. The *company*, which overviews the whole signature procedure and ensures the resolution of any possible dispute related to the signature (e.g., signature repudiation).
2. A domain of *employees* (in general including all the employees of the company) who use social signature to provide integrity and authenticity of the documents they create, and to verify integrity and authenticity of the documents created by other employees of the same domain.

To use social signature, all actors involved in the process have to first carry out the *Registration* procedure, which works as follows.

Registration. First, the company creates an account on Twitter. Clearly, this is done by a person who is authorized to act on behalf of the company. Assume that the username chosen for the account on Twitter is @Company. This account enables the *Twitter Auto Retweets* service, in such a way that all tweets coming from its followers are retweeted.

Next, the employees of the company, selected to use social signature, create also an account on Twitter. Let suppose that an employee chooses @Company_Name_Surname as username. It is not required that all employees complete their registration on Twitter before social signature can be used (clearly, only registered employees can *socially* sign a document). However, it is possible in any time to extend the domain with other employees.

Each time an employee, who was selected from the company to use social signature, completes its registration on Twitter, declare a following relationship to @Company and vice versa (i.e., @Company becomes a follower of the employee account). In this phase, the company is responsible of the verification of the employee identity. Moreover, @Company *tweets* the message #X is Y, where X (which is hashtagged) is the username of the registered employee and Y is an information identifying the employee. Y is typically the name and surname of the employee; however, further information, such as the employee id, is added to manage cases of homonymy. The employee completes this phase by tweeting the message I am an employee of #Company (i.e., the username of the company hashtagged). As it will be clear in the following, the above message exchange is not just syntactic sugar, but has a precise role in the signature procedure. Finally, the employee receives the software that is used to generate social signature. This software is installed on the computer and/or notebook used by the employee. As we will show in the following, this software accesses public data contained in Twitter. This is done by exploiting Twitter APIs.

A real-life example of the registration procedure is summarized in Fig. 1. First, the University of Reggio Calabria creates an account on Twitter with username @unirc. Next, a student of this university creates also an account on Twitter with username @unircLidiaFotia. @unircLidiaFotia becomes a follower of @unirc and vice versa. Finally, @unirc tweets #unircLidiaFotia is Lidia Fotia and @unircLidiaFotia tweets I am an employee of #unirc.

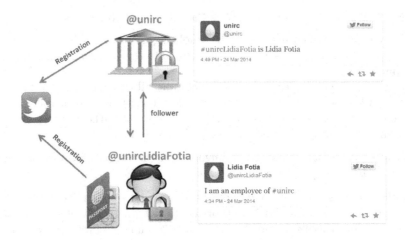

Fig. 1. An example of the registration procedure

Once an employee has completed the registration procedure, he is enabled to create a social signature on a document with scope and validity relevant to her working domain. This is done by the procedure described below.

Signature Generation. First, the employee runs the social signature software and selects the file to sign. Thereafter, the signer is prompted to enter his Twitter username and password. The signature software computes the hash of the file by the cryptographic hash function SHA-256. Let H be the hexadecimal representation of the resulting digest. Now, the software accesses (by a suitable Twitter API) the account of the signer on Twitter with the entered username and password and tweets on behalf of the signer the message `I have signed the document #H`[1]. In this phase, `@Company`, which has enabled the *Twitter Auto Retweets* service, receives and retweets this message. The procedure concludes with the publication of this tweet on the employee's account.

According to the example described in Fig. 1, we summarized in Fig. 2 the generation of the social signature done by the user `@unircLidiaFotia`. The result of this procedure is the generation of a tweet, on the account `@unircLidiaFotia`, which shows the digest of the document. Moreover, the account of the University retweets the same message.

Any employee or the company can verify the social signature generated by any other user through the procedure described below.

Signature Verification. We distinguish two verification modalities. The former, called *global* verification, aims to find the list of employees who have signed

---

[1] Observe that the length of this tweet is always 93 characters, because the hexadecimal representation of the digest needs 64 characters. Thus, it is shorter than 140 characters, which is the maximum tweet length.

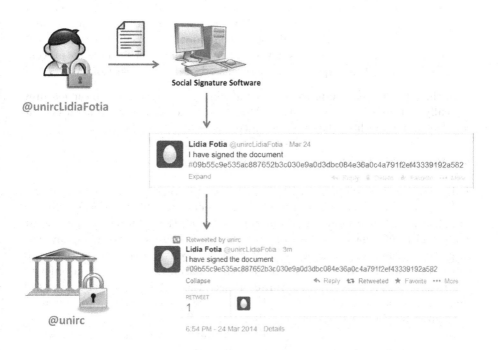

Fig. 2. An example of the social signature generation procedure

a given document. The latter, called *targeted* verification, is run to verify if a given employee has signed a given document. In both cases, the verifier uses the social signature software. Therein, he selects the file whose signature has to be validated. Moreover, the signer is prompted to enter his Twitter username.

In the global verification, the signature software first computes the hexadecimal representation H of the digest of the selected file by SHA-256. Then, the software reads, from the Twitter account corresponding to the entered username, the first tweet posted by the verifier. From this tweet, the (hashtagged) username U of the company is extracted (see the registration procedure). Now, the software finds the hashtag #H in the retweets posted by the account @U. If no retweet with the message I have signed the document #H is found, then the signature verification fails. Otherwise, the signature is considered valid. Observe that more than one tweet (from different accounts) with this message can be found, meaning that more voters have signed the document being validated.

Concerning the targeted verification, the only difference with the global one is that the above retweet is not searched in the account of the company, but in the account of the given employee, thus making this procedure lighter and quicker than the global verification. However, in order to support non repudiation and contrast revocation and impersonation attacks, in the target verification an additional check has to be done. When the signature passes

the target verification process, it is necessary to check that the company
follows the signer, that is, that a following relationship to the signer account
has been declared in the account of the company. Conversely, when the target
verification fails, it is necessary to run the global verification to prevent
repudiation. These aspects will be discussed in detail in Section 4.

In the next section, we prove that social signature provides the basic features
typically required to an e-signature. Moreover, we discuss several attacks that
could be done and how they are disarmed.

4 Security Analysis

This section is devoted to the analysis of the features provided by social signature
and to prove its robustness against a large number of real-life attacks. We discuss
each feature in the following. In our threat model, the attacker cannot add or
compromise information shown on the Twitter accounts of the company and
employees. Moreover, we expect that each actor keeps Twitter access password
secret and that Twitter acts as a trusted third party. Observe that, in order to
contrast attacks aiming to compromise the secretness of Twitter user's password
(like for instance attacks based on phishing or keyloggers), our protocol can be
configured by using a stronger authentication on Twitter [4].

In our analysis, we consider given a document D with a *valid* (i.e., which
passes the verification procedure) social signature.

Document Authenticity. Social signature allows us to be aware of the identity
of the signer of the document D. Indeed, in the verification procedure, the
search for the retweet including the message I **have signed the document**
#H (where, we recall H is the digest of the document) returns also the Twitter
account, say @X, who sent this twitter. Then, a new search in the account
@Company for the hashtag #X returns the tweet #X is Y, where Y is an
information identifying the employee who signed the document (according
to the registration procedure).

Document Integrity. At the end of the signature, the document digest has been
tweeted. Any change of the document produces a change of the digest, so
that finding the retweet with the message I **have signed the document**
#H does not return any result. Observe that the attacker can modify the doc-
ument in such a way that its digest appears on a tweet (for example, cloning
a document already signed). In this case, the message I **have signed the**
document #H', where H' is the digest of the altered document, is found but
it is signed by (thus, associated with) another employee.

Non-repudiation. The signer may attempt to repudiate a signature by deleting
the tweet generated at the signature time on his account. In this case, targeted verification fails. However, after this tweet is generated, it is retweeted
by the company and always shown on its account. As a consequence, the
global verification procedure is able to detect the repudiation attempt and
to contrast it. This is the reason why global verification has to be run when
target verification fails.

Signature Timestamping. It is a nice feature to have the timestamp specifying when the signature is made. In digital signature, this is a (pay-) service provided by a trusted third party. In our case, the signature timestamp is directly provided by Twitter, which reports the time of generation of each tweet, and, thus, of the signature.

Revocation. Revocation is the procedure carried out to withdraw the trust in an employee and thus inhibit him to sign other documents (for example, in case of dismissal). This is done by the company that removes the following relationship towards that employee. This way, any tweet generated by the signature procedure done by this user, is not retweeted by the company. As a consequence, global verification procedure fails. Observe that, in case the target verification procedure is run, then it is also necessary to check that the company follows the signer, in order to prevent an attack of this type.

Impersonation. In this case, the attacker creates a fake profile on Twitter with a username similar to that of the employee to impersonate. For example, considering the scenario shown in Figure 1 and Figure 2, the fake username could be @uniroLidiaFotia, in which the difference with the account of the victim is at the 5-th character. Global verification does not suffer from this attack, because the Tweet of the fake user is not retweeted. In contrast, target verification is vulnerable: indeed, the tweet with the signature is found on the fake account. As a consequence, it is also necessary to check that the company follows the signer, in order to prevent an attack of this type. This way, this check allows us to detect the attack and to find that this account is fake because it is not followed by the company.

5   Related Work

In this section, we give a quick survey on the major signature techniques existing in the literature and, finally, we compare them with our proposal.

Public Key Infrastructure. Digital signatures can not be used in open environments like the Internet, because they have no way to identify the signer. The public key infrastructure (PKI) [21] was designed to permit the binding between the subject and the public key by means of a digital certificate issued by the Certification Authority (CA). PKI relies on a hierarchical architecture and a strong trust-based model. In particular, a digital certificate includes a serial number (i.e. an identifier unique within the CA scope), the subject identity, the issuer identity, the validity period, the certificate policies of applicability, usages for which the key has been authorized by the digital signature of the CA that issued the certificate.

Conditional Signatures. Conditional Signatures were originally introduced by Lee et al. [30] to implement fair exchange of digital signatures in untrusted environments and do not require the card to have a user interface or any special peripheral (like Clarke et al. [20]). Berta et al. [7] propose a method to generate, instead of an ordinary signature, a conditional signature such that it is guaranteed that the condition can not become true before a certain amount of time has passed. This should leave time for the user to move to a trusted terminal for checking the signatures generated by the card and to enforce that the conditions of the fake signatures can ever become true. Since this approach requires the smart card to know the current time but most smart cards have no internal clock, it could be acquired from a secure time servers as described in Berta et al. [8]. Moreover, this proposal requires the user to store every signed message, because this message has to be checked later by means of a trusted terminal. Since it may be infeasible to store large message, this problem can be solved by outsourcing the logging function to an external logserver. Therefore, even though the required hardware is the standard one, a trusted third party is required.

Electronic Signatures. Electronic signature is a data structure that contains some information that must be linked to the signature, like the digital certificate, the cryptographic algorithms or the time at which the signature was generated. International standardization organizations have defined many formats of electronic signatures that include basic forms of electronic signature (ES-BES) and advanced electronic signatures (AdES) [34,17]. AdES formats that include additional validation information allow a relying party to obtain a higher assurance respecting the validity of the certificate used during the signature creation. Therefore, these formats intend to support the verification stage, but do not positively affect the reliability of the creation stage.

Weak Signature. Weak signature was introduced by T. Rabin and Ben-Or [36,35] to solve a problem (Verifiable Secret Sharing [19]) motivated by a question of general multi-party secure computation in the unconditional setting (network of untappable channels). They provide a form of authentication for which the on-line participation of a third party is needed. Check vectors are related to work on authentication codes [26,38] and on universal classes of hash functions [16]. The weak signature scheme relies on the presence of an on-line trusted server that participates in the creation of every signature, and also participates whenever a signed message holder wishes to prove to anyone that a signature is valid. This trusted server stores and retrieves information received from the signing agency and the message holder, and computes certain linear combinations of values it receives. Using the idea of check vectors, T. Rabin [36] presents a weak signature scheme, called Information Checking Protocol. Consider that the intermediary wishes to have a message s signed by the dealer. In the first phase, the original message holder intermediary ends up with the "signed message" s, y, while a third party RCV ends up with the check information a, b. Anyone can determine the validity of the signature by asking RCV to reveal the check information. The signature is weak, because the assistance of this third party is needed to verify a signature. Another signature scheme in the unconditional setting was introduced by Chaum and Roijakkers [18]. It satisfies a stronger set of conditions than Rabin's Information Checking Protocol, at a great increase in communication cost.

Visual Cryptography. Visual cryptography [33] is a type of cryptographic scheme which can decode concealed images without any cryptographic computation. Naor et al. [32] suggest a number of transparency-based methods for visual authentication and identification, and give rigorous analysis of their security. [31] presents human-friendly identification schemes such that a human prover knowing a secret key in his brain is asked a visual question by a verifier, which then checks if an answer sent from the prover matches the question with respect to the key. Ateniese et al. [6] propose a visual cryptography scheme for a set of participants to encode a secret image into many secondary images in such a way that any participant receives one secondary image and only qualified subsets of participants can "visually" recover the secret image, but non-qualified sets of participants have no information, in an information theoretical sense, on the original image. This scheme does not require the participants to perform any cryptographic computation.

Summary. Now, we discuss strengths and weaknesses of the signatures described in the previous section, then we compare them with our proposal.

An advantage of PKI is that a smart card or similar device can store the user's certificate and corresponding private key. In practice, few people use this added security option because smart cards and readers are not widely deployed. Instead, most clients store their private keys on their hard drives, sometimes with encryption but frequently without it [39].

The drawback of conditional signature is to require a significant load for the user, who has to split the signature task into two phases, delaying the effective conclusion of the procedure at validation-time. Electronic signatures are very problematic when it comes to maintaining integrity and security, as nothing prevents one individual from typing another individual's name. Owing to this fact, an electronic signature that does not incorporate additional measures of security is considered an insecure way of signing documentation.

The methods of visual cryptography can be easily broken by attacker exploiting human interaction. Moreover, neither extra hardware or trusted third party is required, whereas the user load can be considered very relevant.

As seen previously, social signature is a lightweight protocol that allows us to know who created an electronic document and to ensure that this document has not been altered since that person created it. Differently from PKI, conditional signature, electronic signature and weak signature, social signature does not rely on certification authority, asymmetric cryptography, or signature device. With respect to visual signature, in social signature the presence of a trusted server (i.e., Twitter) that participates in the creation of the signature is necessary.

6   Conclusion

In this paper, we have proposed a new lightweight e-signature protocol with a good level of security, not using public key cryptography and dedicated devices. The protocol is conceived for closed domains of users, such as the case of document exchanges between citizens and municipal public offices or private companies and employees. As a final consideration we argue that our protocol appears simple to implement, because it does not need any additional infrastructure. The most secure configuration of the protocol requires that the existing Twitter strong authentication is enabled, but we guess that this feature does not add a relevant degree of invasiveness. The overall invasiveness of the procedure is very low, as the signer does not have to manage devices, like smart cards, special PINs or passwords (besides the credentials used to access his Twitter profile), or certificates. Also the timestamping of the document is for-free. Moreover, the implementation cost of our protocol is nearly negligible, as it can be easily understood. Another strong point of our signature is that multiple signatures are implemented in a very easy and flexible way, with no need of planned exchanges of the document being signed, as it happens for PKCS#7 signatures. As a future work, we plan to implement in detail our protocol and experiment it in a real-life domain.

Acknowledgment. This work has been partially supported by the TENACE PRIN Project (n. 20103P34XC) funded by the Italian Ministry of Education, University and Research and by the Program "Programma Operativo Nazionale Ricerca e Competitività" 2007-2013, Distretto Tecnologico CyberSecurity funded by the Italian Ministry of Education, University and Research.

References

1. Directive 99/93/CEE, http://eur-lex.europa.eu/legal-content/EN/ALL/; jsessionid=TCsMT1yBQ965GRJTMG9GnFDxQqYP1W7Y1LFLLkwsmjvWRy1Q15FJ! 527097711?uri=CELEX:31999L0093
2. Twitter (2012), https://dev.twitter.com/docs
3. DPCM 22 Febbraio 2005 (2013), http://www.agid.gov.it/sites/default/files/ leggi_decreti_direttive/dpcm_22_febbraio_2013_-_nuove_regole_tecniche.pdf
4. Twitter authentication (2013), https://blog.twitter.com/2013/ improvements-to-login-verification-photos-and-more
5. Decreto Legislativo 7 Marzo 2005, n. 82 (2015), http://www.funzionepubblica.gov.it/media/672080/ dlgs-822005-aggiornato.pdf
6. Ateniese, G., Blundo, C., De Santis, A., Stinson, D.R.: Constructions and bounds for visual cryptography. In: Meyer auf der Heide, F., Monien, B. (eds.) ICALP 1996. LNCS, vol. 1099, pp. 416–428. Springer, Heidelberg (1996)
7. Berta, I.Z., Buttyán, L., Vajda, I.: Mitigating the untrusted terminal problem using conditional signatures. In: Proceedings of the International Conference on Information Technology: Coding and Computing, ITCC 2004, vol. 1, pp. 12–16. IEEE (2004)
8. Berta, I.Z., Vajda, I.: Documents from malicious terminals. In: Microtechnologies for the New Millennium 2003, pp. 325–336. International Society for Optics and Photonics (2003)
9. Boneh, D.: Elgamal digital signature scheme. In: Encyclopedia of Cryptography and Security, pp. 182–183. Springer (2005)

10. Boneh, D.: Rabin digital signature scheme. In: Encyclopedia of Cryptography and Security, pp. 502–503. Springer (2005)
11. Boneh, D.: Schnorr digital signature scheme. In: Encyclopedia of Cryptography and Security, pp. 541–542. Springer (2005)
12. Buccafurri, F., Fotia, L., Lax, G.: Allowing continuous evaluation of citizen opinions through social networks. In: Kő, A., Leitner, C., Leitold, H., Prosser, A. (eds.) EGOVIS/EDEM 2012. LNCS, vol. 7452, pp. 242–253. Springer, Heidelberg (2012)
13. Buccafurri, F., Fotia, L., Lax, G.: Privacy-preserving resource evaluation in social networks. In: Proceedings of the 2012 Tenth Annual International Conference on Privacy, Security and Trust (PST 2012), pp. 51–58. IEEE Computer Society (2012)
14. Buccafurri, F., Fotia, L., Lax, G.: Allowing non-identifying information disclosure in citizen opinion evaluation. In: Kő, A., Leitner, C., Leitold, H., Prosser, A. (eds.) EGOVIS/EDEM 2013. LNCS, vol. 8061, pp. 241–254. Springer, Heidelberg (2013)
15. Buccafurri, F., Fotia, L., Lax, G.: Allowing privacy-preserving analysis of social network likes. In: 2013 Eleventh Annual International Conference on Privacy, Security and Trust (PST), pp. 36–43. IEEE (2013)
16. Carter, J.L., Wegman, M.N.: Universal classes of hash functions. In: Proceedings of the Ninth Annual ACM Symposium on Theory of Computing, pp. 106–112. ACM (1977)
17. Centner, M.: XML Advanced Electronic Signatures (XAdES). Citeseer (2003)
18. Chaum, D., Roijakkers, S.: Unconditionally secure digital signatures. In: Menezes, A., Vanstone, S.A. (eds.) CRYPTO 1990. LNCS, vol. 537, pp. 206–214. Springer, Heidelberg (1991)
19. Chor, B., Goldwasser, S., Micali, S., Awerbuch, B.: Verifiable secret sharing and achieving simultaneity in the presence of faults. In: 26th Annual Symposium on Foundations of Computer Science, pp. 383–395. IEEE (1985)
20. Clarke, D., Gassend, B., Kotwal, T., Burnside, M., van Dijk, M., Devadas, S., Rivest, R.L.: The untrusted computer problem and camera-based authentication. In: Mattern, F., Naghshineh, M. (eds.) Pervasive 2002. LNCS, vol. 2414, pp. 114–124. Springer, Heidelberg (2002)
21. Cooper, D.: Internet X. 509 public key infrastructure certificate and certificate revocation list (CRL) profile (2008)
22. Cruellas, J.C., Karlinger, G., Pinkas, D., Ross, J.: Xml advanced electronic signatures (xades). World Wide Web Consortium, Note NOTE-XAdES-20030220 (2003)
23. Diffie, W., Hellman, M.E.: New directions in cryptography. IEEE Transactions on Information Theory 22(6), 644–654 (1976)
24. Dobbertin, H., Bosselaers, A., Preneel, B.: RIPEMD-160: A strengthened version of RIPEMD. In: Gollmann, D. (ed.) FSE 1996. LNCS, vol. 1039, pp. 71–82. Springer, Heidelberg (1996)
25. Eastlake, D., Jones, P.: US secure hash algorithm 1 (SHA1). Technical report, RFC 3174 (September 2001)
26. Gilbert, E.N., MacWilliams, F.J., Sloane, N.J.: Codes which detect deception. Bell System Technical Journal 53(3), 405–424 (1974)
27. Harn, L.: New digital signature scheme based on discrete logarithm. Electronics Letters 30(5), 396–398 (1994)
28. Housley, R.: Cryptographic message syntax (1999)
29. Kaliski, B.: Pkcs# 7: Cryptographic message syntax version 1.5 (1998)
30. Lee, B., Kim, K.: Fair exchange of digital signatures using conditional signature. In: Symposium on Cryptography and Information Security, pp. 179–184 (2002)
31. Matsumoto, T.: Human–computer cryptography: An attempt. Journal of Computer Security 6(3), 129–149 (1998)

32. Naor, M., Pinkas, B.: Visual authentication and identification. In: Kaliski Jr., B.S. (ed.) CRYPTO 1997. LNCS, vol. 1294, pp. 322–336. Springer, Heidelberg (1997)

33. Naor, M., Shamir, A.: Visual cryptography. In: De Santis, A. (ed.) EUROCRYPT 1994. LNCS, vol. 950, pp. 1–12. Springer, Heidelberg (1995)

34. Pinkas, D., Pope, N., Ross, J.: Cms advanced electronic signatures (cades). IETF Request for Comments 5126 (2008)

35. Rabin, T.: Robust sharing of secrets when the dealer is honest or cheating. Journal of the ACM (JACM) 41(6), 1089–1109 (1994)

36. Rabin, T., Ben-Or, M.: Verifiable secret sharing and multiparty protocols with honest majority. In: Proceedings of the Twenty-first Annual ACM Symposium on Theory of Computing, pp. 73–85. ACM (1989)

37. Rivest, R.L., Shamir, A., Adleman, L.: A method for obtaining digital signatures and public-key cryptosystems. Commun. ACM 21(2), 120–126 (1978)

38. Simmons, G.J.: Authentication theory/coding theory. In: Blakely, G.R., Chaum, D. (eds.) CRYPTO 1984. LNCS, vol. 196, pp. 411–431. Springer, Heidelberg (1985)

39. Simson, L.: Email-based identification and authentication: An alternative to PKI? (2003), http://u.cs.biu.ac.il/~myghaz/phd/2003.IEEE.EBAI.pdf

40. Taft, E., Pravetz, J., Zilles, S., Masinter, L.: The application/pdf media type. Internet proposed standard RFC 3778 (2004)

41. Zhang, K.: Threshold proxy signature schemes. In: Okamoto, E. (ed.) Download Chapter (586 KB) Information Security . LNCS, vol. 1396, pp. 282–290. Springer, Heidelberg (1998)

Accessibility Issues in E-Government

Eleanor Leist and Dan Smith

University of East Anglia, Norwich, NR4 7TJ, UK
{e.leist,dan.smith}@uea.ac.uk
http://www.uea.ac.uk/computing

Abstract. Government services are almost always monopoly services, and as a result, it is important to maximize inclusion. However, substantial numbers of people are unable or unwilling to use internet services. Usability and accessibility issues are a major deterrent to internet use and are important in users' perceptions of websites. These are particularly important for older people, many of whom have reduced visual acuity, loss of fine motor control and other disabilities that make it more difficult to deal with poorly designed websites. We undertook two sets of experiments, the first involving an assessment of the accessibility and standards compliance of local and national e-government sites in the UK. The second focuses on sites in several other European countries. Results show significant differences between different levels of government and between standards compliance and accessibility.

Keywords: e-government, accessibility, standards, exclusion.

1 Introduction

As we conduct more of our daily activities online, e-government becomes more essential to citizens and to businesses. Governments are sole providers of many services, for example, registering a birth, booking a driving test or paying taxes. Making these services available online gives most people quicker and more convenient access, as well as creating substantial savings [20]. However, the presence of groups of people who are unable or unwilling to use online services makes the change more problematic, the 'actively disengaged' and the 'willing but unable'; the main characteristics of e-government non-users are related to age, education and income [28] [1].

Since many public services are natural monopolies usability and accessibility issues have a disenfranchising effect which is likely to exclude the groups of citizens who are least well equipped to participate in a digital society. Web accessibility guidelines are well developed, but many organisations do not implement them and previous studies have shown a widespread lack of compliance with accessibility guidelines on e-government websites. A related issue is the extent to which e-government sites are using standards-compliant HTML. Standards-compliant HTML is less likely to have accessibility and usability problems and can be rendered appropriately on a wider range of devices, including adaptive technologies and mobile platforms.

A. Kő and E. Francesconi (Eds.): EGOVIS 2014, LNCS 8650, pp. 15–25, 2014.

We describe two sets of experiments, using a set of common e-government tasks in a range of European countries, to test the accessibility of a sample of national and local e-government websites using the WCAG guidelines [29] and to test their compliance with HTML standards.

The structure of this paper is as follows. Section 2 discusses e-government usability issues and some results of previous work in this area. Section 3 describes the methodology used to measure e-government accessibility and section 4 presents the results of the experiments.

2   Service Usability

For e-government services to be successful, they must be usable and easily accessible to consumers. Government sites, in common with the rest of the Web have become more usable over time [21], with the better use of features by designers, better user understanding of conventions and changes in technology. This trend is being helped by the move to standards-based websites, since the standards incorporate many features that aid usability. However, most government (and other) web pages are not compliant with the standards they claim to be written to [14].

Usability measures used for e-government service evaluations may not measure the features normally associated with usability; for example [28], whose usability component comprises a score for help facilities and for user feedback or comment mechanisms. Work on Jordanian government sites [4] included a set of questions about user customisation of the sites, some of which (e.g. font size) are clear usability and accessibility issues, but others do not seem appropriate for e-government sites (e.g. changing the colour scheme).

The satisfaction ratings for e-government services are generally lower than for commercial services (e.g. internet banking); the satisfaction rating was highest for 'declaring income tax' and lowest were for 'becoming unemployed' and other services which might result in a claim for benefits [28]. Of the EU services users, only 47% had their information or transactional needs met in full. Work on US federal e-government shows similar trends; there is low satisfaction (66%) with e-government services compared with commercial services in all sectors surveyed – only ISPs scored lower [2]. There is considerable variation in satisfaction between services, ranging from 75% to 58%; transactional services generally have lower scores than informational services. However, even for poorly-rated services, the satisfaction with the online service is considerably greater than for the paper-based service.

A widely recognised issue in e-government is the difficulty that many users have in finding information (e.g. [9]), which is organised by department, rather than by function. The restructuring of the e-government landscape to facilitate users' tasks is a significant motivation in the UK for both central and local government adoption of cloud-based services.

Extensive research has been carried out on older peoples' use of the internet. It is apparent that the digital divide is a problem for the level of e-government use, with the majority of adults who have never accessed the internet being over the age of 65 [20]. Factors such as ethnicity, education level, income and disabilities can also have a significant effect on usage of the internet [7]. The main barrier to internet use is frustration [12], with causes including failing to remember instructions, inability to use the mouse and preferring words to images [26].

Older users are more inclined to use services which they perceive to be useful and easy to use [24] but they are less likely to use financial services due to a perceived lack of online safety. The lack of trust in online services by older people has been widely reported and there has been work on metrics to identify the aspects of sites that influence older peoples' perception of trustworthiness [15]. Projects such as WAI AGE [3] have investigated improving accessibility using first-hand guidance from older people and guidelines for e-government forms have been developed [22]. Attempts to automatically identify usability problems by adaptively enlarging error sites (e.g. misplaced clicks) show comparable results to one-on-one observations of the users [27].

A survey of e-government sites from Europe and Latin America tested usability with the Neilsen heuristics [14], finding that consistency and standards were the main issues. Work on the usability of online government forms for older people has identified major issues with the web paradigm (i.e. many older users do not have an adequate model of the web to be able to search and navigate sites effectively), the lack online help and real-time assistance, form design, the use of technical or legal language, and trust [22]. The needs of some groups of users (e.g. visually impaired) are not adequately covered by WCAG guidelines [8], as their model of processing is substantially different from the majority [5]. Similar lists of critical page-level issues have been identified in other studies (e.g. for US state websites [6], UK local government [19]).

Many e-government sites require high levels of literacy, making them inaccessible to large segments of the population [10]. Kuzma [18] studied the compliance with UK disability law and WCAG of sites of UK members of parliament and found that only 7% of the sites did not have accessibility problems, with the majority of errors caused by missing alt tags, by insufficient emphasis on important information, and by complex language.

The results of a survey of US local government portals showed that only a small minority of sites met usability standards and passed an accessibility check [30]. Other studies in Malaysia [16] and Dubai [17] found consistent results. Automatic accessibility checkers were used in both studies to measure levels of compliance with WCAG. The Dubai study also found a weak correlation between the accessibility of a website and its evaluation score, measured using a local scale with human assessments of features.

The case for making routine use of usability evaluations for e-government is strong, as successful services are intimately dependent on their users [25]. The issues of poor service usability and the improvement of heuristic usability approaches for e-government are discussed in a case study three Spanish language sites [14], using the g-Quality approach [11]. Text mining of survey results, using a topic model shows similar issues [23]. The major common issues relate to navigation difficulties, missing or hidden information, design consistency and standards compliance.

3   Methodology

The first part of this research was to measure the accessibility of national and local e-government websites, by measuring the accessibility and standards-compliance of pages visited when completing a set of 12 common e-government tasks, which are relevant to a large number of users, covering both local and national government activities. The national level pages are the responsibility of the UK government and the local governments tested are a sample from a range of authorities, covering rural areas, large and small cities, with a mix of reasonably affluent and deprived areas. The second part of the research was to compare the accessibility and standardisation of a wider sample of European countries: France, Germany, the Netherlands and Romania. Seven tasks, applicable across most countries, were used for this experiment and results were gathered using the same methodology; Table 1 shows the tasks.

The tasks used for testing UK sites contain a mix of tasks carried out on national sites (e.g. registering a death and finding e-government statistics) and local sites (e.g. searching for a library book and paying a parking fine). Some tasks can be carried out at both a national and local level, for example, applying for a disabled person's parking permit and reporting a change of address. We have based our choice of national tasks on those listed as most common in European surveys and UK data. For local government tasks we have not had comparable sources of data, so we have identified some from surveys and others by discussion with colleagues.

A number of the chosen tasks are not carried out in the same way across different European countries. For example, parking tickets issued in France have a national number, so fines are paid using a national e-government service, as opposed to a local service in the UK. These differences mean it can be difficult to draw definitive comparisons based on individual tasks. It is also difficult to discover which services are most common on local government sites as, unlike with national government, there are very few statistics available.

We measured standards compliance and accessibility. Firstly, the source code of the website was run through the W3C Validator mark-up checker[1] to assess the level of compliance with standards and to discover the version of markup language being used. Secondly, the page was checked using the AChecker accessibility checker [13], using the WCAG 2.0 AA guidelines.

4   Results and Discussion

The results of the survey show that the national government pages had substantially fewer errors and accessibility issues compared to the majority of local

---

[1] http://validator.w3.org

Table 1. Tasks used to test e-government sites

	All countries		UK only
1	Pay parking or speeding fine	8	Search for a library book
2	Register a death	9	Search for an adult education course
3	Send message to an elected representative	10	Apply for a disabled parking permit
4	Report a change of address	11	Report a problem with a road
5	Pay income (or other) tax	12	Find e-government statistics
6	Add child to school/nursery waiting list		
7	Find information on pension entitlement		

government pages in all cases where we could compare them. The various government organisations almost all require their pages to be declared to a standard, which varies from HTML 3.2, through the XHTML standards, to HTML5, and may change between sections of a site; few organisations seem to look for compliance to their chosen standard(s). For each page visited for a task we recorded the number of HTML errors and WCAG accessibility issues reported, then averaging them. Where a task required a login or citizen identification we stopped the task at that page.

For our 12 UK tasks, we found that the national government portal pages (rooted at https://www.gov.uk) use HTML5 and very few HTML errors were found, most of which were low severity. The number of accessibility problems on these pages is also low, and are mostly due to missing alt text on logos. The majority of problems found on these national pages would be simple to fix. We also sampled some of the less frequently used UK national government services[2] and found much greater variation, particularly with older sites that have not been updated for several years.

In general, local government sites performed worse than the national government pages in terms of both HTML errors and accessibility issues. However, pages from larger authorities (Norfolk, Cambridgeshire and North Yorkshire county councils) were generally found to perform better than those of smaller organisations, possibly due to their being able to recruit and retain staff with higher levels of expertise. The London boroughs performed particularly poorly, with little standardisation; this may be a reflection of the longstanding difficulties that London boroughs have in recruiting and retaining professional staff. There appears to be a correlation between the economic status of the area and the numbers of HTML errors and accessibility problems. Less prosperous areas (e.g. Barking & Dagenham and King's Lynn & West Norfolk) had higher levels of HTML errors or accessibility problems whereas more affluent areas which are seen as desirable places to live (e.g.Cambridge) fared better. However, the small sample size does not allow firm conclusions to be drawn.

---

[2] For 2013, 766 UK national e-government services are listed, but data for many is incomplete; see https://www.gov.uk/performance/transactions-explorer/all-services/by-transactions-per-year/descending

Some results are skewed due to outliers. Pages created by a third party (e.g. capitadiscovery.co.uk for library searches and eadmissions.org.uk for school admissions) had very high numbers of errors or accessibility issues, increasing the average for those tasks.

As with the national government, most of the errors occurring at a local level are low in severity and would require only minimal changes to fix. One authority in our sample is still using HTML 3.2 – superseded in 1999 – as its main standard. The results from our sample show that most local authorities are not consistent in the standards they use, and that the use of obsolete HTML standards is likely to increase the number of accessibility issues found.

Using a chi-squared test, the degree of difference in the number of errors and accessibility problems of local and national pages is found to be highly significant (alpha=0.01). There is also found to be good correlation between the number of HTML errors and accessibility problems observed across all pages tested (R=0.56, alpha=0.01).

The results for the UK tasks are shown in figure 1 and summarised in Appendix A.

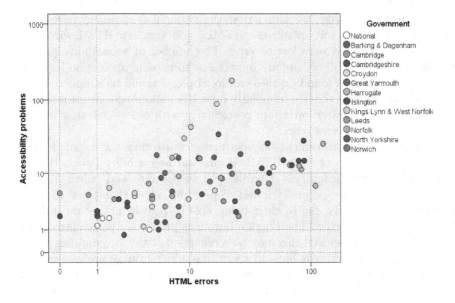

Fig. 1. UK results: mean HTML and WCAG errors (log scales)

Differences between e-government services in the UK and elsewhere restricted the number of tasks we could attempt (see results in table 2). In France, six of the seven tasks could be completed. Results were very similar to those from the UK, with national pages consistently having lower numbers of accessibility problems. The high average number of errors in the table for national pages is

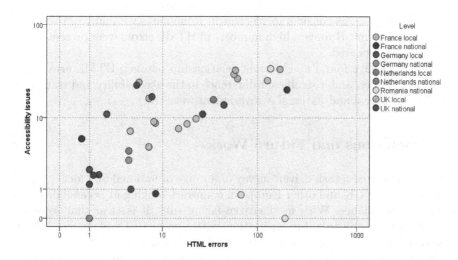

Fig. 2. Europe: mean HTML and WCAG errors (log scales)

Table 2. Results for France, Germany, Romania and the Netherlands

Country	Level	Mean HTML errors	Mean accessibility errors
France	Local	60	26
	National	69	9
The Netherlands	Local	35	16
	National	3	2
Germany	Local	20	15
	National	4	3
Romania	Local	-	-
	National	131	12

due to a single outlier (on impots.gouv.fr). To test the consistency of our local government results, we tried several of the tasks on multiple local government sites in the Rhône-Alpes region. The results suggest that large urban centres (e.g. Grenoble) are likely to have fewest issues, followed by local government authorities, their travel-to-work regions and then by smaller and more isolated authorities.

From the three tasks that we could carry out for Dutch e-government, the local pages had far more issues, whereas the national sites were relatively accessible. Many tasks could not be tested as a login, only available to Dutch residents, is required to access most services.

Most tasks we tested in Germany took place on local sites, all of which had more accessibility problems than national pages. Again, relatively few services were available online, with many pages giving information about how to complete the task by phone or in person. No results were obtained for Romanian local sites as the country is in the early days of e-government provision. Online content is mostly informational, as opposed to transactional. From the sample tested, the accessibility seems considerably better in Romania, with many of the pages having no problems. However, high numbers of HTML errors were present, most of which were repeated.

Overall, we have found a significant relationship between HTML errors and accessibility issues, and a significant difference in the accessibility and standards compliance of local and national e-government websites.

5   Conclusions and Future Work

We have conducted a task-driven survey of a range of national and local government sites in the UK and other European countries, looking at accessibility and standards compliance. With most citizen-facing sites, it is clear that some effort has been put towards standardisation, with a consistent and current HTML version being used on pages across each level of government.

The results show consistent and significant differences in the performance of local and national sites. Similar patterns of HTML errors and accessibility problems were observed in the French sites, although there were more issues in total. In Germany and the Netherlands, the national pages that we could access without a login had relatively few issues, whereas local pages had many more. The Romanian sites had relatively few accessibility problems.; this may be a result of our sampling or may indicate a latecomer benefit, starting e-government development with a better awareness of accessibility issues.

The diversity in government structures between countries make it more difficult to undertake detailed comparisons and to draw consistent conclusions across all countries tested. Many of the services were either not consistently available online, or were provided in a different way, for example, paying a speeding fine or parking ticket at a national level in France and a local level in the UK.

Currently, the issues discovered are likely to be hindering internet use for older people and those with disabilities, increasing exclusion from e-government services. Despite the large numbers of issues, many of them would be easy to correct. Small but vital steps, such as reducing simple errors in HTML and ensuring `alt` tags are included would increase accessibility and would require little effort. It is clear that the use of a mark-up language validator and accessibility checker for all e-government sites could substantially improve their accessibility for a very modest effort. We also note that the characteristics of websites that aid accessibility also – with few exceptions – improve the experience of mobile versions of sites.

It is clear that many government authorities are not using standard tools for checking the accessibility of their websites, making it unnecessarily difficult for a substantial minority of users, many of whom are likely to be reluctant or lacking in confidence in using e-government services.

We are planning further work to look in more detail at selecting suitable e-government tasks that are relevant across a wide range of countries, investigating the relationship between users' usability experiences and reported issues, and undertaking larger surveys to establish the range of variation and relationships to other geographical, economic and social factors that may influence governments' migration to online services.

Acknowledgments. We wish to thank our colleagues Joost Noppen, Kathi Huber and Andreea Bucur for their help with navigating e-government sites. This work was carried out while Eleanor Leist was a MSc Information Systems student at UEA.

References

1. Digital landscape research (2012), https://www.gov.uk/government/publications/digital-landscape-research/digital-landscape-research
2. Acsi federal government report 2013 (2014), http://www.theacsi.org/news-and-resources/customer-satisfaction-reports/customer-satisfaction-reports-2013/acsi-federal-government-report-2013
3. Abou-Zahra, S., Brewer, J., Arch, A.: Towards bridging the accessibility needs of people with disabilities and the ageing community. In: Proceedings of the 2008 International Cross-Disciplinary Conference on Web Accessibility (W4A), pp. 83–86. ACM (2008)
4. AlFawwaz, B.M.: Evaluation of egovernment websites usability in Jordan (2012)
5. AlJarallah, K., Chen, R.C.C., AlShathry, O.: Cognitive-based approach for assessing accessibility of e-government websites. In: Stephanidis, C., Antona, M. (eds.) UAHCI 2013, Part II. LNCS, vol. 8010, pp. 547–554. Springer, Heidelberg (2013)
6. Becker, S.A.: E-government usability for older adults. Communications of the ACM 48(2), 102–104 (2005)
7. Bélanger, F., Carter, L.: The impact of the digital divide on e-government use. Communications of the ACM 52(4), 132–135 (2009)
8. Caldwell, B., Chisholm, W., Slatin, J., Vanderheiden, G., White, J.: Web content accessibility guidelines 2.0. W3C working draft 27 (2006)
9. Choudrie, J., Ghinea, G., Songonuga, V.N.: Silver surfers, e-government and the digital divide: An exploratory study of UK local authority websites and older citizens. Interacting with Computers 25(6), 417–442 (2013)
10. Davey, B., Parker, K.R., Lukaitis, A.: e-government and the elderly: A two country comparison. e-Government 8, 6–2011(2011)
11. Garcia, A.C.B., Maciel, C., Pinto, F.B.: A quality inspection method to evaluate E-government sites. In: Wimmer, M.A., Traunmüller, R., Grönlund, Å., Andersen, K.V. (eds.) EGOV 2005. LNCS, vol. 3591, pp. 198–209. Springer, Heidelberg (2005)
12. Gatto, S.L., Tak, S.H.: Computer, internet, and e-mail use among older adults: Benefits and barriers. Educational Gerontology 34(9), 800–811 (2008)
13. Gay, G., Li, C.Q.: AChecker: Open, interactive, customizable, web accessibility checking. In: Proc. Int.Cross Disciplinary Conf. Web Accessibility, W4A 2010, pp. 23:1–23:2. ACM, New York (2010), http://doi.acm.org/10.1145/1805986.1806019
14. Granizo, C.J., Yanez, P.L., Ramirez, D.P., Machado, P.C.: Usability in e-government sites. In: 2011 Eighth International Conference on Information Technology: New Generations (ITNG), pp. 453–458. IEEE (2011)

15. Holzinger, A., Searle, G., Kleinberger, T., Seffah, A., Javahery, H.: Investigating usability metrics for the design and development of applications for the elderly. In: Miesenberger, K., Klaus, J., Zagler, W.L., Karshmer, A.I. (eds.) ICCHP 2008. LNCS, vol. 5105, pp. 98–105. Springer, Heidelberg (2008)
16. Isa, W.A.M., Suhami, M.R., Safie, N.I., Semsudin, S.S.: Assessing the usability and accessibility of Malaysia e-government website. American Journal of Economics and Business Administration 3(1), 40 (2011)
17. Kamoun, F., Almourad, M.B.: Accessibility as an integral factor in e-government website evaluation: the case of Dubai e-government. Information Technology & People 27(2), 5 (2014)
18. Kuzma, J.M.: Accessibility design issues with UK e-government sites. Government Information Quarterly 27(2), 141–146 (2010)
19. Lines, L., Ikechi, O., Hone, K.S.: Accessing e-government services: Design requirements for the older user. In: Stephanidis, C. (ed.) Universal Access in HCI, Part III, HCII 2007. LNCS, vol. 4556, pp. 932–940. Springer, Heidelberg (2007)
20. PricewaterhouseCoopers LLP: for digital inclusion: The economic case for digital inclusion (2009),
    http://www.parliamentandinternet.org.uk/uploads/Final_report.pdf
21. Loranger, H., Nielsen, J.: Prioritizing Web Usability. New Riders (2006) ISBN-10: 0-321-35031-6
22. Money, A.G., Lines, L., Fernando, S., Elliman, A.D.: e-government online forms: design guidelines for older adults in Europe. Universal Access in the Information Society 10(1), 1–16 (2011)
23. Nariman, D.: Analyzing text-based user feedback in e-government services using topic models. In: IEEE CISIS, pp. 720–725. IEEE Computer Society, Washington, DC (2013), http://dx.doi.org/10.1109/CISIS.2013.129
24. Phang, C.W., Sutanto, J., Kankanhalli, A., Li, Y., Tan, B.C., Teo, H.H.: Senior citizens' acceptance of information systems: A study in the context of e-government services. IEEE Transactions on Engineering Management 53(4), 555–569 (2006)
25. de Róiste, M.: Bringing in the users: The role for usability evaluation in egovernment. Government Information Quarterly 30(4), 441–449 (2013)
26. Sayago, S., Blat, J.: About the relevance of accessibility barriers in the everyday interactions of older people with the web. In: Proceedings of the 2009 International Cross-Disciplinary Conference on Web Accessibililty (W4A), pp. 104–113. ACM (2009)
27. Taylor Sr., A., Miller, L., Nilakanta, S., Sander, J., Mitra, S., Sharda, A., Chama, B.: An error detection strategy for improving web accessibility for older adults. International Journal on Advances in Intelligent Systems 6(3 and 4), 376–393 (2013)
28. Tinholt, D., Colclough, G., Oudmaijer, S., Carrara, W., Tol, T., Schouten, M., van der Linden, N., Cattaneo, G., Aguzzi, S., Jacquet, L., Kerschot, H., van Gompel, R., Steyaert, J., Millard, J., Schindler, R.: Public services online: Digital by default or by detour (2013), doi:10.2759/13072
29. W3C: Web content accessibility guidelines (wcag) 2.0 (2008),
    http://www.w3.org/TR/WCAG20/
30. Youngblood, N.E., Youngblood, S.A.: User experience and accessibility: An analysis of county web portals. Journal of Usability Studies 9(1), 25–41 (2013)

Appendix A: Results for the UK Tasks across a Number of Government Authorities

Government	Standards observed	Mean HTML errors	Mean accessibility errors
National	HTML5, HTML 4.01 Transitional, HTML 4.01 Strict	3.01	4.69
Norfolk	XHTML 1.0 Transitional, HTML 4.01 Transitional	25.35	10.82
Norwich	XHTML 1.0 Transitional	19	8.63
Great Yarmouth	HTML 5, XHTML 1.0 Transitional, HTML 4.01 Transitional	12.65	8.31
King's Lynn & West Norfolk	HTML 5, XHTML 1.0 Transitional, HTML 4.01 Transitional, HTML 3.2	8.51	38.9
Cambridge	HTML 5, XHTML 1.0 Transitional, HTML 4.01 Transitional	2.11	4.18
Cambridgeshire	HTML 5, XHTML 1.0 Transitional, XHTML 1.0 Strict	4.57	4.29
Leeds	HTML 5, XHTML 1.0 Transitional, XHTML 1.0 Strict	19.76	6.09
Harrogate	XHTML 1.0 Transitional, XHTML 1.0 Strict, HTML 4.01 Transitional	85.43	10.88
North Yorkshire	XHTML 1.1, HTML 5, XHTML 1.0 Strict, HTML 4.01 Strict, XHTML 1.0 Transitional	12.27	6.26
Islington	HTML 5, XHTML 1.0 Strict, XHTML 1.0 Transitional	59.21	13.78
Barking & Dagenham	XHTML 1.0 Transitional	18.97	17.08
Croydon	XHTML 1.0 Strict, XHTML 1.0 Transitional, HTML 4.01 Transitional	15.77	18.59

An Interoperability Approach for Enabling Access to e-Justice Systems across Europe

Enrico Francesconi

ITTIG-CNR - via de' Barucci 20, Florence, Italy

Abstract. The creation of a pan-European area of Justice is one of the leading policies of the EU: to this aim the development of e-Justice services across Europe has been promoted within the e-CODEX project. In this paper an overview of the e-Justice platform architecture developed by e-CODEX, as well as the semantic solution conceived to transmit business documents in the domain of Justice within a scenario characterized by different languages and different legal systems, are described.

Keywords: e-Justice, Semantic interoperability, Knowledge representation, e-Delivery, Domain Modeling, Document Modeling.

1 Introduction

Over the last few years the European Union has encouraged policies towards the creation of a pan European judicial area as a main pillar for the creation of a new concept of European citizenship based on the certainty of the law and the effectiveness of rights. In this respect the European e-Justice Strategy [1] and Action Plan [2] promoted the development of the European e-Justice Portal, as well as projects able to create direct services for the citizens able to facilitate access to the information in the field of justice, dematerialization of proceedings, as well as communication between judicial authorities. The e-Justice Portal is now a reality[1], targeted to represent a front end for citizens and companies, for instance to file a claim within the domain of civil law. The aim is to reduce operating costs and procedural deadlines in the administration of Justice, to facilitate the access to cross-border judicial procedures for citizens and, in the end, to create a system of e-Justice in the European multi-language framework.

In this context the e-CODEX[2] project is a Large Scale Pilot in the domain of e-Justice, aiming to implement building blocks for a system supporting cross borders judicial procedures between European Member States and to provide citizens, enterprises and legal professionals with an easier access to transnational justice. In this respect it is not intended to replace national solutions but to provide standards and tools for information exchange and interoperability in

---

[1] http://e-justice.europa.eu (Retrieved on 31/03/2014).

[2] e-Justice Communication via Online Data EXchange (http://www.e-codex.eu) (Retrieved on 31/03/2014).

A. Kő and E. Francesconi (Eds.): EGOVIS 2014, LNCS 8650, pp. 26–40, 2014.

the software tools, respecting the existing diversity. Transport of data and documents is a key target of the e-CODEX platform. In a transnational settings it means transport of information from one country to another, also including communication between the e-Justice Portal and national systems.

In this paper the main features of the e-CODEX system, based on semantic technologies and Web services, will be summed up. In particular the relation with other similar pilots (Section 2) and the architecture of the e-Delivery platform (Section 3) will be presented. Moreover the approach, based on document standards and semantic models, able to provide a semantic interoperability layer for message exchange will be described (Sections 4, 5, 6). In particular (Section 7) such knowledge modeling approach deployed on a specific example is presented. Finally some conclusions and future developments are discussed (Section 8).

2 Related Projects

The e-Justice pilot represented by e-CODEX is not intended to operate in isolation but is able to benefit strongly from the experiences and results of the other Large Scale Pilots (LSPs) and also other pan-European e-Government projects. Especially with regard to the other LSPs, the e-Justice pilot aims to build on existing products and standards already created in the other projects, in particular PEPPOL, STORK and SPOCS.

PEPPOL[3] aims at enabling seamless cross-border e-Procurement, connecting communities through standard-based solutions. To this aim it enables access to the Business Document Exchange Network (BUSDOX), its standards-based IT infrastructure for metadata transport service based on OASIS BDX. It provides services for e-Procurement with standardised electronic document formats, with the aim to facilitate the pre-award and post-award procurement process.

STORK[4] and SPOCS[5] are meant to allow citizens to establish new e-relations across borders. STORK, in particular, is targeted to establish a European eID Interoperability Platform; SPOCS, on the other hand, aims to support small and medium enterprises delivering services in all Member States through the provision of seamless electronic procedures by building cross-border solutions based on each country's existing systems. Both projects use the same e-Delivery solution exploiting the standardization work in the area of Registered E-Mail (REM) using ETSI specifications (ETSI-REM) but also the generalized implementation of transportation standards based on the Web Services Stack and SOAP (OASIS ebMS).

The solutions provided by such LSPs represent the infrastructure which the e-CODEX platform is based on; in this respect, and for explicit mandate of the

---

[3] Pan-European Public Procurement Online (http://www.peppol.eu) (Retrieved on 31/03/2014).

[4] Secure idenTity acrOss boRders linKed (https://www.eid-stork.eu) (Retrieved on 31/03/2014).

[5] Simple Procedures Online for Cross-border Services (http://www.eu-spocs.eu) (Retrieved on 31/03/2014).

EU Commission, the e-CODEX platform is going to represent the convergence solution for the other LSPs.

3   The Architecture of the e-CODEX e-Delivery Solution

The e-CODEX platform for e-Delivery solution will provide facilities for cross border communication via gateways, behind which national domains should stay unchanged. It aims to implement functionalities of reliable messaging delivery between national gateways, including persistence, timestamps to track the chain between sender and receiver, evidences of delivery and acceptance, large message handling, security and encryption of messages.

To guarantee such a reliable messaging between the actual endpoints located within the national domains a so-called "circle of trust", based on legal agreements, is established. Moreover, to provide reliability and non-repudiation between endpoints, the e-Delivery convergence scenario also foresees standardized evidences based on ETSI REM specifications [3]. Gateways will be endowed with routing capabilities able to resolve gataway physical addresses and national competent courts from a central/decentral DB including national filing system IDs for integration into existing national infrastructure.

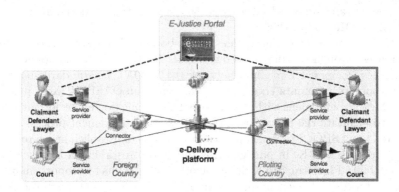

Fig. 1. High level architecture

The high level architecture, based on PEPPOL, is sketched in Fig. 1: it shows a basic architecture of the e-Delivery solution, set up by national gateways which are bilaterally connected to each other, consequently there is no central hub in the middle. National gateways interconnect to the national systems respective applications by adapters (here called 'connectors') which handle the format used by e-CODEX with respect to national oriented communication and formats. The interoperability framework is, on the other hand, represented by an interoperability layer including profiles of secure and reliable transport standards, as OASIS ebMS 3.0 format for message exchange, ETSI-REM evidence format, Web services engines based on Apache Axis2[6] architecture, as well as a semantic layer

---

[6] http://axis.apache.org (Retrieved on 31/03/2014).

necessary for negotiating concepts between different Member States and legal systems (see Section 4).

The open source product Holodeck[7] is used as basic infrastructure to implement business documents exchange using ebMS 3.0 standard. This will serve as the basis for the e-CODEX gateway. The reason for choosing this product is that it is freely useable (open source), easily extensible and natively implements an ebMS 3.0 stack.

The development of 'connectors' between national gateways and national information systems is up to each Member State. Connectors act as an interface between national and European e-Delivery systems, keeping national systems unchanged, nevertheless facilitating message routing according to the schema reported in Fig. 2. In this picture the connector functions, concerning the trust and evidence components as well as metadata and address lookup for forwarding messages to the target gateways, are highlighted. Similarly, the transformation of messages to/from EU format and semantic intermediary functions of the interoperability layer are sketched. The way such semantic intermediary functions are implemented in the project are discussed in the next sections with respect to the foreseen use cases.

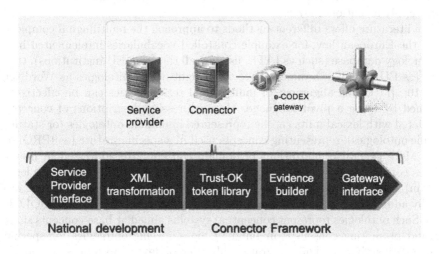

Fig. 2. e-CODEX message routing

4   Semantic Interoperability

For the purposes of e-CODEX message exchange between Member States, having different legal systems and traditions, it is essential to provide a semantic interoperability layer for sharing and harmonizing the meaning of national jurisdiction-dependent concepts. For the piloting phase of the project two use cases have been foreseen: they are related to the exchange of application forms

---

[7] http://holodeck-b2b.sourceforge.net (Retrieved on 31/03/2014).

within the EU Small Claims and European Payment Order procedures, as ruled by the corresponding EU regulations ([4] [5] [6]). Country-dependent legal systems, as well as the diversity of languages, make the exchange of legal information between Member States a challenging task. For this purpose a conceptual model, formalized in an ontology, is necessary for negotiating concepts between different legal systems.

To approach the complexity of the EU multilingual legal scenario, as well as to align concepts of the EU legal domain, one cannot just transfer the conceptual structure of a legal system to another, because of different national legal contexts and legislative cultures within EU Member States [7] [8]. A similar problem arises even with regards to the obligation of EU Member States to implement European Directives into national laws. Far from being a straight transposition, this process usually includes a further step in which European Directives are subject to interpretation which can lead to diverging legislation within the Member States (see [7] for interesting examples). With respect to other domains where conceptual negotiations mainly pertain to linguistic aspects (as for example the e-Health domain), in the e-Justice one, meanings negotiation addresses legal concept nuances in different legal systems and traditions. On the other hand shared interpretation of legal concepts is a pre-condition of EU regulations, which directly apply at national levels.

The literature offers different methods to approach the multilingual complexity of the European law, for example controlled vocabularies implemented in a terminology database (such as IATE, used by all the main EU Institutions), thesauri (as EUROVOC), semantic lexicons or lightweight ontologies as WordNet ([9], [10], [11]). The alignment of multilingual terminologies can be effectively obtained by using a pivot language. More expressive descriptions of concepts associated with lexical units can be represented in domain ontologies (or statute specific ontologies), representing concepts used in a specific statute (as IPROnto [12]). More general organizations of domain concepts are addressed in literature as core ontologies (as LRI-Core [13], LKIF [14] and CLO [15] for the legal domain), while foundational concepts categories, applicable to all domains, are usually addressed in top or foundational ontologies (as SUMO [16] and DOLCE [17]). Such ontologies represent conceptual systems aimed at base-concepts sharing and promoting consensus in building more specific ontologies for specific domains or activities. The integration of different lexical resources (heterogeneous because of belonging to different law systems, or expressed in different languages, or pertaining to different domains) can be carried out in different fashions: 1) generate single resources (merging); 2) compare and define correspondences and differences (mapping); 3) combine different levels of knowledge, basically interfacing lexical resources and ontologies.

The use of a pivot conceptual structure is generally recommended in order to provide a reference for negotiating concepts meaning between Member States, thus providing a layer of legal concepts harmonization in view of the creation of a pan-European judicial area. In this respect the methodological approach chosen in the e-CODEX project is to combine different levels of knowledge, where national legal concepts are reconciled or mapped towards a more general conceptual model.

5 Modeling Semantic Interoperability

e-CODEX uses a 3-levels model towards semantic interoperability: conceptual, logical and physical. The *Conceptual model* is the model for communication and harmonization. It guides and supports business and IT to create the foundation for information exchange, through reuse of experience and application of already known and used concepts. The *Logical model* is the set of data types and code lists ensuring that data definitions are derived methodologically to enhance reusability at the physical level (for e-CODEX the CCTS[8] standards are used). The *Physical model* is the syntax and data formats ensuring mutual understanding between systems of information exchanging partners (XML/XSD and PDF are example of syntax and data formats at physical layer).

5.1 Domain and Document Modeling

The three layers of abstraction introduced so far (conceptual, logical and physical) allow us to identify both the conceptual and technical (data types and syntax) building blocks for describing document types and domain concepts to be exchanged: they represent a methodological framework which is followed by e-CODEX. The main requirement of the project is that, while legal concepts at EU level have different nuances in different legal systems and traditions, e-CODEX documents, pertaining to specific legal procedures, have a structure regulated by the related directives, valid for all the Member States jurisdictions.

Within such framework, proper domain and document modelling have been conceived to address the e-Justice cross-border data/documents exchange as exemplified by the foreseen use cases.

The analysis of the e-CODEX use cases regulations, referred in Section 4, and of the related application forms, identified the following steps and formats for business document exchange, as implemented through the EU e-Justice portal:

- To generate and sign a PDF version of a Web filled form;
- To generate a machine readable version (typically in XML) from the same Web filled form;
- To deliver both signed PDF and XML versions of the form.

In this scenario the descriptions of both domain concepts, addressed in the use cases forms, and form instances are essential requirements for modeling the e-CODEX form generation and delivery. In particular we can distinguish between *Domain Model*, as the model of the scenario to be addressed, and *Document*

---

[8] UN/CEFACT Core Components Technical Specification. Version 3.0. Second Public Review. 16-April-2007.

Model, as the model of a document instance (in our case a form) pertaining to that scenario. Each of them can be furtherly distinguished as follows.

In a bottom-up modeling approach, the Document Model can be viewed according to two layers of abstraction, whose definitions follow those firstly given in literature in the early nineties in [18–20]. The two layers, in fact, are defined as follows:

- The *Document Physical Model* is the collection of the document objects viewed on the basis of their physical, domain independent, function. In e-CODEX it represents the view of a document form in terms of physical components (ex: input fields, check boxes, radio buttons, labels, text boxes, etc.). A specific PDF form or an HTML form are instances of the Document Physical Model.
- The *Document Logical Model* is the collection of the document objects, viewed on the basis of the human-perceptible meaning of their content. In e-CODEX it represents the view of a document form in terms of logical components: ex. Claimant, Claimant name, Claimant address, Court name, etc, as well as their values and relations. A specific XML or an RDF set of triples are instances of the Document Logical Model.

According to the same bottom-up modeling approach, the Domain Model can be viewed according to two layers of abstraction:

- The *Domain Logical Model* is the set of building blocks (data types, code lists, etc.) to describe the documents of a particular domain of interest.
- The *Domain Conceptual Model* is a semantic description of the scenario (entities and relations) of a specific domain. In e-CODEX it allows us to provide meaning to the document physical objects: it gives semantic interpretation to the document elements (physical objects) in terms of logical objects, and it can be represented by element hierarchies (XMLSchema) or ontologies (RDFS/OWL).

Summing up this modeling approach, we can distinguish the following modeling layers and hierarchies:

1. Domain Model
   1.a) Domain Conceptual Model;
   1.b) Domain Logical Model;
2. Document Model
   2.a) Document Logical Model;
   2.b) Document Physical Model.

See also Fig. 3 showing the relationships between Domain and Document Models.

In this view, the two sub-layers of the Document Model are different levels of abstraction (physical and logical) for modeling a document instance. On the other hand, the two sub-layers of the Domain Model are the description of the scenario in terms of concepts and relations between them (Domain Conceptual

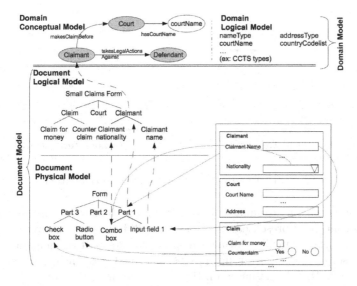

Fig. 3. Relations between Domain and Document Models

Model) as well as data types (Domain Logical Model) according to which you give logical meaning to the document physical components. In other words, they are the semantic instruments to view document physical objects in terms of document logical objects.

6 Technical Implementation of the Modeling Layers

From a technical point of view two strategies for implementing the knowledge modeling proposed in Fig. 3 are being carried out, according to different degrees of complexity, so that they can be viewed in a short or long term.

6.1 Short Term Strategy

In a short term strategy, needed for the e-CODEX piloting phase, the modeling layers are implemented using semantic tools with a limited degree of expressivity. According to this strategy, while the Document Physical Model is the view of an HTML or PDF form in terms of physical objects, the Document Logical Model is the view of such objects as logical components, described by an XML file, compliant to an XMLSchema representing the Domain Model including elements and relations (Domain Conceptual Model), as well as datatype (Domain Logical Model) (Fig. 4a). In Tab. 1 such knowledge modelling and its technical implementation for the e-CODEX short term strategy are reported.

For implementing such modeling strategy, a 'core-team' of data modelers has been established: it is responsible for creating, editing and extending the concept of a shared semantic library. This limited amount of staff members creates the

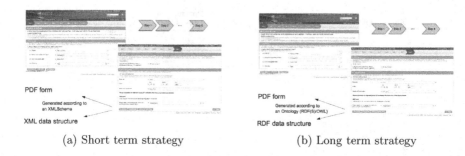

(a) Short term strategy   (b) Long term strategy

Fig. 4. Short and long term strategy form generation

concepts based on the articulated information requirements from the use cases. A created concept is presented to a 'user council' in order to approve a concept for use. The 'user council' is formed by all stakeholders of the semantic library. Finally a 'schema creation group' has been formed, responsible to create and maintain an XML Schema based on the available semantic library.

Table 1. e-CODEX "short term strategy"

Knowledge Modeling	Technical Implementation
Domain Model	
a) Domain Conceptual Model	XMLSchema
b) Domain Logical Model	Data types, code lists (ex. CCTS or specific e-CODEX proprietary datatypes)
Document Model	
a) Document Logical Model	XML file
b) Document Physical Model	HTML or PDF forms

6.2   Long Term Strategy

In a long term, e-CODEX knowledge modeling is supposed to develop a solution with a high degree of expressivity in order to describe the complexity of the scenario to be addressed and to cope with sustainability requirements. For these reasons a more complex knowledge modeling solution can be foreseen.

Table 2. e-CODEX "long term strategy"

Knowledge Modeling	Technical Implementation
Domain Model	
a) Domain Conceptual Model	RDFS/OWL model (ontology)
b) Domain Logical Model	Data types, code lists (ex. CCTS or specific e-CODEX property datatypes)
Document Model	
a) Document Logical Model	RDF file
b) Document Physical Model	HTML or PDF forms

According to this long term solution, the Document Physical Model is the view of an HTML or PDF form in terms of physical objects, the Document Logical Model is the logical view of such objects that can be described by an RDF file able to represent statements over entities, including qualified relations (Fig. 4b). The meaning of such entities and relations can be given by an ontology (Domain Model) of classes and relations (Domain Conceptual Model) as well as datatype and codelists (Domain Logical Model). In Tab. 2 such knowledge modeling and its technical implementation for the e-CODEX long term strategy are reported.

Differently from the short term strategy (Domain Model expressed by an XMLSchema), in a long term strategy the Domain Model is expressed using RDFS/OWL technologies, so to provide a more detailed representation of the meaning of the concepts involved and a more expressive description of the relations between them. An excerpt of concepts and qualified relations between the actors involved in the e-CODEX domain is reported in Fig. 5. It represents an excerpt of the general scenario of a claim including its basic players: Claimant, Defendant and Court, as well as their mutual relationships. In the e-CODEX knowledge modeling language, it represents an excerpt of an e-CODEX Domain Model: it is composed by the Domain Conceptual Model (concepts and relationships) and the Domain Logical Model (data types, code lists, etc. associated to concepts and relationships).

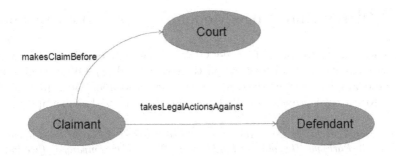

Fig. 5. e-CODEX Domain Model excerpt

An important goal of the Domain Model is to overcome the project finding that "all legislation seems to define its own semantics". e-CODEX noticed that currently each time a legal procedure is taken up for electronic proceeding basic legal concepts have to be analyzed and modeled to match exactly the definition in the legislation at hand. Notwithstanding the necessity for nuances in legal matters, the aforementioned legal concepts are of such generic nature that harmonization seems possible and desirable. Therefore the e-CODEX working group on semantics proposes to develop Core Legal Concepts, as a ground to develop a Domain Model, following the methodology used by the European Commission

DIGIT's ISA Program[9]. The idea is to harmonize data definitions to the benefit of electronic proceedings through the introduction of Core Legal Concepts. Also, such Core Legal Concepts would enable faster electronic deployment of cross border legal procedures.

ISA has in particular provided specific recommendations for concepts identification, both in terms of format and of design rules and management, in order to guarantee persistence and long term maintenance. As recommended by the ISA initiative[10], Core Vocabularies are to be published in multiple formats, including RDF to be useful for linked data applications. This entails that vocabulary terms have to be identified by dereferentiable http URIs.

Following such URIs pattern suggestions for vocabularies, the terms of a Core Legal Concepts vocabulary can be identified by the following hash URI namespace: `http://[URIroot]/def/CoreLegalConcepts#`, where `[URIroot]` is the domain name of the provider. For example the URI for the concept Claim, represented in the Core Legal Concept vocabulary, will be: `http://[URIroot]/def/CoreLegalConcepts#Claim` ; such URI will point to the latest version of related vocabulary. In order to distinguish between different versions of the same vocabulary, as well as different meaning of the same terms in different vocabulary versions, it is recommended that the version date of the vocabulary is added to the vocabulary namespace, according to the following pattern `http://[URIroot]/def/{year}/{month}/{day}/CoreLegalConcepts#`

7 e-CODEX Knowledge Modeling Deployed on Example

In this section a deployment of the e-CODEX knowledge modeling architecture, based on semantic technologies, in particular on RDF(S)/OWL, is shown. A narrative example, here below, concerning a scenario about a dispute leading litigants to start a European small claim procedure, is used as example:

> *Franz von Liebensfels from Klagenfurt rented an Opel Astra on the Internet for use in Portugal. He collected the car from Rental Car company's office in a street in the centre of Lisbon. Due to the existence of damage to the vehicle he decided to go to the company's office at the airport and the employee agreed to the change. The employee inspected the Opel Astra and discovered damage to the windscreen. Mr. Liebenfels assured him that this was already there when he had collected the vehicle. The consumer subsequently saw that his credit card had been charged with the sum of 400 Euro. He decides to file a claim against Rental Car at the court of Lisbon using the European Small Claim Procedure.*

The narrative of Franz von Liebensfels and his car rental, can be generalized and summarized into a more abstract narrative as follows:

---

[9] DIGIT: Directorate-General for Informatics; ISA: Interoperability Solutions for European Public Administration.

[10] PwC EU Services EESV, "D3.1 – Process and Methodology for Core Vocabularies", ISA – Interoperability Solutions for European Public Administrations.

*A claimant from a Member State files a claim against a defendant in another
Member State. The claimant filed the claim at a court in the other Member
State demanding reimbursement of the money taking form his credit card by
the defendant.*

The two narratives at different levels of abstraction are the extensional (real
case) description and intentional (generalization) model, respectively, of a small
claim procedure. In the language of the e-CODEX knowledge modeling they can
be, respectively, represented in terms of:

– Document Model, namely the document description of the specific case including real players and their relations, as well as the document physical
  template that generates the logical description of the real case;
– Domain Model, namely the description of the general scenario of a small
  claim procedure, including actor categories and relations.

In the e-CODEX knowledge modeling approach, the extensional description of
the real case is represented by an e-CODEX Document Logical Model generated
by a document template (Document Physical Model) which, in our narrative
case, is a form pertaining to the Small Claim procedure, properly filled in by
the claimant. The connection between the extensional and intensional representations of a small claim scenario stemming from our example is shown in Fig.
6, where individuals and related concepts are represented at different levels of
abstraction.

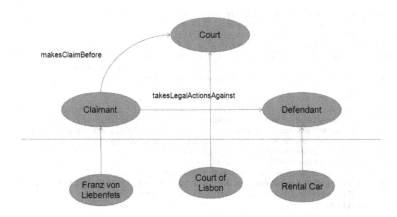

Fig. 6. Relation between extensional (Document Logical Model) and intensional (Domain Model) representations (lower and upper part, respectively) of a small claim
scenario

Here below an RDFS/OWL the Court-Claimant-Defendant scenario and the
RDF/XML serialization of the narrative instance of it, addressed in this paper
where pre-defined URI naming conventions for concepts and documents are used,
are here below respectively reported.

Small Claims Domain Model Excerpt in RDF(S)-OWL/XML

```
<?xml version="1.0"?>
<rdf:RDF
xmlns:rdf="http://www.w3.org/1999/02/22-rdf-syntax-ns#"
xmlns:rdfs="http://www.w3.org/2000/01/rdf-schema#"
xmlns:ESC="http://[URI root]/def/EuropeanSmallClaims#">

    <owl:Class rdf:ID="ESC:Court"/>

    <owl:Class rdf:ID="ESC:Claimant">
        <rdfs:subClassOf rdf:resource="ESC:Person"/>
    </owl:Class>
    <owl:Class rdf:ID="ESC:Defendant">
        <rdfs:subClassOf rdf:resource="ESC:Person"/>
    </owl:Class>
    ...
    <owl:ObjectProperty rdf:ID="makesClaimBefore">
        <rdfs:comment>  Definition of makesClaimBefore property  </rdfs:comment>
        <rdfs:domain rdf:resource="#Claimant"/>
        <rdfs:range  rdf:resource="#Court"/>
    </owl:ObjectProperty>
    <owl:ObjectProperty rdf:ID="takesLegalActionAgainst">
        <rdfs:comment>  Definition of takesLegalActionAgainst property  </rdfs:comment>
        <rdfs:domain rdf:resource="#Claimant"/>
        <rdfs:range  rdf:resource="#Defendant"/>
    </owl:ObjectProperty>
    ...
</rdf:RDF>
```

Small Claims Document Logical Model Excerpt in RDF/XML

```
<?xml version="1.0"?>
<rdf:RDF
xmlns:rdf="http://www.w3.org/1999/02/22-rdf-syntax-ns#"
xmlns:ESC="http://[URI root]/def/EuropeanSmallClaims#">
    <rdf:Description rdf:about="[FormInstanceURI]#id1">
        <rdf:type rdf:resource="ESC#Court"/>
        <ESC:hasCourtName>Court of Lisbon</ESC:hasCourtName>
        <ESC:hasCourtAddress>Rua Polo Sul 43, Lisboa</ESC:hasCourtAddress>
        <ESC:hasCourtCountry>Portugal</ESC:hasCourtCountry>
    </rdf:Description>
    <rdf:Description rdf:about="[FormInstanceURI]#id2">
        <rdf:type rdf:resource="ESC#Claimant"/>
        <ESC:hasClaimantName>Franz von Liebenfels</ESC:hasClaimantName>
        <ESC:hasClaimantAddress>Museumstrasse 12,Klagenfurt</ESC:hasClaimantAddress>
        <ESC:hasClaimantCountry>Osterreich</ESC:hasClaimantCountry>
    <rdf:Description rdf:about="[FormInstanceURI]#id3">
        <rdf:type rdf:resource="ESC#Defendant"/>
        <ESC:hasDefendantName>Rental Car</ESC:hasDefendantName>
        <ESC:hasDefendantAddress>Avenida Sol 1345,Lisboa</ESC:hasDefendantAddress>
        <ESC:hasDefendantCountry>Portugal</ESC:hasDefendantCountry>
    </rdf:Description>
    ...
  </rdf:RDF>
```

8   Conclusions

The e-CODEX project aims to represent an effective implementation of the current e-Justice policies of the European Union towards e-Justice, as well as a basic framework for other pan-European e-Government projects. Legal contents representation and content transport infrastructure are the key activities currently under implementation in a scenario characterized by language and legal systems diversity. Both activities aim to create an interoperability framework based on standards and semantic tools to start and carry out judicial procedures on-line. In particular a legal knowledge modeling approach to promote semantic interoperability for e-Justice in the multilingual and multi-cultural complexity of the EU legal scenarios is proposed and implemented by RDF(S)/OWL technologies. In the next phases of the project particular attention will be payed to the implementation of a secure and reliable data exchanged system, based on evidences and circle of trust, as well as an e-Payment system for a complete on-line finalization of the judicial proceedings.

References

1. European Commission. Towards a European e-justice strategy (2008)
2. European Union Institutions and Bodies. Multi-annual European e-justice action plan 2009-2013 (2009)
3. ETSI. Electronic signatures and infrastructures (esi); registered electronic mail (rem); part 2: Data requirements, formats and signatures for rem. Technical Report ETSI TS 102 640-2, ETSI, v.2.1.1 (2010)
4. The European Parliament and the Council of the European Union. Regulation of the european parliament and of the council of 11 July 2007 establishing a European small claims procedure (July 2009)
5. The European Parliament and the Council of the European Union. Regulation of the European parliament and of the council of 12 December 2006 creating a European order for payment procedure (December 2006)
6. Contini, F., Lanzara, G.F. (eds.): The Circulation of Agency in E-Justice. Interoperability and Infrastructures for European Transborder Judicial Proceedings. Law, Governance and Technology Series, vol. 13. Springer (2014)
7. Ajani, G., Lesmo, L., Boella, G., Mazzei, A., Rossi, P.: Terminological and ontological analysis of European directives: multilingualism in law. In: Proceedings of International Conference on Artificial Intelligence and Law, pp. 43–48. ACM (2007)
8. Van Laer, C.J.P.: The applicability of comparative concepts. Electronic Journal of Comparative Law 2(2) (1998)
9. Fellbaum, C. (ed.): WordNet: An Electronic Lexical Database. MIT Press, Cambridge (1998)
10. Vossen, P. (ed.): EuroWordNet: A Multilingual Database with Lexical Semantic Networks. Kluwer Academic Publishers, Dordrecht (1998)
11. Sagri, M.-T., Tiscornia, D.: Ontology-based models of legal knowledge. In: Wang, S., et al. (eds.) ER Workshops 2004. LNCS, vol. 3289, pp. 577–588. Springer, Heidelberg (2004)
12. Delgado, J., Gallego, I., Llorente, S., Garcia, R.: Ipronto: An ontology for digital rights management. In: Proceedings of the International Conference on Legal Knowledge and Information Systems, pp. 111–120. IOS Press (2003)
13. Breuker, J., Hoekstra, R.: Core concepts of law: taking common-sense seriously. In: Proceedings of Formal Ontologies in Information Systems (2004)
14. Hoekstra, R., Breuker, J., di Bello, M., Boer, A.: Lkif core: Principled ontology development for the legal domain. In: Breuker, J., Casanovas, P., Klein, M., Francesconi, E. (eds.) Legal Ontologies and the Semantic Web. IOS Press (2009)

15. Gangemi, A., Sagri, M.-T., Tiscornia, D.: A constructive framework for legal ontologies. In: Benjamins, V.R., Casanovas, P., Breuker, J., Gangemi, A. (eds.) Law and the Semantic Web. LNCS (LNAI), vol. 3369, pp. 97–124. Springer, Heidelberg (2005)

16. Niles, J., Pease, A.: Towards a standard upper ontology. In: Proceedings of the 2nd International Conference on Formal Ontology in Information Systems, pp. 2–9 (2001)

17. Gangemi, A., Guarino, N., Masolo, C., Oltramari, A., Schneider, L.: Sweetening ontologies with DOLCE. In: Gómez-Pérez, A., Benjamins, V.R. (eds.) EKAW 2002. LNCS (LNAI), vol. 2473, pp. 166–181. Springer, Heidelberg (2002)

18. Esposito, F., Malerba, D., Semeraro, G.: Multistrategy learning for document recognition. Applied Artificial Intelligence, an International Journal 8(1), 33–83 (1994)

19. Tsujimoto, S., Asada, H.: Major components of a complete text reading system. Proceedings of the IEEE 80, 1133–1149 (1992)

20. Tang, Y.Y., De Yan, C., Suen, C.Y.: Document processing for automatic knowledge acquisition. IEEE Transation on Knowledge and Data Engineering 6(1), 3–20 (1994)

An Efficient Homomorphic E-Voting System over Elliptic Curves

M. Àngels Cerveró, Víctor Mateu, Josep M. Miret,
Francesc Sebé, and Javier Valera

Dept. of Mathematics, Universitat de Lleida
Jaume II, 69, 25001, Lleida, Spain
{mcervero,vmateu,miret,fsebe,jvalera}@matematica.udl.cat

Abstract. The homomorphic tallying paradigm provides efficient e-voting solutions when implemented using the multiplicative homomorphic property of the ElGamal cryptosystem. However, that is not the case when implemented over the Elliptic Curve ElGamal cryptosystem (EC-ElGamal) due to the need to solve a knapsack problem for obtaining the election result. In this paper, we present a homomorphic tallying based e-voting system implemented over the Elliptic Curve ElGamal cryptosystem that includes a redundancy system which allows to obtain the election result in a fast way.

1 Introduction

Remote voting systems allow an election to be carried out without requiring its participants to move to the polling place. Instead, participants can cast their ballots through the Internet. A remote voting system should provide the following security features:

- *Authentication:* only people in the electoral roll can vote.
- *Unicity:* each participant can vote once at most.
- *Privacy:* a vote must keep detached from the identity of the voter who cast it.
- *Fairness:* no partial results are revealed.
- *Verifiability:* correctness of the process can be checked.
- *Uncoercibility:* nobody can prove that a voter voted in a particular way.

These security properties are obtained by making use of cryptography. Solutions for remote voting can be classified into three main paradigms: *blind signature based, mix-type* and *homomorphic tallying*.

In the *blind signature based* paradigm [1,2,3], a voter composes her ballot and authenticates against an authentication server. That server checks that the participant appears in the electoral roll and that she has not voted before. In that case, the authentication server blindly signs the participant's ballot (the encrypted vote). After that, the participant casts her ballot to the polling station

A. Kő and E. Francesconi (Eds.): EGOVIS 2014, LNCS 8650, pp. 41–53, 2014.

through an anonymous channel. The polling station only accepts ballots that have been digitally signed by the authentication server. At the end of the voting period, the received ballots are decrypted and tallied.

The *mix-type* paradigm [4,5,6,7,8] resembles a traditional voting process. A participant generates her ballot, encrypts it under the election public key and digitally signs it. After that, the ballot is cast to the polling station which will first validate the digital signature and will next check that this is the first ballot cast by that participant. Once the voting period has ended, the polling station shuffles and re-encrypts (mixes) the collected ballots so that the relation between a ballot and the identity of the participant who cast it is broken. For verifiability purposes, the polling station has to prove in zero knowledge that the mixing process has been performed honestly. Finally, the mixed ballots are decrypted and tallied.

In the *homomorphic tallying* paradigm [9,10,11,12,13,14], a participant generates her vote and encrypts it under some public key cryptosystem with a homomorphic property. Next, she digitally signs her ballot and casts it to the polling station. Once all the ballots have been received, the polling station aggregates them into one or more packages by making use of the homomorphic property of the employed cryptosystem. After that, the packages are decrypted and the election result is obtained from the aggregated cleartexts. In such a system, votes have to be coded so that an election result can be obtained from the cleartext of the aggregated packages. It is necessary that each participant proves in zero knowledge that her vote has been properly composed.

It is well known that homomorphic tallying systems do not scale well as the number of candidates increases. When ballots are aggregated into packages, the system has to avoid cleartext overflowing. In the particular case of multiplicative homomorphic cryptosystems in which an aggregation translates to cleartext multiplication, the cleartext of the aggregated packages grows very fast in size. As a result, the amount of ballots that can be aggregated into a single package is rather small. On the other side, additive homomorphic cryptosystems allow a larger amount of ballots to be aggregated. In these systems, obtaining the final election result requires solving a knapsack problem which is a hard problem when the remote voting system is implemented over elliptic curve cryptography.

1.1   Contribution and Plan of This Paper

In this paper, a remote voting system using the Elliptic Curve ElGamal (EC-ElGamal) cryptosystem is presented. Votes are coded in such a way that the knapsack problem to be solved for vote decoding can be solved in a fast way. As a result, our system can deal with elections with a large amount of participants and candidates.

The paper is structured as follows: Section 2 presents some basic concepts of elliptic curve cryptography and the EC-ElGamal cryptosystem. The proposed system is explained in Section 3. After that, Section 4 is dedicated to prove the security of the system while Sections 5 and 6 are devoted to the experimental results and conclusions.

2   Preliminaries

Given a finite field $\mathbb{F}_p$, $p \neq 2, 3$ prime, an elliptic curve E defined over $\mathbb{F}_p$ is an equation of the form

$$E : y^2 = x^3 + ax + b, \tag{1}$$

with $4a^3 + 27b^2 \neq 0$. The set of points of the curve, denoted $E(\mathbb{F}_p)$, is composed of the points $(x, y) \in \mathbb{F}_p \times \mathbb{F}_p$ satisfying Equation (1) together with the *point at infinity* $\mathcal{O}$. The chord-tangent method permits to endow the set $E(\mathbb{F}_p)$ with an addition operation $+$ so that $(E(\mathbb{F}_p), +)$ has an *abelian group* structure whose identity element is $\mathcal{O}$. Given this group, the *elliptic curve discrete logarithm problem* (ECDLP) [15] consists of, given to points P and Q in $E(\mathbb{F}_p)$, find an integer d that satisfying $Q = d \cdot P$. The ECDLP is computationally hard when the cardinality of $E(\mathbb{F}_p)$ has a large prime factor.

2.1   The Elliptic Curve ElGamal Cryptosystem

The *Elliptic Curve ElGamal* (EC-ElGamal) cryptosystem is composed of the following procedures.

1. *Set up:* A finite field $\mathbb{F}_p$ is first selected. After that, two integers a and b defining an elliptic curve E over $\mathbb{F}_p$ (see Eq. 1) are chosen so that the cardinality of $E(\mathbb{F}_p)$ has a large prime factor q. Finally, a point P of order q is taken as a generator of the order q cyclic subgroup of $E(\mathbb{F}_p)$. The values (p, E, P, q) are made public.
2. *Key generation:* Given the set up parameters, a private key is generated by randomly choosing an integer d in the range $[1, q-1]$. Next, its related public key Q is computed as $Q = d \cdot P$.
3. *Encryption:* A plaintext M consisting of a point of $E(\mathbb{F}_p)$ is encrypted under public key Q by computing

$$E_Q(M) = C = (A, B) = (r \cdot P, M + r \cdot Q),$$

   where r is an integer selected randomly in the range $[1, q - 1]$.
4. *Decryption:* If the private key d is known, a ciphertext C can be decrypted by computing

$$D_d(C) = B - d \cdot A.$$

   The cleartext M is obtained as a result.

The EC-ElGamal cryptosystem has an homomorphic property. Let $C_1 = (A_1, B_1)$ and $C_2 = (A_2, B_2)$ be two ciphertexts encrypting M_1 and M_2, respectively. They are aggregated by computing,

$$C = C_1 + C_2 = (A_1 + A_2, B_1 + B_2).$$

The decryption of C will provide $M_1 + M_2$ as a result.

3   Our Proposal

In this section, we describe a new proposal for an elliptic curve based homomorphic remote voting system. First of all, we enumerate the involved parties:

- *Participants:* They are the voters who will emit a vote. Each participant has a public key pk and its corresponding secret key sk.
- *Polling Station (PS):* It is the coordinator component of the system. It manages the electoral roll and is responsible for collecting the votes. It will next aggregate them into packages that will be decrypted and scrutinized. Finally, it will publish the election result.
- *Bulletin Board (BB):* It is an element on which the PS publishes data which become worldwide available.
- *Key Storage Trusted Party (KSTP):* It is responsible for creating the private/public election key pair. It generates and privately stores the private key, while the public key is made public. When required, it decrypts the aggregated ballot packages.

These parties interact with each other during the three stages of an election: *Set Up*, *Voting* and *Opening*. These stages are detailed next.

3.1   Set Up

During the set up period, the KSTP chooses an elliptic curve E defined over some finite field $\mathbb{F}_p$ and next creates a secret key d. The public key Q is next made public (on the BB) together with the remaining parameters of the EC-ElGamal cryptosystem (p, E, P, q). Also during this period, the PS publishes the electoral roll and some points in $E(\mathbb{F}_p)$ used to represent each of the candidates. The electoral roll includes the public key of each participant.

Let us consider an election with m candidates and N participants. Let n be an integer which represents the amount of ballots that are aggregated into a package.

The m candidates (we represent each candidate by means of an integer ranging from 1 to m) are divided into groups of size four, in such a way that the first group contains the candidates from 1 to 4, the second group contains the candidates from 5 to 8 and so on. In this way, an amount of $t = \lceil m/4 \rceil$ groups is obtained. Next, two lists composed of elliptic curve points are generated. These lists are called *the classic list*, $\mathcal{M}^C$, and *the redundancy list*, $\mathcal{M}^R$. The points in these lists are:

$$\mathcal{M}^C = \left\{ P, \quad (n+1) \cdot P, \quad (n+1)^2 \cdot P, \quad (n+1)^3 \cdot P \right\},$$
$$\mathcal{M}^R = \left\{ P, \quad P, \quad (n+1)^2 \cdot P, \quad (n+1)^3 \cdot P \right\}.$$

Both lists are published on the BB by the *PS*. Next, each candidate j is represented by a pair of points (M_j^C, M_j^R), with $M_j^C \in \mathcal{M}^C$ and $M_j^R \in \mathcal{M}^R$. Table 1 shows the distribution of the candidates into groups and their final representation as points of $E(\mathbb{F}_p)$.

Table 1. Representative points for the candidates

Group 1		Group 2		...	Group t	
$M_1^C = P$	$M_1^R = P$	$M_5^C = P$	$M_5^R = P$		$M_{m-3}^C = P$	$M_{m-3}^R = P$
$M_2^C = (n+1)\cdot P$	$M_2^R = P$	$M_6^C = (n+1)\cdot P$	$M_6^R = P$		$M_{m-2}^C = (n+1)\cdot P$	$M_{m-2}^R = P$
$M_3^C = (n+1)^2\cdot P$	$M_3^R = (n+1)^2\cdot P$	$M_7^C = (n+1)^2\cdot P$	$M_7^R = (n+1)^2\cdot P$		$M_{m-1}^C = (n+1)^2\cdot P$	$M_{m-1}^R = (n+1)^2\cdot P$
$M_4^C = (n+1)^3\cdot P$	$M_4^R = (n+1)^3\cdot P$	$M_8^C = (n+1)^3\cdot P$	$M_8^R = (n+1)^3\cdot P$		$M_m^C = (n+1)^3\cdot P$	$M_m^R = (n+1)^3\cdot P$

| Candidates from 1 to 4 | Candidates from 5 to 8 | Candidates from $(m-3)$ to m |

The value m does not need to be a multiple of 4. In that case, the last group only contains $(m \bmod 4)$ candidate representatives.

The following sections detail how ballots are generated, aggregated and unpacked.

3.2 Voting

The voting process starts when a participant i wants to emit her vote by electing a candidate. Each released vote has to go through four stages: *candidate choice, electoral roll checking, vote coding verification* and *vote packing*.

1) Candidate Choice: Let M_j^C and M_j^R be the curve points representing the choice of the participant i. She emits her vote V_i by performing the following steps:

- *Choice Encryption:* Create two lists V_i^C and V_i^R, each one able to store up to t ciphertexts (t is the total number of groups). V_i^C is the classic list of votes and stores the encryption of classic points while V_i^R is the redundancy list of votes and stores the encryption of the redundancy ones. Being $g = \lceil j/4 \rceil$ the group of the selected candidate represented by the points M_j^C and M_j^R, the vote V_i of participant i is of the form

$$V_i = (V_i^C, V_i^R) = \left((V_{i,1}^C, \ldots, V_{i,t}^C), (V_{i,1}^R, \ldots, V_{i,t}^R) \right),$$

where $\forall\, l \in [1,t]$,

$$V_{i,l}^C = \begin{cases} E_Q(\mathcal{O}), & l \neq g, \\ E_Q(M_j^C), & l = g, \end{cases} \quad \text{and} \quad V_{i,l}^R = \begin{cases} E_Q(\mathcal{O}), & l \neq g, \\ E_Q(M_j^R), & l = g, \end{cases}$$

being E_Q the EC-ElGamal encryption function. Notice that only the position g of each list contains an encryption of a valid candidate point. The other positions are an encryption of the point at infinity.
- *Ballot signature:* Compute $sig_{sk_i}(V_i)$, where sig_{sk_i} is a digital signature of V_i.
- *Ballot casting:* Send $B_i = \{V_i, sig_{sk_i}(V_i)\}$ to the PS.

2) Electoral Roll Checking: When PS receives a ballot, it must verify the validity of its digital signature and check that the participant who emitted it is in the electoral roll and that he has not voted before. If any of these conditions is not met, the ballot is discarded. Otherwise, the PS asks the participant to prove that her ballot was correctly generated.

3) Vote Coding Verification: The PS must ensure that a received ballot is an encryption of a well coded vote. The participant i has to prove that all the cleartexts in it belong to a range of valid values. This verification is done by means of the *Zero Knowledge Proof* described in [16]. Being V_i^C and V_i^R the two lists in the vote V_i, the participant has to demonstrate that:

- All the ciphertexts in V_i^C are an encryption of a point in the set

$$\mathcal{S}^C = \left\{ P, \ (n+1)\cdot P, \ (n+1)^2 \cdot P, \ (n+1)^3 \cdot P, \ \mathcal{O} \right\}.$$

  The data generated for proving this composes the list

$$ZKP_i^C = (ZKP_{i,1}^C, \ldots, ZKP_{i,t}^C),$$

  being $ZKP_{i,j}^C$ the Zero Knowledge Proof ensuring that the cleartext in $V_{i,j}^C$ is on the set $\mathcal{S}^C$.
- All the ciphertexts in V_i^R are an encryption of a point in the set

$$\mathcal{S}^R = \left\{ P, \ (n+1)^2 \cdot P, \ (n+1)^3 \cdot P, \ \mathcal{O} \right\}.$$

  The data generated for proving this composes the list

$$ZKP_i^R = (ZKP_{i,1}^R, \ldots, ZKP_{i,t}^R).$$

- The addition of the two ciphertexts $V_{i,l}^C + V_{i,l}^R$ is an encryption of a point in the set

$$\mathcal{S}^+ = \left\{ 2\cdot P, \ (n+2)\cdot P, \ 2(n+1)^2 \cdot P, \ 2(n+1)^3 \cdot P, \ \mathcal{O} \right\}.$$

  The data generated for proving this composes the list

$$ZKP_i^+ = (ZKP_{i,1}^+, \ldots, ZKP_{i,t}^+),$$

  and proves that the same position in both lists encrypts the same candidate in the corresponding group.
- The addition of all ciphertext $\sum_{l=1}^t \left(V_{i,l}^C + V_{i,l}^R \right)$ is an encryption of a point in the set $\mathcal{S}^+$. This proof ZKP_i^T ensures the participant i has voted for just one candidate.

The complete Zero Knowledge Proof of participant i is given by the set

$$ZKP_i = (ZKP_i^C, ZKP_i^R, ZKP_i^+, ZKP_i^T).$$

Any ballot that passes this proof has been correctly coded. In that case, the PS publishes the signature, the encrypted ballot and its Zero Knowledge Proof data on the BB.

4) Vote Packing: Each ballot is composed of $2t$ ciphertexts, distributed between lists V_i^C and V_i^R. Each individual ciphertext is homomorphically aggregated into the corresponding package. So, the system keeps $2t$ packages storing up to n votes:

$$\mathcal{P}_l^C = \sum_{i=1}^{n} V_{i,l}^C \quad \text{and} \quad \mathcal{P}_l^R = \sum_{i=1}^{n} V_{i,l}^R, \qquad \forall\, l \in [1,t].$$

The classic package $\mathcal{P}_l^C$ aggregates all the votes located at position l of the classic lists V_i^C and the redundancy package $\mathcal{P}_l^R$ stores the votes at the same position in the redundancy lists V_i^R.

We call *meta-package* $\mathcal{P}$ the list of packages $\mathcal{P} = \left(\mathcal{P}_1^C, \ldots, \mathcal{P}_t^C, \mathcal{P}_1^R, \ldots, \mathcal{P}_t^R\right)$.

3.3 Opening

Once the election has finished, it is time to decrypt the ballots and tally the votes. This process is composed of four steps: *meta-packages decryption, unpacking, scrutiny* and *publication*.

1) Meta-Packages Decryption: When the voting period is over, the PS has a set of $\ell = \lceil N/n \rceil$ encrypted meta-packages, where N is the number of participants that effectively emitted a vote and n is the size of the packages. In order to get the plaintext votes, these meta-packages $\mathcal{P}^h$, $h \in [1, \ell]$, are sent to the KSTP, which decrypts them (it decrypts all the packages in each meta-package). Finally, the KSTP returns the decrypted meta-packages $\widehat{\mathcal{P}}^h$ to the PS so that they can be unpacked and tallied.

2) Unpacking: An homomorphic remote voting system needs an additional decoding step in which the plaintext of the aggregated packages is processed so as to obtain the amount of votes for each candidate. In particular, the meta-packages of our system consist of a list of t classic and t redundancy packages. That is

$$\widehat{\mathcal{P}}^h = \left(\widehat{\mathcal{P}}_1^{C,h}, \ldots, \widehat{\mathcal{P}}_t^{C,h}, \widehat{\mathcal{P}}_1^{R,h}, \ldots, \widehat{\mathcal{P}}_t^{R,h}\right)$$

where $\forall\, l \in [1, t]$

$$\begin{cases} \widehat{\mathcal{P}}_l^{C,h} = \sum_{j=1}^{4} x_{4(l-1)+j}^h \cdot M_{4(l-1)+j}^C, \\ \widehat{\mathcal{P}}_l^{R,h} = \sum_{j=1}^{4} x_{4(l-1)+j}^h \cdot M_{4(l-1)+j}^R, \end{cases} \tag{2}$$

being $x_{4(l-1)+j}^h$ the votes received for the candidate $4(l-1)+j$ and aggregated to the meta-package $\widehat{\mathcal{P}}^h$.

In order to get the amount of votes $x_{4(l-1)+j}^h$ in (2), we propose to process the coded packages and solve a set of knapsack problems over the group $E(\mathbb{F}_p)$. Our solution implements a *Meet-in-the-Middle* (MITM) algorithm to solve the redundancy packages.

For the sake of simplicity, the decrypted packages for the candidates from 1 to 4 are of the form

$$\widehat{\mathcal{P}}_1^C = x_1 \cdot P + x_2(n+1) \cdot P + x_3(n+1)^2 \cdot P + x_4(n+1)^3 \cdot P,$$
$$\widehat{\mathcal{P}}_1^R = x_1 \cdot P + x_2 \cdot P + x_3(n+1)^2 \cdot P + x_4(n+1)^3 \cdot P.$$

During a preprocess time, we compute the list of elliptic curve points $\mathcal{A} = (0 \cdot P, 1 \cdot P, \ldots, n \cdot P)$. These are the $n+1$ possible points that can be reached for the first two candidates in package $\widehat{\mathcal{P}}_1^R$. Then, for each point $k \cdot P \in \mathcal{A}$ we compute all the possible combinations of x_1 and x_2 such that $k \cdot P = x_1 \cdot P + x_2 \cdot P$. With those successful combinations (x_1, x_2), we also compute the points $x_1 \cdot P + x_2(n+1) \cdot P$. We store the key-value pair $\big(x_1 \cdot P + x_2(n+1) \cdot P, \ (x_1, x_2)\big)$ in a hash table $\mathcal{H}_1$.

On the other hand, we also compute all the feasible combinations of (x_3, x_4) and the corresponding points $x_3(n+1)^2 \cdot P + x_4(n+1)^3 \cdot P$ are also stored in a hash table $\mathcal{H}_2$. This precomputed data can be used for decoding all the redundancy packages. This is because all of them have coded the candidates in the same manner.

So as to unpack $\widehat{\mathcal{P}}_1^R$, we compute the point $\widehat{\mathcal{P}}'^R = \widehat{\mathcal{P}}_1^R - k \cdot P$, for each $k \cdot P \in \mathcal{A}$ until $\widehat{\mathcal{P}}'^R$ is found in $\mathcal{H}_2$. When this happens, the correct values for x_3 and x_4 are obtained. We get the values x_1 and x_2 by checking the point $\widehat{\mathcal{P}}_1^C - [x_3(n+1)^2 \cdot P + x_4(n+1)^3 \cdot P]$ in the hash table $\mathcal{H}_1$.

The unpacking process described is applied to all the t pairs of classic-redundancy packages of each decrypted meta-package.

3) Scrutiny: When each meta-package $\widehat{\mathcal{P}}^h$ has been decoded, the PS only needs to sum the votes obtained from each package to finally scrutiny the election result. The total amount of votes for candidate j is

$$\sum_{h=1}^{\ell} x_j^h,$$

where $\ell = \lceil N/n \rceil$ is the total number of meta-packages and $(x_1^h, \ldots, x_m^h)$ are the values obtained from the meta-package $\widehat{\mathcal{P}}^h$.

4) Publication: After obtaining the final result of the voting process, the PS publishes the election data on the BB. This data comprises the final result of the election and all the information needed to verify the process. The BB exposes the votes received for each candidate and the encrypted homomorphic meta-packages together with their capacity n.

4   Security

In this section we prove that our system achieves the security requirements given in Section 1.

Authentication: The system has to ensure that only people in the electoral roll can cast a vote. This fact is guaranteed by means of the digital signature attached to each ballot. The digital signature provides three properties to the ballot it is linked to:

- Authentication: the signature has been cast by the participant who owns the associated pair of public and private keys.
- Integrity: any modification to the ballot invalidates the signature so that any unfair alteration of the ballot by a third person can be detected. This is ensured assuming the collision resistance of the involved hash function.
- Non-repudiation: the participant who signed a ballot can not deny having cast it.

Hence, the signature associated to each ballot ensures that the participant is who he says to be and he is on the electoral roll, that the vote is his and that the content of the vote has not been altered.

The electoral roll and the encrypted ballots are publicly available on the BB so that anybody can check that all participants have been authenticated.

Unicity: The system must ensure that:

1. Each participant can vote only once;
2. Each ballot contains just one vote. Multiple votes for the same candidate or multiple votes for different candidates are not allowed in a ballot.

The first issue is solved by casting digitally signed ballots. In this way, ballots are authenticated and the system can keep a register of all the participants that have already voted. If a participant sent two or more ballots, the system would only accept the first one.

The second issue is solved by means of the Zero Knowledge Proof generated by the voters in the *vote coding verification* step. Each pair (V_i, ZKP_i) ensures the following aspects regarding V_i:

- The classic and the redundancy ciphertexts are encryptions of the same candidate.
- There is only one voted candidate.

Privacy: The vote content is kept private since all the ballots are encrypted using EC-ElGamal cryptosystem and aggregated homomorphically into meta-packages.

The EC-ElGamal cryptosystem is secure under the assumed intractability of the elliptic curve discrete logarithm problem. No one, except from the KSTP, who owns the private key, can decrypt a single ballot or a meta-package. The decryption of the meta-packages is performed by the KSTP only after the voting process is concluded. In addition, the homomorphic aggregation of the encrypted votes decouples any relation between the participants and their votes. Finally, the Zero Knowledge Proof does not leak any information about the encrypted votes.

Fairness: Assuming the KSTP keeps the private key secret until the voting stage is concluded, no vote is decrypted before the opening stage.

Verifiability: The verifiability of our system holds on four points:

- The electoral roll is public. Anyone can check that all the ballots received during the election come from valid participants by verifying the attached digital signatures.
- The BB publishes the Zero Knowledge Proof data of each ballot, so that anyone can also verify them.
- The homomorphic packing can be verified from the list of received ballots and the list of meta-packages. Anyone can homomorphically aggregate the ballots and check the results against the published meta-packages.
- The decryption step is also performed verifiably by the KSTP [17].

Uncoercibility: It can be provided by applying any *coercion-resistance* solution like [18], which solves this issue by using a system of registration and credentials for the voters. That system allows to check electoral roll (only listed participants can emit their vote) without revealing if a particular participant voted. Moreover, it decouples the content of the vote from the voter so that no attacker can link its attempted coercion with the final result of the election.

5   Experimental Results

We have developed a test program to check the time and memory consumption of the proposed e-voting system. This program has been implemented in $C++$ using the $Crypto++$ library and run over a *Debian 8.0 Jessie* OS in a PC with an *Intel Core i5 650 3.2GHz* CPU with 6GB of RAM.

The unpacking algorithm described in Section 3.3 has a $O(n)$ linear cost per package ($O(t{\cdot}n)$ per meta-package). Notice that, in order to decode each package, we only need to check the $n+1$ points stored in the array $\mathcal{A}$, subtract them from the point representing the corresponding package and test whether the result is in the hash map $\mathcal{H}_2$. After this is done, we only need to look in $\mathcal{H}_1$ for the final combination of votes.

We have simulated several examples of e-voting processes with different number of candidates and package sizes in order to study the time and memory costs of the proposed system. Table 2 presents the time needed to unpack a complete meta-package containing 100, 250, 500 and 1000 aggregated votes. The tests have been done for 4, 10, 20 and 30 candidates. We can see that our system decodes the homomorphic packages very efficiently, including large packages storing 1000 votes for an election with 30 candidates.

On the other hand, Table 3 shows time consumption of the preprocessing stage and the memory requirements to store all the data needed to decode a single package. Notice that these costs are completely independent of the number of candidates of the election because all the packages belonging to a single meta-package are coded in the same way. We can see that the time and space requirements can be perfectly assumed so that any commodity PC could afford them. Note that the preprocessing computations can be carried out before the election starts.

Table 2. Unpacking time for different number of candidates and meta-packages size

Number of Candidates	Meta-Package size n	Unpacking time (ms)
4	100	1,17
	250	2,95
	500	5,98
	1000	12,15
10	100	1,22
	250	2,98
	500	6,14
	1000	13,12
20	100	1,22
	250	3,02
	500	5,93
	1000	12,16
30	100	1,45
	250	3,06
	500	6,05
	1000	12,31

Table 3. Preprocessing time and Memory requirements for meta-packages

Meta-Package size n	Preprocessing time (s)	Memory (MB)
100	1,06	1,53
250	6,78	9,41
500	28,03	37,42
1000	116,15	149,22

By comparing our proposal with that presented by Peng et al. [14], we can see that our unpacking algorithm is much more efficient than that in [14] (also implemented in $C++$ using $Crypto++$ and executed over the same PC). The proposal of Peng et al. uses the multiplicative homomorphic property of ElGamal with 1024 bits long public keys. Its main drawback is that the maximum capacity of the packages it can manage is rather small. Table 4 presents the results obtained with that multiplicative system. For several numbers of candidates, the table shows the maximum package size and the time required to decode each package. Observe that our system is more efficient and can manage much larger packages than [14].

Although the proposal in [14] is faster than our method during the encryption and decryption phases when the number of candidates is large (see Table 5), their whole e-voting process is slower than ours. For example, in an election with 30 candidates and 1000 voters, our system just needs to decrypt a single meta-package, while [14] needs to decrypt up to 7 packages.

The most expensive stage of our method is the Zero Knowledge Proof required to prove a ballot was properly coded.

Table 4. Package size and unpacking time for a multiplicative homomorphic system

Number of Candidates	Maximum package size n	Unpacking time (ms)
4	364	20,50
10	209	14,10
20	165	12,00
30	149	11,40

Table 5. Comparison of the encryption and decryption times (ms) between our EC-ElGamal system and the multiplicative ElGamal system in [14]

	Number of Candidates	Presented method	Peng et al. [14] method
Encryption time	4	0.0018	
	10	0.0052	0.0057
	20	0.0087	
	30	0.0138	
Decryption time	4	0.0009	
	10	0.0026	0.0030
	20	0.00436	
	30	0.0070	

6 Conclusion

A new homomorphic tallying e-voting system using the EC-ElGamal cryptosystem has been presented. It allows to use the benefits of elliptic curve cryptography while offering an affordable ballot package decoding time. The homomorphic unpacking stage can be performed efficiently by taking advantage of a redundant information technique. Moreover, the cost of the homomorphic decoding of a package is linear $O(n)$ with the amount n of aggregated ballots.

The presented system would benefit from advances in methods to prove a proper coding of votes encrypted under the EC-ElGamal cryptosystem.

Acknowledgments. Research of the authors was supported in part by grants MTM2010-21580-C02-01 (Spanish Ministerio de Ciencia e Innovación), 2014SGR-1666 (Generalitat de Catalunya) and IPT-2012-0603-430000 (Spanish Ministerio de Economía y Competitividad).

References

1. Chaum, D.: Security without identification: transaction systems to make big brother obsolete. Communications of the ACM 28(10), 1030–1044 (1985)
2. Fujioka, A., Okamoto, T., Ohta, K.: A practical secret voting scheme for large scale elections. In: Zheng, Y., Seberry, J. (eds.) AUSCRYPT 1992. LNCS, vol. 718, pp. 244–251. Springer, Heidelberg (1993)

3. Ohkubo, M., Miura, F., Abe, M., Fujioka, A., Okamoto, T.: An improvement on a practical secret voting scheme. In: Zheng, Y., Mambo, M. (eds.) ISW 1999. LNCS, vol. 1729, pp. 225–234. Springer, Heidelberg (1999)
4. Sako, K., Kilian, J.: Receipt-free mix-type voting scheme: A practical solution to the implementation of a voting booth. In: Guillou, L.C., Quisquater, J.-J. (eds.) EUROCRYPT 1995. LNCS, vol. 921, pp. 393–403. Springer, Heidelberg (1995)
5. Jakobsson, M.: A practical mix. In: Nyberg, K. (ed.) EUROCRYPT 1998. LNCS, vol. 1403, pp. 448–461. Springer, Heidelberg (1998)
6. Sebé, F., Miret, J.M., Pujolàs, J., Puiggalí, J.: Simple and efficient hash-based verifiable mixing for remote electronic voting. Computer Communications 33(6), 667–675 (2010)
7. Peng, K.: An efficient shuffling based eVoting scheme. J. Syst. Softw. 84(6), 906–922 (2011)
8. Mateu, V., Miret, J.M., Sebé, F.: Verifiable encrypted redundancy for mix-type remote electronic voting. In: Andersen, K.N., Francesconi, E., Grönlund, Å., van Engers, T.M. (eds.) EGOVIS 2011. LNCS, vol. 6866, pp. 370–385. Springer, Heidelberg (2011)
9. Cohen, J.D., Fischer, M.J.: A robust and verifiable cryptographically secure election scheme. In: 26th Annual Symposium on Foundations of Computer Science, pp. 372–382 (1985)
10. Sako, K., Kilian, J.: Secure voting using partially compatible homomorphisms. In: Desmedt, Y.G. (ed.) CRYPTO 1994. LNCS, vol. 839, pp. 411–424. Springer, Heidelberg (1994)
11. Cramer, R., Gennaro, R., Schoenmakers, B.: A secure and optimally efficient multi-authority election scheme. In: Fumy, W. (ed.) EUROCRYPT 1997. LNCS, vol. 1233, pp. 103–118. Springer, Heidelberg (1997)
12. Hirt, M., Sako, K.: Efficient receipt-free voting based on homomorphic encryption. In: Preneel, B. (ed.) EUROCRYPT 2000. LNCS, vol. 1807, pp. 539–556. Springer, Heidelberg (2000)
13. Peng, K., Aditya, R., Boyd, C., Dawson, E., Lee, B.: Multiplicative homomorphic E-voting. In: Canteaut, A., Viswanathan, K. (eds.) INDOCRYPT 2004. LNCS, vol. 3348, pp. 61–72. Springer, Heidelberg (2004)
14. Peng, K., Bao, F.: Efficient multiplicative homomorphic E-voting. In: Burmester, M., Tsudik, G., Magliveras, S., Ilić, I. (eds.) ISC 2010. LNCS, vol. 6531, pp. 381–393. Springer, Heidelberg (2011)
15. Hankerson, D., Menezes, A.J., Vanstone, S.: Guide to Elliptic Curve Cryptography. Springer (2004)
16. Cramer, R., Damgård, I.B., Schoenmakers, B.: Proofs of partial knowledge and simplified design of witness hiding protocols. In: Desmedt, Y.G. (ed.) CRYPTO 1994. LNCS, vol. 839, pp. 174–187. Springer, Heidelberg (1994)
17. Chaum, D., Pedersen, T.P.: Wallet databases with observers. In: Brickell, E.F. (ed.) CRYPTO 1992. LNCS, vol. 740, pp. 89–105. Springer, Heidelberg (1993)
18. Juels, A., Catalano, D., Jakobsson, M.: Coercion-resistant electronic elections. In: Chaum, D., Jakobsson, M., Rivest, R.L., Ryan, P.Y.A., Benaloh, J., Kutylowski, M., Adida, B. (eds.) Towards Trustworthy Elections. LNCS, vol. 6000, pp. 37–63. Springer, Heidelberg (2010)

Exploring the Determinants of Citizens' Intention to Participate in the Development of e-Government Services

Her-Sen Doong[1] and Hui-Chih Wang[2]

[1] Department of Management Information Systems, College of Management,
National Chiayi University, Chiayi 60054, Taiwan
hsdoong@mail.ncyu.edu.tw
[2] Department of Business Administration, College of Management,
National Taiwan University of Science and Technology, Taipei 106, Taiwan
hcwang1@gmail.com

Abstract. The EGS (Electronic Government Services) impacts greatly on the relationship between citizens and their governments, so governments seek to manage and develop these services more effectively. By integrating the 'involvement' and 'innovativeness' theories into the expectation disconfirmation paradigm, this study investigates the significance of the role of expectation disconfirmation on the intention to participate towards the EGS. 320 Taiwanese samples were used. Our findings indicated that positive disconfirmation of the EGS leads to a high involvement with the EGS. A citizen's involvement and disconfirmation together increases the citizen's satisfaction with the EGS and thus the participation intention to develop the EGS. A citizen's innovativeness moderates the relationship between their satisfaction and participation intention. Practical implications and future research suggestions were proposed accordingly.

Keywords: Expectation-disconfirmation theory, Electronic Government Services.

1 Introduction

The importance of the EGS (Electronic Government Services) has always been of interest to governments and to researchers because of its influence on the relationship between citizens and their governments [8, 25]. The EGS is also a key driver of a government's effectiveness and as such is a useful tool with which to increase citizens' satisfaction with government performance [17, 25]. The Internet has allowed the governments of today to enhance the efficiency of the EGS and many have provided Internet-enabled EGS to their citizens, thus facilitating better services [20, 21].

Governments have displayed an interest in the exploration of the determinants of citizens' intentions to participate in the EGS development. Initial acceptance is obviously the first stage for EGS success. The citizen participation (i.e. feedback

A. Kő and E. Francesconi (Eds.): EGOVIS 2014, LNCS 8650, pp. 54–62, 2014.

from citizens then enables governments to enhance the EGS) is crucial for the long term operation of the EGS. The EDT (expectation-disconfirmation theory) is one of the reference theories used to explain users, system usage behaviour [5, 16, 23]. In order to demonstrate the significance of the role of disconfirmation (where the use of EGS results in an outcome different from prior expectation) in shaping a citizen's intention to participate in the EGS development, this study proposes a research model integrating 'involvement' and 'innovativeness' theory into EDT. The research findings have the potential to benefit promotion of the EGS and its' implementation tactics.

This remainder of this paper is organised as follows: Section 2 reviews literature used to formulate the research hypotheses and model; Section 3 describes the research methodology; Section 4 presents the data analysis; and Section 5 contains a discussion of the conclusion and practical implications of the research.

2   Theoretical Background and Research Hypotheses

2.1   Expectation-Disconfirmation Theory

Oliver [18] advocated the use of EDT in the discipline of marketing in order to investigate sources of consumer satisfaction with services and products. EDT suggests that while an individual may feel satisfied, they will go through three stages. Initially the individual may have generated an expectation at the pre-purchase stage, based on product information. The individual uses the product and then has experience of product performance. A comparison of expectation and actual experience is made and a 'disconfirmation' is established. A positive disconfirmation leads to a high satisfaction level and this satisfaction may lead to a repurchase of the product. Alternatively, if a lower than expected product performance, a negative disconfirmation, is experienced, then the individual experiences dissatisfaction.

Using EDT, this study proposes the research model depicted in figure 1. A citizen's satisfaction with the EGS and their participation intention towards the EGS will also be discussed in stages. Citizens may receive the EGS promotion information from governments and form their initial expectation at this pre usage stage. They use the EGS for a period of time, thus acquiring EGS performance perceptions based on actual experience. Citizens have a positive disconfirmation towards the EGS if it has performed higher than expected; citizens have a negative disconfirmation towards the EGS if it's performance is lower than expected. Positive disconfirmation toward the EGS enhances the citizens' satisfaction with the EGS, persuading citizens to have a higher level of intention to provide feedback to the government, enabling the government in the revision of the EGS and participation in the development of the EGS. Thus, the following hypotheses are provided:

- H1: Citizens' EGS disconfirmation will have a significant effect on their satisfaction with the EGS.
- H4: Citizens' satisfaction with the EGS will have a significant effect on their participation intention towards the EGS development.

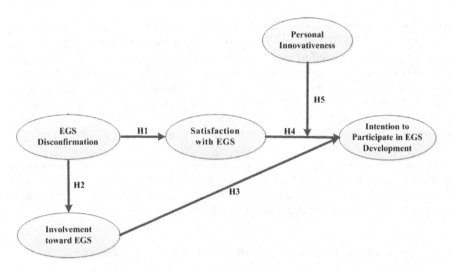

Fig. 1. Research Model

2.2   Involvement

Involvement refers to the interest that an individual displays toward a product class; whether or not the product meets the individual's important values or goals [4]. Individuals may form expectations toward the EGS based on the government's promotion information. After usage, individuals generate disconfirmations toward the EGS. The service is perceived to be useful if there is positive disconfirmation [23]; citizens use the expectation generated by the governments' EGS promotion information as the benchmark to judge whether or not the EGS meets their important values or goals. If citizens have a positive disconfirmation, they may become highly involved in the EGS, as they perceive it to be important to them. Therefore, the following hypothesis is proposed:

- H2: Citizens' EGS disconfirmation will have a significant effect on their involvement with the EGS.

Previous studies have revealed the effects of an individual's involvement on user's systems adoption and usage behaviour [13]. Baronas and Louis [3] find that a user's level of involvement contributes to their system acceptance level. Blili et al. [6] demonstrate the impact of end user involvement on the success of end user computing implementation in organisations. Doll and Torkzadeh [10] indicate personal involvement to be a determinant of end user satisfaction in the context of end user software usage.

In the context of the EGS, this study argues that involved citizens behave differently to those who are not involved. Highly involved citizens provide feedback to governments so that they can refine the EGS. The following hypotheses are provided:

- H3: Citizens' involvement toward the EGS has a significant effect on their intention to participate in the development of the EGS.

2.3   Personal Innovativeness

Innovativeness is conceptualized here as innovative behaviour or the early adoption of new products or services [11]. The higher the innovativeness of an individual, the more likely they are to be an innovative consumer across a wide range of products and services [12]. Individuals with a high degree of personal innovativeness may be referred to as innovators. Those with a low degree of personal innovativeness may be referred to as adapters. The relationship between a person's innovativeness and their level of information systems (IS) and innovative service usage behaviour has been widely researched in a number of different contexts. Agarwal and Prasad [1] demonstrate how personal innovativeness determines a person's perception, defined as 'perceived usefulness and perceived ease of use, of IS. Yi [24] finds that personal innovativeness determines IT enabled innovation acceptance. Many researchers have indicated the moderating effect of personal innovativeness on the relationship between an individual's perception and their intention to adopt IT and IS. For example, Agarwal and Prasad [2] confirm personal 'innovativeness' to have a moderating effect on antecedent behaviour as well as consequent individual perception of new IT.

Innovators tend to enjoy using new services at their early stage and to share their experiences of usage. This study argues that, in the context of EGS development, citizens with a low level of personal innovativeness will be more sensitive to levels of satisfaction, compared to citizens with a high level of personal innovativeness. That is, satisfaction with the EGS will be more significant to the adaptive citizen's relationship to participation intention. Consequently, it is hypothesized:

- ● H5: Citizens' level of innovativeness will moderate the association between their satisfaction with the EGS and an intention to participate in the development of the EGS.

3   Research Methodology

3.1   Instrumentation Construction

Existing validated scales drawn from previous literature have been employed to assess the constructs used in the research model. The EGS disconfirmation is defined as a cognitive belief that derives from EGS usage and it refers to the extent to which the performance of the EGS meets a citizen's expectations. The EGS disconfirmation is measured with a measurement scale adapted from Bhattacherjee [5] that has been appropriately modified to fit the EGS context. The satisfaction with EGS construct measures citizens' feelings about using the EGS and has been measured with tools adapted from the Spreng and Olshavsky's scale [22]. Involvement toward the EGS refers to citizens' perception of the relevance of the EGS, to themselves with respect to their inherent needs, values and interests. Olsen's scale [19] has been adapted to measure this. Personal Innovativeness has been here defined as the tendency to learn about and use the information technology or service. Measurement tools have been adapted from Goldsmith and Hofacker's [1991] Domain Specific Innovativeness. Intention to participate in the EGS development was measured using the scale developed by Davis et al. [9], modified to fit the context of the EGS.

The preliminary version of instruments was tested for content validity by two professors and by a government officer. A pilot study was then undertaken to identify any unclear items or wording in the questionnaire.

3.2   Subjects

The empirical data is made up of 320 valid and complete samples. Of the respondents, 168 are male and 152 are female. 42%, 26%, 18% and 12% respectively were under 30 years of age, 31-40 years old, 41-50 years old and over 50 years of age.

4   Data Analysis and Results

4.1   Measurement Model

The scale validation was first examined by analysing the goodness-of-fit, using LISREL version 9.1. Bollen [7] suggest that the ratio of χ^2 to the degrees of freedom for a model should be less than 5 and prior literature, for example Hair et al. [2006], suggests that the value of the non-normed fit index (NNFI), the normed fit index (NFI), the goodness-of-fit index (GFI) and the comparative fit index (CFI) should all exceed 0.9.

In this study, χ^2/df is 3.28, NNFI is 0.97, NFI is 0.96, CFI is 0.97 and GFI is 0.90. This indicates an adequate fit between the measurement model and the observed data. Acceptance levels were also exceeded as the root mean square error of approximation (RMSEA) is 0.06 and the adjusted goodness of fit indices (AGFI) is 0.87. These fit indices provide adequate evidence of a model fit.

4.2   Reliability and Validity of the Scale

Construct reliability is assessed using Cronbach's alpha. High internal consistency is demonstrated as all the alpha values are greater than 0.7. Construct validity is assessed by evaluating the standardized factoring loadings of the hypothesized items. All indicator factor loadings exceeded 0.7 and were significant at the level of $p < 0.01$.

The composite reliability (CR) of each scale was at least 0.8 and all average variance extracted (AVE) exceeded 0.5, thus exceeding the variance due to measurement error for that construct.

4.3   Model Fit and Hypotheses Testing

Goodness-of-fit of the hypothesized model was examined first. The result of the analysis demonstrates the overall model fit indices for the research model to be in excess of their respective acceptance levels: NFI, NNFI, CFI, GFI and AGFI were 0.95, 0.97, 0.96, 0.91 and 0.87 respectively. This indicates a good fit between the hypothesized model and the observed data.

Figure 2 demonstrates the significance of the individual pathways and the explanatory power of the research model. All the hypothesized associations were significant at $p < 0.01$. As depicted in figure 2, the EGS satisfaction ($\beta = 0.36$, $p < 0.01$) is the strongest predictor of the intention to participate in the EGS development. This is followed by involvement towards the EGS ($\beta = 0.28$, $p < 0.01$). The EGS satisfaction and involvement together explain 22% of the variance in the participation intention toward the EGS. In this way, hypotheses H3 and H4 are supported.

The hypothesis testing also reveals the EGS disconfirmation to influence a citizen's satisfaction with the EGS ($\beta = 0.46$, $p < 0.01$): 21% of the satisfaction variance can be explained. The EGS disconfirmation also has a significant effect on a citizen's involvement toward the EGS ($\beta = 0.35$, $p < 0.01$) and explains 12% of the variance. Thus hypothesis H2 is supported.

In order to test hypothesis 5, the difference between path coefficients is examined. The results indicate a citizen's level of innovativeness to moderate the association between satisfaction with the EGS and intention to participate in the EGS development ($t=1.98$, $p<0.05$). In this way, hypothesis H5 is supported.

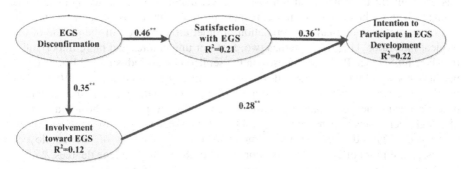

*p-value < 0.05; **p-value < 0.01

Fig. 2. Analysis results for the research model

5   Conclusions and Implications

The aim of this study was to gain an understanding of the determinants of a citizen's intention to participate in the development of the EGS. The results have been shown to support the research hypotheses and to clarify the roles of disconfirmation in the formation process of a citizen's intention to participate towards the EGS development.

This study is an initial step towards the integration of the expectation disconfirmation paradigm with personal involvement and investigates the citizen's decision making process in the context of the EGS. The research results indicate that increasing a citizen's positive disconfirmation level is a critical factor in increasing a citizen's willingness to refine the EGS. The expectation-disconfirmation' paradigm cannot be ignored with respect to the EGS development. Governments need to be aware of their citizens' disconfirmation levels. As citizens may lack an understanding of the benefits that the EGS may provide, it is critical that they are provided with adequate promotional information, so that they can develop realistic expectations of the EGS. Governments also need to recognise the different uses that the EGS can be put to, providing customised functions for different sectors of society.

The most crucial challenge for a government who wishes to encourage its' citizens to participate in the development of the EGS is the maximisation of their 'positive disconfirmation'. Furthermore, our research also indicates the significance of a citizen's level of innovativeness as it is a moderator of the association between satisfaction with the EGS and intention to participate in the EGS development. Innovative citizens have been found to enjoy sharing their experiences: They will devote time to providing feedback that helps governments develop the EGS, even if they are dissatisfied. If governments decide to encourage their citizens to provide ideas and feedback about the EGS, this study offers a valuable tool with which to select target groups most likely to yield successful outcomes.: by targeting highly innovative citizens in the EGS implementation stage, the development of e-government services may be accelerated. The Taiwanese government already uses this model of implementation. For example, the city of Hsinchu is always used by this government to promote an innovative government service, as its' population is younger, better educated, earns more, is more proficient in the use of new technology and more professional than the population of other cities. They fit the profile of the 'typical innovator' [14]. Hsinchu has two, first-tier universities and more importantly, the Hsinchu Science Park that focuses on the semiconductor industry and has received investments totalling USD 1.8 billion from central government since 1980. The park's objective is to attract a critical mass of high tech industries and individuals in order to form synergistic industry clusters. By 2005, the park had hosted a total of 382 high tech firms and has employed 114,836 workers with an average age of 30 years and balanced between male and female. Two thirds of the employees possessed a junior college level education at least: 28,604 had college degrees, 25,510 had bachelor degrees, 20,793 had master degrees and 1,335 had PhD qualifications. Over 4,000 had studied overseas. Employees have founded or participated in the development of 111 Park firms. Also, the park workers with an average age of 30 years have much involvement with the government requirements, such as income tax, the registration of vehicles and properties, marriage and birth certificates, so they are more likely to have already sufficient involvement with the new e-Government services: If the Taiwanese government plans to pilot the implementation of the new e-Government services, Hsinchu would appear to be an excellent possibility.

This research is not without its' limitations: Convenience sampling has been used; future studies may seek government funding in order to improve the generalizability of the findings. This study examined intention instead of actual behaviour. Future studies may wish to provide further insights by testing the actual usage of e-Government services. Further, this study used cross-sectional data collection methods and only one country was examined. It is recommended that future studies collect longitudinal data across different countries in order to reveal the citizens' participation intentions and their variation over time and space.

References

1. Agarwal, R., Karahanna, E.: Time Flies When You're Having Fun: Cognitive Absorption and Beliefs about Information Technology Usage. MIS Quarterly 24(4), 665–694 (2000)

2. Agarwal, R., Prasad, T.: A Conceptual and Operational Definition of Personal Innovativeness in the Domain of Information Technology. Information Systems Research 9(2), 204–215 (1998)
3. Baronas, A.M.K., Louis, M.R.: Restoring a Sense of Control during Implementation: How User Involvement Leads to System Acceptance. MIS Quarterly 12(1), 110–124 (1988)
4. Beatty, S.E., Smith, S.M.: External Search Effort: An Investigation across Several Product Categories. Journal of Consumer Research 14, 83–95 (1987)
5. Bhattacherjee, A.: Understanding Information Systems Continuance: An Expectation-Confirmation Model. MIS Quarterly 25(3), 351–370 (2001)
6. Blili, S., Raymond, L., Rivard, S.: Impact of Task Uncertainty, End-user Involvement, and Competence on the Success of End-user. Information and Management 33, 137–153 (1998)
7. Bollen, K.: Structural Equations with Latent Variables. Wiley, NY (1989)
8. Chan, C.M.L., Lau, Y.M., Pan, S.L.: E-Government Implementation: A Macro Analysis of Singapore's e-Government Initiatives. Government Information Quarterly 25(2), 239–255 (2008)
9. Davis, F.D.: Perceived Usefulness, Perceived Ease of Use, and User Acceptance of Information Technology. MIS Quarterly 13(3), 319–340 (1989)
10. Doll, W.J., Torkzadeh, G.: A Discrepancy Model of End-User Computing Involvement. Management Science 35(10), 1151–1171 (1989)
11. Dowling, G.R.: Consumer Innovativeness. In: Earl, P.E., Kemp, S. (eds.) The Elgar Companion to Consumer Research and Economic Psychology, pp. 111–115. Edward Elgar, Cheltenham (1999)
12. Flynn, L.R., Goldsmith, R.E.: Identifying Innovators in Consumer Service Markets. Service Industries Journal 13(3), 97–109 (1993)
13. Garfield, M.J., Taylor, N.J., Dennis, A.R., Satzinger, J.W.: Modifying Paradigms: Individual Differences, Creativity Techniques and Exposure to Ideas in Group Idea Generation. Information Systems Research 12(3), 322–333 (2001)
14. Gatignon, H., Robertson, T.S.: A Propositional Inventory for New Diffusion Research. Journal of Consumer Research 11(4), 849–867 (1985)
15. Goldsmith, R.E.: Using the Domain Specific Innovativeness Scale to Identify Innovative Internet Consumers. Internet Research 11(2), 149–158 (2001)
16. Hong, S.J., Thong, J.Y.L., Tam, K.Y.: Understanding Continued Information Technology Usage Behavior: A Comparison of Three Models in the Context of Mobile Internet. Decision Support Systems 42(3), 1819–1834 (2006)
17. Lean, O.K., Zailani, S., Ramayah, T., Fernando, Y.: Factors Influencing Intention to Use e-Government Services among Citizens in Malaysia. International Journal of Information Management 29(6), 458–475 (2009)
18. Oliver, R.L.: A Cognitive Model for the Antecedents and Consequences of Satisfaction. Journal of Marketing Research 17(3), 460–469 (1980)
19. Olsen, S.O.: Repurchase Loyalty: The Role of Involvement and Satisfaction. Psychology & Marketing 24(4), 315–341 (2007)
20. Pieterson, W., Ebbers, W.: The Use of Service Channels by Citizens in the Netherlands: Implications for Multi-channel Management. International Review of Administrative Sciences 74(1), 95–110 (2008)
21. Reddick, C.G.: Citizen Interaction with e-Government: From the Streets to Servers? Government Information Quarterly 22(1), 38–57 (2005)

22. Spreng, R.A., MacKenzie, S.B., Olshavsky, R.W.: A Reexamination of the Determinants of Consumer Satisfaction. Journal of Marketing 60(3), 15–32 (1996)
23. Thong, J.Y.L., Hong, S.J., Tam, L.Y.: The Effects of Post-adoption Beliefs on the Expectation-Confirmation Model for Information Technology Continuance. International Journal of Human-Computer Studies 64(9), 799–810 (2006)
24. Yi, M.Y., Fiedler, K.D., Park, J.S.: Understanding the Role of Individual Innovativeness in the Acceptance of IT-based Innovations: Comparative Analyses of Models and Measures. Decision Sciences 37(3), 393–426 (2006)
25. Yildiz, M.: E-government Research: Reviewing the Literature, Limitations, and Ways forward. Government Information Quarterly 24(3), 646–665 (2007)

E-mail Responsiveness in the Public Sector

Hanne Sørum

The Norwegian School of Information Technology
Schweigaardsgate 14, 0185 Oslo, Norway
hanne.sorum@nith.no

Abstract. During the last decade, the scope of digital communication between citizens and the public sector has increased rapidly, and consequently, the use of Web technologies has replaced traditional face-to-face interactions and other conventional and accepted modes of communication and exchange. The aim of online dialogues is to provide the public with certain accepted standards and values of efficiency and effectiveness and thereby create more efficient communication channels with users, such as citizens and businesses. By shedding light on this fact, the present study investigates response time and quality with reference to e-mail inquiries to municipalities in Norway. The findings indicated that, in general, there is a short response time in the public sector. The quality of answers provided was relatively high, but a large variance was noticed in the profundity and complexity of the answers. It was observed that seventeen percent of the municipalities did not respond to the e-mail inquiry. A potential for possible improvements is also connected with the use of autoreplies, a function which has been implemented by only ten percent of the municipalities. The study offers suggestions and methods by which governments can improve their performance in the interest of enhanced service quality in the public sector.

Keywords: eGovernment, service quality, responsiveness, e-mail inquiries, municipalities.

1 Introduction

With the emergence of technology, the Internet has changed writing styles in the 21st century. People have swiftly transitioned from using pen and paper as writing technologies to computers and online tools. The year 2014 heralded a decade of revolutionary advances in Web technologies, which had endorsed the emergence of innumerable innovative and advanced modes of interaction. Since the start of the millennium in 2000 and the dot-com bubble, the market witnessed numerous innovations and user-centred Web solutions. This phenomenon emerged in both the private and public sectors, and all the evidence is only indicative of further enhancement in the use of technologies in the future. Although some dot-com projects were more successful than others, many valuable lessons were learnt during the course of this radically pioneering decade, and these lessons were considered significant for the advancement of the public sector.

A. Kő and E. Francesconi (Eds.): EGOVIS 2014, LNCS 8650, pp. 63–72, 2014.
© Springer International Publishing Switzerland 2014

The use of ICT in government has changed the way of communication in government [1] and website has become the primary interface between public sector organisations and the users [2]. In this regard, Verdegem and Verleye [3] opined that "New information and communication technologies (ICT) offer the government new possibilities for providing citizens and businesses with better, more efficient services." (p. 487). In line with the increasing use of Web technologies, users also became more demanding and knowledgeable. This necessitated providing additional solutions to citizens/businesses and augmented use of Web technologies in terms of organisational management, usability on the Web and security issues. Moreover, quality of services with the intention of inspiring trust and confidence among users is also important, along with creation of public values in an eGovernment context.

Public values in eGovernment can be described in various ways and different approaches can be applied in such assessment. By focusing on municipalities (local websites) Karkin and Janssen [2] studied values by emphasising aspects such as accessibility, citizen engagement, transparency, responsiveness, dialog and balancing of interest. The value is not necessarily directly related to the actual quality of the website, but rather the effects driven by the website and information/services provided. Furthermore, based on a literature review in regards to public values, Bannister and Connolly [4] developed a typology of values driven by ICT that can be applied in a public sector setting. These values were associated to aspects such as serving the citizens, respect for the citizens, social inclusion and transparency. Satisfying the user's requirements and needs are the main issue in provision of online information and digital services, which in the end may also create organisational values.

We also witness that an increasing use of digital self-services reduces, to a large extent, manual registration, paper-based forms and traditional face-to-face interaction. In this regard, values in government (perceived from an organisational perspective) can be created by reducing costs, in connection with goods and services provided towards citizens and businesses [5]. Consequently, the role of government is to act as facilitator for enabling satisfaction, effectiveness and efficiency in the public sector [6], which can, as demonstrated, be approached from both a user and an organisational perspective.

On the subject of eGovernment information and services provided on the Web and in creation of public values, various features such as trust [7] privacy [8] and usability issues [9] are viewed as significant in relation to use and user adoption. Accessibility requirements are also perceived as particularly important in a public sector setting, in order to be able to include all users in a digital society and provide equal access to everyone [10]. In this regard, prior research contributions [11] has determined that "e-Government research has paid much attention to e-Government service adoption from the supplier side - the government - while mostly overlooking the user side of e-Government, such as citizens and businesses." (p. 222). Although we can argue for the importance of value creation from a government perspective (e.g. efficiency, effectiveness, reducing costs etc.), we also need to be aware of the users and their individual requirements and needs. In this regard, online communication and new ways of interaction between government bodies and the users are of particular importance.

As stated by Gauld et al. [12], e-mail communication in an eGovernment context facilitates and expedites real-time communication and replaces in many cases paper and postal services. In regards to online communication and response time in public sector organisations, Andersen et al. [13] state that: "Assessing e-government responsiveness is one of the major gaps in the currently dominant e-government maturity models." (p. 439). Consequently, not many studies has taken a user-centred approach in regards to responsiveness towards citizens/businesses, in the up taking use of ICT and digital communication in eGovernment environments. According to Karkin and Janssen [2] there is also a lack of research concerning website evaluation from a public value perspective. We need to satisfy the website users by providing great services and fulfill their expectations and needs in provision of online information and digital services. Quality in services is also favored as an important contributor in this, impacting aspects such as satisfaction and loyalty [14]. Response to e-mail inquiries can be regarded as one type of service delivered by public sector organisations, although it is rather related to a manual service, than a digital service integrated in the website.

In order to fill in a research gap, the present study aims to contribute to this unexplored area, by focusing on eGovernment (municipalities) in Norway and the responsiveness towards the users. "From the government's perspective, e-mail responsiveness is an important component in assessing public sector service efficiency, effectiveness, and transparency against internally stated service commitments and external benchmarks and standards. From a user/citizen perspective, e-mail responsiveness is a critical component of satisfaction." [13, p. 441].

Regarding this, we also witness that e-mail correspondence has become a favored way to interact with government bodies, from both a user and an organisational perspective. Such communication has a low cost, is in most cases secure and the message is available for the receiver immediately after it is sent. As a result of this, we need to ensure an informative and trustworthy dialogue between government bodies and the users. Accordingly, the following research question is addressed in this paper:

- *How do municipalities in Norway perform with reference to e-mail inquiries?*

In order to provide an answer to this question, the present research focuses on response time and quality of e-mail inquiries to municipalities in Norway (N=428).

We find that the public sector in Norway has implemented numerous strategies and set itself ambitious goals within the last decade, with respect to digitalisation of information and services, e.g. [8,10]. Norway also aims to be the world leader with regard to innovation, technical standards and a user-centred focus in the field of ICT. In addition, ranks consistently high in international benchmarking studies, although Norway is a relatively small country with about five million inhabitants. In line with this, we witness that the central government spends considerable resources in development and facilitation for use of Web technologies in a public sector setting.

Consequently, as a result of the challenging and impressive ambitions of the government in terms of digitalisation of the entire public sector in Norway [10], government bodies constantly strive to fulfill their requirements and obligations on this front.

These requirements primarily pertain to the responsibility that municipalities in Norway have to their citizens and other stakeholders for provision of online information and services.

The rest of this paper is organised as following: Section 2 describes the method employed in the current research study and Section 3 examines the findings. Section 4 provides a discussion of the findings and Section 5 presents the concluding remarks. In addition, suggestions for upcoming research contributions are also provided.

2   Method

The empirical data presented in this paper is based on an e-mail survey conducted in December 2013 among municipalities in Norway. Response time and the quality of e-mail inquiries are the key points covered by this study. Norway has 428 municipalities spread all over the country. Some of these municipalities are small in size as well as population, while others have a population of over 100,000 residents and cover a larger geographic area. The country is divided into 428 municipalities of varying sizes in terms of area and population. Some municipalities have a scattered population, while others have relatively densely populated areas (such as in the main cities). The tasks of the municipalities are many and varied, but their chief responsibility is related to guarding the citizens' interests with reference to welfare, daily life, housing, politics and the environment.

The survey design is identical to a study conducted in Denmark in 2010 [13]. A similar study was also undertaken in Australia and New Zealand [12]. The aim of the present study therefore, was to replicate these studies, not only with the objective of examining Norway as a separate case, but also with the intention of providing an opportunity to compare responsiveness in the public sector in different countries.

The websites of all 428 municipalities were accessed in order to procure e-mail addresses for use in this study. The addresses were collected and registered manually by the researcher and this task was completed a week before the e-mail was distributed to the service department of each municipality. The researcher opted to make use of an official e-mail address, similar to e-mail addresses utilised by organisations for inquiries from citizens and businesses. An official e-mail address in Norway typically begins with "post" (e.g. post@xxxx.kommune.no).

In total 428 e-mails were distributed after normal working hours (around 07.00 p.m.) on a Wednesday to the 428 municipalities in Norway. These mails were sent out within a time period of fifteen minutes. For the purpose of the present study, a Gmail-account was created, which was registered to a firm named *JP Frakt* and all the e-mails were signed by a man named *Jens Pedersen*. The subject title of the e-mail was as follows: *"Retrieval of shipment"*.

In order to examine response time and quality, all e-mails contained the following text (translated in English from Norwegian):

> *"Hello,*
> *I have to pick up a shipment from your office.*
> *Can you tell me where you are located and what your opening hours are?*
> *Sincerely, Jens Pedersen, JP Shipping".*

One month after the e-mail was circulated to the municipalities, the data collected was registered in an Excel document. All the mails received (answers from the municipalities) were opened and the answers were categorised, based on the name of the municipality, response time to the e-mail inquiry and quality of the answers. Every single registration was completed manually by the researcher and then analysed.

This paper merely provides descriptive results of the findings and therefore, no statistical tools were employed for this study. The researcher will provide additional in-depth results in forthcoming research contributions. A comparison with the results from the Danish study [13] and the evidence from Australia and New Zealand [12] is either not performed in the present paper. Consequently, the aim of this paper has been to highlight and explore a relevant research topic, and provide a contribution (paper) that can inspire for future research studies within an eGovernment context.

3   Findings

In total 428 e-mails were distributed, which is the same as the number of municipalities in Norway at the end of year 2013. Effectively, all the municipalities were therefore covered by this study.

The findings shows that 47 out of 428 municipalities used the autoreply function in order to confirm that they had received the e-mail. The autoreplies were received immediately after the e-mail was sent out, except in a few cases, where the autoreplies were received the next day. Including municipalities using this automatic response function for e-mails, 364 municipalities (85%) responded to the e-mail inquiry. Ten of the municipalities from which an autoreply was received did not respond to the e-mail inquiry in any form whatsoever, and opted not to answer the questions, although it was confirmed that the e-mail was received by the municipality.

Concerning this, the study showed that there were considerable differences in the mail text included in the autoreplies. Some of the municipalities provided detailed replies, including value added information in their replies such as expected response time, and also that the mail would be forwarded to the right person in the organisation etc. Similarly, other municipalities simply confirmed that the e-mail was received by means of a short text, without any additional information. Thus, it was perceived that the standard format of text in the autoreplies varied considerably and in some cases, the content of the text was significant because it was more informative and descriptive than in other cases.

Furthermore, seventeen percent of the municipalities in Norway did not respond to the e-mail inquiry. Ideally, all the municipalities were obligated to respond to the inquiry sent by e-mail, as this was categorised as a request to a public authority, and the contents of the e-mail were characterized as accessible information that could be effortlessly answered without difficulty and without expending considerable time or resources in the process.

Table 1 provides an overview of response time versus number of responses with respect to the e-mail inquiries. A normal working day for all municipalities and employees in Norway extends from 08.00 a.m.-16.00 p.m. Monday-Friday. Hence, the response time for the study is calculated from 08.00 a.m. (The percentages are calculated from N = 428).

Table 1. Response time to e-mail inquiries

Response time	Number	Percentage
Before 08.00 a.m.	33	8%
08.00-10.00 a.m.	205	48%
10.00-12.00 a.m.	64	15%
12.00-14.00 p.m.	16	4%
14.00-16.00 p.m.	11	3%
24 hours and more	25	6%

The findings concerning response time reveal that 33 municipalities responded to the e-mail inquiry before the start of the working day at 08.00 a.m. Furthermore, 205 of the municipalities answered within two hours after opening hours and 64 of the municipalities answered after two hours, but within four hours. Sixteen municipalities had a response time of between five to six hours, while eleven municipalities required more than six hours for providing an answer, but less than eight hours for responding to the e-mail inquiry.

To sum up, it was confirmed that 329 out of the 428 Norwegian municipalities responded to the e-mail inquiry within one day. The majority of the municipalities responded within two hours or less, including the opening hours of 08.00 a.m. However, we also witness that 25 municipalities did not provide an answer within 24 hours, and some of them spent considerable longer time than others.

Apropos the quality of answers, the municipalities were asked two questions in the e-mail with respect to the following topics: (1) The opening hours of the municipality and (2) directions to reach the offices of the municipality. Table 2 indicates the number of responses elicited by each of the questions from the municipalities. (The percentages are calculated from N = 428).

Table 2. Overview of quality of answers provided

Question(s) answered	Number	Percentage
One question	57	13%
Both questions	220	51%
Answered, but with no relevance	87	20%

Table 2 shows that 57 municipalities out of 428 (13%) replied to merely one of the two questions addressed in the e-mail, while 220 municipalities (51%) answered both the questions. Contrastingly, twenty municipalities did not answer any of the questions at all, but instead preferred to ask questions in their replies to the e-mail. A majority of these questions referred to matters such as the contact person (a common question was: "Who is your contact person in the organisation?") and directions for driving (questions were on the lines of: "In order to give you directions to reach the offices of the municipality, we would like to know from which direction you would be coming.").

Regarding the municipalities which only answered one question, it was observed that a majority of them provided an answer to the location (street address), but did not respond to the query on the opening hours of the municipality. Moreover, a vast difference in the quality of the responses was noted in the study. Although 220 of the 428 municipalities answered both questions requested in the e-mail, some of them provided brief answers, while others offered comprehensive descriptions. Furthermore, some of the municipalities provided maps to their location with detailed directions. This bore testimony to the fact that some of the municipalities clearly spent more time in answering the queries than the others.

The study further disclosed that employees in the service department of the municipality predominantly replied to the e-mail inquiry. However, in a few of the cases, the replies were received from the same municipality and these were answered by different employees in the municipality.

With reference to the question in the e-mail concerning directions to reach the offices of the municipality, many of the respondents interpreted this question to signify the road address or the office address. It followed therefore that some of the respondents provided only the address, rather than suitable directions to reach the offices of the municipality. In Table 2 no distinction is drawn between those respondents who offered only the road address, those who sent detailed directions to reach the offices of the municipality and/or both. The question was considered as answered, on condition that they provided some approximate information that could be useful and practical on the subject of directions to reach the offices of the municipality. In a few cases, the municipalities also offered GPS coordinates to the location of their offices, which could be seen as an added value.

It is noteworthy that not a single municipality stated that the e-mail inquiry appeared to be lacking in seriousness and/or classified the inquiry as spam mail.

4   Discussion

In view of the fact that Norway aims to be an international leader in digitalisation within the public sector [10], it is safe to make an assumption regarding the superior quality of public sector services delivery by government bodies to citizens and businesses. In this regard, e-mail responsiveness towards the users is perceived as important within an eGovernment context [13]. This study aims to fill in a research gap by addressing the research question: *How do municipalities in Norway perform with reference to e-mail inquiries?*

The empirical findings in the present paper indicate that, in general, municipalities in Norway take a short time to respond e-mail inquiries. Although there was a short response time among the respondents in this study, as discussed earlier 74 of the municipalities did not reply to the e-mail inquiry at all. The fact that nearly 20% of the municipalities did not provide an answer is testimony to a potential for improvement in public sector service delivery quality. This is because in principle, there should ideally be zero no-replies in the context of eGovernment. Public sector organisations which are listed on a website with an e-mail address should priorities their response to users [14]. In most cases, government bodies act as a service institution towards citizens/businesses and should, therefore, fulfill the users' expectations and needs in any communication channel.

In this regard, we find that the goal of the central government is to provide public values [2,4] and encourage efficiency and effectiveness of public sector services [5], by using Web technologies. Digitalisation strategies and goals, e.g. [8,10] should, therefore, trigger reflection and guide all practices for facilitation of great user satisfaction and frequently use. Although a majority of the municipalities were responsible and provided responses within two hours, the ultimate aim for eGovernment would be that all inquiries are answered within a minimum of response time. What constitutes as a minimum time in this context can of course be discussed, but an inquiry should be answered as quickly and accurately as possible. Responsiveness will also depend on the individual inquiry and its complexity, but inquiries such as in this study, should be answered immediately and with great precision as regards to key details concerning goods delivery/collection.

The use of information and communication technologies serves to create greater efficiency of services for users [3]. This is perceived as being of vital significance in the context of eGovernment along with trust [7] in the context of eGovernment information and services. In a public sector setting we also found that respect for the citizens [4] and dialogue [2] is vital contributors to value creation and facilitation for user satisfaction [13]. Concerning e-mail inquiries and responsiveness, response time and quality of answers provided will most likely have an impact on such aspects. In line with this, quality in services is found to be important in a public sector setting [15] and response to e-mail inquiries can be viewed as a type of service provided towards citizens and businesses, although it is related to a manual service and not a digital service integrated to the website.

The study also proved that there were noticeable differences between the municipalities in respect to the level of quality. Most of the municipalities replied to the e-mail inquiries by responding with concise and short answers to the questions asked in the e-mail. Fifty-seven municipalities replied to merely one of the two questions addressed in e-mail, while 220 municipalities answered both the questions. Some of the municipalities provided detailed replies, including value added information in their replies, which comprised maps in various formats, links to relevant websites, phone numbers and detailed directions to reach the offices of the municipality.

It was also established that municipalities with high quality websites possessed a noteworthy advantage by providing detailed contact information and descriptions, and including links in e-mail responses without problems. Therefore, such websites could provide users with additional value, besides facilitating organisational effectiveness and efficiency [5]. The use of automatic feedback (autoreplies) was implemented by remarkably few municipalities, despite the fact that this function involves a simple technical adaptation. With only a few keystrokes, this function has the ability to provide users with a confirmation for e-mails that are received by an organisation. Although prior research found that the users appear to perceive no significant difference between receiving no reply and receiving a generic auto-reply [16], we can discuss whether the autoreply function should be a standard within a public sector setting. In all probability, this might most likely serve to increase the perception of service quality within government bodies in regards to responsiveness.

Consequently, in order to move the public sector forward, it is therefore imperative to have a discussion on the methods by which governments can improve their performance in regards to services, as well as in creation of public values [2]. Respect for the users (citizens and businesses) is also found to a significant contributor [4].

Based on the findings in the present study, three recommendations are put forth: (1) Swift and speedy responses to e-mail inquiries are fundamental and indispensable to improving public sector service delivery, particular within eGovernment environments. In connection with this, there is a substantial potential for improvement in the use of autoreplies in e-mail communications with citizens and businesses to enhance and accelerate public sector service quality. (2) The public sector should strive to ensure that they meticulously provide answers to users for each and every e-mail inquiry, in order to inspire trust and ensure user satisfaction among citizens and businesses. (3) Finally, prioritisation of resources pertaining to website quality improvements, would contribute remarkably towards increasing efficiency and effectiveness of dialogue with users, through specific measures such as including useful Web-links in e-mail responses and presenting contact details on the website.

5   Conclusion

Drawing on empirical data collected from the 428 municipalities in Norway, this study affirmed that the response time to e-mail inquiries was relatively short, in most cases. However, the e-mail responses given by the municipalities demonstrated that there was room for improvement in the quality of answers, the use of autoreplies and provision of value added information, which could conveniently be included in the format of the autoreplies. Future research studies could concentrate on response time and quality of e-mail inquiries to the public sector in Norway, in comparison with other countries which have conducted similar surveys e.g. [12,13]. Moreover, in order to extensively examine and determine responsiveness within the public sector, municipalities and other similar public institutions could be compared with reference to response time and quality, in addition to differences and similarities between geographic areas, number of inhabitants and type of e-mail inquiries.

The data collected for the purpose of the present study will be further analysed and presented in forthcoming research contributions.

References

[1] Hong, H.: Government websites and social media's influence on government-public relationships. Public Relations Review 39(4), 346–356 (2013)
[2] Karkin, N., Janssen, M.: Evaluating websites from a public value perspec-tive: A review of Turkish local government websites. International Journal of Information Management 34(3), 351–363 (2014)
[3] Verdegem, P., Verleye, G.: User-centered E-Government in practice: A comprehensive model for measuring user satisfaction. Government Information Quarterly 26(3), 487–497 (2009)

[4] Bannister, F., Connolly, R.: ICT, public values and transformative gov-ernment: A framework and programme for research. Government Information Quarterly 31(1), 119–128 (2014)

[5] Esteves, J., Joseph, R.: A comprehensive framework for the assessment of eGovernment projects. Government Information Quarterly 25(1), 118–132 (2008)

[6] Hu, G., Shi, J., Pan, W., Wang, J.: A hierarchical model of e-government service capability: An empirical analysis. Government Information Quarterly 29(4), 564–572 (2012)

[7] Ozkan, S., Kanat, I.E.: e-Government adoption model based on theory of planned behavior: Empirical validation. Government Information Quarterly 28(4), 503–513 (2011)

[8] Datatilsynet, "Strategi for godt personvern i digitalisering av offentlig sektor" (2013), https://www.datatilsynet.no/Global/04_planer_rapporter/ Strategi%20for%20et%20godt%20personvern%20i% 20digitaliseringen%20av%20offentlig%20sektor.pdf

[9] Choudrie, J., Wisal, J., Ghinea, G.: Evaluating the usability of developing countries' e-government sites: a user perspective. Electronic Government 6(3), 265–281 (2009)

[10] Ministry of Modernisation, "eNorway 2009 - the digital leap" (2009), http://www.regjeringen.no/upload/FAD/Vedlegg/ IKT-politikk/eNorway_2009.pdf

[11] Lee, J., Kim, H.J., Ahn, M.: The willingness of e-Government service adoption by business users: The role of offline service quality and trust in technology. Government Information Quarterly 28(2), 222–230 (2011)

[12] Gauld, R., Gray, A., McComb, S.: How responsive is E-Government? Evidence from Australia and New Zealand. Government Information Quarterly 26(1), 69–74 (2009)

[13] Andersen, K.N., Medaglia, R., Vatrapu, R., Henriksen, H.Z., Gauld, R.: The forgotten promise of e-government maturity: Assessing responsiveness in the digital public sector. Government Information Quarterly 28(4), 439–445 (2011)

[14] West, D.M.: e-Government and the transformation of service delivery and citizen attitudes. Public Administration Review 64(1), 15–27 (2004)

[15] Cheng, Y.-H.: Evaluating web site service quality in public transport: Evidence from Taiwan High Speed Rail. Transportation Research, Part C, 957–974 (2011)

[16] Mattila, A.S., Andreau, L., Hanks, L., Kim, E.E.: The impact of cybe-rostracism on online complaint handling: Is "automatic reply" and better than "no reply"? International Journal of Retail & Distribution 41(1), 45–60 (2013)

Business Intelligence Systems as Management, Accountability and Transparency Tools for the Government: The Case of Platform Aquarius

Ethel Airton Capuano

Ministry of Planning, Budget and Management, Brasília, Brazil
eacapuano@terra.com.br

Abstract. This paper shows the case of Platform Aquarius, a new Web-based Government Business Intelligence System (GBIS) to enable the public transparency with information on the public funding of research and development (R&D) in Brazil. This multidisciplinary project is an initiative of the Ministry of Science, Technology and Innovation (MCTI) to integrate data of federal government agencies in the field of science, technology and innovation (ST&I). Platform Aquarius has the tools necessary for the publication of Open Government data and the presentation of the essential managerial and analytics information in dashboards that are useful to the access of the average citizen in the Web. Important lessons can be elicited from the project, such as the complexity of data governance model necessary to deal with data of several science and technology federal agencies.

Keywords: Platform Aquarius, government business intelligence system, public transparency, science and technology public policies, public accountability.

1   Introduction

Business Intelligence (BI) systems have been a class of computing application aimed to corporate environment concerned with better decision taking processes in contexts of business performance improvement [1]. Whilst we cannot speak on strategies in government departments mainly because of the short-lived tenure of the ministers [2], [3], [4], [5], the use of this kind of technology in government is starting to show some interesting results in the wave of public policies to implement Open Government Data (OGD), such as the law of free access to the government information passed recently in Brazil [6].

As noted in other democratic countries, the free access to the government information has become more effective after the broad diffusion of information and communication technologies (ICT) in the 1990's with the coming of the Internet and the World Wide Web. Thus, recognizing the social empowerment of the ICT concerning the scrutinizing of the government against corruption and poor performance, the 5th article of the Brazilian law prescribes that is the duty of the State to ensure the right to information access that will be freed by means of objective and agile procedures, in a transparent way, with clear and easy language.

A. Kő and E. Francesconi (Eds.): EGOVIS 2014, LNCS 8650, pp. 73–90, 2014.
© Springer International Publishing Switzerland 2014

This paper shows a new approach of BI systems that leverages OGD in a new way of disclosing public information in order to improve the people capacity to know the *arcana imperii* without the need to know the rites of the public bureaucracy and its systems metadata. The case studied is a project aimed to the implementation of this approach in the Brazilian Federal Government called "Platform Aquarius"[1], a Government Business Intelligence System (GBIS) initiative of the Ministry of Science, Technology and Innovation (MCTI) that integrates data of several agencies in the area of science, technology and innovation (ST&I). This BI platform has the tools necessary for the publication of OGD and the presentation of the essential managerial and analytics information in dashboards that are also more useful to the average citizen in the Web.

GBI systems could be the main tool of "active transparency" in government, the kind of transparency initiative that do not expect the citizen to ask some information to the government, but to disclosure, in advance, the public information in a proactive way. The policy goal could be achieved by means of integrating data of legacy systems to yield performance indicators and insights to improve the public governance in a democracy. In this paper we present the political saga, the ICT issues, the complex ontology components concerning the public sector bureaucracy, and the outcomes of the project "Platform Aquarius" in the Brazilian Ministry of Science, Technology and Innovation (MCTI), trying to elicit useful knowledge on BI project management in the public sector.

2   Political Dream *versus* Technical Reality

It is useful for the understanding of the project context to present a brief retrospective of the BI project started in 2011 by a new managerial team empowered in the MCTI after the presidential election of 2010.

2.1   Motivation

According to Drucker [7], the entrepreneur always searches for change, responds to it, and exploits it as an opportunity. The political initiative underpinning the project Platform Aquarius was plenty of an eagerness for change and a sense of opportunity to improve the strategic management in the MCTI in 2011. The sponsor of the project Platform Aquarius was the newly appointed minister of MCTI, who accomplished a Senator mandate in the previous legislative period.

The political speech of change is due to the historical poor performance of the ST&I policies in Brazil (excepting the human resources training in master and doctorate degrees) and the need to improve the innovation level in the Brazilian native industry. By this point of view, the project Platform Aquarius was an entrepreneurship in the very sense of Drucker's management thought not because of the ICT approach, but due to the sense of opportunity of a new government with some compromise with public transparency.

This sense of political opportunity to exploiting the ST&I databases in order to improve public policies in that arena is also due to the success of a prior initiative not

---

[1] See the Web Portal in: http://aquarius.mcti.gov.br/app/home/

yet achieved by any other country: the "Platform Lattes".[2] In fact, the Platform Lattes, operated by the National Council of Scientific and Technological Development (CNPq), integrates personnel catalog and scientific production data of almost all the Brazilian and some foreign researchers and technologists in the country (this database has cataloged more than one million people). The sponsor's team of the Platform Aquarius also counted on some professional civil servants of the Federal Government that managed the project Platform Lattes in 1999.

Information systems like this, in Brazil, is due to the centralized government tradition that carries out a large sum of public revenues to the Federal Government budget, turning the ST&I development almost a federal issue itself.

2.2   Requirement Engineering Issues

In this large scale scenario of public transparency, the project Platform Aquarius, according to the *metaphora* of Flyvbjerg, Bruzelius and Rothengatter [8] about complex projects, is a "new animal" challenging the "brave new world" of information management pointed out by Loshin [9]. It is a corporate BI project with a goal of integrating data of all the main government databases on ST&I in the country, as well as some interesting open information sources from other countries.

There is a common understanding amongst project management experts that to be complex a project must be very large and costly and have a long term implementation scheduling [8]. Large (and costly) projects require long time to be implemented and the problem lies exactly in this point, when we have politicians and technicians (government bureaucrats) in its leadership. The political time and the technical time are quite different, because of the different world vision of politicians and bureaucrats [10]. In short, politicians are driven upon values and interests and bureaucrats upon facts and information; politicians are also moved by pressures of lobbies and bureaucrats are moved onto the public interest within a structural epistemology also called "instrumental rationality" [11].

In the case of Platform Aquarius, while the political leadership had in mind, initially, a project scheduled in no more than six months, the project developers estimated no less than two years to launch just the first "knowledge panels" of the system's development cycle.

Other issue not well addressed in the first stage of the project was the quality of the data, "quality" here understood in the broadest technical sense of the Information Science and of the Computer Science. Although bureaucrats in the government understand the need to implementing data quality control processes in order to turn this intangible asset onto a real value to the public sector organizations, this practice is still in its infancy even in the private companies. Wende [12] pointed out that only 8% of them implemented a data governance initiative in their companies, and that 17% of them did it only in the project step. Santos [13], with a similar research in Brazil, shows that more than 80% of the ICT professionals do not use a data quality methodology in their companies.

The concept of "data quality" is also a complexity factor in an information system project, with different meaning for different people, and Santos suggests a "best of

---

[2] See the "Platform Lattes" Web Portal in: http://lattes.cnpq.br

breed" data quality concept: a concordance measure between the data visions presented in the information systems and the phenomenon represented by the same data in the real world, that is a notion closer to the attribute "reliability" [12]. However, in a complex information system like Platform Aquarius, integrating data from several independent government agencies, the first issue is not data quality, but data governance, because the main difficulty to put the first release of the systems available to the users is to gather the data.

The third issue the developers had to deal in the project Platform Aquarius referred to the management model of the initiative, which in the Brazilian Federal Government means to deal with several stakeholders with different political biases and interests. The first ST&I government agency involved in the project, besides MCTI, was that having an immediately available (and important) data source: the National Council of Scientific and Technological Development (CNPq). The General Comptroller of the Union (CGU), that is the agency aimed to the internal control of the government, also participated with some data on public expenditure, as well as the Ministry of Planning, Budget, and Management with an entire dataset on "convênios" (that is a kind of intergovernmental agreement between the Federal Government and other federated governments and third sector organizations in order to implement public projects of mutual interest).

The project team also experienced some difficulties facing the project management model involving three organizations, one having the MCTI as the beneficiary of the project, the Center for Strategic Management and Studies (CGEE) as the ICT solution integrator, and a third sector organization [14] as a solution provider aimed to research and development (R&D) on Knowledge Engineering and to the software development.

With the aim of not to locking the MCTI to a proprietary BI technology, the political sponsors of the project presented the requisites of using only open source software to compose the systems and of taking the help of a hackers community to improve the code and exploit ST&I open data like the "apps for ..." contests do worldwide. However, these non functional requisites could not to be matched mainly because of the tight schedule of the project set out by the Minister of Science, Technology and Innovation, who was the project sponsor.

As we show in the following, these non functional requisites and the natural complexity of BI systems caused severe impact on the first project schedule of six months. In order to contribute to the BI epistemology in the public sector, we hope that the experience with the project "Platform Aquarius" could be of utility for the next brave developers of BI systems in the public sector.

3   Information Architecture for Public Transparency

An information architecture to leverage a policy of public transparency is not a special one concerning BI technology. What makes this kind of project very special is the institutional environment where it takes place, which is much more complex than the corporate environment in the private sector. The first difficulty is to get the data from several government agencies that are not politically engaged or, at some extent, really interested in the project. Information integration is a very hard task in a corporate model where the branch companies do not submit to the command of the holding company. In fact, in an institutional point of view the ST&I agencies are independent of the MCTI, shaping a public governance architecture like the one implemented by the US Government research system.

Thus, the experimental information architecture developed to the Platform Aquarius followed an institutional policy to deal with a set of independent ST&I agencies. The selected methodology to accomplish with this complex task was based on ontology. The development team had in mind that a good ontology map could be useful to the acknowledgement of the agencies linked to the MCTI and the intricacies of their R&D programs and projects funded by the Federal Government. The GBI ontology planned was twofold: domain ontology and application ontology.

However, due to the short time schedule of the project, the ontology was developed not as planned in the first step of the project, but in parallel with the systems development. The exploitation of the domain ontology, perhaps with a Knowledge Engineering methodology such as CommonKADS [15], was postponed to the next phase of the project to be developed in the years ahead.

3.1 ST&I Public Governance

In Brazil, the expenditures in research and development (R&D) perform 1.1% of the Gross Domestic Product (GDP), 45% of this budget having the public sector as the source of funding. According to the UNESCO Institute for Statistics [16], its share of the world research and development (R&D) expenditure (by the GERD criterion) was 1.8% in 2007, performing investments of nearly USD 15.0 billion.

The budget of the MCTI in 2013 provides public funds of USD 4.1 billion to promote the development of science, technology and innovation (ST&I) in several ways, using eight linked agencies, fourteen research institutes, and one state-owned company (see these organizational structure in MCTI website: http://www.mcti.gov.br). Federal agencies and institutes cover together a wide spectrum of scientific research in the country, dealing with R&D projects on space, advanced electronics, nuclear energy, astronomy, astrophysics, information and communication technology, and other areas of scientific knowledge. Therefore, the National Council of Scientific and Technological Development (CNPq) and the National Fund for Scientific and Technological Development (FNDCT) have the "lion share" of the ST&I budget in the Federal Government: 54,6% in 2013 (an amount of money that is equivalent to USD 2.2 billion).

In fact, public governance on ST&I is provided by the MCTI as the central body responsible for the making, coordination and evaluation of the public policies, programs and some information systems projects such as "Portal Innovation" and "Platform Aquarius". The budget for the agencies is proposed by the Government and approved by the Congress and the responsibility of the MCTI is limited to the overview of the agencies and the ST&I projects funded by them, meaning that the know-how for operating the ST&I policies is mainly in the agencies.

These administrative structure and management model makes the institutional and procedural ontology very complex, where some information and business rules are stored in databases well known to the "Platform Aquarius" team – the "backbone systems" of the Federal Government in Brazil, such as the Financial Management Integrated System, and a lot of ST&I information and business rules, are not under the governance of the MCTI.

3.2   Data Governance

The search for literature carried out to support decision taking in data governance along the development of "Platform Aquarius" was not much productive in the Computer Science area. By the other hand, the Information Science has shown an abundant paper production concerning information sources and its quality, a similar data governance approach in the context of the project that could surplus the lack of enough knowledge in the Computer Science. We also assumed, for the purposes of the project, data quality as a subject area of data governance.

Wende [12], for example, assumes a concept of "data governance" adapted from the concept of "IT governance" [17], stating that data governance specifies the framework that defines the decision rights and the accountability to encourage wishful behavior in the use of data. However, the empirical researches on data governance are still scarce and very limited in scope, lacking of analysis on the interaction of several actors and roles in corporate environment.

Other difficulty is that general data governance models do not seem to fit all the organizations, which has driven corporate data managers to develop specific model to each organizational context [12]. However, Fischer [18] pointed out as success critical factors to data governance the need of:

a) clear assignment of the "data owner";
b) recognizing the value aggregated to data by means of the data governance;
c) data policies and procedures assumed by the company as a whole (by all business units).

Data governance in the public sector organizations requires an approach very different from the one envisioned to the companies in the private sector. Figure 1, inspired on the corporate data governance model of Wende [12], tries to show the essential entities that shape the structure of a standard department (ministry) in the Brazilian Federal Government, such as MCTI. Instead of a corporate governance level at the head of the organization, we have, in a department (ministry), a political governance level, that is called "governability", a kind of governance based on the political forces that support the minister as a sponsor of the project.

The governance level below, in the Wende's model, deals with data governance and ICT governance, while in the governance model of a typical ministry in Brazil we have a huge set of institutional constraints based on the law (including the Constitution), presidential decrees, and normative acts of the minister itself. These constraints are the outcomes of past public policies on the organizational structure of the government (which we call "corporate" policies), organization of the bureaucracy functions (or "systems"), human resources management, business processes management, ICT management, data and information management, etc.

These legal constraints can be seen as a "manual" to the application of a regulatory policy inside the public sector, which is the core of a democratic state of rights. Due to the "Napoleonic" administrative tradition, there is a set of rules that defines the expected behavior of the political representatives and public servants in Brazil. This means that whilst charged in power by a legitimate political regime, neither the ministry nor the public servants can do what is not stated by the law. It is because of this institutional (legal) system that the set "business rules" (called "institutional governance"), stands above the "political-executive governance" level.

The "political-executive" governance level is at the midway between the political level *(politikón)* and the technical level *(techné)* of the Public Administration. This means that a ministerial "Executive-Secretary" (Deputy Minister) must deal with political drivers and institutional constraints at the same time, doing what is possible to do within the legal framework.

Below the hierarchical level of political-executive governance there are several management branches (functions) organized under the notion of "systems", which are managed by an "Undersecretary of Planning, Budget, and Management" in a position just below the Executive-Secretary.

As the Figure 1 shows, the standard governance architecture of the ministries does not empower data governance, which is just an operational function in the management model. However, in the near future perhaps data governance will be an important management subject for the corporate governance level at the ministries in Brazil because of the Open Government Data (OGD) agreement, according to which the country is now a signatory. The Law of Information Access will also contribute to the empowerment of the data governance as an important corporate function in the Federal Government when the top managers will understand that an active transparency policy could be more cost-effective than a passive transparency policy.

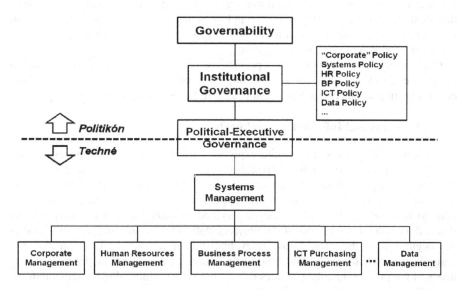

Fig. 1. Governance Model in the Standard Brazilian Ministries (Source: the Author)

The operational function of ICT management, in a typical Brazilian ministry, represents a very small workforce and is strongly limited by legal and public policies constraints, where the main ICT service providers have to be the state-owned companies. Because of these constraints, ICT management function ends up to be confined to the ICT purchasing processes.

In the project Platform Aquarius, a data governance framework was proposed in order to answer questions like the following: What are the actors, activities and roles concerning the implementation of data governance? Who is responsible/accountable for what procedure? Which is the best way to solve a data quality issue in a given business context? When an actor must relate a problem to another authority level in the governance structure? How each member of the team must behave in benefit of data governance at all? Why one procedure is preferred rather another one?

One important outcome of this step of the project was a Responsibility Assignment Matrix (RAM), where each data governance activity and procedure is associated to members of the data governance team who are accountable/responsible for its accomplishment, or who have to be consulted or informed in some control milestones. The data governance model proposed to manage the Platform Aquarius is a document which presents a workflow to implement data quality analyses and assessment, using the criteria proposed by Pipino, Lee and Wang [19], and also states some procedures on how a data analyst must proceed accordingly. An important issue of decision making, when an analyst finds a problem in the data, is to evaluate whether it is the case of going on with the data flow and to approve the publication in the knowledge panels or to hold the data in standby.

Integrating data from government agencies creates a problematic data flow where the data owner is never in the project sponsor team, nor in the BI system's supporting team, requiring different approaches to solve problems with data. Because of the political responsibility of data published by the government and taking into account that Platform Aquarius data governance policy is not to substitute the data owners in the agencies, when a data analyst find a problem he/she has to consult the colleague in the agency to implement (if so) a solution.

Considering the complexity of the project, the corporate strategy for data quality in the project Platform Aquarius will be implemented in a long term schedule, with continuous improvement, such as the approach of Sebastian-Coleman [20].

3.3   Experimental Information Architecture

Experimental BI systems also require experimental information architectures. In fact, it is hard to preview all of the difficulties to be overcome when dealing with data sources in a BI project: data sources considered useful, but inaccessible for any reason (political, economical, technical, etc); disappointed data sources (estimated as useful data sources before the start of the project and evaluated as useless after a more detailed analysis in the course of the project); data sources evaluated as not useful in the beginning of the project, but re-evaluated later as useful; data sources only partially useful that require additional data sources to complement the information needs of the project (i.e., data sources that do not allow drilling down queries into the "grain" of the business data); and so on.

In the case of Platform Aquarius BI project this reality was previewed and considered as of some risk to the project management. This difficulty was to be solved with some research on data governance and information architecture in order to allow the modeling of a standard information architecture also useful to the project in the future.

Meanwhile, an experimental (and provisional) three tier information architecture was arranged to deal with the first steps of the project. This architecture consisted of the following static components:

I.   Staging Layer: a set of data files received from the data sources managers by e-mail (the files formats were mainly of data sheets and text editors); indeed, this layer is like the Operational Data Store (ODS) layer proposed by Inmon, Imhoff and Battas [21] to implement Data Warehouse systems;

II.   Knowledge Layer: a set of integrated BI tools that run like a software "engine" to produce intelligence data to the system's layer above;

III. Dashboard Layer: it is the system user interface responsible for presenting the managerial and strategic information to the users in the Web; this intelligence information set is shown in several visual ways such as line, pie, and bar graphics, and other Knowledge Representation models useful for management purposes, like gauges and textual insights (such as "Did You Know?" style questions and answers).

It is important to point out that the "Knowledge Layer" tools were able to deal with several BI technical environments such as On Line Analytical Processing, Rule-Based Systems, Statistics, Data Mining, and Text Mining.

3.4   Standard Information Architecture

The design of a sustainable information architecture to support the further development of the Platform Aquarius, with more connected data sources in the future, was one of the main functional requirements of the project. For the sake of concept simplification, this information architecture is called "standard" with the hope that it could be (scientifically) generalized to support each new data source connection. In fact, this "ideal" information architecture was to be one of the most important subject of R&D in the project because of the uncertainty concerning data.

Whilst the Platform Aquarius has not yet a number of connected data sources that allow us to identify a standard information architecture to support its operations in any case, the architecture model shown in Figure 2 already shows the most important components estimated to properly run Government BI Systems (GBIS) in the future. Basically, three information architecture components make this model more complete than the provisional (experimental) architecture:

I.   Web Connection Layer: consisting of simple data services based on FTP network protocols and more sophisticated connection services like Web Services, this is the first layer of the architecture responsible for the process of accessing remote data sources;

II.   Data Staging Layer: an operational data computing environment like an Operational Data Store (ODS) responsible for the first stage of raw data processing, concerning Extract, Transform, and Load (ETL), in order to make them useful for the layers above in the information architecture;

III. Data Warehousing Layer: consisting of several Data Marts properly integrated in order to allow the above Knowledge Engineering layer to analyze data and discover interesting data patterns useful to support the decision making processes in the ST&I public policy management;

IV.   Knowledge Engineering Layer: despite limited to some tools used in the first version of the Platform Aquarius, such as Natural Language Processing (NLP) applications, this is an information and technology architecture layer that can evolve significantly in the next years with the availability of new BI engines in the market; for instance, it is expected the using of Geographical Information Systems (GIS) in order to show the share of the federal ST&I public expenditures in each state of the federation;

V. Knowledge Representation Layer (Dashboard): responsible for the visual presentation of information to the users in the Web, consisting of all the useful visualization tools that can be put on the Knowledge Engineering Layer to yield a way to make the top managers and citizens more knowledgeable in the decision making processes.

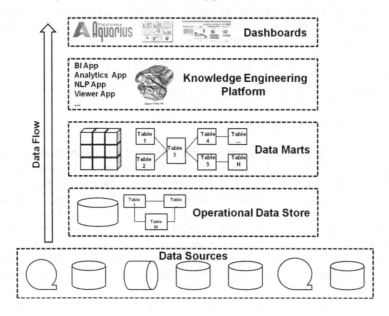

Fig. 2. The Platform Aquarius Standard BI Architecture (Source: Pacheco *et al.*)

The two-way data flow in this information architecture is intended to make the drill-down search operation available to the users in a transparent style. For instance, when a MCTI top manager will ask for some information about expenditures in some government ST&I program, then he/she could know in more detail also who benefits with these funds. Actually, the system has to search (drill-down) some detailed documents in a textual base stored in the "Data Staging" Layer. Thus, reasoning on the data flow through the information architecture, the Data Warehousing Layer certainly must have the documents index stored in its database.

In practice, some BI operations are more important in a context of government than in the private sector. Whilst some system requirements like "to drill-down to the documents" could sound a little weird to a traditional (private sector oriented) BI system, they are invaluable for exercising democracy, especially in developing countries too much vulnerable to political corruption. In these countries, the public money transfer from a ministry or government agency to a certain company can be of interest to the scrutiny of the citizens because of the risk of misappropriation of public funds to finance political campaigns or embezzlement.

4   Government Information to the Citizens

The Platform Aquarius BI systems (Figure 3) include four "knowledge panels" (http://aquarius.mcti.gov.br/app/): Expenditure Panel ("Painel de Dispêndio", in Portuguese), Sector Funding Panel (Painel de Fundos Setoriais), Agreements Panel (Painel de Convênios), ST&I Public Policies Monitoring Panel (Painel de Monitoramento de Políticas de CT&I). Each knowledge panel shows graphics and insights on a ST&I thematic area in order to support the processes of monitoring and evaluating public policies investments and outcomes.

However, considering the main objective of the Platform Aquarius is to provide transparency in the government, there is a hope the information and insights published in the MCTI Web Portal can leverage a wide debate in the scientific community about several aspects of the ST&I public funding nowadays.

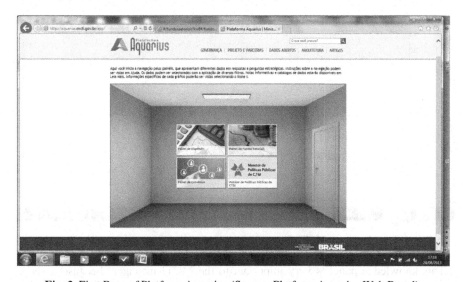

Fig. 3. First Page of Platform Aquarius (Source: Platform Aquarius Web Portal)

The knowledge panels allow the citizens to access the data and information from the National System of Science, Technology and Innovation (SNCTI) already organized by themes. Also, they provide "knowledge services" to give the top managers in the public sector informational support for the monitoring and decision making processes related to major policies, initiatives, and programs in science, technology and innovation (ST&I) funded by the Ministry of Science, Technology and Innovation (MCTI). Such information may be available in spreadsheets, graphs, mental maps or topic lists, depending on their nature.

4.1   MCTI General Expenditures

The expenditure panel shows the evolution of the MCTI and its nine Federal Government agencies expenditures in their mission of granting funding for the R&D initiatives. Internet users have five options of graphs in this knowledge panel:

I.   Time series on general expenditures (including some administrative expenditures to the maintenance of the Ministry's bureaucracy): one line graph showing the MCTI expenditures as a whole, meaning the Ministry and its nine agencies' total budget in the past years since 2005 (Figure 4);
II. Efficiency of the business processes: showing the operational pace of the MCTI's activities to implement the projects along the year; it is common to see every year, in this line graph, a very low commitment level of the budget in the second half of the year means that MCTI business processes performance could be late (graph on the right side, top of the Figure 4);
III. Budget share by agency: showing the budget of each ST&I agency.

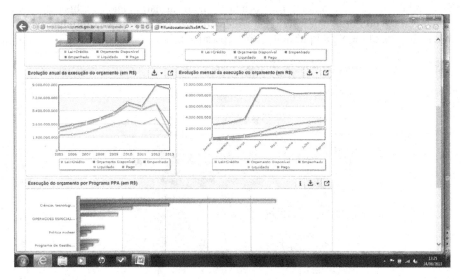

Fig. 4. Time Series on MCTI Expenditures (Source: Platform Aquarius Web Portal)

This knowledge panel is very important to the MCTI managers because it shows management insights to improve the business policies and operational processes. It is shown an objective indicator of the management efficiency: the path of the expenditures along a fiscal year, paying special attention to the "execution lag" between the budget allowance and the real time when the projects and activities are performed and the money spent. This indicator, in (cumulated) percent of the year budget spent until a month, shows how is the efficiency of the managers in executing the whole budget of the MCTI (with its agencies). So, a low inclination in the line (graph in the right side of the Figure 4) of the budget implementation is a strong evidence of inefficiency, that is commonly either the consequence of a lack of planning or the late release of funds.

Another important information search approach of all the knowledge panels in the Platform Aquarius is the "Strategic Questions" application. This feature provides Internet users with another link to more detailed information such as, on MCTI general expenditures panel, the name of the MCTI business partners contracted to perform operational processes. This search application allows the citizens to scrutinize the contracted partners and the amount of money spent in purchasing products and services for the maintenance of the MCTI.

Ultimately, the coming of the Non-Governmental Organizations (NGO) to the "market" of the execution of public policies, after the Bresser Administrative Reform in the 1990's, has brought a more flexibility to the government operations but also a sort of scandals of political corruption because of the unnatural birth (born of overnight) of a number of this kind of organization only to receive federal funds.

4.2   Funding by ST&I Sector

The Sector Funding Panel (Figure 5) is aimed to the encouragement and supporting of researchers in several universities, institutes, companies and non-profit institutions in the country. Since its beginning, the sector funds are the main instrument to leverage the federal system of Science, Technology and Innovation (ST&I) by enabling the implementation of new research projects in universities and research centers in order to encourage the knowledge creation and transfer to the companies. Their goal is to ensure the stability of funding to the research sector and create a new model of management with the participation of several social segments.

Fig. 5. ST&I Research Project Portfolio (Source: Platform Aquarius Web Portal)

One feature of this research funding system, applauded by some and condemned by others, is that it avoids the concentration of activities in a few science and technology fields and enables the distribution of its benefits through several knowledge areas: aeronautical, agribusiness, Amazon, waterway, biotechnology, energy, space, hydrology, information technology, infrastructure, mining, oil and gas, health, and transportation. There are two more sector funds called "Green-Yellow" (Verde-Amarelo) and "Funttel" (dedicated to research on telecom).

The graph in the left side of the Figure 5 shows a three line time series with: the year budget, the amount of funded projects, and the average cost of the projects.

4.3 Scholarships

The "Scholarships Panel" presents information on the application of the National Council of Scientific and Technological Development (CNPq) funds for scholarships to support scientific and technological research. Queries of Internet users can be made on this panel in the Web from the following strategic issues:

- overview of the implementation of the scholarships;
- geographical distribution of scholarships;
- key terms associated with scholarships;
- profile of fellows (age, sex, area of knowledge, mode of scholarship, etc);
- implemented scholarships, containing detailed report of the awarded grants;
- impact on social networks, by searching the conceptual terms related to scholarships frequently found in tweets of the official channels (in the Twitter media) with the application of several "conceptual filters" concerning time (year), knowledge area, and geographical distribution of the funds.

4.4 Institutional Agreements

This knowledge panel is referred to the transfer of funding to public and private institutions qualified as MCTI's research partners (http://aquariusp.mcti.gov.br/app/#/convenios?bc=17). For the Federal Government, it is important to monitor this process of research funding because of the risk of corruption involving money transfer from the ministries to third sector organizations in order to decentralize operations.

One interesting feature of this knowledge panel is the topic map application showing the most frequent research branches funded by MCTI. In the first view of the topic map, the central node gathers the topics of the funded projects in circular orientation. Each node is connected by an edge that links it to another node, showing the frequency the two research topics appear together.

The central node tag shows the main subject of the research projects funded in a year, which is the most frequent topic found in the funding transfer transactions. This node is surrounded by the next (circular) level of nodes representing the most common tags related to the main research subject. And directly related to this second level of tags are the next level of nodes, which presents the terms that appear less frequently in the funding transfer documents; and so forth. This kind of technology implements the mental maps as suggested by Ontoria, de Luque and Gómez [22].

4.5 Scientific Production Cataloged in the Platform Lattes

This knowledge panel is based on the *curricula vitae* of the scientists and technologists registered in the Platform Lattes, providing information concerning bibliographical records, including artistic and cultural publications. Queries can be made by Internet users from strategic issues such as:

- characteristics of the scientific & technological (S&T) production;
- profile of the authors;

- regional (geographical) distribution of the S&T production;
- evolution of annual S&T production;
- annual evolution of the national S&T production;
- keywords associated with S&T production.

Users can search desired information on the panel by applying various filters drilling down the database by: year, knowledge area, and geographical distribution. The panel also provides to the Internet users CSV files containing details of the output items recorded in the Platform Lattes.

4.6   Monitoring ST&I Public Policies

Whilst this ST&I Public Policies Monitoring Panel is not a GBIS component, it shows informational contents useful to ST&I policymakers in the Federal Government such as:

- consolidated information, statistics, and new indicators about ST&I policies to express, beyond the view of the financial resources invested, the profile of the outcomes and public values produced by the funded initiatives; and
- qualified information to developing studies, analyzes, and reports on the monitoring and tracking of the actions funded by the MCTI.

This panel also encourages a culture of transparency within and outside the MCTI by ensuring publicity to the results obtained from the monitoring and evaluation carried out by the ministry. It is divided into 5 main topics:

I.   Section "Policies and Programs" (Políticas e Programas) presents policy documents about ST&I programs and plans and information on participation of the society;

II.   In the section "Financial and Budgetary Resources" (Recursos Orçamentários e Financeiros), the citizen will find information on the MCTI budget and the implementation of ST&I programs and actions;

III. In the section "National Indicators on ST&I", one can find the macro indicators on the ST&I in the country;

IV.   In the section "Policy Monitoring and Evaluation" (Monitoramento e Avaliação de Políticas), there are available documents (including legal documents) on proceedings of the Standing Committee on Monitoring and Evaluation (Comissão Permanente de Monitoramento e Avaliação); and

V.   Section "Reports, Studies and Analysis" (Relatórios, Estudos e Análises) presents information for monitoring and evaluating the ST&I policies.

In short, Platform Aquarius GBIS provides the Internet users a wide sort of information on ST&I initiatives funded by the Federal Government in Brazil, classified in the Table 1 by type of information representation frame showing: time series on budget and project funded; distribution of funds and benefits; efficiency indicators; strategic questions and answers; and other kind of relevant information.

Table 1. Knowledge Panels and Information Frames in the Platform Aquarius

Knowledge Panel		Type of Information Representation Frame				
#	Name	Time Series	Share Graphs	Efficiency Indicators	Strategic Questions	Others
1	MCTI Expenditure Panel	1	1	3	7	
2	Funding by ST&I Sector	1	6		6	
3	Institutional Agreements	2	2	2	5	1
4	Scholarships	4	4		6	5
5	ST&I Production in the Platform Lattes		2		7	3
	Total	8	15	5	31	9

5   Conclusions and Lessons Learned

With this project experience, we conclude that Government Business Intelligence Systems (GBIS) can be too much complex because the public sector has corporate structure and management models that make the development of this kind of computational information systems a very hard task to be accomplished. Countries like USA and Brazil, which have a federative political system, operate their public policies with a set of several government agencies that have their own mission, management culture, political priorities, and business system databases with different data models and technologies. There is no need to say that corporate ICT projects, in that kind of fragmented political environment, make the data integration, in a GBIS project, a daunting mission that can last several years to be accomplished.

The political system also strengths this institutional fragmentation trend because each agency involved in the implementation of a project like GBIS is led by a political leader representing a different political party integrated in the government coalition or a different political trend in the President's political party. In short, the political scenario that best features the GBIS project management model is that presented by Weil and Ross [17] about ICT governance: a feudal model.

Consequently, data governance represents a formidable challenge in GBIS project. For instance, data quality assurance arises as a complex process with a workflow that may pass through the boarders of several government agencies and requires a team of data quality experts in the whole ETL data flow to support the system maintenance. The communication team who has to manage the relationship between the GBIS "owner" and its data suppliers (other ministries and agencies) must also be qualified to negotiate on a daily basis in order to avoid political frictions in the BI operations. Third Nature [23], for example, shows that 70% of the BI project costs, in a three year Total Cost of Ownership (TCO) perspective, are due to labor costs, and it is easy to understand that data governance requirements is responsible for a significant share of this costs.

Another important lesson learned is a paradox: GBIS are long term strategic project with short term top leaders sponsorship, because the state ministries (or department secretaries) tenure is far shorter than the top executives (Chief Executive Officers - CEOs) tenure in the private companies. Berlinski, Dewan, and Dowding [2], for instance, point out that a Minister in the United Kingdom government stay (in average) only 25-28 months in the Office. Ferraz and Azevedo [5] show that an average Brazilian Health Minister tenure is only of 15 months, far less than the average of 33 months of Health

Ministers tenure observed in other 22 countries researched, and both ministers tenures are too much less than a CEO tenure in a big company of the healthcare industry, that is more than nine years. Cleary and Reeves [4] concentrate this kind of research to show that in the last seven years (since 2005) the UK ministries tenure has down to just 1.3 years! Chang, Lewis and McCarty [24] do the same for the case of the USA concerning the tenure of the political appointees to the government. In Brazil, a state minister's tenure is only 21 months long in average [3], an issue which requires a new corporate BI project management approach concerning sponsorship and leadership.

Because of this issue, it remains only two ways to support a GBIS project in a ministry or agency in democratic countries: (i) make the project be "bought" by the managers near to the "street-level" public servants, in a bottom-up approach; or (ii) implement the project in a four or five years presidential mandate, with priority in the President's agenda, in a top-down approach.

Despite of these difficulties, Platform Aquarius follows the democratic trend presented in the accurate analysis of Davis [25], Fioretti [26] and Stephenson [27], and in the study case presented by Demeyer, Kresin, Oosteren, and Gallyas [28], on the economic exploitation of government's information based on the laws of free access to information.

References

1. Dhar, V., Stein, R.: Seven Methods for Transforming Corporate Data into Business Intelligence. Prentice Hall (1997)
2. Berlinski, S., Dewan, T., Dowding, K.: The Length of Ministerial Tenure in the UK 1945–1997. Political Economy and Public Policy Series, Suntory and Toyota International Centres for Economics and Related Disciplines, London (2005), http://sticerd.lse.ac.uk/dps/pepp/pepp16.pdf
3. Capuano, E. A.: Profissionalização da administração pública e modelos institucionais de convivência entre políticos e burocratas nos governos democráticos do século XXI. In: CLAD sobre la Reforma del Estado y de la Administración Pública, XVI Congreso Internacional del, Asunción, Paraguay, 8 - 11 Nov. (2011).
4. Cleary, H., Reeves, R.: The "Culture of Churn" for UK Ministers and the Price We All Pay. Research Briefing, June 12 (2009), http://www.demos.co.uk/files/Ministerial_Churn.pdf
5. Ferraz, M.B., Azevedo, R.T.: Ministers of Health: short-term tenure for long-term goals? São Paulo Medical Journal 2(129), 77–84 (2011), http://www.scielo.br/pdf/spmj/v129n2/a05v129n2.pdf
6. Capuano, E.A.: Gobierno y datos abiertos: la sociedad descubriendo los secretos del Estado en el siglo XXI. In: XVII Congreso Internacional del CLAD sobre la Reforma del Estado y de la Administración Pública, Cartagena, Colombia, October 30-November 2 (2012)
7. Drucker, P.F.: Innovation and Entrepreneurship: Practice and Principles. HarperCollins (1985)
8. Flyvbjerg, B., Bruzelius, N., Rothengatter, W.: Megaprojects and Risk: an Anatomy of Ambition, Cambridge (2010)
9. Loshin, D.: The Infrastructure for Information Management: A Brave New World for the CIO. White Paper. SAS Institute (2013), http://www.sas.com/resources/whitepaper/wp_62504.pdf
10. Aberbach, J.D., Putnam, R.D., Rockman, B.A.: Bureaucrats and Politicians in Western Democracies. Harvard University, Cambridge (1981)
11. Dusek, V.: Philosophy of Technology: an Introduction. Blackwell (2006)

12. Wende, K.: A Model for Data Governance - Organising Accountabilities for Data Quality Management. In: 18th Australasian Conference on Information Systems, Toowoomba, Queensland, Australia, December 5-7 (2007)
13. Santos, I.M.F.: Uma Proposta de Governança de Dados Baseada em um Método de Desenvolvimento de Arquitetura Empresarial. Rio de Janeiro: UNIRIO. Dissertação de Mestrado (2010), http://np2tec.uniriotec.br:9090/ppgi/banco-de-dissertacoes-ppgi-unirio/ano-2010/uma-proposta-de-governanca-de-dados-...-empresarial/view
14. Pacheco, R.C.S., Sell, D., Todesco, J.L., Montenegro, F.B., Salm Jr., J.F.: Plataforma de Gestão Estratégica à Governança Pública em CT&I. Congresso ABIPTI 2012, Brasília, DF, 14 a 16 de agosto de (2012), http://www.researchgate.net/publication/23072 9104_Plataforma_de_Gesto_Estratgica__Governana_Pblica_em_CTI
15. Schreiber, G., Akkermans, H., Anjewerden, A., De Hoog, R., Shadbolt, N., Van de Velde, W., Wielinga, B.: Knowledge Engineering and Management: The CommonKADS Methodology. MIT, Cambridge (2000)
16. United Nations Educational, Scientific and Cultural Organisation (August 2011), Nr. 15, (UNESCO): Global Investments in R&D. UIS Fact Sheet http://www.uis.unesco.org/FactSheets/Documents/fs15_2011-investments-en.pdf
17. Weil, P., Ross, J.: IT Governance: How Top Performers Manage IT Decision Rights for Superior Results. Harvard Business Review (2004)
18. Fisher, T.: The Data Asset: How Smart Companies Govern Their Data for Business Success. John Wiley, Hoboken (2009)
19. Pipino, L.L., Lee, Y.W., Wang, R.Y.: Data Quality Assessment. Communications of the ACM 45(4ve), 211–218 (2002)
20. Sebastian-Coleman, L.: Measuring Data Quality for Ongoing Improvement. Morgan Kaufmann (2013)
21. Inmon, W.H., Imhoff, C., Battas, G.: Building the Operational Data Store. John Wiley & Sons (1995)
22. Ontoria, A., De Luque, A., Gómez, J.P.R.: Aprender con mapas mentales: una estrategia para pensar y estudiar. Narcea (2008)
23. Third Nature: Lowering the Cost of Business Intelligence with Open Source: a Comparison of Open Source and Traditional Vendor Costs. Third Nature (2010), http://www.pentaho.com/assets/pdf/CdWb6vEk6eTGuPa7FX3C.pdf
24. Chang, K., Lewis, D., McCarty, N.: The Tenure of Political Appointees. In: 2001 Annual Meeting of the Midwest Political Science Association, April 19-22 (2001), http://people.vanderbilt.edu/.../Papers/turnover0329.pdf
25. Davis, T.: Open data, democracy and public sector reform: a look at open government data use from data.gov.uk. MSc Dissertation submitted for examination in Social Science of the Internet, at the University of Oxford, in the Summer (2010), http://www.practicalparticipation.co.uk/odi/report/
26. Fioretti, M.: Open Data: emerging trends, issues and best practices. Open Data, Open Society Project Report. Pisa (Italy): Scuola Superiore Sant'Anna (2011), http://www.lem.sssup.it/WPLem/odos/odos_report_2.pdf
27. Stephenson, W.D.: Data dynamite: how liberating information will transform our world. Data 4 All (2011)
28. Demeyer, T., Kresin, F., Oosteren, C., Gallyas, K.: Field note Apps for Amsterdam. The Journal of Community Informatics 8(2) (2012), http://cijournal.net/index.php/ciej/article/view/850/906

Process-Based Knowledge Extraction
in a Public Authority: A Text Mining Approach

Saira Andleeb Gillani[1] and Andrea Kő[2]

[1] CoReNeT, Mohammad Ali Jinnah University, Islamabad, Pakistan
sairagilani@yahoo.com
[2] Corvinno Technology Transfer Center Ltd.
ako@corvinno.hu

Abstract. Processes in public administration are complex and changing fast, according to the changes in the regulatory environment. Public servants have to face with the challenge of getting a job role specific knowledge, which is embedded into the processes or available in other unstructured sources, like in public policies. Even though much of government regulations may now available in digital form, due to their complexity and diversity, identifying the ones relevant to a particular context is a non-trivial task. Our paper will discuss a text mining solution to extract, organize and preserve knowledge embedded in organizational processes to enrich the organizational knowledge base in a systematic and controlled way, support employees to easily acquire their job role specific knowledge. The solution has been tested for the case of an agricultural service at public authority. The context of the case is sampling in controlling food safety and quality.

Keywords: knowledge extraction, text mining, process mining, semantic process management.

1   Introduction

Regulatory, social and economic environment are complex and changing continuously that cause increase demand for public servants in getting the necessary job-specific knowledge in right time and right format. Employees in the public sector have to follow these changes, improve their competencies according to it.

Even though much of government regulations may now available in digital form, due to their complexity and diversity, identifying that ones, which relevant to a particular context is a non-trivial task. Another important knowledge source is processes, which contain rich, but in many case embedded, hidden knowledge. Complex organizations, like public authorities use to model and manage their processes with the help of business process management (BPM) tools[1]. These applications are used to describe the organizational processes, together with the required information and other resources (amongst other human resources) needed to perform each activity. From the organizational knowledge assets view responsibility for the execution of each activity has key importance[2]. The RACI matrix (Responsible, Accountable, Consulted,

A. Kő and E. Francesconi (Eds.): EGOVIS 2014, LNCS 8650, pp. 91–103, 2014.

Informed) is used for grouping role types, bridging the organizational model and the process model. Knowledge belonging to the job roles has to be explored to have clear view about job role types of the tasks[3].

Processes and their embedded knowledge have significant role in providing a suitable support for employees and at the same time they help to offer improved quality in public services, they facilitate to manage the complexity of the environment.The increasing popularity of semantic web and a variety of participatory tools such as web/text/opinion mining systems, online social networking, blogs, wikis, and forums, present to public administration decision-makers, governance bodies and civil society actors the possibility of bringing about significant changes in the way future societies will function. The emerging technological environment is transforming information processing and knowledge-sharing among public administration participants and also within civil society.

The rapid growth of the internet and the world wide web led to an enormous amount of machine readable documents online. This increasing text data come from different domains and has been growing exponentially for several centuries. Approximately, 85% business information is present in digital text format [4]. This unstructured digital text data contains ambiguous relationships. Typical logic based programming models cannot find concealed information that is present in such data. Therefore, there is a need of such a paradigm that can disclose the hidden information and interesting patterns by means of methods which dynamically handle the large number of words and structures of natural language in a scalable way and also able to handle vagueness and fuzziness of text data. According to Hearst [5], "text mining is the discovery by computer of new, previously unknown information, by automatically extracting information from different written resources. A key element is the linking together of the extracted information together to form new facts or new hypotheses to be explored further by more conventional means of experimentation". Text mining is a new area of research in computer science and it is inherently interdisciplinary that have strong connections with adjacent fields such as data mining, machine learning, knowledge management and computational linguistics. Text mining is different from data mining in this sense that in data mining interesting patterns are extracted from structured data (databases) while text mining processes semi structured (XML files) or unstructured data (natural language text) and extracts hidden meaningful information.

Our paper will discuss ProMine text mining solution to extract, organize and preserve knowledge embedded in organizational processes to enrich organizational knowledge base in a systematic and controlled way, support employees to easily acquire their job role specific knowledge. ProMine is developed in Prokex project (EUREKA_HU_12-1-2012-0039) aiming to develop an integrated platform for process-based knowledge extraction. ProMine solution has been tested for the case of an agricultural service at public authority. The context of the case is sampling in controlling food safety and quality.

The paper is structured accordingly. Section 2 gives an overview of the text mining state of the art. Section 3 discusses Prokex framework, while section 4 details ProMine solution. Section 5 illustrates the ProMine approach and section 6 summarizes our proposal and prospects for future study.

2   The State of the Art in Text Mining

In this section, different approaches of text mining that are available to efficiently organize, classify, label, and extract relevant information for today's information-centric users, have been discussed. The research community is working to develop text mining approaches for the main analysis tasks, like preprocessing, information extraction, categorization or classification of documents, clustering to group similar text documents, and information visualization.

Preprocessing
A huge collection of our digital data is in textual form. This textual data is in natural language which is unstructured form. It is very difficult to extract rules from unstructured data and therefore, such data cannot be used for prediction or any other useful purpose. When text mining techniques are applied to such unstructured huge data, another problem of pattern overabundance can occur. When these immense number of patterns are generated; it is very difficult to find out the only relevant result sets. Therefore, to perform text mining, it is necessary to pass this data through a process in which different refinement techniques are applied and this process will make sophisticated refinements. Then this refined data will be transformed in such a form that will be more appropriate to extract knowledge. This process is called "preprocessing" of data. Research community is working on different preprocessing techniques. Some techniques of preprocessing are discussed here.

Wang [6] described five different preprocessing approaches to create an intermediate form of text documents for text mining. These approaches are: Full Text Approach in which a set of words is selected from a text document and this set of words represents the whole document. This set of words representation is also called as a "bag of words". For further refinement in data stop words can be removed from this set of words. The second approach is keywords/index data approach [7-8]. This approach refines each "bag of words" by referring a keyword list. Keywords are extracted by using different schemes like frequency based weighing scheme [9] or key word extraction based on CRF (conditional random fields) [10]. One drawback of this approach is the removal of rich data of the document which can be useful for text mining. Prototypical document is a third approach of preprocessing. This is the full text approach and composed of two components. One is Part of Speech (POS) tagging and other is Term Extraction. In POS, automatically, tags are assigned to words in a document. The second component Term Extraction is domain dependent. This term may be a word or a phrase. Another preprocessing approach is Multi-Term text phrase [11] is co-occurrence of a set of words in raw data. Wang [6] described the Concept approach as a last preprocessing approach. After extracting key terms and their syntax relationship from raw text, more semantically meaningful concepts are extracted.

Hotho[4] defined three main methods of preprocessing of text data. First is tokenization, in which stream of words is prepared by removing different grammatical symbols (punctuation marks), white spaces and tabs from each text document. The resulting document of words is called a dictionary. Then to reduce words, some other methods, filtering, lemmatization, stemming and keywords selection are applied to this dictionary. By filtering, stop words are removed. Lemmatization is a process in which noun words are mapped into singular form and verbs are mapped into infinite tenses. But this process is error prone, so mostly used stemming method for this purpose. In stemming, word is reduced to its root word. Porter stemming [12] is one of the well known stemming algorithm. The third method of preprocessing is keyword selection. This method is also used to further reduce words from the dictionary. Different techniques are used for keywords selection. Hotho[4] used entropy for this purpose. Words having low entropy mean frequently occurence in documents. So an importance of a word in a given domain can be checked by finding entropy. In another keyword selection technique, distance between every two words is measured and most related keywords having minimum distance are selected [13].

Wang [14] proposed three text preprocessing approaches. First is a pruned bag of single-words approach which is different from a conventional bag of single-words approach in two aspects. It removes common words from all documents because these words do not generate useful classification rules. It also removes very rare words that are present in some documents. A minimum and maximum threshold values are selected for removing such words. The second approach is emerging pattern based bag of single-words. This approach is based on traditional emerging pattern approach in which frequency of an itemset can be increased by moving this itemset from one database to another database. In text mining, a document consists of different records and each record represents a document with its predefined class label. By dividing the document base into small databases with respect to their predefined classes, emerging patterns can be extracted. A third approach is bag of frequent itemset. In this approach, single word is represented as a single item and frequent itemset is represented as wordset. From a given document base a set of frequent wordsets can be generated.

All above research work shows that most text mining techniques are based on the idea that a text document can be represented by a set of words. If each document is to be considered a linear vector, then for each word of the document, a numerical value is stored which shows its importance in the document. All above research work done in preprocessing field, shows that various preprocessing methods gradually find out a representative set of words on which text mining techniques can be applied to find out interesting patterns of knowledge. Some major preprocessing techniques are discussed in the following section.

Information Extraction

Many researchers are integrating different information extraction methods, natural language processing techniques and Knowledge Discovery from Databases (KDD) to discover useful knowledge from unstructured or semi-structured data.

Karanikas and Tjortjis[15] presented a new text mining approach, TextMiner which involved information extraction and data mining. This approach consists of two main components, one is text analysis and other is data mining. In text analysis component after applying preprocessing techniques on text, they extracted events and terms from a document and then convert this information to structured form. And in second component they performed data mining by developing a new clustering algorithm to discover structure within the document. They applied their approach for financial domain.

Nahm and Mooney [16] integrated the text mining with information extraction and data mining. They used an automatically learned information extraction system to extract structured database from document corpus and then KDD tools are applied to mine this database. This system suggested a method of learning word to word relationship across fields by integrating data mining and information extraction. By using this system, experiments were conducted to construct soft matching rules from textual databases via information extraction. Through this system, they extracted multiple relationships in single document extraction. The main drawback of Nahm and Mooney's system is time complexity for rule discovery. The second limitation of this solution is the RAPIER information extraction system, which they used. RAPIER does not deal with the relationships of attributes because it is a field level extraction system [17]. RAPIER also handles only single slot extraction of semi structured data.

Popowich[18] developed an enterprise healthcare application which processed on structured and unstructured data associated with medical insurance claims. In this work, the author combined text mining with Natural Language Processing (NLP) techniques to find dependencies between different entities with textual information. By using NLP techniques, the author defined a text-based concept creation algorithm and developed an NLP Concept Matcher. This system is not fully automated because human involvement is required in the investigation of resulting claims.

3   PROKEX Framework Overview

The goal of the PROKEX solution[19] is to extract, organize and preserve knowledge embedded in organizational processes in order to (1) enrich organizational knowledge base in a systematic and controlled way (2) support employees to easily acquire their job role specific knowledge, (3) help to govern and plan the human capital investment. PROKEX IT solution integrates a) organizational process management tool, b) learning management tool, c) real-time data monitoring and processing tool and d) data and text mining tools for developing a knowledge base (domain ontology) and the interfaces which are responsible for the communication between these components.

The novelty of the solution is based on process mining, namely dynamically analysing processes with data and text mining techniques to extract knowledge from them, in order to connect them toorganizational knowledge base, where the process structure will be used for building up the knowledge structure. In our approach knowledge base is an ontology, which provides the conceptualization of a certain domain. The main innovation lies in new algorithms for the extraction and integration of the static and dynamic process knowledge and a novel integration architecture that enables smooth integration of the e-learning methods in the process execution models. The focus is on the job training, since it increases organizational knowledge assets, creates productivity at the organizational level and is also a source of innovation and therefore long-term competitiveness of organizations. Our paper discusses in detailed the data and text mining component of the solution, as it is highlighted in figure 1.

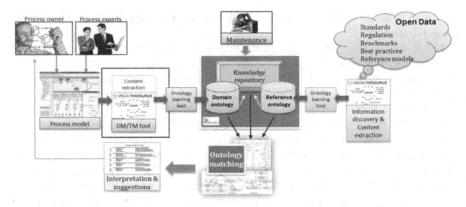

Fig. 1. General overview of Prokex solution

3.1   Prokex Text Mining Component Overview

In this section, a Prokex text mining framework (ProMine) for knowledge element extraction from the contextual data is presented. On the basis of these knowledge elements, the domain specific ontology will be created. This framework uses several text mining and data mining techniques to extract knowledge and identify the relationship between specific activities and job role specification competencies. Figure 2 illustrates the overall components and processes of the proposed framework. The framework can be described by five major steps: text extraction, text preprocessing, text transformation, word selection, association mining. The outcome of ProMine will be used in domain ontology mapping process. ProMine has the capabilities to perform all the tasks shown in figure 2.

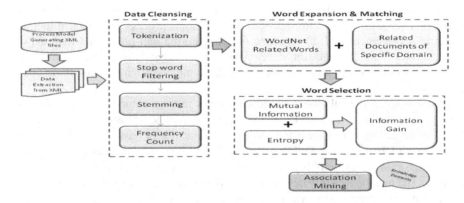

Fig. 2. ProMine: AText Mining Framework

3.2   Text Extraction

ProMine text mining solution is a part of Prokex framework, which is a combination of process modelling and text mining. The input data required for text mining component comes from process model in the form of XML files. These XML files contain a specific type of tag for a description of an activity. Every activity is described in a separate activity tag. At the first step of this framework, the pertinent information from these input files is extracted automatically. After extracting specific text, this text is saved in different text files.

3.3   Preprocessing / Text Cleansing

The next step is to clean the extracted text and this preprocessing module ensures that data is ready for analysis process. According to the literature, different preprocessing techniques can be applied at this step. In ProMine the following preprocessing methods are involved in text cleaning.

Tokenization: First, tokenization is applied to the text and converts a stream of characters into streams of words, which are our processing unit.

Stop Words Filtering: To reduce the dimensionality of tokenized data, stop word filter is applied. In this process most frequent but unimportant words are removed.

Stemming: After applying stop words filtering, list of words is further reduced by the method of stemming which reduced words to their stems. More frequently used stemmer is porter stemmer [12]. But this stemmer has some drawbacks like over stemming and under stemming. In overstemming it stems "process", "processed", "processing", "procession" to "process". To overcome the shortcomings of porter stemmer, we have applied a new method of stemming in ProMine. In this stemming method, first we apply porter stemmer on the text and in this process we get the list of all conflated forms of a single word from input text and also resulting stem word of porter. After getting this list and stem word, we check the co-occurrence of these words within our domain related documents. In this way, to some extent we overcome the overstemming of porter stemmer.

Frequency Count. To find most interesting terms, a method of frequency count is applied. For extracting maximum important keywords, we have set minimum threshold.

3.4   Word Expansion and Matching

At the end of preprocessing step, a list of keywords is created. This list of words came from a file that is generated by a process model. Single file cannot provide enough information for generating knowledge elements that we need for domain specific ontology. In order to enrich vocabulary of required knowledge elements, we extract similar words (synonyms) from WordNet dictionary developed by Princeton University[20]. WordNet is a semantic database, which provides a set of synonyms of a given word and these synonyms are linked by semantic relations [21]. We have used WordNet to expand a concept's vocabulary for extracting useful knowledge elements. For every keyword, we get a set of synonyms from WordNet and generate a list of words of that keyword as shown in figure 3.

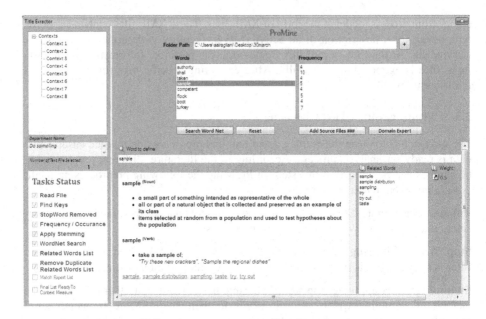

Fig. 3. ProMine: Data Extraction & Word Expansion

However, WordNet has different senses of a word so; many irrelevant words (can not a part of specific domain) are also generated. To overcome this ambiguity, we filter the candidate word senses by using specific domain related documents that may be glossaries or legal documents or any type of documents. If any word does not occur in related documents or its recurrence is below than a defined threshold, then this word will drop from the list. In this way all irrelevant words from the list of synonyms are dropped. WordNet database has no compound words/multiword terms (all pairs in which keyword is used as the first word) represents concepts so are more informative as compared to single words. Therefore, at this step, multiword terms are also stretched from the given corpus because these multiword terms represent concepts that are more important to get meaningful knowledge elements.

3.5   Feature Ranking and Selection

Though, we have removed ambiguity of unrelated terms (conceptually, not related to a specific domain) from a set of related terms (from WordNet) of a give keyword by using the last module (Word Expansion and Matching) our framework. However, the resultant word list consists of tens or hundreds of terms (single and compound words) created from a moderate-sized collection of documents of a specific domain. This high dimensionality of the feature space is the major particularity of text domain. These unique terms or potential keywords are considered as feature space, these lists of words can be considered as high dimensional and sparse vectors. In high dimensionality data sets, data points (features) are very far from each other due to sparsely filled space [22]. In literature, researchers use feature selection methods to reduce high dimensionality. Feature selection is a method to choose a minimum subset of features that satisfy an evaluation criterion. Literature has proved that feature selection reduces the dimensionality of feature space and it also removes redundant, irrelevant, or noisy data. By reducing dimensionality, performance of algorithms can be improved.

In our proposed framework, at his stage, we are reducing feature space by selecting more informative words from word lists by using a feature ranking method that is based on Information Gain (IG). We find out IG for all potential terms and remove all those terms that have low information gain than a predefined threshold. First, we calculate entropy, which is the measure of unpredictability and provide the foundation of IG. Entropy is defined as

$$E(x) = -\sum_{x \in X} P(x) \log P(x) \qquad (1)$$

Where $P(x)$ is the probability of each keyword in the domain related documents.

After calculating we find out Mutual Information (MI) of keyword with each potential similar word. We can find MI by following formula

$$MI(x, y) = \frac{P(x,y)}{P(x)*P(y)} \qquad (2)$$

Where x represents keyword and y represents related word.

Now on the basis of entropy and mutual information we can find out the information gain (IG) which will decide which term should be included in our final list of words. The information gain of term x is defined to be

$$IG(x) = f(MI)*E(x)*E(y)/W(x) \qquad (3)$$

Where f is the frequency of mutual occurrence; w is the weight of keyword that can be found by frequency count of that word in all documents. All these steps are shown in figure 4.

At the end of this step, we have a final list of words having all informative relative words in a keyword. In this way, at the end, all keywords have their own lists of related words which we will use as transactions for association mining.

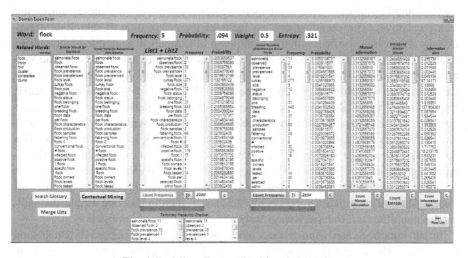

Fig. 4. ProMine: Feature Ranking & Selection

3.6   Association Rule Mining

At the end of the last step, we have a list of words against each keyword. At this step we have to find out concept relationships among these words. By using contextual information, we can find out more semantic relations among these words that can further used for ontology enrichment. In literature, different data mining techniques have been used for contextualization. Mei et al. [23] used vector space context to provide semantic annotations for frequent patterns while Tsatsaronis, G., et al. [24] used decision support subsystem which is based on if then rules for medical research-ers to efficiently access scientific literature for designing clinical trial protocol. Mei et al. [25] proposed a general contextual probabilistic latent semantic analysis (CPLSA) model for contextual text mining. We used association rule extraction to generate more meaningful and human understandable patterns/relations from these lists of words. Each list of words, acts as a set of frequent item (keyword) set and we take all lists of key words of a same activity. For each frequent item set, all association rules have to find that satisfy already defined threshold minimum confidence. These resulted relations as knowledge elements will be used for ontology enrichment.

4   ProMine Case – Sampling in Controlling Food Safety

In Prokex project we aimed to inspect the complex process of the food supply chain. ProMine case focused on one part of the process: the sampling. The reason for select-ing this domain is the complexity of the related tasks and the problems occurring during the everyday execution.

The real complete process starts with the planning of sampling meaning about 3000 product/parameter pairs and 100.000 samples during a year. The planning of sampling is centrally prepared; the execution is done by a staff of approx. 1000 people organized regionally. The detailed timing and task breakdown of the individual sam-pling events is done by the regional management.

The sampling process (our main focus process) starts with the preset timing and task breakdown. The sampling process includes the preparation of sampling, execu-tion described by specific regulations, shipping of samples to accredited laboratories, related documentation and input in the Public Authority internal IT system. The sam-pling process ends at the point when the samples are arriving to the laboratories. Complexity of sampling is caused by the small differences depending on the scope. Depending on the goal of the investigation and the parameters of sampling, different portions, methods, devices and documentations have to be used, on top of it the goals and parameters may also change in line with some high-risk events in the food chain. Sampling process is a very good candidate for data and text mining, because the re-lated regulations are various and changing fast. The domain of food safety is a strongly regulated environment: EU legislation, national legislation and in-house Public Authority regulations are deeply described, thereby causing strong difficulty for the sampling staff to have always fully updated and actual information.

In our sampling case, from process model XML file was generated in which some descriptions about the different steps of "execution of sampling" were given. ProMine take this XML as an input source, extract text from some specified tags that contain a description of the sampling process and save this extracted text into different text files (each for different subprocesses of sampling). After extracting text, preprocessing techniques that are mentioned in section 3.3 are applied on this source and find out all key terms of each subprocess. Now each key term is sent to WordNet for expanding the list of related words to find more information elements related to the sampling process. After finding related words of a keyword, then these related words along with a keyword match with domain related documents and find some more relevant single and compound words. In this way, a long list of related words of keyword comes as an output. Next step is to filter out words, which have less domain related information. We used the information gain method to rank all words, and by defining a threshold we select most informative words as shown in figure 5. At the end, to extract knowledge elements from these lists of related words, we applied association rule mining. We consider each list of words as one transaction and all words as frequent item set. By applying association mining, we will generate find strong relations among words in the form of association rules from the frequent itemsets. These relations are finally used for ontology enrichment.

An example of these generated association rules:

Vaccinated, flocks, infection -- >lower 85%

This rule tells us that in 85% of text these three words (vaccinated, flock, infection) occurred within 3 consequent words, the word "lower" co-occurs within 4 words. So in this way we can get information from this rule that in vaccinated flocks, infection chances are low.

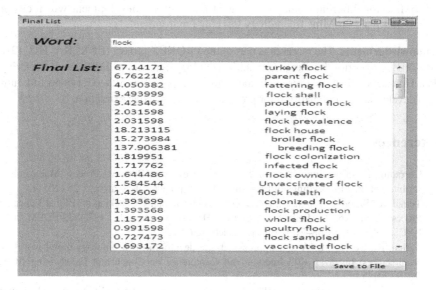

Fig. 5. ProMine: Final Related list of Words

5   Conclusion

In this paper we have discussed an innovative approach for process-based knowledge extraction. ProMine is a text mining component of Prokex framework, which was developed in Prokex project (EUREKA_HU_12-1-2012-0039). ProMine support to extract, organize and preserve knowledge embedded in organizational processes to enrich the organizational knowledge base in a systematic and controlled way, support employees to easily acquire their job role specific knowledge. The novelty of the ProMine solution is based on process mining, namely dynamically analysing processes with data and text mining techniques to extract knowledge elements from them, in order to connect them to organizational knowledge base, where the process structure will be used for building up the knowledge structure. In our approach knowledge base is the ontology, which provides the conceptualization of a certain domain. The main innovation lies in new algorithms for the extraction and integration of the static and dynamic process knowledge and a novel integration architecture that enables smooth integration of the e-learning methods in the process execution models. The focus is on the job training, since it increases organizational knowledge assets, creates productivity at the organizational level and is also a source of innovation and therefore long-term competitiveness of organizations.

ProMine solution has been tested for the case of an agricultural service at public authority, in the case of sampling in controlling food safety and quality. By applying ProMine in PROKEX, the sampling staff receives a useful tool for easily retrieving relevant knowledge related to the specific process they are actually running and valuable feedback about the embedded knowledge in processes.

Future work includes further improvement of Porter stemmer and additional testing of ProMine for different domains. The next phase of the development will focus on the integration of ProMine to ontology learning environment.

Acknowledgements. The research is part of the PROKEX project (EUREKA_HU_12-1-2012-0039, supported by Research and Technology Innovation Fund, New Szécsényi Plan, Hungary), which is a research and innovation program of the Corvinno Ltd, aimingto develop integrated platform for process-based knowledge extraction.

References

1. Corradini, F., et al.: Innovation on Public Services using Business Process Management. In: International Proceedings of Economics Development & Research, p. 25 (2011)
2. Ternai, K., Szabó, I., Varga, K.: Ontology-Based Compliance Checking on Higher Education Processes. In: Kő, A., Leitner, C., Leitold, H., Prosser, A. (eds.) EGOVIS/EDEM 2013. LNCS, vol. 8061, pp. 58–71. Springer, Heidelberg (2013)
3. Ternai, K., Torok, M.: A new approach in the development of ontology based workflow architectures. In: 2011 17th International Conference on Concurrent Enterprising (ICE). IEEE (2011)
4. Hotho, A., Nürnberger, A., Paaß, G.: A Brief Survey of Text Mining. In: Ldv Forum (2005)
5. Hearst, M.: What is text mining, vol. 7, p. 2011 (retrieved February, 2003)
6. Wang, Y.: Various approaches in text pre-processing. TM Work Paper No, 2 (2004)

7. Feldman, R., Hirsh, H.: Mining Associations in Text in the Presence of Background Knowledge. In: KDD (1996)
8. Feldman, R., Dagan, I., Hirsh, H.: Mining text using keyword distributions. Journal of Intelligent Information Systems 10(3), 281–300 (1998)
9. Salton, G., Buckley, C.: Term-weighting approaches in automatic text retrieval. Information Processing & Management 24(5), 513–523 (1988)
10. Zhang, C.: Automatic keyword extraction from documents using conditional random fields. Journal of Computational Information Systems 4(3), 1169–1180 (2008)
11. Ahonen-Myka, H.: Finding all maximal frequent sequences in text. In: Proc. of the ICML 1999 Workshop on Machine Learning in Text Data Analysis. Citeseer (1999)
12. Porter, M.F.: An algorithm for suffix stripping. Program: Electronic Library and Information Systems 14(3), 130–137 (1980)
13. Kardan, A.A., Farahmandnia, F., Omidvar, A.: A novel approach for keyword extraction in learning objects using text mining and WordNet. Global Journal of Information Technology 3(1) (2013)
14. Wang, Y.: Novel Approaches to Pre-processing Documentbase in Text Classification. Citeseer (2012)
15. Karanikas, H., Tjortjis, C., Theodoulidis, B.: An approach to text mining using information extraction. In: Proc. Knowledge Management Theory Applications Workshop (KMTA 2000) (2000)
16. Nahm, U.Y., Mooney, R.J.: Text mining with information extraction. In: AAAI 2002 Spring Symposium on Mining Answers from Texts and Knowledge Bases (2002)
17. Chang, C.H., et al.: A survey of web information extraction systems. IEEE Transactions on Knowledge and Data Engineering 18(10), 1411–1428 (2006)
18. Popowich, F.: Using text mining and natural language processing for health care claims processing. ACM SIGKDD Explorations Newsletter 7(1), 59–66 (2005)
19. Gabor, A., Török, M.: Prokex Deliverable D2.1 Process Model Selection. Integrated Platform for Process-based Knowledge Extraction (2014)
20. Miller, G.A.: WordNet: a lexical database for English. Communications of the ACM 38(11), 39–41 (1995)
21. Luong, H., Gauch, S., Wang, Q.: Ontology Learning Using Word Net Lexical Expansion and Text Mining (2012)
22. Milenova, B.L., Campos, M.M.: O-cluster: Scalable clustering of large high dimensional data sets. In: Proceedings of the 2002 IEEE International Conference on Data Mining, ICDM 2003. IEEE (2002)
23. Mei, Q., et al.: Generating semantic annotations for frequent patterns with context analysis. In: Proceedings of the 12th ACM SIGKDD International Conference on Knowledge Discovery and Data Mining. ACM (2006)
24. Tsatsaronis, G., et al.: PONTE: a context-aware approach for automated clinical trial protocol design. In: Proceedings of the 6th International Workshop on Personalized Access, Profile Management, and Context Awareness in Databases in Conjunction with VLDB (2012)
25. Mei, Q., Zhai, C.: A mixture model for contextual text mining. In: Proceedings of the 12th ACM SIGKDD International Conference on Knowledge Discovery and Data Mining. ACM (2006)

Combining Knowledge Management and Business Process Management – A Solution for Information Extraction from Business Process Models Focusing on BPM Challenges

Katalin Ternai[1], Mátyás Török[2], and Krisztián Varga[3]

[1] Corvinno Technology Transfer Center Ltd.
kternai@corvinno.com
[2] Netpositive Ltd.
torok.matyas@netpositive.hu
[3] Corvinus University of Budapest
kvarga@informatika.uni-corvinus.hu

Abstract. In today's dynamic environment all organizations need up-to-date knowledge for their operations that are based on business processes. Complex organizations use business process management (BPM) tools to model and manage these processes. BPM applications tends to model the organizational processes, together with the required information and other resources needed to perform each activity. BPM yields an overall context, but it is still static.

Our paper presents a solution to extract, organize and preserve knowledge embedded in organizational processes to enrich organizational knowledge base in a systematic and controlled way utilized in the PROKEX project. The proposed solution is to extract the knowledge from information stored in the process model in order to articulate, externalize and transfer it. Our paper focuses on the BPM aspects of the solution as we want to investigate it from the information systems perspective.

The novelty of the solution is based on the connection between process model and corporate knowledge base, where the process structure will be used for building up the knowledge structure. Common form of knowledge base is the ontology, which provides the conceptualization of a certain domain. By using the ontology and combining it with the process models, we connect knowledge management and business process management in a dynamic, systematic and well-controlled solution.

Keywords: semantic business process management, knowledge extraction, knowledge management, knowledge gap.

1   Introduction

Complex organizations model and manage their processes with the help of business process management (BPM) tools. These applications help to describe the organizational processes, together with the required information and other resources needed to perform each activity. BPM yields an overall context, but it tends to be static.

A. Kő and E. Francesconi (Eds.): EGOVIS 2014, LNCS 8650, pp. 104–117, 2014.
© Springer International Publishing Switzerland 2014

Project PROKEX proposes a solution to extract, organize and preserve knowledge embedded in organizational processes to enrich organizational knowledge base in a systematic and controlled way, support employees to easily acquire their job role specific knowledge.

Business processes are defined as sequence of activities. From the human resource management view it is required to define unambiguously, who is responsible for the execution of each activity. The RACI matrix (Responsible, Accountable, Consulted, Informed) is used for grouping role types, bridging the organizational model and the process model. We need to acquire knowledge belonging to the job roles, in this sense RACI assigns only job role types to the tasks.

The proposed solution is to extract the knowledge from information stored in the process model in order to articulate, externalize and transfer it. Since the business process models are used for the execution of processes in a workflow engine, another very important source for gathering useful knowledge are real-time instantiations of the business processes, that gives a view on the dynamic knowledge, usually represented in the form of different business rules.

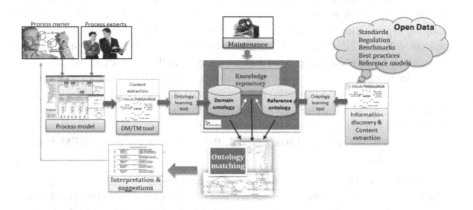

Fig. 1. General overview of Prokex solution http://prokex.netpoitive.hu/

The goal of the paper is to introduce a solution to extract, organize and preserve knowledge embedded in organizational processes in order to enrich organizational knowledge base in a systematic and controlled way; support employees to easily acquire their job role specific knowledge and help to govern and plan the human capital investment (1. Figure).

The novelty of the solution is based on the connection between process model and corporate knowledge base, where the process structure will be used for building up the knowledge structure. Common form of knowledge base is the ontology, which provides the conceptualization of a certain domain.

2   The State of the Art in SBPM

2.1   Business Process Management

Nowadays business process modeling is an integral part of many organizations to document and redesign complex organizational processes. One of the most promising tendencies in application development today is business process design based software development. Software development methodologies have traditionally been driven by programming and not organizational concepts, leading to a semantic gap between the software system and its operational environment. Business process modeling aligns the business goals and incentives with the IT software design process.

As a forerunner of BPM, in the early 1990s, the idea of Business Process Reengineering (BPR) brought business processes to the center of interest and lifted the subject of design from the supporting IT systems to business processes, to the perspective of business experts. The term is originated from Hammer & Champy's BPR paradigm [1-2].

It has been common sense to first determine business requirements and then to derive IT implementations, to develop software according to ideal processes as determined by business logic. Business processes have to perform well within ever-changing organizational environments. It can be expected that Business Process Management will only come closer to its promises if it allows for a better automation of the two-way translation between the business level and the software systems.

In order to obtain a full view of the capabilities of BPM, we have to start out from the overview of the BPM lifecycle. Among the vast number of BPM lifecycle models available [3], we chose to build upon the most concise and probably one of the most popular model of van der Aalst.

According to the proposed basic model, the four elements of the BPM Lifecycle are the following:

Process Design: The organizational processes concerning the subject are identified, top level visualization of the processes are laid down. Several modeling standards and tools are aiding this phase, as we will have a deeper look among them in the following sections.

System Configuration: This phase provides a more thorough overview of the processes, ideally taking into consideration all possible aspects required for the implementation of the underlying IT infrastructure. One very important dimension of the configuration is business-IT alignment, and also the synchronization of roles and responsibilities of the organizational structure concerning the processes. This stage has many obstacles in real-life implementations due to the inhomogeneous nature of the IT and organizational architectures of different enterprises.

Process Enactment: Processes are inaugurated in real life circumstances, and form the IT point of view being deployed into Business Process Management Systems/Suites (BPMS), workflow engines or other software instances. Recently, in a state-of-the-art organization, this deployment holds some extent of automation. The current focus of BPM theory is concerned with raising this level of automation in turning electronically modeled processes into effective IT supporting infrastructure.

Diagnosis: In an ever-changing business environment it is inevitable to have appropriate feedback on the operational environment of the processes. Diagnosis activities range from monitoring, analysis of the effectiveness – or other KPIs – of enacted processes, and also after identifying and analyzing possible failures and bottlenecks, the revision of the process design, making BPM a continuous, cyclic function of the organization. This phase has a wide body of literature within the BPM community, it is supported by many diagnostic standards, but it falls out of the scope of our interest.

2.2   BPM and Workflow Management

BPM standards and specifications are based on established BPM theory and are eventually adopted into software and systems. BPM standards and systems are also what Gartner [4-5-6] describes as "BPM-enabling technologies".

In the industry, there is a growing awareness of the emerging term service-oriented architecture (SOA). BPM is a process-oriented management discipline aided by IT while SOA is an IT architectural paradigm. According to Gartner [6], BPM "organizes people for greater agility" while SOA "organizes technology for greater agility". Processes in SOA (e.g. linked web services) enable the coordination of distributed systems supporting business processes and should not be confused with business processes.

There is also some confusion between the Workflow Management (WfM) and BPM terms. While often treated synonymously, BPM and workflow are, in fact, two distinct and separate entities. According to one viewpoint, workflow is concerned with the application-specific sequencing of activities via predefined instruction sets, involving either or both automated procedures (software-based) and manual activities (people work) [7]. BPM is concerned with the definition, execution and management of business processes defined independently of any single application. BPM is a superset of workflow, further differentiated by the ability to coordinate activities across multiple applications with fine grain control.

Other research views BPM as a management discipline with Workflow Management supporting it as a technology [8]:

- Business process management is a process-oriented management discipline. It is not a technology;
- Workflow is a flow management technology found in business process management suites and other product categories.

Another viewpoint from academics is that the features stated in WfM according to Georgakopoulos et al. [9] is a subset of BPM defined by van der Aalst [11] with the diagnosis stage of the BPM life cycle as the main difference.

However, in reality, as we have observed, many BPMS are still very much workflow management systems (WfMS) and have not yet matured in the support of the BPM diagnosis, some providers of software tools have updated their products' names from "WfM" to the more rewarding "BPM" [5].

2.3   Classification of BPM Standards

The most logical way to make sense of the myriad of BPM standards is to categorize them into groups with similar functions and characteristics. For this reason, we propose a cleaner separation of features found in standards addressing the process design and process enactment phase into three clear-cut types of standards:

Graphical Standards: This allows users to express business processes and their possible flows and transitions in a diagrammatic way. Graphical standards are the highest level of expression of business processes.

Graphical standards allow users to express the information flow, decision points and the roles of business processes in a diagrammatic way. Graphical standards are currently the most human-readable and easiest to comprehend without prior technical training. Unified Modeling Language activity diagrams – UML AD [12], Business Process Model and Notation - BPMN [13], Event-driven Process Chains – EPC [14], Role-Activity Diagrams (RADs) Petri-nets and flow charts are common techniques used to model business processes graphically [15].

These techniques range from common notations (e.g. flow charts) to standards (e.g. BPMN). And of the standards, UML AD and BPMN are currently the two most expressive, easiest for integration with the interchange and execution level, and possibly the most influential in the near future. For this reason, we will focus more on UML AD and BPMN, followed by a brief description of the other graphical business process modeling techniques.

Execution Standards: It computerizes the deployment and automation of business processes. Execution standards enable business process designs to be deployed in BPMS and their instances executed by the BPMS engine. There are currently two prominent execution standards: BPML and BPEL (Business Process Execution Language). Of the two, BPEL is more widely adopted in several prominent software suites (e.g. IBM Websphere, BEA AquaLogic BPM Suite, SAP Netweaver, etc.) even though BPML can better address business process semantics.

Interchange Standards: It facilitates portability of data, e.g. the portability of business process designs in different graphical standards across BPMS; different execution standards across disparate BPMS, and the context-less translation of graphical standards to execution standards and vice versa.

As mentioned earlier, interchange standards are needed to translate graphical standards to execution standards; and to exchange business process models between different BPMS's [16]. Some practitioners thought these interchange standards as "the link between business and IT", but we do not agree with this assertion because an interchange standard is a translator from a graphical standard to an execution standard [17]. There are currently two prominent interchange standards: Business Process Definition Metamodel (BPDM) by OMG and XML Process Definition Language (XPDL) by the WfMC.

2.4   Semantic Interoperability and Process Ontologies

2.4.1   Semantic Business Process Management
The main challenge in Business Process Management is the continuous, two-way translation between the business requirements view on the process space and the

actual process space, constituted by the IT systems and resources. Semantic Business Process Management (SBPM) is a new approach of increasing the level of automation in the translation between these two levels, and is currently driven by major players from the BPM and Semantic Web Services domain [18].

Business Process Management is the approach of managing the execution of IT supported business operations from the managerial process view. BPM should provide a uniform representation of a process at a semantic level, which would be accessible to intelligent queries or for compliance checks [19]. It is expected, that the BPM notation should cover every aspect of the characterized processes available at the managerial level.

Semantic process management was created with the purpose to overcome the obstacles of standard BPM techniques, and also to incorporate its principles with semantic technologies, primary with the ontology-based development. Hepp at. al, along with Koschmider and Oberweis identified the challenge in traditional process management, that it only contributes models for the business experts and managerial level, completely lacking or only marginally addressing technical details of implementation. This way process models are inadequate for automatic machine processing, working implementations are only possible after further supplementary transformation [20-21]. The main focus of semantic process management is consequently the narrowing of the gap between the business and IT views of organizational phenomenon with the utilization of semantic technologies such as ontologies, reasoning mechanisms and semantic web services. Hepp et al. did not demonstrate concrete applications, only introduced a theoretical framework.

There is a considerable advance in the past decade in the domain of SBPM, many experimental projects have been concluded successfully. The unambiguous and rapid alignment between process models and IT solutions is targeted by the SUPER project, one of the most extensive R+D project under the FP7 initiative of the European Union (Semantics Utilised for Process Management within and between Enterprises) [22]. Another result of this effort is the development of the Web Service Modeling Ontology (WSMO) [23], as well as the Semantic Business Process Execution Language (SBPEL). Gábor and Szabó extends the standard BPM life cycle to SBPM life cycle and gives examples to existing applications to the phases [24].

Several approaches have been discussed to enhance both the act of creating conceptual models as well as the execution of the models by using semantic schema in the area of business process management [20]. The paradigm of current SBPM research is to provide as much compatibility to existing tools and standards as possible. This means, that processes behind of a business model should be represented in terms of SBPM environment, and it should be possible to create executable processes configured within an SBPM environment.

During the phases of development and implementation, conceptual models are used to support the requirements engineering process. Furthermore, conceptual models facilitate tasks such as the exploration, negotiation, documentation, and validation of requirements. This allows exploring and correcting possible errors at an early stage [25]. Conceptual modeling captures the semantics of an application through the use of a formal notation, but the descriptions resulting from conceptual modeling are intended to be used by humans and not machines. The conceptual foundations of these approaches show several similarities, but the actual realizations on various technical platforms are not discussed in detail. The realization of the alignment of conceptual models and semantic schema on a technical level needs to be elaborated in details. Our approach tries to provide a feasible implementation pattern based on the extension of process ontologies to resolve this issue.

2.4.2   Process Ontology

Ontologies are state-of-the-art constructs to represent rich and complex knowledge about things, their properties, groups of things, and relations between things. The use of web-based ontologies and their contribution to business innovation has received a lot of attention in the past years [26]. Ontologies provide the means to freely describe different aspects of a business domain, basically provide the semantics and they can describe both the semantics of the modeling language constructs as well as the semantics of model instances [27]. With web-based semantic schema such as the Web Ontology Language (OWL) [28], the creation and the use of specific models can be improved, furthermore the implicit semantics being contained in the models can be partly articulated and used for processing.

Apart from the representation of business domains, ontologies are utilized in many other practical areas of software development from 3D construct definition to software localization and internationalization. The generation, processing and visualization of ontologies are supported by an extensive set of tools and frameworks. This general but formalized representation can also be used for describing the concepts of a business process. We attempt to undertake this task and provide an extension for the standard ontology definition in the form of an annotation scheme to enable ontologies to cover all the major aspects of business process definition. From now on, we refer to ontologies as process ontologies [29-30].

According to our current knowledge, process ontologies have no precise definition in academic literature. Some refer to it simply as a conceptual description framework of processes [30]. In this interpretation process ontologies are abstract and general. Contrary, task ontologies determine a smaller subset of the process space, the sequence of activities in a given process [31].

In our approach, a formal process ontology is a domain ontology built upon the knowledge domain of processes. Ontology definition is the key element in turning process models into working software, providing a visual and textual representation of the processes, data, information, resources, collaborations and other measurements. We are primarily interested in the automatic generation of workflow systems based on BPM defined ontologies, while preserving the capability of discussion with non-technical users. The core paradigm of our approach is to represent the business incentives extended with all the implementation details of processes using ontology languages and to employ machine reasoning for the automated or at least semi-automated translation. We discuss how to establish the links between model elements and ontology concepts in order to realize reusability. Automatic generation of workflow processes allows us to redeploy processes in a flexible manner whenever business requirements change. This method also permits interoperability between different implementation frameworks supporting the process ontology annotation scheme.

2.5   Ontology Languages

In the context of our research, process models as process knowledge resources can be disseminated through the Web. The Semantic Web domain has given us standards such as RDF and OWL to support the semantic interpretation. The knowledge representation of process models needs to be transformed into those Semantic Web standards.

The Web can be viewed as a large distributed repository for the process models. However, distributed models are originally from different autonomous systems and stored in various schemas. Technologies facilitating interoperability of heterogeneous models such as ontology and semantic annotation, are required when organizing the knowledge in such a repository.

The OWL Web Ontology Language [27] is designed for use by applications that need to process the content of information instead of just presenting information to humans. OWL facilitates greater machine interpretability of Web content than that supported by XML, RDF, and RDF Schema (RDF-S) by providing additional vocabulary along with a formal semantics.

OWL-S is an ontology of services that provides users and agents with the possibility to discover, invoke, compose, and monitor Web resources offering particular services and having particular properties [32]. The motivations of the applications of OWL-S are automatic Web services discovery, automatic Web services invocation and automatic Web service composition and interoperation.

3   Prokex BPM Component Overview

In this section we provide a short overview of the modeling components utilized during the PROKEX project to obtain the necessary knowledge of the observed organizations. We have conducted process audits at several organizations: government agencies, profit-oriented companies and companies of the financial sector.

Our inspection concentrated on a small number of business processes. It was not our aim to build a complete process map of these organizations, but to acquire enough information to validate our approach in diverse circumstances.

3.1   Use Case: "Food Safety Inspection – Sampling" Process

Based on the challenges of the common agricultural policy and the demand for a consistent management of professional policy, the Agricultural Management has been rearranged. Another goal of the reform has been to provide an access to the necessary information for the farmers faster than before, and to make administration more efficient. Accordingly, all the agricultural administrative departments, which had been independent before, were integrated on 1 January 2007.

The application of an integrated "from the soil to the table" approach and view was implemented, covering each element of the food chain, including feed production and marketing, the primary production, processing, storing, transporting and marketing of food. With the consistent and complete surveillance of the whole chain kept in one hand, the highest level of food safety could be implemented.

In our use case, we demonstrate the Prokex BPM component via the "Food safety inspection – Sampling" process. The sampling process starts by the pre-set timing and task breakdown, and it includes the preparation of sampling, execution described by specific regulations, shipping of samples to accredited laboratories, related documentation. The sampling process ends at the point when the samples are arriving to the laboratories.

The main process of sampling is simple but complex as well, because of the small differences depending on the scope of the sampling. Depending on the goal of the investigation and the parameters of sampling, different portions, methods, devices and documentations have to be used, on top of it the goals and parameters may also change in line with some high-risk events in the food chain.

The domain of food safety is a strongly regulated environment: EU legislation, national legislation and organizational regulations are deeply described, thereby causing strong difficulty for the sampling staff to have always fully updated and actual information.

Nevertheless sampling is a critical phase in the whole process as if the sampling is not happening fully in line with regulations and documentation is not complete and accurate, even though laboratories may provide a prefect work and results from a scientific standpoint the results may not be relevant and useful from a food safety and control standpoint.

Challenges we face and plan to provide a solution by PROKEX:

- Sampling staff doesn't always have fully updated knowledge about sampling requirement details;
- Related regulation and documentation is very long and detailed;
- Because of the different sources and form of Information, documentation is not well structured to enable staff members to easily find relevant pieces of information;
- Sampling staff often works based on routines learned from the past even if the related process has been changed in the meantime.

By analyzing the tasks and implementing a structured knowledge base in PROKEX sampling staff will receive a useful tool for easily retrieving relevant knowledge related to the specific process they are actually running.

3.2   Modeling Environment

The business process models have been implemented using the BOC ADONIS modeling platform. The main application area of ADONIS is Business Process Management. We have selected this modeling platform because of its popularity in modeling practice. However, our approach is principally transferable to other semi-formal modeling languages.

ADONIS is a graph-structured Business Process Management language. The integral model element is the activity. The ADONIS modeling platform is a business meta-modeling tool with components such as modeling, analysis, simulation, evaluation, process costing, documentation, staff management, and import-export. Its main feature is its method independence.

The RACI model support for identifying roles within the processes and associate them with the process activities has a built-in support for EPC in Adonis.

3.3   Initial Modeling of the Processes

The basis of our multi-dimensional approach is a general control-flow oriented business process model. The process modeling starts with the close observation of an existing, real-life process at the given organization. We conducted interviews with all of the stakeholders of the company, reviewed the process development meetings and materials prepared during the actual project. We also inspected the underlying IT infrastructure.

The ever-recurring problem of capturing processes is the level of granularity. Setting this appropriate level can be thought of as an optimization problem in itself. If a process model is too superficial, it will not contain enough information to draw conclusions, conduct redesign or utilize it in any other ways. A modeling architecture with unnecessarily frittered details or a model with inhomogeneous granularity results in a confusing process architecture, and consumes unnecessary resources to create, maintain and manage. Ternai et al. collects the parameters have to be set in order to use a process model as a base of semantic transformations [33], we used those guidelines in this work, too.

Throughout our work, the level of granularity in modeling a process is set to grant the ability to attach corresponding concepts like roles or information objects to the model. In the sampling process it means, that we have modeled the main tasks, and identified the relevant information required to those tasks. At this point, the information is unstructured, and has various, heterogeneous sources.

3.4   Complementary Modeling Layers

After finalizing the basic process flow, the specific activities within the process model have to be aligned with roles and responsibilities. We capture a view of the inner stakeholders of the organization. We start by collecting all the roles that are related to the given process, and gradually examine, which roles have any relation with a given activity. This task is carried out on the theoretical ground of the RACI responsibility matrix. We determine, which are the explicit roles being played by which stakeholder at the level of a given activity. More precisely, we define according to the RACI, which role is Responsible for the performing of the activity, which role is Accountable for it, which are the roles needed to be Consulted during the execution of the activity, and who to be Informed about the advance, obstacles, completion or other information related to the given activity.

This knowledge is the basis of the PROKEX project's proposed outcome, namely to be able to present the knowledge items required by a person in a given role, or in a broader perspective, in a given position.

There are two additional modeling dimensions that play an important part in enriching process information. Many organizations have a well-structured IT infrastructure map, and in a higher-level process model, IT architecture elements are assigned to the process model at activity level. Modeling tools incorporate sub-models of the company's IT infrastructure. In this sub-model we define the major systems, tools or resources, which are going to play an active role in our processes.

Documents are also essential artifacts of business processes, different documents serving different roles are being created, transferred, and utilized as a source of knowledge and information. These documents have to be taken into account throughout the complete BPM lifecycle, and this way also incorporated to the complex process models.

In the sampling process it means, that we have identified the main roles in the process, and assigned them to the tasks, and to the RACI matrix. We have modeled the IT system model and investigated the unstructured information gathered in the previous step.

3.5   Complex Process Model

As a last step of capturing the inspected processes, we undertake a 360 degree semantic annotation. In other words, we supplement the models with every available, explicit knowledge items at activity level.

This action is carried out in three levels:

- Domain experts and practitioners provide direct, structured knowledge items at the level of activities;
- As a second layer, an accurate, thorough description of the activity is recorded which can be treated as unstructured information;
- The third layer relies on related documentation: guidelines, official procedures, best-practices, related legislation, etc.

Concerning the modeling implementation of the semantic annotation, the first level knowledge items can be directly placed in Adonis EPC process models as information objects. The information contained in underlying, non-structured form most undergo a semantic transformation to identify the knowledge elements or concept groups.

We are preserving the level of granularity set forth in our initial process models. It has to remain unchanged, since this granularity applies to all other modeling dimensions as well.

In the sampling process, structured information was provided by domain experts, and we modeled that as 'Information objects' connecting them to activated in the process model. All the information gathered via process meetings was populated to the description attribute to the relevant activities; this is layer two. And in the third layer, we have investigated the regulations and connected them to the activities as well.

3.6   Multidimensional Process Knowledge–Process Coupling via Semantic Transformations

The resulting complex process models contain interconnected, multi-dimensional information on the following areas of the recorded processes:

- process structure, process hierarchy
- organizational structure, roles and responsibilities at activity level
- mapped explicit knowledge

- IT architecture
- document structure

In order to make use of this holistic process-space, we need to apply semantic transformations to the models. We are aiming to provide a machine-readable representation for further utilization in the form of ontologies.

Since the complex process models hold both process knowledge and domain knowledge, we have to conduct these transformations respectively.

Process ontology instances can be created automatically by XSLT transition. The process model hierarchy is represented in OWL format, and the additional structure of interconnected elements can also be transferred following a semantic annotation scheme. As far as our knowledge extends, there are no industry standards expressing the full requirements of such a process structure annotation, but an ad-hoc processing of such a markup is possible [34]. The PROKEX project intends to develop a reference architecture satisfying some aspects of automatic processing.

The creation of domain ontology also holds several challenges. The above described first level structured knowledge can be easily transformed into OWL ontologies, but the underlying levels need further elaboration. We are striving to provide automatic ways to create ontology knowledge elements or concept groups by means of applying text-mining techniques, but some extent of domain expert knowledge seems to be inevitable for transforming unstructured knowledge from the recorded processes. Another article under the PROKEX project tackles this issue in details "Process-based Knowledge Extraction in a Public Administrative Authority: A Text Mining Approach" is to create an ontology from the originating SBPM. [10]

4   Conclusion

Our approach proposes a solution to extract, organize and preserve knowledge embedded in organizational processes to enrich organizational knowledge base in a systematic and controlled way, support employees to easily acquire their job role specific knowledge. We have identified the requirements in the business process modeling level to be able to use the process model as a base of creating a domain ontology from the information in it.

Our overall aim is to create a supporting infrastructure capable to conduct multidimensional queries especially for the purpose to support employees to easily acquire their job role specific knowledge.

The novelty of the solution is based on the connection between process model and corporate knowledge base, where the process structure will be used for building up the knowledge structure. The whole solution can be fully understood by investigating the articles to be written from project Prokex and its text-mining part. We focused on the business process modeling challenges of the solution.

References

1. Hammer, M., Champy, J.: What is reengineering? Information Week 372, 20–24 (1992)
2. Hammer, M., Champy, J.: Reengineering the Corporation: A Manifesto for Business Revolution. HarperBusiness, New York (1993)

3. Jeston, J., Nelis, J.: Business process management: Practical Guidelines to Successful Implementations. Routledge (2008)
4. Hill, J.B., Cantara, M., Deitert, E., Kerremans, M.: Magic quadrant for business process management suites. Gartner Research, Stamford (2007)
5. Hill, J.B., Kerremans, M., Bell, T.: Cool Vendors in Business Process Management. Gartner Research, Stamford (2007)
6. Hill, J.B., Sinur, J., Flint, D., Melenovsky, M.J.: Gartner's position on business process management. Gartner Research Group (2006)
7. Csepregi, L.: BPM and Workflow revisited (2010)
8. Hill, J.B., Pezzini, M., Natis, Y.V.: Findings: confusion remains regarding BPM. Gartner Research, Stamford (2008)
9. Georgakopoulos, D., Hornick, M., Sheth, A.: An overview of workflow management: from process modeling to workflow automation infrastructure. Distributed and Parallel 2(3), 119–153 (1995)
10. Gillani, S.A., Kő, A.: Process-Based Knowledge Extraction in a Public Authority: A Text Mining Approach. In: Kő, A., Francesconi, E. (eds.) EGOVIS 2014. LNCS, vol. 8650, pp. 91–103. Springer, Heidelberg (2014)
11. Van der Aalst, W.M.: Don't go with the flow: Web services composition standards exposed. IEEE Intelligent Systems 18, 72–76 (2003)
12. Object Management Group [OMG]: Unified Modeling Language (OMG UML), Infrastructure - Version 2.4 (2010), http://www.omg.org/spec/UML/2.4/Infrastructure/Beta2/PDF/
13. Object Management Group [OMG]. BPMN Fundamentals (2005)
14. Scheer, A.-W.: ARIS – House of Business Engineering: Konzept zur Beschreibung und Ausführung von Referenzmodellen. In: Becker, J., Rosemann, M., Schütte, R. (eds.) Entwicklungsstand und Entwicklungsperspektiven der Referenzmodellierung: Proceedings zur Veranstaltung vom 10. März 1997, pp. 3–15. Münster, Institut für Wirtschaftsinformatik, Westfälische Wilhelms-Universität, Münster (1997) (in German)
15. Tsohou, A., Kő, A., Lee, H., Al-Yafi, K., Weerakkody, V., El-Haddadeh, R., Irani, Z., Medeni, T.D., Campos, L.M.: Supporting Public Policy Making Processes with Workflow Technology: Lessons Learned From Cases in Four European Countries. International Journal of Electronic Government Research (IJEGR) 8(3), 63–78 (2012), http://www.igi-global.com/article/supporting-public-policy-making-processes/70076, ISSN: 1548-3886
16. Mendling, J., Neumann, G., Nüttgens, M.: Yet Another Event-driven Process Chain. Enterprise Modelling and Information Systems Architectures 1(1) (October 2005)
17. Koskela, M., Haajanen, J.: Business process modelling and execution: tools and technologies report for the SOAMeS project. VTT Research Notes No. 2407, VTT Technical Research Centre of Finland, Espoo (2007)
18. Ternai, K., Török, M.: Semantic modeling for automated workflow software generation – An open model. In: 2011 5th International Conference on Software, Knowledge Information, Industrial Management and Applications (SKIMA). IEEE (2011)
19. Weber, R.: Ontological Foundations of Information Systems. Coopers & Lybrand Research Methodology Monograph, vol. 4, Coopers & Lybrand, Melbourne (1997)
20. Hepp, M., Leymann, F., Domingue, J., Wahler, A., Fensel, D.: Semantic Business Process Management: A Vision Towards Using Semantic Web Services for Business Process Management. In: IEEE International Conference on e-Business Engineering, pp. 535–540 (2005)

21. Koschmider, A., Oberweis, A.: Modeling semantic business models. In: Rittgen, P. (ed.) Handbook of Ontologies for Business Interaction. Idea Group, Harpenden (2008)
22. Belecheanu, R., Cabral, L., Domingue, J., Gaaloul, W., Hepp, M., Filipowska, A., et al.: Business Process Ontology Framework. SUPER research project deliverable D1.1 (2007), SUPER project website: http://www.ip-super.org/res/Deliverables/M12 /D1.1.pdf (retrieved November 11, 2013)
23. Fensel, D., Lausen, H., Polleres, A., de Bruijn, J., Stollberg, M., Roman, D., et al.: Enabling Semantic Web Services: The Web Service Modeling Ontology. Springer (2006)
24. Gábor, A., Szabó, Z.: Semantic Technologies in Business Process Management. In: Integration of Practice-Oriented Knowledge Technology: Trends and Prospectives, pp. 17–28. Springer, Heidelberg (2012)
25. Wand, Y., Weber, R.: Information systems and conceptual modeling - a research agenda. Information Systems Research 13(4), 363–372 (2002)
26. Cardoso, J., Hepp, M., Mytras, M.D.: The Semantic Web: Real-World Applications from Industry. Springer (2007)
27. Murzek, M., Kramler, G.: Business Process Model Transformation Issues (2006), Wissenschafterinnenkolleg Internettechnologien: http://www.wit.at/people/murzek/ publications/Murzek_Kramler_2006_ModTransIssues.pdf   (retrieved January 2014)
28. McGuinness, D.M., van Harmelen, F.: OWL web ontology language overview (2004) W3C: http://www.w3.org/TR/2004/REC-owl-features-20040210/ (retrieved December 2013)
29. Török, M., Leontaridis, L.: Ontology based workflow architecture implementation for SMEs - case study. In: eChallenges e-2011 Conference Proceedings (October 2011)
30. Ternai, K., Török, M.: A New Approach in the Development of Ontology Based Workflow Architectures. In: 17th International Conference on Concurrent Enterprising - Conference Proceedings. Approaches in Concurrent Engineering, June 20-22. Ralf Zillekens Druck- und Werbeservice, Stolberg (2011), ISBN: 978-3-943024-04-3
31. Herborn, T., Wimmer, M.A.: Process Ontologies Facilitating Interoperability in eGovernment - A Methodological Framework. In: Hinkelmann, K., Karagiannis, D., Stojanovic, N., Wagner, G. (eds.) Proceeding of the Workshop on Semantics for Business Process Management at the 3rd European Semantic Web Conference, Budva, Montenegro, pp. 76–89 (2006)
32. Benjamins, V.R., Nunes de Barros, L., Valente, A.: Constructing Planners through Problem-Solving Methods. In: Proceedings of KAW 1996, pp. 14.1–14.20 (1996)
33. Martin, D., Burstein, M., Hobbs, J., Lassila, O.: OWL-S: Semantic Markup for Web Services (November 2004) W3C Consortium: http://www.w3.org/Submission/ OWL-S/ (retrieved December 2013)
34. Ternai, K., Szabó, I., Varga, K.: Ontology-based compliance checking on higher education processes. In: Kő, A., Leitner, C., Leitold, H., Prosser, A. (eds.) EGOVIS/EDEM 2013. LNCS, vol. 8061, pp. 58–71. Springer, Heidelberg (2013)
35. Gábor, A., Kő, A., Szabó, I., Ternai, K., Varga, K.: Compliance Check in Semantic Business Process Management. In: Demey, Y.T., Panetto, H. (eds.) OTM 2013 Workshops. LNCS, vol. 8186, pp. 353–362. Springer, Heidelberg (2013)

Persistent Storage and Query of E-government Ontologies in Relational Databases

Jean Vincent Fonou-Dombeu[1], Nicholas Mwenya Phiri[1], and Madga Huisman[2]

[1] Vaal University of Technology, Department of Software Studies
Private Bag X021, Andries Potgieter Blvd, Vanderbijlpark
1900, South Africa
{fonoudombeu,mwenyaphiri13}@gmail.com
[2] North-West University, School of Computer,
Statistical and Mathematical Sciences
Private Bag X6001, Potchefstroom
2520, South Africa
Magda.Huisman@nwu.ac.za

Abstract. Over the past eight years, building ontologies for semantic-driven e-government applications has been a subject of interest to e-government researchers. However, only a few has focused on the persistent storage and query of ontologies of the e-government domain. In this paper, 3 selected e-government ontologies are persistently stored and queried in relational databases. The OWL and RDF codes of these ontologies generated with Protégé or downloaded from the Internet are parsed with Jena API (Application Programming Interface) and loaded into MySQL RDBMS (Relational Database Management System). Thereafter, SPARQL queries are written to extract information from the created ontology databases. Experiments show that (1) the Jena parser scales well and could successfully parse and store e-government ontologies of different sizes into relational databases, and (2) the response times of SPARQL queries written in Jena to MySQL ontology databases are proportional to the sizes of the ontologies.

Keywords: E-government, Semantic Web, Ontology Storage, Ontology Query, Protégé, Jena API, MySQL, SPARQL.

1   Introduction

The Semantic Web is an evolution of the current World Wide Web in which data and resources are represented on the basis of their meaning rather than web links as is done in the current Internet. This provides the web with content that is understood by both humans and computers. In particular, the content of the Semantic Web is represented with ontology in such a way that computers can automatically reason it to extract useful information for users. Therefore, ontology is the backbone of any Semantic Web application. Ontology is defined as an explicit specification of a conceptualization [1]. A conceptualization defines an

A. Kő and E. Francesconi (Eds.): EGOVIS 2014, LNCS 8650, pp. 118–132, 2014.
© Springer International Publishing Switzerland 2014

abstract and simple view of a domain of interest that is being represented purposively. Examples of domains are medicine, biology, e-commerce, e-government, etc. Ontology represents the semantic content of a domain using its constituents including the concepts, objects, entities and relationships between them [1].

Over the past eight years, building ontologies for semantic-driven e-government applications has been a subject of interest to e-government developers and researchers. In [2] the Federal Enterprise Architecture (FEA) Reference Model Ontologies (FEARMO) and the FEA capacities advisor ontologies are presented. The FEARMO is set of 5 ontologies derived from the FEA e-government reference model of the United States (US) government, whereas, the FEA capacities advisor ontologies is a set of 6 ontologies developed to provide US government agencies with advises on the available capacities that could support e-government initiatives.

The semantic components of the Italian e-government architecture, the Estonian semantic interoperability architecture and the Palestinian interoperability framework are presented in [3], [4] and [5], respectively. The Italian e-government architecture [3] includes an ontologies repository, which is composed of a set of ontologies and schemas that describe the services and information semantics. The ontology component of the Estonian semantic interoperability architecture [4] is a set of domain ontologies that describe objects including web service operations, business processes and data structure. The Palestine interoperability framework [5] includes a government ontology formed of a set of 15 domain ontologies which describe data concepts, services and processes of the Palestine government.

Various different aspects of e-government have been modelled in academic research studies using ontologies [6], [7], [8], [9], [10], [11]. In [12], a life-event ontology is used to model the e-services integration processes. A framework for services integration based on specific ontologies is proposed in [7], whereas, the mapping of various ontologies to a predefined e-government system reference model is established in [8]. The issue of services interoperability is also addressed in [9], [10], [11], with e-government specific ontology models.

Several European based e-government projects have used ontologies to describe and specify the public administration domain as well as the e-government services delivery processes. The OneStopGov project uses life-event ontology to model public services [13] while the issue of composition, reconfiguration and evaluation of e-services is addressed in the OntoGov project [14] with various kinds of ontologies. The real-estate transactions are described with a set of ontologies in the Reimdoc project [15]. Another set of ontologies is used in the SAKE project [16] to model the public administration workflow and business processes, and to describe the structure of information or metadata as well as the concepts related to the performance evaluation of the public administration's processes. The Government Enterprise Architecture (GEA) ontology [17], [18], created from the GEA object model [19], is developed in the SemanticGov project to model the public administration semantic as well as the overall e-government domain. The SmartGov project [20] presents the e-government services ontology that models the business process and social aspects of e-government services delivery. Another interesting work is done in the Estrella project [21] where the Legal Knowledge Interchange Format (LKIF) core ontology is built to describe basic legal concepts; aiming at supporting the translation, alignment and harmonization between national jurisdictions of European countries. The Access-eGov [22] project uses a set of ontologies to model the e-services integration process. Semantic interoperability solutions for local governments are proposed in the TerreGov [23] project with a set of ontologies.

In light of the above, ontologies have been used intensively in the e-government domain. However, the important Semantic Web research topic of database to ontology mapping which is divided into two sub-branches, namely, ontology storage in and construction from Relational Databases [24], [25], [26] has not yet been addressed in e-government research. This study aims at filling this gap in the current semantic-based e-government literature. In fact, one of the functions of Semantic Web applications is to reason the ontologies in order to extract domain knowledge that is semantically rich and that is of interest to users. This demands that ontologies be stored with appropriate techniques. Further, it is argued that an efficient storage of ontology in a Semantic Web application provides greater benefits [26]. Therefore, storing ontology in Relational Database has been a subject of interest to the Semantic Web community since its inception as a research discipline [24]. In this paper, 3 selected e-government ontologies are persistently stored and queried in relational databases. The OWL (Web Ontology Language) and RDF (Resource Description Framework) codes of these ontologies generated with Protégé or downloaded from the Internet are parsed with Jena API and stored into MySQL RDBMS. Thereafter, SPARQL queries are written to extract information from the created ontology databases. Experiments show that (1) the Jena parser scales well and could successfully parse and store e-government ontologies of different sizes into relational databases and (2) the response times of SPARQL queries written in Jena to MySQL ontology databases are proportional to the sizes of the ontologies.

The rest of the paper is organized as follows. The Semantic Web technologies and platforms for storing and querying ontologies are presented in Section 2. Section 3 describes the experiments and results of the application of ontology storage and query techniques on e-government ontologies. Related studies are discussed in Section 4 and the last section concludes the paper.

2   Semantic Web Technologies for Persistent Storage and Query of Ontologies

This section discusses existing ontology repositories, the languages and platforms for representing, storing and querying ontologies.

2.1   Ontologies Repositories

Ontology storage and reasoning are important topics of research in Semantic Web [25]. As a result, there is a number of ontology repositories developed for

Semantic Web applications. Figure 1 presents a diagrammatic representation of existing ontology repositories according to their storage models. They are classified into two major categories, namely, native stores and database based stores (Figure 1). Native stores are built on the file system, whereas, database based repositories use relational databases as the back-end store [25]. It has

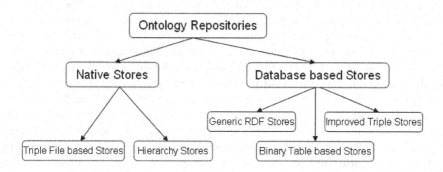

Fig. 1. A taxonomy to classify ontology repositories [25]

been demonstrated that the database repositories are the most efficient, due to the maturity of the Relational Database technology [24], [25], [26]. In fact, Relational Database research has been in existence for more than 30 years and current Relational Database Management Systems (RDBMS) provide sophisticated functionalities such as query optimization, transaction processing, access control, logging and recovery [25], [26]. Therefore, this study implements the Generic RDF store with Jena API and Improved triple store with MySQL.

A generic RDF store uses a relational table of three columns (Subject, Property, Object) to store the statements of an RDF graph of an ontology. In addition to the relational table used to represent RDF statements, generic RDF stores use symbol tables to encode URIs and literals with internal unique IDs. Contrary to generic RDF stores, improved triple stores use different tables to manage RDF statements [25]. More information on the Triple File based, hierarchy and Binary Table based stores can be found in [25]. The next subsection discusses the platforms and languages for editing and representing ontologies.

2.2   Semantic Web Ontology Languages and Platforms

The Semantic Web domain provides various languages for the formal representation and description of e-government service workflow processes, Web services operations and documents processing using ontologies; they include Extensible Markup Language (XML), RDF, RDF schema (RDFS), DARPA Agent Markup Language (DAML), and OWL [27]. Several software platforms are also used for ontology edition including WebODE, OntoEdit, KAON1, Protégé, and so forth [28]. In addition to the software platforms used for the edition of ontologies, APIs (Application Programming Interface) such as OWL API [29], Jena API

[30], Sesame [31], Minerva [39], etc., also exist and which provide facilities for the database storage and query of ontologies. The platforms for storing ontologies and the query languages are presented in the next subsection.

2.3   Ontologies Storage Platforms and Query Languages

Developing e-government systems using Semantic Web technologies consists of modelling and specifying the public administration system, the services (tax return, social grants, etc.) that it delivers to the public (citizens, businesses, etc.) and the services delivery processes, using ontologies. These ontologies must be further written formally with Semantic Web ontologies languages such as XML, RDF, DAML, and OWL [28]. The resulting formal ontologies should then be stored in a traditional relational database management system (RDBMS) such as Oracle, MySQL, PostgreSQL, etc. [30] and access through semantic web services [8], [11] in the daily running of e-governments applications to provide answers to citizens' requests. The Semantic Web domain has developed a set of languages for the technical implementation of these semantic-based queries. These languages include: RDQL, Semantic Web Rule Language (SWRL) [32], XSLT, SPARQL, etc. [33]. The next section describes the experiments and results of the study.

3   Experiments

3.1   Data Set

Three ontologies, namely, OntoDPM (Ontology of Development Projects Monitoring)[34], CGOV (central government ontology)[35] and FEARMO (Federal Entreprise Architecture Reference Model Ontologies) [2] were used in this study. This ontologies were chosen after a thorough search of e-government ontologies on the Internet using ontology search engines such as Swoogle and Watson as well as searches in linked data repositories including LOV(Linked Open Vocabularies) and LOD (Linked Open Data). Unfortunately, the search produced only a few e-government ontologies codes amongst which the CGOV and FEARMO were the largest is terms of classes, properties and instances. The OntoDPM was built by the authors [34] and has more classes, properties and instances than other e-government ontologies discovered.

The OntoDPM ontology was developed as a knowledge base model for a web-based application for e-government monitoring of development projects in developing countries. In fact, in developing countries, almost every government department is somehow involved in the implementation of a programme aiming at improving the welfare of its people. These programmes are commonly called development projects and include infrastructure development, water supply and sanitation, education, rural development, health care, ICT infrastructure development and so forth. Thus, an application that could interface all the activities related to development projects implementation in a developing country could bring tremendous advantages; particularly, such a web-based e-government application would improve the monitoring and evaluation of projects and provide transparency, efficiency and better delivery to populations. The OntoDPM was built to support the Semantic Web development of such a web-based e-government application [34]. The OntoDPM is constituted of 30 classes, 19 properties and 18 Instances. It describes the key concepts of the domain of development projects monitoring in developing countries (people, stakeholder, financier, monitoring indicator, reporting technique, etc.), the activities carried out in the domain (training, discussion, fieldwork, visit, meeting, etc.) and the relationships between the constituents of the domain.

Table 1. Part of description logic representation of the OntoDPM ontology

$DevelopmentProject \sqsubseteq Programme \; \Pi \; \forall \; focuses \; Community$
$DevelopmentProject \sqsubseteq \exists \; involves \geq 1 \; (Person \sqcup$
$Financier \sqcup Stakeholder \sqcup Community)$
$DevelopmentProject \sqsubseteq \exists \; implements \geq 1 \; DeliveryActivity$
$DevelopmentProject \sqsubseteq monitors \geq 1 \; (MonitoringIndicator \sqcup$
$Reporting \sqcup Accounting)$
$ProjectStaff \sqsubseteq isA.Person \; \Pi \; \exists \; affiliates = 1 \; (Municipality \sqcup$
$Department \sqcup Agency)$
$CommunityWorker \sqsubseteq isA.Person \; \Pi \; \exists \; affiliates \; Municipality$
$CommunityWorker \sqsubseteq isA.Person \; \Pi \; \exists \; resides \; Community$
$TraditionalLeader \sqsubseteq isA.Person \; \Pi \; \exists \; resides \; Community$
$PrivateCompany \; \Pi \; \exists \; delivers \geq 1 \; DeliveryActivity$
$CommunityBasedOrganization \sqsubseteq owns \; Community$
$Donor \sqsubseteq Financier \; \Pi \; \forall \; hasContribution \; ContributionLevel$
$Government \sqsubseteq \exists \; hasDivision.(Municipality \sqcup Department \sqcup Agency)$

Table 1 shows a part of the Description Logic (DL) representation of the On-toDPM ontology. The full DL version of the OntoDPM is provided in [34]. In this study, the formal representation of the OntoDPM ontology in OWL is created with Protégé, parsed into an RDF graph and stored into MySQL RDBMS.

The central government ontology (CGOV) is the ontology of the UK central government. Its RDF code is downloadable from the UK government open data repository [35]. It is formed of 46 classes and 46 properties. A view of the classes and properties of the CGOV generated with the tool for ontology documentation named Parrot [36] is shown in Figure 2. It classes mainly describe the structure of the central government of the UK in terms of physical and organizational components such as Cabinet, Civil Service Committee, Government Department, etc. (Figure 2). In this study, the RDF code of the CGOV ontology is directly parsed with Jena API and stored into the MySQL RDBMS.

The FEARMO [2] ontology is a set of 5 modules namely Performance, Business, Services, Technology and Data reference models ontologies; these ontologies were developed to enable the interoperability of the US governments federal agencies; they basically provide common reference models for modeling federal agencies business processes, thereby, supporting their interoperability. The FEARMO ontology is constituted of 314 classes, 141 properties and 783

Central Government Ontology

ⓒ Classes (46)

Advisory NDPB, Assistant Parliamentary Counsel, Cabinet, Cabinet Committee, Civil Service, Civil Service Committee, Civil Service Post, Committee, Corporation Sole, Deputy Director, Deputy Parliamentary Counsel, Devolved Government, Devolved Government, Director, Director General, Executive agency, Executive NDPB, Government, Government, Government Department, Great Officer of State, Honorific Post, Machinery of Government Change, Minister, Minister of State, Ministerial Committee, Ministerial department, Monitoring NDPBs, Non-departmental public body, Non-Disclosure, Non-ministerial department, Parliamentary Counsel, Parliamentary Counsel, Parliamentary Under-Secretary, Permanent Secretary, Post, Principal Secretary of State, Salary Range, Secretariat, Senior Assistant Parliamentary Counsel, Senior Civil Service Post, Sinecure, Tenure, Tribunal NDPB, UK Public body, Working Time

Ⓟ Properties (46)

Attends Cabinet, Cabinet, Cabinet Attendee, Cabinet Committee, Cabinet Committee Of, Cabinet Of, Chair, Chairs, Currency, Deputy Chair, Deputy Chair Of, Deputy Head of Government, Deputy Head of Government, Devolved From, Devolves To, For Every, Formed At, Full-Time Equivalent, Full-time Equivalent Salary, Government Organisation Of, Head of Government, Head of Government, Lower Bound, Member of Cabinet, Member of Cabinet, Organisation, parent department, Post, Post, Post, Postholder, Postholder, related body, Salary, Salary Excluding Benefits, Salary Including Benefits, Salary Range, Served By, Serves, Supported By, Supports, Tenure, Terms of Reference, Time Period, Upper Bound, Working Time

Fig. 2. A view of the central government ontology generated with Parrot

instances. The next subsection describes the the implementation, storage and query of the e-government ontologies presented above.

3.2   Experimental Results

The experiments were carried out on a computer with the following characteristics: Windows 8.1 Pro 64-bit operating system, Intel (R) CPU 2160, 1.80 GHz, 4 GB RAM and 160 GB Western Digital SATA HDD hard drive. Figure 3 shows the screenshot of the Protégé implementation of the OntoDPM ontology based on its Description Logic representation (see part in Table 1). The OntoDPM ontology is saved from Protégé as an OWL file. The OWL syntax provides facilities for representing ontology elements such as inheritance, instance, slots, domain and range of a slot, etc. For instance in the OntoDPM ontology, community worker, community leader, traditional leader, and project staff are subclasses of the person class (Table 1). This inheritance relationship is represented in OWL syntax with the following OWL code generated with Protégé.

```
<owl:Class rdf:about="#ProjectStaff">
    <rdfs:subClassOf rdf:resource="#Person"/>
</owl:Class>
<owl:Class rdf:about="#CommunityLeader">
    <rdfs:subClassOf rdf:resource="#Person"/>
</owl:Class>
<owl:Class rdf:about="#CommunityWorker">
    <rdfs:subClassOf rdf:resource="#Person"/>
</owl:Class>
<owl:Class rdf:about="#TraditionalLeader">
    <rdfs:subClassOf rdf:resource="#Person"/>
</owl:Class>
```

Fig. 3. Screenshot of the protégé implementation of the OntoDPM ontology

Similarly, in the OntoDPM ontology, department, agency and municipality are divisions of government (Table1). The relationship between government and its divisions can be represented in Protégé with the property hasDivision. Then, the domain of the hasDivision property will be the government class and its ranges, the department, agency, and municipality classes. The hasDivision property and its domain and ranges are represented in OWL with the following code generated with Protégé.

```
<owl:ObjectProperty rdf:about="#hasDivision">
    <rdfs:domain rdf:resource="#Government"/>
    <rdfs:range rdf:resource="#Agency"/>
    <rdfs:range rdf:resource="#Department"/>
    <rdfs:range rdf:resource="#Municipality"/>
</owl:ObjectProperty>
```

The OWL file of the OntoDPM ontology along with the RDF and OWL files of the CGOV and FEARMO ontologies, respectively are further parsed into RDF graphs and stored persistently in the MySQL RDBMS using Jena API [37]. Jena uses an interface called OntModel to parse ontology file (RDF and OWL files in this study) to a RDF graph. To store statements of the RDF graph in a RDBMS such as MySQL, Jena implements an interface called Store which formats and configures the database for RDF storage [37]. A sample Jena code for parsing the OWL file of the FEARMO ontology into an RDF graph is given below.

```
1. String inputFileName = "C:\\EgovOntologies\\FEARMO.owl";
2. OntModel parser =
3. ModelFactory.createOntologyModel(OntModelSpec.RDFS_MEM_RDFS_INF);
4. InputStream input = FileManager.get().open(inputFileName);
5. if (input == null) {
6.    throw new
7.    IllegalArgumentException("File: "+inputFileName+" not found");
8. }
9. parser.read(input, null);
```

The first line of the above code defines the input file to be parsed into an RDF graph; in this case, the FEARMO.owl file. The parser is formatted in lines 2 and 3 as an OntModel interface object. The input file is connected to the InputStream and parsed into an RDF graph with the read() method of the OntModel interface in lines 4 an 9, respectively. Thereafter, The RDF graph obtained is loaded into MySQL RDBMS with the following Jena code.

```
1. StoreDesc storeDesc =
2.    new StoreDesc(LayoutType.LayoutTripleNodesHash,
3.    DatabaseType.MySQL);
4. SDBConnection connection =
5.    new SDBConnection(DB_URL, DB_USER, DB_PASSWD);
6. Store store = SDBFactory.connectStore(connection,storeDesc);
7. Model dbLoader = SDBFactory.connectDefaultModel(store);
8. dbLoader.add(parser);
```

The database type to be connected to, i.e., MySQL is set in lines 1, 2 and 3 of the above code. The connection is established in lines 4 and 5 using predefined parameters including the URL of the database, the user name and password for connection to the database. The lines 6 and 7 format the database for the storage of the RDF graph hold in the parser. The RDF graph is loaded into the database in line 8.

Figure 4 depicts a screenshot of MySQL workbench with a view of the FEARMO ontology database as well as the databases for the CGOV and OntoDPM ontologies. In fact, the top left side of Figure 4 shows all ontology databases created in MySQL from the Jena application including centralgovernmentdb, developmentprojectdb and fearmodb, for the CGOV, OntoDPM and FEARMO ontologies, respectively. The Jena application creates four tables for the persistent storage of an ontology in MySQL RDBMS, namely, nodes, prefixes, quads, and triples as shown on the left side of Figure 4 for the FEARMO ontology database. The right part of Figure 4 displays the records of the nodes table of the FEARMO ontology database. Similar results were obtained with

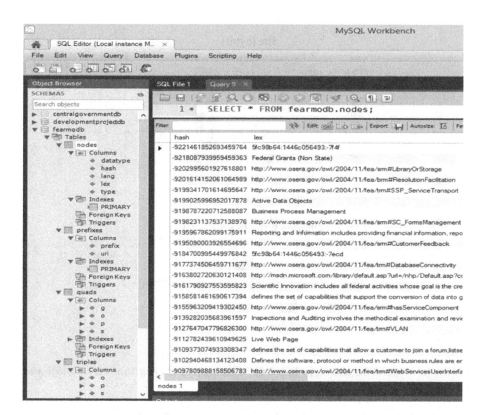

Fig. 4. Screenshot of e-government ontology databases stored in MySQL RDBMS

the OntoDPM and CGOV ontologies. The charts in Figure 5 show the size of the ontologies as well as the times needed to parse and load them into MySQL RDBMS . The differences in sizes of the ontologies (Figure 5, (a)) compared to the parsing and loading times (Figure 5, (b)) demonstrate that the Jena parser is scalable and could successfully parse and store e-government ontologies of different sizes into relational databases. As expected, Figure 5 shows that bigger ontologies take more time to be parsed and loaded into a relational database.

Finally, SPARQL queries are written in Jena to query the ontology databases created in MySQL RDBMS. Overall, 15 SPARQL queries were run on the three ontology databases, i.e., 5 queries per database. The response time of each query was recorded and the average response time per database calculated.

An example of SPARQL query run on the developmentprojectdb database is provided below.

```
PREFIX foal: <http://OntoDPM/>
SELECT ?CommunityWorker
WHERE {foal:CommunityWorker ?p ?o}
```

The query retrieves from the OntoDPM ontology database, namely, developmentprojectdb, all the properties and objects of the CommunityWorker class.

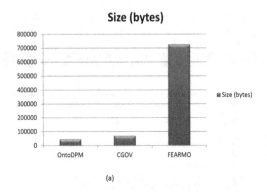

(a)

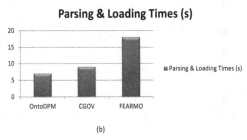

(b)

Fig. 5. (a) Sizes of ontologies in bytes; (b) Parsing and loading times of ontologies in seconds

Figure 6 depicts the chart of query response times for all the three ontology databases. It can be noticed that the smallest average response times of queries was recorded on the OntoDPM ontology (6.2 seconds), followed by the CGOV ontology (6.6 seconds). The highest average response time was recorded with the FEARMO ontology (18 seconds). In light of the above, one can conclude that the response time of a SPARQL query written in Jena to a MySQL ontology database is proportional to the size of the ontology (Figure 5). The next section discusses related studies.

4   Related Work

There is a growing interest among Semantic Web researchers on the topic of Ontology storage and query in relational databases. A method for direct storage and query of OWL ontology in relational database is presented in [38]. The method consists of mapping the OWL syntax to a certain number of relational database tables including class, property, property characteristics, property restrictions and instance for the persistent storage of ontology.

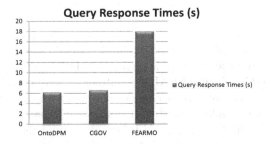

Fig. 6. Average response times of SPARQL queries on ontology databases

In [39], another tool for storing, inferencing and querying ontology in relational database, namely, Minerva is presented. Minerva is composed of four modules including the Import, Inference, Storage and Query modules. Similar to Jena API, the Import module of Minerva consists of an OWL parser and a translator. The parser parses OWL documents into an in-memory model and the translator load this model into the back-end RDBMS such as MySQL, Oracle, IMB DB2 and Derby. Another similarity with Jena is that the query language supported by Minerva is SPARQL.

A small ontology of 7 classes and 2 properties, namely, Computer Graphic (CG) ontology is stored in MySQL RDBMS via Jena in [40]. Further, an inference engine is developed in a client/server mode with Jena and JSP to enable remote execution of queries on the MySQL ontology database.

Different approaches for mapping OWL syntax to a relational database are proposed in [41] and [42]. In [41], the OWL ontology constructs are mapped into relational data tables. An original OWL file is firstly parsed into a DOM (Document Object Model) XML document. The resulting model is imported with Jena, loaded into the IBM DB2 RDBMS and queried. A method for mapping OWL 2 ontology to relational database, namely, OWL2ToRDB is proposed in [42]. OWL2ToRDB technique uses a so-called hybrid approach to directly map each ontology concept to a relational database schema based on its semantic description. Additionally, metadata tables are used to store ontology constructs that do not have a direct equivalent in database schema.

A method for efficient storage and query of RDF data in triple stores is presented in [43]. The method consists of mapping an RDF graph into a triple table. The triple table is further partitioned in a way that minimizes the cost of self-joins operations on the triple table for query optimization.

Other interesting literatures on ontology storage and query in relational database are provided in [24] and [25]. The problem of database to ontology mapping is introduced in [24] with clear motivation, benefits and challenges of each of its subproblems, namely, ontology storage into databases and ontology construction from databases. In [25], existing ontology repositories are discussed and compared.

5   Conclusion

In this study, 3 e-government ontologies, namely, OntoDPM, CGOV and FEARMO were parsed and stored in MySQL RDBMS via Jena API. Protégé was used to generated the OWL code of the OntoDPM, whereas, the RDF and OWL codes of the CGOV and FEARMO ontologies were downloaded from the Internet. Thereafter, the Jena parser was used to parse the ontologies codes into RDF graphs that were loaded into MySQL ontology databases. Finally, SPARQL queries were written in Jena to extract information from the created ontologies databases. A measurement of the execution time of the Jena application, showed that the Jena parser is scalable and could successfully parse e-government ontologies of different sizes and that large ontologies take more time to be parsed and loaded into the databases. Further, experiments showed that the response times of a SPARQL queries on MySQL ontology databases are proportional to the sizes of the ontologies.

The future direction of the research would be to repeat the experiments with other Semantic Web toolkits for storing and querying ontologies in relational databases such as Minerva [39], Sesame [31], etc. and draw a performance comparison of these tools. Furthermore, it would be interesting to look into integrating and mapping multiple e-government ontologies into a single database as well as the deployment of these ontologies within a full Semantic Web application through semantic web services.

References

1. Gruber, T.R.: Toward Principles for the Design of Ontologies used for Knowledge Sharing. International Journal of Human-Computer Studies 43, 907–928 (1993)
2. Allemang, D., Hodgson, R., Polikoff, I.: Federal Reference Model Ontologies (FEARMO). White Paper (2005)
3. Baldoni, R., Fuligni, S., Mecella, M., Tortorelli, F.: The Italian e-Government Service Oriented Architecture - Strategic Vision and Technical Solutions. In: 6th EGOV Conference, Regensburg, Germany, pp. 79–88 (2007)
4. Luts, M.: Estonian Semantic Interoperability Initiative. SEMIC.EU publications (2004)
5. Jarrar, M., Deik, A., Farraj, B.: Ontology-Based Data Process Governance Framework–The Case of e-Government Interoperability in Palestine. In: IFIP International Symposium on Data-Driven Process Discovery and Analysis (SIMPDA 2011), pp. 83–98 (2001)
6. Salhofer, P., Stadlhofer, B., Tretter, G.: Ontology Driven E-government. El. J. of E-government 7, 415–424 (2009)
7. Chen, D., Nie, G., Liu, P.: Research Knowledge Sharing of E-government Based on Automatic Ontology Mapping. In: 6th Wuhan International Conference on E-Business, Business, China, pp. 105–111 (2008)
8. Gugliotta, A., Cabral, L., Domingue, J., Roberto, V.: A Conceptual Model for Semantically-Based E-government Portal. In: International Conference on e-Government 2005 (ICEG 2005), Ottawa, Canada (2005)

9. Xiao, Y., Xiao, M., Zhao, H.: An Ontology for E-government Knowledge Modelling and Interoperability. In: IEEE International Conference on Wireless Communications, Networking and Mobile Computing (WiCOM 2007), Shanghai, pp. 3600–3603 (2007)

10. Sabucedo, L.M.A., Rifon, L.E.A.: Semantic Service Oriented Architectures for E-government Platforms. American Association for Artificial Intelligence (2006)

11. Sabucedo, L.M.A., Rifon, L.E.A., Corradini, F., Polzonetti, A., Re, B.: Knowledge-Based Platform for E-government Agents: A Web-based Solution Using Semantic Technologies. J. of Expert Systems with Applications 5, 3647–3656 (2010)

12. Sanati, F., Lu, J.: Multilevel Life-event Abstraction Framework for E-government Service Integration. In: 9th European Conference on E-government 2009 (ECEG 2009), London, UK, pp. 550–558 (2009)

13. Torodovski, L., Kunstelj, M., Cukjati, D., Vintar, M., Trochidis, I., Tambouris, E.: OneStopGove: D13 – Life-event Reference Models, Deliverable No. 13 (2007)

14. Apostolou, D., Stojanovic, L., Lobo, T.P., Miro, J.C., Papadakis, A.: Configuring E-government Services Using Ontologies. In: Funabashi, M., Grzech, A. (eds.) Challenges of Expanding Internet: E-Commerce, E-Business, and E-Government. IFIP, vol. 189, pp. 141–155. Springer, Boston (2005)

15. Ortiz-Rodriguez, F., Villazon-Terrazas, B.: EGO Ontology Model: Law and Regulation Approach for E-government. In: Workshop on Semantic Web for E-government 2006, Workshop at the 3rd European Semantic Web Conference, Budva, Serbia, Montenegro, pp. 13–23 (2006)

16. Butka, P., Gabor, A., Ko, A., Mach, M., Ntioudis, S., Papadakis, A., Stojanovic, N., Vas, R., Zelinsky, T.: Semantic-enable, Agile, Knowledge-based e-Government (SAKE). Deliverable No. 3 (2006)

17. Goudos, S.K., Peristeras, V., Tarabanis, K.: Mapping Citizen Profiles to Public Administration Services Using Ontology Implementations of the Governance Enterprise Architecture (GEA) models. In: 3rd Annual European Semantic Web Conference, Budva, Montenegro, pp. 25–37 (2006)

18. Goudos, S.K., Peristeras, V., Lutas, N., Tarabanis, K.: A Public Administration Domain Ontology for Semantic Discovery of e-Government Services. In: 2nd IEEE Conference on Digital Information Management 2007 (ICDIM 2007), Lyon, France, pp. 260–265 (2007)

19. Peristeras, V., Tarabanis, K.: Reengineering Public Administration through Semantic Technologies and the GEA Domain Ontology. In: AAAI Spring Symposium, Semantic Web meets eGovernment (SWEG). Stanford University, California (2006)

20. Fraser, J., Adams, N., Mckay-Hubbard, A., Macintosh, A., Canadas, R.: A Framework for e-Government Services. Deliverable No. 71 (2003)

21. Breuker, J., Hoekstra, R., Boer, A., van der Berg, K., Sartor, G., Rubino, R., Wyner, A., Bench-Capon, T., Palmirani, M.: OWL Ontology of Basis Legal Concepts (LKIF-Core). Deliverable 1.4 (2006)

22. Hreno, J., Bednar, P., Furdík, K., Sabol, T.: Integration of Government Services using Semantic Technologies. Journal of Theoretical and Applied Electronic Commerce Research 6, 143–154 (2011)

23. Barthes, J.P., Moulin, C.: Impact of e-Government on Territorial Government Services. Deliverable No. 1.4 (2005)

24. Spanos, D.E., Stavrou, P., Mirou, N.: Bringing Relational Databases into the Semantic Web: A Survey. Semantic Web Journal 3, 169–209 (2012)

25. Heymans, S., Ma, L., Anicic, D., Ma, Z., Steinmetz, N., Pan, Y., Mei, J., Fokoue, A., Kalyanpur, A., Kershenbaum, A., Schonberg, E., Srinivas, K., Feier, C., Hench, G., Westzstein, B., Keller, U.: Ontology Reasoning with Large Data Repositories. In: Ontology Management, pp. 89–128. Springer US (2008)
26. Keet, M.: Using and Improving Bio-ontologies Stored in Relational Databases. Extended Abstract of the Talk Held at SBIOLBD, EPFL, Lausanne, Switzerland (2006)
27. Laclavik, M.: Ontology and Agent Based Approach for Knowledge Management. PhD Thesis, Institute of Informatics, Slovak Academy of Sciences (2005)
28. Calero, C., Ruiz, F., Piattini, M. (eds.): Ontologies for Software Engineering and Software Technology. Springer, Heidelberg (2006)
29. Knublauch, H., Fergerson, R.W., Noy, N.F., Musen, M.A.: The Protégé OWL Plugin: An Open Development Environment for Semantic Web Applications. In: McIlraith, S.A., Plexousakis, D., van Harmelen, F. (eds.) ISWC 2004. LNCS, vol. 3298, pp. 229–243. Springer, Heidelberg (2004)
30. Wilkinson, K., Sayers, C., Kuno, H., Reynolds, D.: Efficient RDF Storage and Retrieval in Jena2. In: 1st International Workshop on Semantic Web and Databases (SWDB), Berlin, Germany, pp. 131–150 (2003)
31. Watson, M.: Practical Artificial Intelligence Programming with Java, 3rd edn., pp. 57–72 (2008)
32. Zhang, W., Wang, Y.: Towards Building a Semantic Grid for e-Government Applications. WSEAS Transactions on Computer Research 3, 273–282 (2008)
33. Bailey, J., Bry, F., Furche, T., Schaffert, S.: Semantic Web Query Languages. In: Encyclopedia of Database Systems, pp. 2583–2586 (2009)
34. Fonou-Dombeu, J.V., Huisman, M.: Semantic-Driven E-government: Application of Uschold and King Ontology Building Methodology for Semantic Ontology Models Development. International Journal of Web and Semantic Technology (IJWesT) 4, 1–20 (2011)
35. CGOV: Central Government Ontology. An Ontology of the UK Central Government, http://reference.data.gov.uk/def/central-government
36. Silvio, P., Shotton, D., Vitali, F.: Tool for the Automatic Generation of Ontology Documentation: A Task-Based Evaluation. International Journal on Semantic Web and Information Systems (IJSWIS) 9, 21–44 (2013)
37. Rajagopal, H.: JENA: A Java API for ontology management. IMB Corporation, Colorado Software Summit (2005)
38. Wang, S., Zhang, X.: A Highly Efficient Ontology Storage and Query Method Based on Relational Database. In: IEEE International Conference on Electrical and Control Engineering, Yichang, China, pp. 4253–4256 (2011)
39. Zhou, J., Ma, L., Liu, Q., Zhang, L., Yu, Y., Pan, Y.: Minerva: A Scalable OWL Ontology Storage and Inference System. In: Mizoguchi, R., Shi, Z.-Z., Giunchiglia, F. (eds.) ASWC 2006. LNCS, vol. 4185, pp. 429–443. Springer, Heidelberg (2006)
40. Zhong, L., Zheng, M., Yuan, J., Jin, J.: The Jen-Based Ontology Model Inference and Retrieval Application. Intelligent Information Management 4, 157–160 (2012)
41. Gali, A., Chen, C.X., Claypool, K.T., Uceda-Sosa, R.: From Ontology to Relational Databases. In: Wang, S., et al. (eds.) ER Workshops 2004. LNCS, vol. 3289, pp. 278–289. Springer, Heidelberg (2004)
42. Vysniauskas, E., Nemuraite, L., Paradauskas, B.: Preserving Semantics of OWL 2 Ontologies in Relational Databases Using Hybrid Approach. Information Technology and Control 41, 103–115 (2012)
43. Yan, Y., Wang, C., Zhou, A., Qian, W., Ma, L., Pan, Y.: Efficient Querying RDF Data in Triple Stores. In: World Wide Web Conference, Beijing, China, pp. 1053–1054 (2008)

Application of Process Ontology
to Improve the Funding Allocation Process
at the European Institute of Innovation and Technology

Matteo Arru

European Institute of Innovation and Technology
1117 Budapest, Neumann Janos utca 1/E, Hungary
Department of Information Systems, Corvinus University of Budapest
1093 Budapest, Fővám tér 13-15., Hungary
matteo.arru@eit.europa.eu

Abstract. This studio explains the application through the application of the ProKEx architecture is used to improve the process of allocation of funding at the European Institute of Innovation and Technology (EIT). The mission of the EIT is to grow and capitalize on the innovation capacity and capability of actors from higher education, research, business and entrepreneurship from the EU and beyond through the creation of highly integrated Knowledge and Innovation Communities (KICs). This case offers the scenario of a complex application where a fragmented process with several actors is dealing with the different domains of knowledge of each KIC. Starting from the Business Process Model, applying text-mining techniques we extract the ontology elements from the activity description and converted into an Ontology of the process domain. By the critical analysis of the information contained in the model, we gain the relevant information to improve the current approach.

Keywords: semantic business process management, ontology matching, European Institute of Innovation and Technology, European funding.

1   Introduction

Organization Resilience in the Private and in the Public Sector

Organizations are subject, in the modern era, to continuous changes in their structure due to a reference environment very competitive. This is due to stress from the external market but also because is necessary to implement human resources policy that motivate and retain those resources that are important asset for the organization.

Public Administrations are not exception to this phenomenon as the public service, as we know it today have different characteristics from the public administration model that prevailed at the beginning of the twentieth century including:

- Respect for the rule of law.
- A commitment to serving the public good.
- An expectation that public servants will exhibit integrity, probity and impartiality in serving the public trust.

A. Kő and E. Francesconi (Eds.): EGOVIS 2014, LNCS 8650, pp. 133–147, 2014.
© Springer International Publishing Switzerland 2014

The model was clear and simple - characteristics that continue to hold great intellectual appeal. Reality, however, is rarely as simple as theory. The classic model falls short of being able to address an increasing number of issues that reflect today's reality and other important element have to be considered:

- The need for flexibility.
- The interactions between politics and policies.
- New forms of accountability. (Bourgon, 2007)

Furthermore the more the business in which operate is knowledge intense, the more the need of leverage on human capital is important and the management of it is strategically critical for its success and subsistence.

One of the main threats is, in this context, the staff movement. The conduction of the changes is not exhaustive - only some parts are affected. The main challenge is the exhaustive knowledge articulation in order to provide the organization with up-to-date knowledge.

Business Process Modelling
The adoption of Procedures and Business Process Modelling are common practice in every organization that wants to increase its resilience, however is not clear to what extent such model is able to describe the knowledge necessary to operate the process in an efficient way.

Trough ProKEx[1] we propose a solution to overcame the dualism procedural approach versus Domain approach by providing tools where iteratively the two approach mutually feed each other. It provides a solution to extract, organize and preserve knowledge embedded in organizational processes to enrich organizational knowledge base in a systematic and controlled way, support employees to easily acquire their job role specific knowledge.

Structure of the Article
In this article, we provide an overview of the ProKEx project and we illustrate the case study of the European Institute of Innovation and Technology.

We give a general overview of the project including overarching objectives, status of the arts of the technologies in this area, specific characteristics of the solution proposed and the constructions blocks.

In the case study, we will illustrate the application related to the process of "Allocation of funding" highlighting the motivation of studying this case in the context of Semantic Business Process Management.

---

[1] The research is part of the ProKEx - "Corporate Knowledge Management Supported by Semantic Process Ontology Technology") project (EUREKA_HU_12-1-2012-0039, supported by Research and Technology Innovation Fund, New Szécsényi Plan, Hungary), this article recalls the main deliverable of the project.

2   The ProKEx Project

2.1   General Objectives

According to the Lisbon Strategy the EU aims to become the most competitive and dynamic knowledge-based economy in the world. (European Commission, 2000) To achieve this goal the strategy outlines taking advantage of the growth and employment opportunities afforded by new technologies. Development and adoption of new technologies result in increased investment in knowledge, skills and infrastructure. Human capital is considered a crucial input for the development of new technologies and a necessary factor for their adoption and efficient use, but also a prerequisite for employability. (De la Fuente & Ciccone, 2002)

Complex organizations use to model and manage their processes using Business Process Management (BPM) tools. These applications help to describe the organizational processes, together with the required information and other resources (amongst other human resources) needed to perform each activity. Business processes are defined as sequence of activities. From the Human Resource Management view it is required to define unambiguously, who is responsible for the execution of each activity in terms of the RACI matrix (Responsible, Accountable, Consulted, Informed), bridging the organizational model and the process model. Usually BPM methodologies' requirements are satisfied with the definition of the type of job role, this is emphasized in the RACI matrix. The ProKEx approach explicitly differentiates between the task (as element of the process) and the job role (associated with, or assigned to the task). Job role is interpreted as a bridge between the task (to be executed) and the actor (in case of ProKEx always a human resource). Human resource always have at least to organizational attributes: position and job role, they may relate to each other several ways (1:1, 1:m, n:1, m:n). The knowledge (often cited as competences) relates to the job role, what is considered as content. The knowledge elicitation, extraction refers to the content, while the type of the job role has more organizational aspects than knowledge management. In order to include properly the job role knowledge into the process model, we use the extended RACI matrix, that is the description of task from knowledge perspective is added to the RACI, and this extension is processed later in the system. In brief, one of the overall objectives of BPM is the transformation of informal knowledge into formal knowledge and facilitates its externalization and sharing (Kalpic & Bernus, 2006).

The relevant and internalized knowledge is embedded and strongly related to the roles as building element of the organizational structure. In dynamic environment both the roles and required competencies are changing, therefore the knowledge elicitation[2], articulation cannot be independent from the permanently updated business process model; hence, the business process model is one of the most important ingredients of the knowledge to be captured.

---

[2] Knowledge elicitation is the process within Knowledge Capture where hidden or tacit knowledge is being articulated. Frequently but not exclusively selected experts are encouraged to articulate their knowledge.

The proposed solution is to extract the knowledge from information stored in the process model in order to articulate, externalize, represent and transfer (re-use) it. Since the business process models are often used for the execution of processes in a workflow engine, another very important source for gathering useful knowledge are real-time instantiations of the business processes, that are giving a view on the dynamic knowledge, usually represented in the form of different business rules. The expected impact is the preservation and efficient management of corporate intellectual capital, a better return on investment in human capital that will lead to the more efficient execution of processes and consequently higher profit. The expected impact is the preservation and efficient management of corporate intellectual capital, a better return on investment in human capital.

The goal of the proposed project is to develop a solution to extract, organize and preserve the knowledge embedded in organizational processes in order to:

— enrich organizational knowledge base in a systematic and controlled way,
— support employees to easily acquire their job role specific knowledge,
— help to govern and plan the human capital investment.

In order to achieve this goal a complex IT solution and method is developed which integrates:

• organizational process management tool,
• learning management tool,
• real-time data monitoring and processing tool,
• data and text mining tools for developing knowledge base (domain ontology) and
• the interfaces which are responsible for the communication between these components.

On-the-job training is put on the focus, since it increases productivity at the firm level and is a source of innovation and therefore long-term competitiveness of firms, too.

The novelty of this approach is based on the connection between process model and corporate knowledge base, where the process structure will be used for building up the knowledge structure. Common form of knowledge base is the ontology, which provides the conceptualization of a certain domain. (Gruber, 1993)

The main innovation lies in new algorithms for the extraction and integration of the static and dynamic process knowledge and a novel integration architecture that enables smoothly integration of the eLearning methods in the process execution models.

However, the capability of the ontology to describe the process knowledge domain is very much related to the way the model has been generated, therefore for this project we apply a Semantic Business Process Management approach.

The main challenge in Business Process Management (BPM) is the continuous translation between the business requirements view and the IT systems and resources. Semantic Business Process Management (SBPM) is a new approach of increasing the level of automation in the translation between these two levels, and is currently driven by major players from the BPM, and Semantic Web Services area. The core paradigm of Semantic Business Process Management is to represent the distinct levels using ontology languages and to employ automated translation. (Török & Ternai, 2011)

The approach of this study will provide a paradigm to evaluate the level of alignment between process requirements and domain requirements and providing input to the domain expert to revise critically the process and to enrich the Business Process Model.

2.2   Technology State of the Art

The various Business Process Management solutions offer different modelling approaches, but the basic logic behind the modelling methods remains the same. The different approaches include the definition of activities, descriptions, and responsible positions or roles for execution. To integrate the different approaches, the main market leaders agreed to create a standard modelling method, BPMN, which latest version is v2.0. (Object Management Group, s.d.)

Innovative e-learning solutions are combined with semantic technology to have solid knowledge base in knowledge elements structuring. Common form of knowledge base is the ontology, which provides the conceptualization of a certain domain. E-learning solutions started to include semantic interpretation of knowledge areas, ontology based adaptive testing. (Kismihók & Vas, 2006)

Real-time data processing has become very important recently since the number of the information that are produced daily (business transactions, process measurements, web activities, to name but a few) is growing constantly and the ability for processing them not only in the batch mode (once per week/day), but rather in the real-time is crucial for the competitive advantage. Currently, the real-time processing tools in the industry (like these from Tibco, IBM, Oracle) are not taking into account the connection between static and dynamic process data.

Moreover, existing solutions have not been integrated in the learning context yet, which gives us the chance to develop a very competitive and useful solution. In fact, the objective is to describe and manage data in a static context.

However, companies have to manage huge and growing volume of content. The amount of information that must be retained to comply with rules and regulations is expected to grow from 25% of the digital universe last year to 35% in 2012 (Wray, 2009).

To utilize the embedded knowledge of the content data, web and text mining solutions are applied, that is one of the reasons of their increasing popularity recently. Free software, like Rapid Miner and R are the more popular in data and text mining based on the KDnuggets Poll in 2013 (Piatetsky, RapidMiner and R vie for first place, 2013) However due to the introduction of commercial versions of those tools shows an increase of adoption of those software: 29% of the users used only commercial software, 30% only free software, and 41% both. RapidMiner, R, and Excel were again the most popular tools. W. European data miners had the highest percentage of free tool use, 35%, while E. Europe has only 29%. Ratio of the projects, which did not apply text analytics / text mining in the past 12 months is decreasing (33.7% in 2014, 34.7% in 2011 and 45% in 2010) (Piatetsky, How much did you use text analytics or text mining in the past 12 months?, 2014).

2.3   Characteristics of the Solution

The proposed solution envisages a comprehensive procedure whose unique feature is the integration of different partial technologies, owned by the participants to the project [3] , as business process modelling, semantic technology, real-time data processing, knowledge elicitation, representation and transfer; data and text mining technologies mainly support the knowledge extraction.

The technologies involved are mainly open source elements since the interoperability is a crucial pre-condition of the application. The added value comes from the realization and integration. While the case studies and scenarios are very different, the architecture is loosely coupled and, depending on the local circumstances, elements can be replace without radical changes in the structure and usability. The source of knowledge extraction is the business process model, including its instantiation online. The on-time data processing and analysis methods are used for the generation of the dynamic knowledge, e.g. in the form of business rules. The appropriate text mining solution produces the content and the structure that is then uploaded to the ontology-based application. For example, one of the business case aims to create an e-learning application based on the ontology instantiated, or an application to map knowledge gaps in an organization.

The proposed complex approach will cope with these challenges, through a semi-automatic solution, which applies the advanced text-mining technology for annotation that helps to identify specific activities, and the required competency areas. Text selection (e.g. job role description) is semi-automatic, controlled by the process structure. Text-mining solutions identify the relationship between the specific activities and job role specific competencies. The structure of the job role competencies and the structure of the organization and business processes should be mapped. The result of the analysis is a domain specific ontology that will be used as the basis of structuring the content. The domain ontology is always industry specific; therefore, industrial benchmark will be used to validate the results.

2.4   How Does It Work

The ProKEx solution is a composite infrastructure where different technologies are employed in different phases of the process as shown in Fig. 1. Despite of the specific business application there are four main elements that constitute the technology and that implement the iterative translation from the process to the ontology domain.

- A process model
- Translation to a domain model
- Content development and exploitation of the ontology
- Feed back to the process model

---

[3] Netpositive Ltd., Corvinno Nonprofit Public Ltd, Nissatech Innovation Center doo Niš.

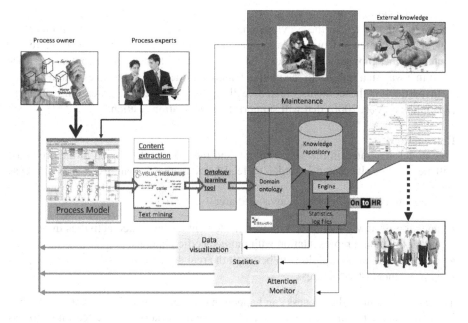

Fig. 1. The Big Picture

Business Process Modelling

Business Process Modelling is the graphic representation of an organisation's business processes. In this first phase, the business process is formalized using SBPM tools (in Fig. 2 an example of modelling of one of the macro activities of the business case). Process modelling aims at graphically describing the process flow and providing information to company so that even complex processes remain transparent. Detailed processes are grouped in process groups and sub-groups; event-driven process chains are often used at the lowest level of the process hierarchy. By definition, each elementary task should have an organizational actor to perform it. A well-described process model contains all the relevant tasks and their description. (Ternai, Török , & Varga, 2014)

In the description of each task is stored the information about the content of the work. Relation with other task, roles, resources, input and output are contextualizing the activity role in the process. Supporting documents, (e.g. regulations) enrich the description of the activities.

Ontology Building

In the second phase all the relevant information extracted from the process models and related documents will be processed and analysed. Text- and data mining techniques are employed for knowledge extraction from the context data. Those knowledge elements will be the basis to create the new specific domain ontology.

The technology behind this phase is described more in details in the article "Process-based Knowledge Extraction in a Public Administrative Authority: A Text Mining Approach" is to create an ontology from the originating SBPM. (Gillani & Kő, 2014)

Content Development
The ontology created in the previous phase will be the basis for the development of the relevant contents. Corvinno's system called STUDIO will be used to store the content in the knowledge repository. The ontology will ensure that content is structured in a way that reflects to the unique features of the selected business models.

In particular, the contents created, will be used to feed an e-Learning platform (Kismihók & Vas, 2006) that will support the organization resilience.

Retroaction
The model generated in the second phase and the content developed in the previous, will be then re-elaborated in order to feed back in the Semantic Business Process Model.

The main type of retroaction envisaged are:

- injection of newly identified knowledge element to the related activities in order to enrich the model representation with more specific contents,
- improvement of the ontology to better fit the real domain,
- improvement of the process.

The improvement of the process can happen in different ways: direct expected benefit is improvement by increasing the match between workers knowledge and process required knowledge. Looking at the process in terms of knowledge exploitation, will help the process owners to identify waste[4] and areas of development for the existing process that could bring to a change of the approach or more generally to a process reengineering. Those improvements of the process can happen jointly with knowledge management tools that use the ontology generated within this project too.

3   The European Institute of Innovation and Technology

3.1   The Mission of the EIT

The European Institute of Innovation and Technology (hereinafter referred to as 'EIT') is a new independent community body established by Regulation (EC) No 294/2008 of the European Parliament and the Council of 11 March 2008 (EC Regulation 294/2008, 2008) and based in Budapest. The EIT aims at addressing Europe's innovation gap to rapidly emerging as a key driver of EU sustainable growth and competitiveness through the stimulation of world-leading innovations with a positive impact on economy and society.

The EIT is a European Institute promoting and performing high-level programs in postgraduate education, research and wider knowledge transfer to industry and society. It acts as a catalyst of good practice for the European scientific and industrial communities by promoting an original European dimension from its very foundation and contributing to the structuring of the European Knowledge Area. (Rubele, 2006)

---

[4] In this context with "waste", we refers to the Lean acceptation (also known as "muda"): any human activity that absorbs resources but creates no value. (Womack & Jones , 2010).

The EIT should be an institution, performing programs in the fields of education, research, and innovation – especially technological. It will be managed at the Union level making it fully an European undertaking, but actually built on knowledge communities typically seconded from existing organizations (Universities, research centers, companies) (EC, 2006) The mission of the EIT is to grow and capitalize on the innovation capacity and capability of actors from higher education, research, business and entrepreneurship [5] from the EU and beyond through the creation of highly integrated Knowledge and Innovation Communities (KICs).

The EIT and Its Knowledge Innovation Communities (KICs)

Since it was founded in 2008, the EIT has sustained the first three KICs that have already trained more than 1,000 young entrepreneurs, incubated more than 100 new companies, and developed a wide range of new products and services.

Each kick have created productive partnerships among hundreds of companies, universities and research institutes mobilizing European capital to produce innovation on a large scale leveraging the initial EU investment to attract three times as much capital from partners and other funding sources.

The KICs are selected by means of a bid in which groups of educational, research and business partners comes together and commit to a long term strategic plan to achieve innovation impact in one of the defined areas that the Parliament decides. Once selected by the EIT Governing Board each KIC constitutes a legal entity and sign with the EIT a Framework Partnership Agreement for a period of 7 years.

Under the provision of such agreement, each KIC every year presents a business plan that is evaluated by the EIT Governing Board that will lead to the allocation of funding for the following year on a competitive base.

The Continuous Research of Excellence

The EIT continuously face this challenge positioning in an area where the expectation is very high (Romeo, 2013), according to its Regulation the EIT shall seek to become a world-class body for excellence in higher education, research and innovation [6] (EC Regulation 294/2008, 2008).

The EIT have in focus the research of innovative practice to implement and simplify its processes and organization. In this context, EIT has initiate knowledge management program and a simplification agenda to overcome the limit of traditional funding approaches. (EIT, 2013)

3.2   The Process for the Annual Allocation of Funding

The process for the "Allocation of funding" is lasting about one year (in terms of lead-time) and involves different actors: EIT Officers, Governing Board Members, KICs and experts.

---

[5] Higher education, research, business and entrepreneurship are known as "knowledge triangle "too.

The macro phases of such process are:

- Definition of policies and guidelines
- Analysis of KICs past performance
- Analysis of KIC annual business plan
- Hearings of the KIC in a multiannual perspective

This process is very critical because is the formal process that allocate most of the budget of the EIT. Compared to other similar programs, the allocation is made based on competitiveness.[7] The impartiality of the process and even more the equal treatment of the participant is particularly important, however the KICs are very different in terms of the expertise domain and strategy. A blended approach is therefore necessary that takes in consideration different aspect of those very peculiar projects. The novelty of the approach, the connatural experimental nature of this exercise, and the relative youth of the EIT as institution, result particular risk because the process scenario is very variable. However, the need of a qualitative and accountable process shall be guarantee. Furthermore the EIT is soon be growing its structure and have to understand what kind of resources it needs to better support its processes, what expertise should be in-house and what shall be externally procured.

Definition of Policies and Guidelines
In the first phase the EIT to guarantee the rules that will governing the competition among the KICs. The actors that mainly intervene in this phase are the EIT Headquarter and EIT Governing Board. The first provide a synthetic view of lesson learned from previous years' experience and the regulation that frame the relationship with the partners in order to propose to the governing board elements to the EIT steering body to discuss and define the criteria that will rule the annual exercise.

Based on those decisions the EIT shall draft the guidelines for the preparation of the business plan and the rules for the allocation of funding exercise.

Analysis of KICs Past Performance
To produce an assessment of the KICs past performance the EIT-HQ analyze the outputs of the assessment of the reporting for the previous years and give an evaluation based on the rules defined in the previous phase. In the analysis of the past performance the EIT Head Quarter and in particular the KIC Project Officers and Continuous monitor Officer evaluate the KICs past performance by taking in account also the previous assessment on the reporting performed by experts in the previous years and the information collected during the management of the relationship with the KICs. Other elements that concurs to the evaluation of the KICs past performance are the level of consumption of the budget allocated in the previous years and the competitive review of the contribution of the KICs to the overall objectives of the EIT by comparing their performance in terms of contribution to the Core Key Performance Indicators (KPI)[8].

---

[7] The EIT Governing Board defines the percentage of competitive funding yearly.

[8] A Core KPIs is a KPI that the KIC measures and that concur to the achievement of the overall strategy of the EIT. The definition and the calculation modalities of such KPIs are uniform and commonly agreed by the KICs.

The evaluation in this phase is mainly performed by EIT staff. EIT need to know if there are knowledge gaps that need to be filled.

Analysis of KIC Annual Business Plan

Experts are contracted to evaluate the business plan presented by the KICs according to the three pillars (education, entrepreneurship and research) and to the merit of the thematic area of each KIC. Experts then provide an outlook of the quality of such proposal according to the rules defined by the EIT Governing Board.

Every year the KICs commit to specific objectives in terms of implementation of activities that will contribute to the overall strategy of the KIC.

In this phase, experts are selected and contracted to evaluate the activities that the KIC decides to carry out in the following year. The evaluators are assessing the business plan produced by the KICs according to the modalities that the EIT Governing Board has defined in the first phase by carrying out an evaluation according to the different domains. Although the process is quite stable, the EIT Head Quarter has to adapt it according to the decision of the Governing Board for the specific year[9]. The composition of the experts' panel in particular may be different by incorporating experts in other domains, such management, operations, finance or knowledge triangle integration... according to the areas the Board decides in the specific year is important to investigate.

In addition, the number of experts in each domain can change in order to moderate the dependence from individuals and to have a complete coverage of the domain in which the KIC operates and the specific contents of the proposed business plan.

This one of the areas where the adoption of the ProKEx platform will provide a concrete benefit in order to understand if the disposed knowledge is sufficient to perform an appropriate and independent assessment.

Hearings of the KIC in a Multiannual Perspective

During the hearings of the Governing Board, the EIT present factual data about the evolution of the KICs on a multiannual perspective and each KIC's board is requested to illustrate and promote the annual plan in the context of the multiannual implementation of the activities of the KICs. The Governing Board members therefore provide their evaluation that is consolidated with the evaluation of past performance, of the assessment by experts of the business plan, and calculate the final funding that have to be allocated to each KIC. While the assessment of the business plan was focusing on analysing the contents of the business plan, the exercise of the assessment of the past performance address the capacity in implementing such a plan, with the hearings the KICs are evaluated in terms of the expected long-term impact. In preparation of the hearings the EIT Headquarter consolidate the figures about the activities of the KICs with a multiannual perspective and prepare a risk assessment report for the Governing Board. The EIT Governing Board is composed by high professional and successful managers in all three areas of the Knowledge triangle that have no necessarily competence in the domain in which the KICs are operating but with a broad experience in

---

[9] The business case has been taking in consideration the 2014 Allocation of funding implemented in 2013.

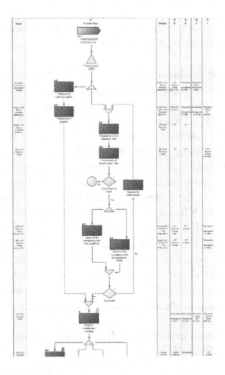

Fig. 2. Analysis of KICs Business Plan

evaluating business cases. During the hearings, in particular, the KICs management is invited to explain the strategy they want to implement in the following year and how this is going to influence Europe in the long-term perspective committed with the KIC Initial Proposal. This is another important point where the ontology can provide important support to contextualize information related to a domain to people that are not expert in the field.

The evaluation of the Board concurs together with the evaluation of the past performance and the technical assessment of the business plan to a final score that is used to elaborate the final funding to each of the KICs. The total funding is composed of a part of structural funding fixed and equal to each KIC and a part that is allocated in a competitive manner through this exercise. The Governing Board together with the final allocation also provide the KICs recommendations for the adaptation of the business plan. In fact, the business plan of the KICs have to be amended to reconcile, the final budget allocated, by taking in consideration those recommendations.

The EIT KIC Officers revise the new version of the business plan to secure that all recommendations have been receipt. With the finalised version of the document, the EIT and the KICs sign the Annual Grant Agreement that will rule the modalities for the funding disbursement.

4   Conclusions

Relevance of the Business Case

The business case is very interesting in terms of provisions to the ProKEx project for several reasons. First of all the process is very well documented (as it should be auditable) and is subject to different regulations (internal to the institute and coming from EU Financial rules) that are formalized. This is very helpful in the word expansion & matching phase that supports the translation from the process model to the domain ontology. To be a top-class process in this application, it requires a wide range and very specialized competences. Because this results in a process very fragmented in terms of activities and roles, the ProKEx project can have a complex scenario to address. The other element that make of the EIT allocation of funding process particularly enticing to test ProKEx is the extension and variety of the knowledge domain involved: there is the domain of the financial rules of the European institutions, the three vertical pillars domains, the thematic domain of the KICs and, of course, the process itself.

Benefit for the EIT

The EIT on the other hand will benefit of the process because can identify area of improvement and simplification of the process, in particular the selection of the resources necessary to perform the evaluation is where we expect the most important benefits. The EIT will advantage of an objective approach to the identification of the right mix of competencies necessary to provide a comprehensive and independent assessment that will secure and improve the guidelines.   The KICs are different not only for the domain in which operate, but also in terms of organisation, history, value and culture. Using the proposed approach will help homogenise the diversities. In the evaluation of the process, furthermore the methodology will provide a unique compliance check with the several requirements this process is subject.

Benefit for the Public Administrations

By generalizing the concept, the adoption of Semantic Business Process Management applying the ProKEx framework in the public administration is a promising approach can provide the several benefits including:

- to improve compliance of the procedures;
- to increase the resilience of the organizations;
- to provide tools to evaluate a domain to non-experts;
- to reduce the fragmentation of roles and process or optimize the management of this level of complexity;
- to improve of the quality of the processes in terms of:

— guarantee high objectivity to the evaluation processes;
— developing efficiency even where diversity and variety is considered a value to preserve.

References

Bourgon, J.: Responsive, responsible and respected government: towards a New Public Administration theory. International Review of Administrative Sciences (2007)

De la Fuente, Á., Ciccone, A.: Human capital in a global and knowledge-based economy. European Commission, Directorate-General for Employment and Social Affairs Unit A.1 (2002)

EC: Communication: from the Commission to the European Council "Implementing the renewed partnership for growth and jobs. Developing a knowledge flagship: the European Institute of Technology". Commission of the European Communities (2006), http://eur-lex.europa.eu/LexUriServ/site/en/com/2006/com2006_0077en01.pdf (retrieved)

EC Regulation 294/2008. REGULATION (EC) No 294/2008 OF THE EUROPEAN PARLIAMENT AND OF THE COUNCIL of 11 March 2008 establishing the European Institute of Innovation and Technology. Official Journal of the European Union(L97/1) (April 9, 2008)

EIT. EIT 2014-2016 Triennial Work Programme - From High-Level Goals to Achieving Impact (2013), http://eit.europa.eu/fileadmin/Content/Downloads/PDF/TWP/EIT_Triennial_Work_Programme_2014-2016.pdf (retrieved)

European Commission. Precidency Conclusions Lisbon European Council 23 nd 24 March 2000 (March 23,24, 2000), http://www.consilium.europa.eu/uedocs/cms_data/docs/pressdata/en/ec/00100-r1.en0.htm

European Commission. Proposal for a regulation of the European Parliament and of the Council amending Regulation (EC) No 294/2008 establishing the European Institute of Innovation and Technology. Brusselles (November 30, 2011), http://eit.europa.eu/fileadmin/Content/Downloads/PDF/EC_SIA/proposal-for-regulation_en.pdf

Gillani, S.A., Kő, A.: Process-Based Knowledge Extraction in a Public Authority: A Text Mining Approach. In: Kő, A., Francesconi, E. (eds.) EGOVIS 2014. LNCS, vol. 8650, pp. 91–103. Springer, Heidelberg (2014)

Gruber, T.: A Translation Approach to Portable Ontology Specifications. Knowledge Acquisition 5(2), 199–220 (1993)

Kalpic, B., Bernus, P.: Business Process Modelling Through the Knowledge Management Perspective 10(3) (2006), doi:10.1108/13673270610670849

Kismihók, G., Vas, R.: Ontology Based Adaptive Examination System in E-Learning Environment. In: 28th Int. Conf. Information Technology Interfaces, ITI 2006, Cavtar, Croatia (2006)

Object Management Group (n.d.). BPMN v2.0. Business Process Model and Notation, http://www.omg.org/spec/BPMN/2.0/

Piatetsky, G.: RapidMiner and R vie for first place (June 03, 2013), Retrieved from KD Nuggets: http://www.kdnuggets.com/2013/06/kdnuggets-annual-software-poll-rapidminer-r-vie-for-first-place.html

Piatetsky, G.: How much did you use text analytics or text mining in the past 12 months? (February 2014), Retrieved from KDnuggets: http://www.kdnuggets.com/polls/2014/text-analytics-text-mining-use.html

Romeo, E.: Horizon (2020): the ambitious new UE program for research and innovation (2013), http://www.lyonbiopole.com/: http://www.lyonbiopole.com/News/Horizon-2020-The-futur-UE-ambitious-programme.html (retrieved)

Rubele, R.: European Institute of Technology: how to move forward. EURODOC (2006), http://scs.sa.infn.it/rubele/EURODOC/EIT_rapid_note.pdf (retrieved)

Ternai, K., Török, M., Varga, K.: Combining knowledge management and business process management – A solution for information extraction from business process models focusing on BPM challenges. In: Kő, A., Francesconi, E. (eds.) EGOVIS 2014. LNCS, vol. 8650, pp. 104–117. Springer, Heidelberg (2014)

Török, M., Ternai, K.: Semantic modeling for automated workflow software generation – An open model. IEEE Xplore (2011)

Womack, J., Jones, D.: Lean Thinking: Banish Waste and Create Wealth in Your Corporation, 2nd edn. Free Press (2010)

Wray, R.: Internet data heads for 500bn gigabyte. The Guardian (May 18, 2009), http://www.guardian.co.uk/business/2009/may/18/digital-content-expansion (retrieved)

Extending Computerized Adaptive Testing to Multiple Objectives: Envisioned on a Case from the Health Care

Christian Weber and Réka Vas

Corvinno Technology Transfer Center, Budapest, Hungary
{cweber,rvas}@corvinno.com

Abstract. In the age of information, only personalized learning and education enables the adaption to always changing requirements. In health care, labor forces are especially in a continuous need of improvement and adaption. Maintaining an optimal care sets a dual goal in the education of health professionals: adapt to scientific developments while retaining the compliance with changing laws and regulations.

Computerized adaptive testing (CAT), as a dynamic approach to education, is providing here the right adaptivity by optimizing time and precision of learning and scaling to the ability of the learner.

This paper will provide an overview on the current state of CAT and connected methodologies and shed light on the potentials for the next generation of adaptive testing, which can support the emergence of novel ways of education. Its strength is shown on a scenario from the health care sector.

Keywords: Computerized adaptive testing, CAT, item response theory, IRT, health care, survey, differential item functioning, educational objectives, education and training.

1 Testing Individual Improvement in a Medical Context

Education and continuous improvement is becoming a fixed, yet extending, part of the daily live. Workers have to develop further skills and experiences, to cope with their work and be ready to breach into new areas of their working domains to compete in changing markets and social environments. While decisions on outdated knowledge may lead already to unsuccessful projects, no other area is more thoroughly affected by the results of personal decisions than the health care sector.

There is a lack of adequate education in the daily work of doctors and care takers. A societal consent exists that healthcare professionals have to keep improving their knowledge within their working routine, yet the educational offers are seldom fit to the workers and their personal requirements. While graduated workers like doctors, are habituated to be in a self managed educational process, care takers are often missing guidance for their learning profiles, facing the variety of medical topics.

Providing guidance through adaptive learning within the daily practice, could here be a solution to close the existing gap. But it comes with demands:

A. Kő and E. Francesconi (Eds.): EGOVIS 2014, LNCS 8650, pp. 148–162, 2014.

1. **The time is restricted**, which applies to the available time for learning activities, as well as to the time of domain experts like doctors, designing and evaluating testing items and detecting the educational need.
2. **The learning has an educational context.** Each area to test on, has a domain context but also an educational context, resulting in cases with different goals:
   (a) National and international regulations on the job are mandatory knowledge areas, tolerating no lacks or errors, captured as **"must-know" items**.
   (b) Knowledge extensions, grasping new developments or personalized specializations are important but optional educational goals as **"should know" items**. For detected learning needs, the "time to learn" is more important than the "time to test", favoring an extended detection of educational gaps, while challenging the traditional adaptive testing goal of a short test.
3. **The learning has a cultural context.** Jobs throughout the medical professions are coming with a strong human relation. Knowledge and skills are mixed with a human context in regards to the cultural background, influencing the educational utilization of the care taker, which is also connected to the influence of learning types.

This paper will shed light on the possibilities for an adaptive education, to fit to the needs of the medical workers and provide an insight on how to create the right educational feedback in line with personal learning requirements. In this regards, this paper will first address the current state in and the potential path to an adaptive testing, to then motivate a new multiple objectives vision for upcoming solutions.[1]

2   From Classic to Adaptive Testing

For an adaptive test, in contrast to a classical linear test, the number of test items and the order of questions is only determined during the test itself. The goal is to determine the knowledge level of the test taker as precisely as possible with a number of questions as low as possible. It does not require deep analysis to realize that in contrast, linear tests have always been constructed to meet the requirements of testgivers.

Selecting the adequate examination method or setting up a good test is far from being an easy task. A test that is much too easy or much too difficult is a waste of time. If the test is too easy for the candidate, it is likely to invite unwanted candidate behavior such as thoughtless mistakes. On the other hand, questions that are much too hard also produce generally unreliable test results, as candidates will give up early and cease to seriously attempt to answer the questions, resorting to guessing, response patterns and other forms of unwanted behavior.

According to traditional testing methods, all candidates should get absolutely the same questions. This way the results and the performance of candidates can be easily and clearly compared. Adaptive testing breaks away with this approach. Every candidate may receive entirely different question and not even the order of questions is

[1] This work is created in the frame of the Eduworks project, support by the European Commission within the Marie Curie Initial Training Network Programme of the FP7 People Programme, in cooperation with the Corvinno Technology Transfer Center.

defined in advance. This means, answers of previous questions determine which questions will be asked in the following steps.

An adaptive methodology was first applied in psychology and Alfred Binet worked out the first form of adaptive testing in 1904 [1]. He developed intelligence tests that aimed at diagnosing the individual, rather than the group, this way eliminating the issue of fairness, requiring everyone to take the same test. He realized he could customize the test to the individual by rank, by ordering the items according to their difficulty. He would then start testing the candidate by estimating the level of the candidate's ability and asking a subset of items (questions) that he believed to meet this ability level. If the candidate succeeded, Binet proceeded to give successively harder item subsets, until the candidate failed frequently. In the opposite case, if the candidate failed the initial question or item subset, then Binet would administer successively easier item subsets until the candidate succeeded frequently.

Binet's procedure has been improved and refined by many authors, like Lord (1980) [2] Henning (1987) [3] and Lewis and Sheehan (1990) [4]. In their approaches, items are stratified by their difficulty level, and subsets of items are formed at each level. The test starts with administering subsets of items and it goes on with moving the difficulty up or down in accordance with the success rate on each subset.

3   Computerized Adaptive Testing as a New Type of Learning

Reckase developed the first computer aided adaptive testing in 1974 [5], fusing the potentials of IT systems with adaptivity and a user centric strategy to overcome the limitations of linear testing. In case of computer adaptive testing (CAT), it is not the test-givers task anymore to select the items, define the order of further items and evaluate results, as the computer will execute all these tasks. The candidate gets administered questions automatically, with a difficulty level that is accordant to his estimated ability level, with which examination stress is reduced and a suitable level of motivation is assured. But the most important feature is, that the time of testing is much shorter, as shown by Welch and Frick [6].

Linacre [7] provides a detailed description of the theoretical background, major types and logic of operation in adaptive testing. Several methodological approaches have been developed for CAT which evolved from the principles of psychometric measurement. Nowadays CAT has reached a broad application from local education [8] till mobile solutions on smart devices [9]. From the numerous variations, Item Response Theory (IRT) (Wainer & Mislevy, 1990) [10] and Knowledge Space Theory (Falmagne et al., 1990) [11] have spread the most.

The main characteristics of CAT – independently from the approach – are:

- The test can be taken at the time most convenient to the examinee; there is no need for mass or group-administered testing, thus saving physical space.
- As each test is tailored to an examinee and no two tests need be identical, which minimizes the possibility of copying.
- Questions are presented on a computer screen, one at a time.

- Once an examinee keys in and confirms his answer, he is not able to change it.
- The examinee is not allowed to skip questions, nor is he allowed to return to a question which he has confirmed his answer to previously.
- The examinee must answer the current question in order to proceed onto the next.
- The selection of each question and the decision to stop the test are dynamically controlled by the answers of the examinee [12].

3.1 Dichotomous Test Items

Providing the simplest version of adaptive testing, dichotomous items (multiple choice questions) are weighted along a linear scale and answers can only have two values a time (true or false).

Gershon [13] suggests, that the first item, and perhaps all items, should be a bit on the easy side, giving the candidate a feeling of accomplishment in a situation of challenge. If there is a criterion pass-fail level, then a good starting item has a difficulty slightly below that.

3.2 Polytomous Test Items

In case of tests consisting of polytomous items, answers can have more than two values. Typically the test-taker would not be able to recognize any difference between a strictly dichotomous question and a polytomous question. The difference is in the scoring. False answers (distractors) may be more correct than others, and so are given greater scores (or credits). Naturally, the correct option is given the greatest score. At the same time, selecting questions for a test from a set of polytomous items, requires more care, since it is not possible to define the difficulty of all items with intermediate levels which indicate different ability levels.

Since polytomous items are more informative regarding the candidate performance than dichotomous items, polytomous CAT administrations usually comprise fewer items. At the same time writing polytomous items, and developing defensible scoring schemes for them, can be difficult.

4   Measuring Abilities with CAT – Psychometrics and Methodologies

A CAT-based system cannot operate adequately without an objective measurement model that enables the evaluation of results. Most of the computer-adaptive testing systems are based on the models of Rasch [14] and Wright [15].

Almost all ability tests are based on the hypothesis that abilities can be ranked along one single dimension. But in the average, no test is exactly one-dimensional. If candidates are to be ranked relative to each other or relative to some criterion levels of performance, an approximation to unidimensionality has to be achieved. When a new item is entered to the test-bank it has to be decided how to determine the difficulty level of the new item and how to preserve the unidimensionality of the test. In most of the cases the estimation of the difficulty of new items could be reduced to a matter of maintaining a consistent stochastic ordering between the new and the existing items in the bank [14]. Instead of defining the real difficulty level, the difficulty level and ranking of the new item is defined by comparing it to old items in the bank. The primary goal is to maintain a consistent stochastic ordering. Its most spread tool is the Rasch model [16].

The essence of the dichotomous Rasch model is that it presents a simple relationship between the test-takers and the items. Each test-taker is characterized by an ability level expressed as a number along an infinite linear scale of the relevant ability. The local origin of the scale is chosen for convenience. The ability of test-taker n is identified as being B_n units from that local origin. Similarly, each item is characterized by a difficulty level that is expressed as a number along the infinite scale of the relevant ability. The difficulty of an item i is identified as being D_i units from the local origin of the ability scale. Accordingly, the relationship between test-takers and items is expressed by the dichotomous Rasch model [14]:

$$\log(P_{ni1} / P_{ni0}) = B_n - D_i , \qquad (1)$$

where Pni1 is the probability that test-taker n succeeds on item i, and Pni0 is the probability of failure. Wright [15] suggested here in 1988 an algorithm which is easy to implement, and could be successfully employed at the end of each learning module to keep track of student progress.

4.1 Item Response Theory (IRT)

The Item Response Theory (IRT) were connected to CAT by Wainer and Mislevy in 1990 [10] and is a statistical framework in which examinees can be described by a set of ability scores that are linking the actual performance on test items and the examinees abilities. In this regards, it is extending the use of the Classical Test Theory (CTT), where characteristics of the test-taker and the test could not be separated.

For a classic, linear test structure, CTT and IRT could perform similar, when used for pre-testing test items, and offer the same quality, with CTT being more invariant than IRT methodologies [17, 18]. Nevertheless, for CAT, where tailoring, adaptive test builds are the focus of interest, IRT-based methodologies are mandatory to enable the system to provide test items in an adaptive and personalizing manner [19].

Each item can be associated with one or more of the following parameters – the difficulty level, the discriminatory power and the guessing factor. The difficulty level describes how difficult and complex an item is, the discriminatory power explains how well the test item differentiates students of different proficiency level, while the guessing factor is the probability that a student can answer correctly by simply guessing. Before each test, the test bank must be balanced and checked that there are not over-represented or under-represented knowledge areas. Finally the values of test item parameters must be defined. The progress of testing under IRT is given in Figure 1.

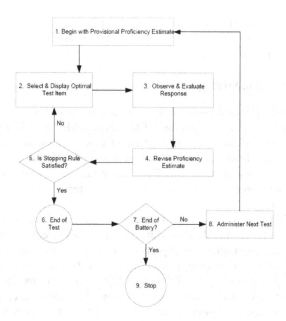

Fig. 1. Process of Adaptive Testing (Thissen and Mislevy, 1990 [12])

5   Calibration and Organization of the Item Bank

The item bank - independent of its local implementation – is one of the most vital parts of a CAT system. To enable a stable functionality and to decide which item should be presented to the test-taker, in terms of knowledge and testing context, the underlying item bank and connected parameters have to be calibrated. Especially in an environment with tight time restrictions and a complex background, as within the health care sector, the constant definition and classification of test items, is a limiting factor to the long term usability of a system. Even more, the knowledge to evaluate items may be distributed among different experts of different expertise with a differing vision on the difficulty of items. This appeals and requires a self calibrating solution, to create and continuously adopting the difficulty of the items, based on real testing feedback. As not only the preparation and support but also the actual administering of the test is a task under time limitation, a calibration of items would benefit from happening online and in parallel to the online testing.

Even though concepts for an online calibration in parallel to the actual testing exist, a majority of calibration is still done before the productive testing [20]. Human experts are handling and managing the calibration of the item-bank based on their knowledge, acting as knowledge area or testing expert. To succeed in the planning and organization the experts have to decide on how to calibrate the parameters of the IRT methods [21].

In a manual frame, the estimation of the difficulty has to be assessed in cooperation with testers and experts, and should be evaluated in the same environment. As experts like doctors in the medical context, have very limited time for additional duties, each improvement regarding calibration time is a direct benefit. Here, online calibration strategies are an alternative to address parametric IRT requirements for calibration, in parallel to the actual testing [22].

5.1 Online Calibration Strategies

Online calibration assigns values to the item parameters over time, even if there is no information about the items at beginning of the testing. Makransky proposed in 2009 [20] online calibration strategies, with a phase of random item administration at the beginning of the test, till sufficient information is available to use e.g. Fisher's information function. To overcome the initially missing item level, the core goal of each strategy is to define a process on how to fill the parameters while preventing an artificial bias on the items.

An online calibration is especially valuable in frames where no experts or pre-testers are available for an initial calibration, e.g. in medical areas, where the checking of the items through high qualified experts is already a costly and time consuming task. The benefit of an online calibration comes with the need for a high amount of initial test takers to reach a full CAT functionality, which also means that the initial testers are starting in an environment different from the following up tests. To cope, the test could be designed to lower or ignore the counting of items in the initialization phase, at the cost of a longer test.

Two-Phase Strategy. The strategy splits in two phases. At the start of the testing process, items are administered randomly, starting with a difficulty parameter of 0 for each item. Based on the derived difficulty parameter calibration, the items are then administered in the form of a CAT. The transition point between the random and CAT phase is triggered if an average number of taken test items is reaching a threshold.

Multi-phase Strategy. The multi-phase strategy is a higher level strategy, including the two-phase strategy. Each higher level phase starts with a random selection phase, followed by a CAT sub-phase. To prevent a biasing of the items, the first higher level phase is entirely presented in a random fashion. For each cycle of the higher level phases, the proportion of the actual CAT-based administration is increasing till reaching a CAT-only phase.

Continuous Updating. The continuous updating starts with a random phase, gathering the feedback on administered items over time. If an item is administered a predefined number of times, it is added to a set of CAT enabled items and could be used in following CAT phases. The system passes through cycles of random item presentation and CAT, calibrating after each cycle. In this manner the item level is improving constantly till the complete item bank is calibrated. In practical application the continuous updating is the strategy offering the best compromise for a stable and qualitative calibration, while the other strategies are valuable in specific IRT methodology and testing case combinations [20].

5.2 Differential Item Functioning

The cultural background of a person could not only color an answer, but also decide about the potential to assess a specific ability. If for a test item, persons possessing the same backing ability but, coming out of different cultural contexts, have different potentials to answer, the item is showing Differential Item Functioning (DIF). More generalized it could be expressed as Measurement Invariance (MI), expressing that a specific item is measured different among different specific groups in an organizational context. Vandenberg and Lance [23] underlined, that a missing assessment of differences across assumptions, like for created test items, could lead to an inaccurate reasoning.

The cultural context of a person could be an important feedback in regards to skills, labor aspects like communication skills and corporate culture and learning types. This is especially true in professions with a strong human relation, like medical professions. Instead of following the default procedure of deleting affected items, this motivates an alternative focus on the handling of DIF with a goal oriented modeling of items and structures, making use of the additional knowledge.

A way to cope with it, is a modeling solution, proposed by Makransky and Glas, where items with a detected DIF are virtualized and instanced with the same content but a different context parameterization. The DIF item gets virtually multiplied, as shown in Figure 2. Each virtual item is flagged with a parameter grasping the context of the item and the sub-items.

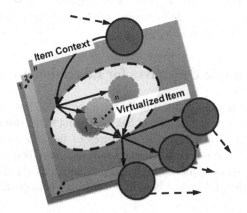

Fig. 2. Virtualizing DIF items to act in a given context

5.3 Ontology Enhanced Item Banks

An item bank could be seen as a database of testing items and realized by a database software solution, storing the items with their connected parameters and statistical properties. In terms of adaptivity to the testers ability and the relations to knowledge areas, CAT is providing a contextual and context-aware experience and does, especially for broad but complex knowledge areas as the medical knowledge domain, profit from a semantically enhanced, ontological representation of content and relations. Two approaches exist within the literature to connect ontological benefits and item bank related CAT requirements:

Ontological Item Bank Extraction. For a long term use of online testing systems, a regular flow of new test items is needed to prevent the memorization and propagation of the content inside of the groups of test takes. To cope with the need to constantly provide new items, an automatic or semi-automatic creation of items is beneficial. Ying and Yang [24] proposed here the design of a course material knowledge ontology, storing the structure and the concepts of courses and materials. Through the contextualization of the material structure, the system is able to parse learning material to new question items, while incorporating levels of understanding like within the revised Bloom Taxonomy [25].

Backing the Item Bank with Domain Knowledge. A second approach to an ontology connected item bank, is to back the collection of items with modeled information about the domains behind the test items. Through the structure and relations of the domain knowledge, the system is able to optimize the process of item administration, following related concepts and evaluating stored conceptualizations about the test taker and contexts. Soylu und Vandewaet designed an ontology to store concepts about the learner, knowledge areas and access rights [26].

The ontology, which will be used as a starting point for the following up, is focusing on the connection and relation of knowledge domains, tasks, activities, competences and curricula. The connected domains are detailed into concepts, theorems and basic examples, as presented in [27–29].

6   CAT in Multiple Objectives for Educational Feedback

The connection of testing and education is often motivated but rarely underlined by real methodological concepts. A solution has to connect to the results, gathered by the adaptive test, as well as to connect to measures of the indicators, involved in the process. In an isolated test environment, the test is the main focus, but seen in an educational view, the context of the testing is education. Assessing the abilities of a test taker is a must, but the global goal is to improve his or her education on a long term development.

The previous sections gathered and motivated the background for a system to address the needs for adaptive testing in learning environments, as found in health care related professions, with multiple time restrictions and different and potentially conflicting learning goals. Still the question is how to connect the testing and the test results to an educational feedback in the form of evaluations and materials. The better the educational feedback is fitting the user, the higher are the chances for improvement and the motivation to continue this type of education, which resul in a reuse of the test items and a pay-back of the connected creation and maintaining efforts.

As seen in the previous sections, the testing methodologies and measurements are created based on the notion of a single testing goal. In real applications a test motivation could cluster in different tasks or learning goals under contexts like cultural differences, learning types and skill or expertise obligations. The test taker becomes a learner and in this way must play multiple roles in such a system. Accordingly, the process not only includes the discovery of a current state but also a feedback process, embedded in a loop of improvement.

The exploration of connected and extended requirements, captured within the ontology, as well as the analysis of tracked process parameters, yields the power of a new solution, defining a triangle of actors for a novel process: "Educational Objective", "Education Strategy" and "Testing Strategy", enabled by an ontological extension on the item bank. The vision for a multi objective testing will connect to the existing and proven Studio approach, making use of a functional domain ontology implementation, providing a riche context for the parameters of the item bank [27–29].

6.1   A Vision for Multiple Objectives as Learning Cases within the Health Care Environment

As shown in the initial motivation in Section 1, there are a number of requirements, which are specially fitting to medical professions and specifically to care takers. Based on these requirements and backed and motivated by the CAT connected methodologies, highlighted in the sections before, three "Objective Classes" are extracted in the following, fitting to the requirements and proposing how to adapt CAT in medical education under different objectives, to enable an educational feedback cycle.

"Must Know" Objective. A "must know" item captures a knowledge element or skill in which the test taker should not fail in any circumstances. It pictures a fixed regulation, created by a higher instance. In the medical context it captures an official health regulation, which could cause a life threatening situation or trigger legal measures, but it could also implement a commitment in connection with the corporate identity.

Table 1. "Must know" objective overview

Objective	Educational strategy	Testing strategy
Must know	Learner should under no circumstances have a lack in this field. Feedback content is extensive and far reaching on the topic.	Failing an element marked as "must know" or sub-elements, fails all following elements. Elements marked as related and "must know" will be assessed.

If an element is marked as "must know", a false answer will trigger the fail of the complete sub-tree of following up items, from a general to a detailed level. Failing on the detail level will trigger the same fail event, as the "must know" flag is an all-or-nothing signaler. As there is a possibility that a fail also signals a knowledge lack in related regulations, the testing strategy will make use of the underlying ontological relations, e.g. the relation "is_element()" and "belongs_to()", to discover other marked curriculums in the connected curriculum group, as shown in [30].

The resulting feedback to a failed group, headed by an element with the "must know" flag, is to present the complete material capturing the regulations which were tested in the CAT iterations.

"Should Know" Objective. Out of the educational view, a "should now" item is connecting to knowledge areas which are an extension to the core knowledge needed to improve on the job. In the context of a care taker, new medicaments, exotic diseases and knowledge outside of the medical specialization are "should know" items.

Table 2. "Should know" objective overview

Objective	Educational strategy	Testing strategy
Should know	Learner has optional knowledge domains to improve on. With the feedback on in which details an area failed, user adapted education content could be provided.	Failing an element marked as "should know" or sub-elements, will trigger testing on related areas to detect and constraint the educational feedback.

An element marked as "should know" will for a negative answer act as a starting point to assess if the educational feedback could be limited in favor of the later educational time. The system will make use of the connections to the curriculum, evaluating which other curriculum is part of the current group of related elements. Defining an additional threshold against the percentage of sub-elements needed to fail an area, could limit the educational feedback material, reducing the time needed for learning.

The gathered, failed items and related items with the "should know" marker will be used to organize the feedback material in a way that it fits to the core of the unknown items, leaving out related but unnecessary content, e.g. could a failed item about types of strong pain killers trigger the center article as an educational feedback, while removing the general content about pain, when this part were answered correctly in related areas. Skipped content could be made available as linked material.

"Learning Context" Objective. Learners could be grouped by different learning types, e.g. visual, sensing/practical or sequential/process oriented learners [31]. To improve the educational feedback for different types of learners, items could be biased on purpose as for DIF items. E.g. if a care taker is a visual type, a question about taking the blood pressure could use a visual wording, connecting to the visual memory instead of listing parts of the processes. The educational feedback could then be reorganized to start with the visual part, before explaining the process in details.

Items marked with a "learning context" are virtualized, as seen in the DIF section. Thus multiple parallel elements of the item exists, connected to the same head and child element(s), yet yielding a different context to act on the same underlying ability. If a contextualized item is answered correctly, a predefined modification pack, stored with the item, is loaded. This pack attaches modifiers to the following elements, countering disadvantages based on the learning style and stabilizing the online calibration.

Table 3. "Learning context" objective overview

Objective	Educational strategy	Testing strategy
Learning Context	Learner should get learning material, adapted to their learning style, easing the education.	Failing an element marked with a "learning context" gets virtualized in the number of available contexts. To adopt the context, the element triggers a pattern, modifying the weights of sub-elements to reflect the context.

The general information on the learning type could be used to provide alternate, type-fitting material. The marked items could act as a correction modifier, preventing the concentration of material for topics which were failed based on a learning type mismatch.

7   Conclusion and Outlook

This paper gives an overview about the methodologies and modifications needed to address adaptive learning under restrictions and in a new vision of multiple and differing learning goals. Beside the proven frame and fundamental methodologies connected to CAT, it were shown and motivated that only a specific combination of methodologies will create an adaptive solution, addressing the range of restrictions and demands of professions with rapidly changing backgrounds and learning requirements, as found within the health care sector. While the proposed frame and multi learning goal extension is representing a vision, the conceptualization is reasonable in terms of the used methodologies and the realization is feasible in terms of future implementations making use of the existing and proven Studio software solution [30].

Above the presented considerations for a future implementation, additional limitations have to be addressed and evaluated for a stable, lasting CAT process. E.g. could an overuse of specialized objectives disturb the ability to adapt to the learners level, through interrupting a continuous measurement, as items may be administered based on an objective instead of the item level. Here, the profiling of the test taker [32] could become important to track the learning level of the test taker as the administering is based on previous tests and the known calibration values.

The value of introducing learning objectives into CAT based testing solutions is looking promising and only the start of its potential. Extensions are possible to define additional objective processes, like marking items as inactive based on previous tests or adding additional contexts, like communication types and cultural backgrounds. Despite the potential, the new vision has to be proven based on a practical realization and connected to real world test scenarios for evaluation.

With the strong connection to a context rich background and representation, the presented conception of a needed compilation of methodologies and the vision for a new goal-based adaptive testing, is a fitting complement and extension to the existing implementations of the Studio approach. The next step will be to adapt the new conceptions to the proven adaptive testing frame of Studio. A test field is here the synergic potential to fuse and prove the new vision in existing Studio projects and prototypes, e.g.:

- **ProKEx**[2]**:** As presented in the complementing publications within the frame of the EGOVIS 2014, ProKEx [33, 34] offers a solution to connect organizational processes and process knowledge requirements to the testing and learning capability of the Studio approach. In this frame it is a benefit to label related educational domains with "must know" and "should know" objectives, to give education priority to critical processes.
- **MedAssess**[3]**:** The IT powered core of the MedAssess project, is a further development of the Studio-based OntoHR prototype [35, 36]. It is mixing the ontology-backed testing ability of Studio with the power to match educational profiles to available job profiles in the health care sector. As such it is the prototype for the cases this paper and the perfect application area to test and implement educational objectives.

References

1. Simon, T., Binet, A.: Méthodes nouvelles pour le diagnostic du niveau intellectuel des anormaux. L'année Psychologique 11, 191–244 (1904)
2. Lord, F.M.: Applications of Item Response Theory to Practical Testing Problems. Taylor & Francis (2012)
3. Henning, G.: A guide to language testing: development, evaluation, research. Newberry House Publishers (1987)
4. Sheehan, K., Lewis, C.: Computerized Mastery Testing With Nonequivalent Testlets. Applied Psychological Measurement 16, 65–76 (1992)
5. Reckase, M.: An interactive computer program for tailored testing based on the one-parameter logistic model. Behavior Research Methods & Instrumentation 6, 208–212 (1974)
6. Edwin Welch, R., Frick, T.: Computerized adaptive testing in instructional settings. Educational Technology Research and Development 41, 47–62 (1993)
7. Linacre, J.M.: Computer-adaptive testing: A methodology whose time has come. In: Chae, S., Kang, U., Jeon, E., Linacre, J.M. (eds.) Development of Computerized Middle School Achievement Tests. MESA Research Memorandum No. 69. Komesa Press, Seoul (2000)
8. Čekerevac, Z., Andjetić, S., Petar, Č.: Knowledge assessment and application of computer adaptive testing. Knowledge Assessment and Application of CAT // MEST 1, 16–30 (2013)
9. Triantafillou, E., Georgiadou, E., Economides, A.A.: The design and evaluation of a computerized adaptive test on mobile devices. Computers & Education 50, 1319–1330 (2008)

[2] The ProKEx project (EUREKA_HU_12-1-2012-0039) is supported by the Research and Technology Innovation Fund, New Szécsényi Plan, Hungary, in cooperation with the Corvinno Technology Transfer Center.
[3] The MedAsses project is support by the European Commission within the LEONARDO DA VINCI innovation transfer program of Lifelong Learning (grant no. DE/12/LLP-LdV/TOI/147557), in cooperation with the Corvinno Technology Transfer Center.

10. Wainer, H. Mislevy, R.J.: Item Response Theory, Item Calibration, and Proficiency Estimation. In: Wainer, H., Dorans, N.J., Flaugher, R., Green, B.F., Mislevy, R.J. (eds.) Computerized Adaptive Testing: A Primer, pp. 61–100. Lawrence Erlbaum Associates (1990)
11. Falmagne, J.-C., Koppen, M., Villano, M., Doignon, J.-P., Johannesen, L.: Introduction to knowledge spaces: How to build, test, and search them. Psychological Review 97(2), 201–224 (1990)
12. Thissen, D., Mislevy, R.J.: Testing Algorithms. In: Wainer, H., Dorans, N.J., Flaugher, R., Green, B.F., Mislevy, R.J. (eds.) Computerized Adaptive Testing: A Primer, pp. 101–134. Lawrence Erlbaum Associates (1990)
13. Gershon, R.C.: Test Anxiety and Item Order: New Concerns for Item Response Theory. In: Wilson, M. (ed.) Objective Measurement: Theory into Practice. Ablex, Norwood (1992)
14. Rasch, G.: Probabilistic Models for Some Intelligence and Attainment Tests. MESA Press (1960)
15. Wright, B.: Practical adaptive testing. Rasch Measurement Transactions. Rasch Measurement SIG (1988)
16. Roskam, E.E., Jansen, P.G.W.: A New Derivation of the Rasch Model. In: Degreef, E., Buggenhaut, J.V. (eds.) Trends in Mathematical Psychology, pp. 293–307. North-Holland (1984)
17. Fan, X.: Item response theory and classical test theory: an empirical comparison of their item/person statistics. Educational and Psychological Measurement 58, 357 (1998)
18. Lawson, S.: One-Parameter Latent Trait Measurement: Do the Results justify the Effort? In: Advances in Educational Research?: Substantive Findings, Methodological Developments (1991)
19. Stage, C.: Classical Test Theory or Item Response Theory: The Swedish Experience. Centro De Estudios Públicos, Santiago de Chile, Chile (2003)
20. Makransky, G., Glas, C.A.: An automatic online calibration design in adaptive testing. Journal of Applied Testing Technology 11, 1–20 (2010)
21. Lopez-Cuadrado, J., Arruabarrena, R., Armendariz, A., Perez, T.A., Vadillo, J.A.: Computerized Adaptive Testing, the Item Bank Calibration and a Tool for Easing the Process. Technology Education and Development (2009)
22. Makransky, G.: Computerized adaptive testing in industrial and organizational psychology. Educational Testing Service, Princeton (2012)
23. Vandenberg, R.J., Lance, C.E.: A Review and Synthesis of the Measurement Invariance Literature: Suggestions, Practices, and Recommendations for Organizational Research. Organizational Research Methods 3, 4–70 (2000)
24. Ying, M.-H., Yang, H.-L.: Computer-Aided Generation of Item Banks Based on Ontology and Bloom's Taxonomy. In: Li, F., Zhao, J., Shih, T.K., Lau, R., Li, Q., McLeod, D. (eds.) ICWL 2008. LNCS, vol. 5145, pp. 157–166. Springer, Heidelberg (2008)
25. Krathwohl, D.R.: A Revision of Bloom's Taxonomy: An Overview. Theory Into Practice 41, 212–218 (2002)
26. Soylu, A., Vandewaetere, M., Wauters, K., Jacques, I., De Causmaecker, P., Desmet, P., Clarebout, G., Van den Noortgate, W.: Ontology-Driven Adaptive and Pervasive Learning Environments – APLEs: An Interdisciplinary Approach. In: De Wannemacker, S., Clarebout, G., De Causmaecker, P. (eds.) ITEC 2010. CCIS, vol. 126, pp. 99–115. Springer, Heidelberg (2011)
27. Kő, A., Gábor, A., Vas, R., Szabó, I.: Ontology-based Support of Knowledge Evaluation in Higher Education. In: Proceedings of the 2008 Conference on Information Modelling and Knowledge Bases XIX, pp. 306–313. IOS Press, Amsterdam (2008)

28. Szabó, I.: The implementation of the educational ontology. In: Fehér, P. (ed.) Proceedings of the 7th European Conference on Knowledge Management (ECKM 2006). Academic Conferences Limited (2006)

29. Vas, R., Kovacs, B., Kismihok, G.: Ontology Based Mobile Learning and Knowledge Testing. Int. J. Mob. Learn. Organ. 3, 128–147 (2009)

30. Vas, R.: Educational Ontology and Knowledge Testing. Electronic Journal of Knowledge Management 5, 123–130 (2007)

31. Felder, R.M., Spurlin, J.E.: Applications, Reliability, and Validity of the Index of Learning Styles. Intl. Journal of Engineering Education 21, 103–112 (2005)

32. Triantafillou, E., Georgiadou, E., Economides, A.A.: Applying adaptive variables in computerised adaptive testing. Australasian Journal of Educational Technology 23(3), 350–370 (2007)

33. Arru, M.: Application of Process Ontology to improve the funding allocation process at the European Institute of Innovation and Technology. In: Kő, A., Francesconi, E. (eds.) EGOVIS 2014. LNCS, vol. 8650, pp. 133–147. Springer, Heidelberg (2014)

34. Gillani, S.A., Kő, A.: Process-Based Knowledge Extraction in a Public Authority: A Text Mining Approach. In: Kő, A., Francesconi, E. (eds.) EGOVIS 2014. LNCS, vol. 8650, pp. 91–103. Springer, Heidelberg (2014)

35. Khobreh, M., Ansari, F., Dornhöfer, M., Fathi, M.: An ontology-based Recommender System to Support Nursing Education and Training. In: LWA 2013 (2013)

36. Mol, S., Kismihók, G., Ansari, F., Dornhöfer, M.: Integrating Knowledge Management in the Context of Evidence Based Learning: Two Concept Models Aimed at Facilitating the Assessment and Acquisition of Job Knowledge. In: Fathi, M. (ed.) Integration of Practice-Oriented Knowledge Technology: Trends and Prospectives, pp. 29–45. Springer, Heidelberg (2013)

From Legislation towards the Provision of Services

An Approach to Agile Implementation of Legislation

Tom van Engers[1] and Sjir Nijssen[2]

[1] University of Amsterdam, Leibniz Center for Law
vanEngers@uva.nl
[2] PNA Group
Sjir.Nijssen@pna-group.com

Abstract. Since the spring of 2012 a number of people from the Dutch government, academia and business have joined forces under the label 'Blue Chamber'. The partners' concrete ideas are intended to closely cooperate in the development of an agile implementation of legislation, allowing for a human-centred approach. The principle used is: digital whenever possible, in person when needed. Cooperation and widespread sharing of experiences are the principles that the participants embrace and promote. The emphases can be summarized as follows: 1. Knowledge management by staff responsible for policy and implementation of services. 2.Separating the management of IT systems aimed at supporting the large-scale handling of cases, but linked together. 3. Multidisciplinary knowledge work by focusing policy, service implementation and information supply on knowledge management and the preparation of IT specifications. 4. Capturing reusable and sustainable specifications for service implementation processes and IT. 5. The development of internationally recognized methods and standards.

Keywords: Requirements for legal DNA, requirements for protocol for analysis of laws and regulations, co-creation in law analysis, combining academic research with experiments in large-scale practice.

Track to which the paper is being submitted: Completed research; Legal compliance, knowledge rules, legal shaping and legal impact of innovative government services provision.

1   Introduction

Conditions under which the government must perform its duties are constantly changing due to changes in legislation. The effects of these changes are to be implemented in services to citizens and businesses quickly and effectively. Citizens and businesses may expect reliable and expedient rendering of services. Services that provide answers to their questions, or offer a solution to their specific needs.

In recent decades, much has changed under the influence of digitisation. These changes affect the processes of implementing bodies of government. Both the large-scale processes for handling cases of large groups of citizens, and processes for the

A. Kő and E. Francesconi (Eds.): EGOVIS 2014, LNCS 8650, pp. 163–172, 2014.
© Springer International Publishing Switzerland 2014

treatment of individual cases in complex situations are affected. Examples can be found in the area of benefit provision, granting of subsidies, licensing and taxation. Central government, provincial governments and municipalities strive, as much as possible, to process applications for licenses, benefits and the provision of other public services electronically.

Successive governments have been working on a response to this development. Among other things, this has resulted in a government-wide vision[1] of the provision of services to citizens and businesses. This vision is based on customer-driven public services in which there is a central focus on the requests of citizens and businesses. The implementing bodies are expected to design their processes and services in such a way that they can meet the needs and perspectives of their customers. In other words, efficacy is central. A prime challenge will be to offer the desired effective processing of customer requests in an affordable and efficient manner.

The effective and efficient handling of customer requests requires cooperation between different organisations. This helps diminish the meaning of the boundaries between layers of government and government organisations.

In order to play their part for and on behalf of citizens, it is necessary for the government organisations to design their processes and services in such a way that they can respond to changing conditions, changing customer demands and changes in cooperation with other organisations.

This paper is a report of the competed research of the requirements specification stage of a larger project. Academics and practitioners participating in a unique collaboration with various partner organizations including large public administrations, private parties and a university, joined together in what has become known as 'the Blue Chamber' initiative. The people contributing to this collaborative platform have joined effort to develop a protocol for analysis and modeling of sources of law in such way that their meaning becomes clear and unambiguous, i.e. the impact of regulations on concrete situations can be calculated and consequently serve as the formal requirements for supporting IT systems. We are not naïve about the fact that sources of law written in natural language and being the result of political deliberation processes may have intended and unintended ambiguity, vagueness and imprecision. Obviously multiple interpretations may be used to disambiguate these sources. In our approach we intend to being able to compare different interpretations in a clear and unbiased way, again by calculating the effects of these interpretations on actual or fictive cases.

The collaboration being knowledgeable about the last decades of research in communities such as the AI&Law community, the communities working on knowledge based systems, legal rule ML, SVBR etc., has decided not only to work on a solid method that can be applied in practice, but to also test it on concrete cases within the participating organizations, thus following a 'living lab' research approach. The clear advantage of this is the immediate feedback that we'll get while further developing our method, while the drawback is limited to not going as fast as the participants sometimes want us to go.

---

[1] Established Government-Wide Vision of Services (Vastgestelde Overheidsbrede Visie op Dienstverlening) kst-26643-182 – Official Publications (in Dutch).

This paper consequently has two faces. On one hand it reports on a unique collaboration between people working in the field of large-scale legal information systems, developing their method in an interesting living lab setting. On the other hand this paper reflects the results of a limited time frame that was used to develop just the basis for further development and as such this research result is still preliminary work: it marks the conclusion of the requirements specification stage. We believe however that sharing this with the reader might still be useful, both as a scientific result as well as a practice that might be useful in a pragmatic sense. As far as the scientific results we claim that at least we have come up with a good set of validated requirements for the method that we aim to develop and of which we hope to report in our next annual report.

2   Development and Requirements

In recent years, it has been the tendency for implementing bodies to refrain from concealing the rules in layers of IT systems, but to opt instead for an approach in which these rules are defined in such a way in IT systems that they can be more easily implemented and maintained. In legislation, the trend is to model information, rules and processes in an integrated fashion. This translation of legislation into integrated knowledge and process models is used as a specification for processes and IT systems. 'Rule-based or knowledge-based working', 'rule management', 'Knowledge as a Service' (KaaS) and 'agile implementation of legislation' are names that are used to describe this approach.

The approach aims to provide greater flexibility and agility in the implementation of new laws and/or regulations.

So far, however, there has not been proper support for the design of rule-based systems: the analysis and interpretation of legislation in a uniform and coherent manner. Such an approach is essential in order to achieve integrated information, rules and process models with which the desired flexibility and agility in the provision of information can be realized. The approach is therefore a prerequisite for the realization of a customer-oriented service and for securing collaboration between organisations (interoperability). The observations below from daily implementation practice illustrate the lack of a 'clear and coherent method of analysis for the interpretation of legislation by implementing bodies':

a. Translating legislation into customer-driven service and product requirements for the implementation of processes and applications is usually quite time-consuming.
b. The (contents of) services and processes is not sufficiently traceable to the legislation.
c. Up till now, the translation of legislation into service and product requirements has often proved to be a process difficult to control. The procedure is not clear and is in part implied and depends on the individual 'translator'. Analysis usually takes place from their own discipline (legal, implementation, information science or IT). The required expertise is in short supply.

d. Adequate support which allows for intelligent searching of the corpus of legislation is currently lacking and there is only limited support for adequately managing the results in conjunction.

3   Towards an Approach to an Agile Implementation of Legislation

In legislation rights and obligations are defined: among citizens, citizens towards the government and vice versa. Legislation contains concepts, rules and conditions that directly affect the actions of citizens, businesses and government organisations. These terms, rules and conditions form the basis for the services and processes of public implementing bodies. For the following reasons, it is important to be able to distill concepts, rules and conditions from the legislation in an unambiguous and repeatable manner:

A. It promotes legal certainty for citizens and prevents unnecessary disputes and proceedings in court.
B. It enhances the transparency of government. The government can show that what they are doing is in accordance with the democratically established legislation. This includes providing insight into the rules that give the authorities a margin of discretion to do justice in special cases.
C. It simplifies implementation of legislation in services and processes. Thus, orders from politics and public demands can be accommodated more rapidly.
D. It improves an implementing body's capacity to, as part of ex ante feasibility tests, to provide feedback on proposed changes in legislation. This contributes positively to the effectiveness and efficiency of the implementation.
E. It provides insight into the coherence of the complex of legislation. Consequently, generic and specific elements in processes and services can more easily be distinguished. This offers possibilities for reuse, not only within an organisation, but also between organisations.

In short, the added value of a repeatable approach to the organisation of the implementation of legislation comes from the ability to transform legislation into legitimate and meaningful services for citizens and businesses and to perform this in a truthful, efficient, multidisciplinary and timely fashion.

4   The Approach in a Nutshell

At the heart of the approach is that laws and regulations, as legislative source[2], are transformed in a traceable way in a concise number of well-defined steps

---

[2] Legislative sources: laws and regulations (formal law and subsequent subordinate regulations and policies), jurisprudence and doctrine.

(transformation by humans), into demands on the design of services. It is of paramount importance in this context that knowledge is properly managed and that the traceability from the requirements to the legislative source is supported. The knowledge that is already inherent in legislation is marked for sharing as a traceable source when going through the transformation process. This calls for ancillary methods and techniques.

Steps in the approach are:

Step 1:   Analysis of (changes in) legislation and implementation policies;
Step 2:   Analysis of the objectives of the implementing body and the organisational units involved;
Step 3:   Design of the products and services of the implementing body;
Step 4:   Design of standardized (data processing) activities;
Step 5:   Assign services to the departments.

See Fig. 1.

The approach was based on a careful analysis of legislation and implementation policies. Consequently, products and services are developed and unambiguous and precise requirements concerning the design of organisational units and applications are drawn up from a business perspective in the shape of functional descriptions.

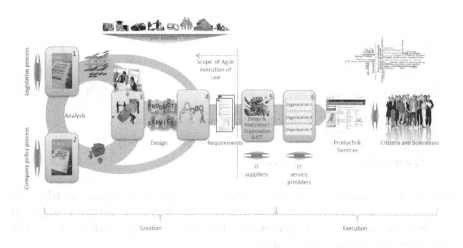

Fig. 1. Agile execution of law

5   Legal DNA

In formulating laws and regulations, the legislature will have concrete situations in the so-called 'harsh' reality in mind. The relevant aspects of reality are legally expressed in legislation, in the shape of goals, target groups and conditions.

Legislation is given further content in practical implementation, based on which services are performed for citizens and businesses. The goals, target groups and conditions in legislation are translated into products and services. In the protocol, at the core of the analysis of legislation is the identification of the legal DNA. This is depicted in Fig. 2.

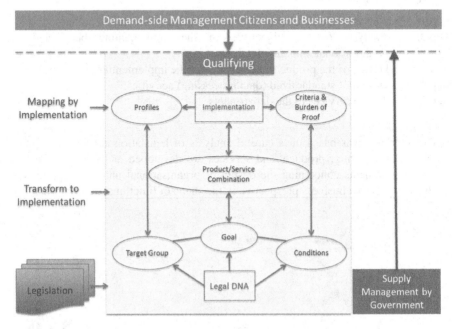

Fig. 2. From legislation towards implementation

6   Legal DNA: The Protocol

Legislation is written using natural language. Natural language is rife with ambiguities, which lends it – if left unadjusted – less well to the definition of precise and clear functional system requirements. This in contrast to a formal language[3] with an unambiguous syntax and semantics.

In addition, certain things are taken for granted in legislation and therefore left implicit. Furthermore, the legislator often chooses to describe the prescriptive content from the perspective of just one of the parties concerned.

In order to achieve uniform and verifiable requirements for the establishment of business units and service applications, analysis is needed which leads to the explicit formulation of implicit rules and transformation into unambiguous language.

---

[3] One symbol has just one single meaning.

In this context, 'Legal DNA' is used as a source. This concerns the legal information contained by legislation and forms the foundation for the combinations of goals, target groups and conditions

This 'Legal DNA' encodes the following:

1. The purpose of legislation;
2. The target group and the conditions that must be met in order to qualify for the target group;
3. The product to be delivered and/or the service to be provided and the conditions to be met to obtain them;
4. The procedural conditions which apply;
5. The authority to provide a service and/or product;
6. The concepts with which target group, goals and conditions are described;
7. The legal facts of which there must exist a clear comprehension.

In Fig. 3, the legal DNA of the aliens act is used as an example.

Upon mapping the legal DNA, a repeatable, multidisciplinary protocol is utilized.

Legal draughtsmen, implementation policy advisers and experts from the primary process collaborate with information and process engineers and architects in transforming legislation to specifications to be used by the organisation and IT. The steps as outlined in section 4 are followed in this process. For each step, the results are documented, making them reusable and ensuring that underlying interpretation or design decisions are always traceable.

Ideally, the protocol, which is extensively described in a further detailed description (soon to be released), would be applied to every kind of legislation: from formal law to policy guidelines, without distinguishing between new legislation and amendments to existing legislation. The protocol offers the opportunity to gain insight into the impact of new rules on the service implementation practice already during the development process. Thus, the approach contributes to the improvement of ex ante feasibility tests.

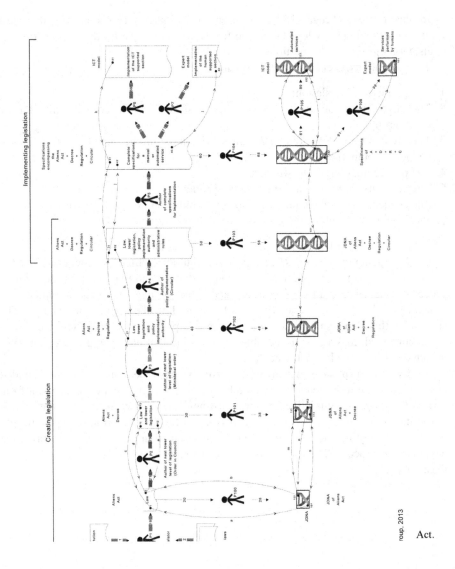

Fig. 3. The establishment of rule-based services – legal DNA of the Aliens Act

7   Summary

The 'Blue Chamber' group has made a first attempt to arrive at a well-founded, repeatable protocol for the systematic translation of legislation into implementation practice, by mapping of the legal DNA. Goals, target groups and conditions – among others – which are present in legislation, are made more manifest in the legal DNA. This constitutes the foundation for further elaboration into automated implementation of the analysed legislation on the one hand and human-oriented implementation on the other. By using the DNA as a source for implementation and incorporating changes to legislation into the DNA, a sustainable framework for the implementation of public services is created. In addition, the goal of a service is clearly indicated, as well as the target audience of the service and the conditions to be met by citizens or businesses to qualify for a specific service, or obligations to be satisfied, respectively.

Because goals, target groups and conditions are directly traceable to the legislation, the legitimacy of government action is ensured and as a consequence, the effort that is taken to keep these services in accordance with the legislation, diminishes.

The result of the generic and systematic transformation of legislation into services and products can be converted into automated implementation and administration or into specifications for the provision of information. Naturally, the aforementioned principle is taken into account: 'digital whenever possible, in person when needed'.

The method for making implementation frameworks using legal DNA and the applicable protocol, is being developed at the Dutch Tax and Customs Administration and the IND (Immigration and Naturalisation Service), in collaboration with science and business partners. The aim is to arrive at a scientifically supported and practically relevant method. Current expectation is that around the end of 2013 a preliminary version can be presented of the method and results of experimental application. The aim is to subsequently share the results at an applicable congress. Working towards this congress, we are quite willing to divulge the available intermediate results, such as processed documents, methods developed and the experiences gained thus far. The bibliography as enclosed below is an extract of the main sources that we used or developed during the course of the project.

The Blue Chamber invites other government organisations to take note of the results to date, and to join us in our mission to achieve a well-supported approach to the agile implementation of legislation.

Acknowledgments. The authors acknowledge the group effort of the Blue Chamber. They express their recognition to the other members for allowing them to focus mainly on the research and development efforts. However, without the guidance, practical testing and feedback from the other members of the Blue Chamber this paper would not exist. At present, the partners participating in the Blue Chamber are: the Dutch Tax and Customs Administration, the Immigration and Naturalisation Service, the Leibniz Center for Law of the University of Amsterdam, the PNA Group and Business KnowHow Services.

The participants of the respective organisations (using the order as listed above): Diederik Dulfer, Mariette Lokin, Peter Straatsma; Maarten Appunn, Christiane

Buschman, Robert van Doesburg, Theo Lodder, Jorke van der Pol, Rani Wierda; Tom van Engers; Hennie Bouwmeester, Bas van de Laar, Maurice Nijssen, Sjir Nijssen; Harrie van Houtum.

References

1. Algemene Zaken Aanwijzingen voor de regelgeving, Regeling van de Minister-President van 18 November 1992, Stcrt. 1992, 230, laatstelijk gewijzigd bij regeling van 1 April 2011, Stcrt. 2011, nr. 6602
2. Boer, A.: Legal Theory, Sources of Law, & the Semantic Web. Frontiers in Artificial Intelligence and Applications, vol. 195. IOS Press, Amsterdam (2009)
3. Cimiano, P., Pinto, H.S. (eds.): EKAW 2010. LNCS, vol. 6317. Springer, Heidelberg (2010)
4. Boer, A.W.F., Van Engers, T.M.: Legal Knowledge and Agility in Public Administration. Intelligent Systems in Accounting, Finance and Management 20(2), 67–88 (2013)
5. Corbin, A.: Legal Analysis and Terminology. Yale Law School (1919)
6. Corbin, A.: Jural Relations and Their Classification. Yale Law School (1921)
7. Crosby, A.W.: The Measure of Reality: Quantification and Western Society, 1250-1600, 245 p. Cambridge University Press (1997)
8. Van Engers, T.: Knowledge Management, The Role of Mental Models in Business Systems Design (2001)
9. Van Engers, T.M., Nijssen, S.: Bridging Social Reality with Rules. Paper Presented at IRIS (Internationals Rechts Informatik Symposion), Salzburg, to be published in Jusletter-IT (February 2014)
10. Van Engers, T.M., Nijssen, S.: Connecting People: Semantic-Conceptual Modeling for Laws and regulations. Paper Accepted for Presentation at and to be Included in the Proceedings of the IFIP EGOV 2014 Conference, to be held in Dublin, Ireland, September 1-4 (2014)
11. Hohfeld, W.N.: Fundamental Legal Conceptions as Applied in Judicial Reasoning, Cook, W.W. (ed.) (2010) ISBN-13: 978-1-58477-162-3
12. Nijssen, G.M.: A Framework for Discussion in ISO/TC97/SC5/WG3, 78.09/01 (1978)
13. Nijssen, G.: A Framework for Advanced Mass Storage Applications. In: Conference Medinfo, pp. 1–21, Tokyo (1980)
14. Nijssen, S., Valera, S.: An Architecture Ecosystem for the Whole Systems Perspective, Including System Dynamics, Based on Logic & Set Theory and Controlled Natural Languages, Working paper for the OMG Architecture Ecosystem SIG (2012)
15. Nyquist, C.: Teaching Wesley Hohfeld's Theory of Legal relations. Journal of Legal Education 52(1 and 2) (March/June 2002)

Breaking the Barriers of e-Participation: The Experience of Russian Digital Office Development

Samuil Gorelik[1], Vitaly Lyaper[1], Lyudmila Bershadskaya[1], and Francesco Buccafurri[2]

[1] ITMO University, St. Petersburg, Russia
{samgor46,bershadskaya.lyudmila}@gmail.com, vitaly@lyaper.com
[2] University of Reggio Calabria, Italy
bucca@unirc.it

Abstract. Digital signature is the key factor of e-government and e-participation processes, as it is the main security mechanism we have to use to implement the dematerialization process. The scope of digital signature is definitely not restricted to the e-government setting, existing a large number of contexts (like e-commerce, e-banking, etc.) where the need of strong authentication of people arises, so that digital signature may be a full solution ensuring both the identity of the user and the integrity of the digital document the user signs. On the other hand, open government and e-participation development is strongly connected to citizens' engagement in online services and connections through web portals. As a consequence, the authentication systems and its characteristics (such as simplicity, usability, security, etc.) are very important for the success of the digitalization process. Unfortunately, often registration procedures do not fully satisfy the above properties, thus introducing an obstacle to the diffusion of e-participation. For instance, this is the case of online services and e-participation portals in Russia.

In this paper, we deal with this problem, by referring to the Russian system as a case study, and by proposing a protocol of distant primary registration to solve the abovementioned drawbacks. Such useful experience could be exported to other cases in the sphere of electronic services development, to fully involve citizens in the electronic society.

Keywords: e-participation, digital signature, advanced digital signature, non qualified digital signature.

1   Introduction

Digital signature (D-signature) is the key issue of a number of innovative processes involving different components of the economic-social-administrative system. In particular, e-government activities should receive from D-signature a strong hint to enlarge significantly their action and their effectiveness. The scope of D-signature is definitely not restricted to the e-government setting, existing a large number of contexts (like e-commerce, e-banking, etc.) where the need of strong authentication of people arises, so that D-signature may be a full solution ensuring both the identity of the user and the integrity of the digital document the user signs.

A. Kő and E. Francesconi (Eds.): EGOVIS 2014, LNCS 8650, pp. 173–186, 2014.
© Springer International Publishing Switzerland 2014

On the other hand, open government and e-participation development is strongly connected to citizens' engagement in online services and connections through web portals. As in case of the initial registration of the signer at the Certification Authority, in case of qualified electronic signature, we can argue that every other (weak) type of e-signature must involve a registration phase, which is of course the most invasive step of the entire signature life-cycle. Thus, the registration phase of an e-signature protocol is definitely the most critical phase to analyze at design time, to guarantee a good level of usability. As a matter of fact, the authentication systems and its characteristics (such as simplicity, usability, security, etc.) are crucial for the success of the digitalization process. And strong authentication should require the use of e-signatures, even weaker than qualified D-signature. Indeed, in case of electronic interactions like C2C, C2B, B2C, it is necessary to evaluate risks for the sides participating in interaction and to select technological decisions that provide legality and "reasonable" protection of interests of participants. "Reasonableness" is defined as a situation which doesn't exclude some security incident, but provides acceptable level of the cost on creation of threat protection technology.

Unfortunately, often registration procedures do not fully satisfy the above properties, thus introducing an obstacle to the diffusion of e-participation. For instance, this is the case of online services and e-participation portals in Russia.

In this paper, we deal with this problem, by referring to the Russian system as a case study, and by proposing a protocol of remote primary registration to solve the abovementioned drawbacks. Such useful experience could be exported to other cases in the sphere of electronic services development, to fully involve citizens in the electronic society. As a further contribution, specifics of using of not qualified D-signature in electronic interactions such as C2C and C2B (except for financial systems where a special legislation exist) from legal and technical points of view are discussed. The special emphasis is placed on the organization of systems of remote primary registration.

As a first step, we analyze the notion of non-qualified electronic signature mainly from a legal point of view, by referring to the European legal system, by choosing in particular the Italian experience that implement the European notion of advanced electronic signature, just to overcome the limits of full digital signature in terms of usability and expensiveness.

The structure of the paper is the following: Section 2 consists of information about technologies used to define e-signatures protocols, in Section 3 the case of Italian non-qualified electronic signature, then in Section 4 the Russian experience of digital office implementation is described in detail, Section 5 includes some practical issues for future research, Section 6 summarizes authors' results.

2   Background and Literature Review on E-signature

The prominent technology used to define protocols of e-signature is based on both asymmetric cryptographic techniques and, possibly, the usage of a secure external device (like a smart card or an USB token) for the generation process. The first step of the signature generation process is the computation, on the document to sign, of a cryptographic hash function, like SHA-256 or RIPEMD-160. The result is called digest (typically 256 bits wide) of the document. The properties of the hash function guarantee that the digest can substitute the original document in the signature generation process since the probability of having two distinct documents producing the same digest is negligible. Consequently, the problem of finding a document colliding on a digest of another distinct document is unfeasible, so that an attacker cannot corrupt a signed document without the signature detects it. The digest is computed on the PC by the signature software (typically supplied by the certification authority) and sent to the smart card embedding the private key of an asymmetric cryptographic cipher, typically RSA. The smart card is then enabled by the user (typically by inserting a secret PIN) to encrypt the digest by RSA with the private key, thus producing the digital signature. It is finally sent by the smart card to the signature software running on the PC in order to produce the cryptographic message (typically in PKCS#7 [1] format). The robustness of RSA (used with enough large keys, typically 1024 bits) and the security used to manage the private key, allow us to give the so-obtained digital signature the power of non-repudiable proof of both the identity (guaranteed by a public-key X.509 certificate granted by a trusted certification authority - included into the PKCS#7 message) of the provenance of the signed document and the statement of what the document itself represents. PKCS#7 is a standard defined by RSA describing a general syntax for data that may have cryptography applied to it, such as digital signatures and digital envelopes. PKCS#7 and X.509 guarantee the interoperability of software for verifying signed documents. Indeed, the verification of a document D is done by (1) re-computing the digest I of the document D using the same hash function as exploited in the signature generation process (this information is included in the PKCS#7 message), (2) computing J as the result of the decryption of the signature F done by means of the same algorithm as the generation step (as indicated in the PKCS#7 message) with the public key of the subscriber (included in the X.509 certificate, which is another component of the PKCS#7 message), and (3) checking that the decrypted digest J coincides with the computed digest I. Clearly, the complete verification has to check both validity, trustworthiness and non-revocation of the certificate, but we do not focus on this step since it is not involved in the attack here presented.

PKCS#7 is a standard defined by RSA describing a general syntax for data to which cryptography may be applied, such as digital signatures and digital envelopes. PKCS#7 supports several different content types: data, signed data, enveloped data, signed-and-enveloped data, digested data, and encrypted data.

- The data content type represents a sequence of bytes.
- The encrypted-data content type consists of encrypted content of any type.
- The digested-data content type consists of content of any type and a message digest of the content.
- The signed-data content type consists of content of any type and encrypted message digests of the content for zero or more signers and it is used to represent digital signatures.

• The enveloped-data content type is intended to represent digital envelopes, combining encrypted data sent to one or more recipients and the information (the content-encryption keys) needed by each recipient in order to decrypt the content.

• Finally, the signed-and-enveloped-data content type represents digital envelopes providing data with "double encryption", i.e., an encryption with a signer's private key followed by an encryption with the content-encryption key.

Any of the content types defined in PKCS#7 can be enveloped for any number of recipients and signed by any number of signers in parallel.

The signed-data content type is intended to be used for digital signatures, and it constitutes the basis upon the cryptographic message is built. Such a content type consists of (i) a given content of any of the types defined in PKCS#7 and, for each signer, (ii) both an encrypted message digest of the content (i.e., of the document) representing the signer's digital signature on the content, and (iii) other signer-specific information (concerning, for example, certificates and certificate-revocation lists). Additional information can be signed in order to authenticate attributes other than the content, such as the signing time.

Besides PKCS#7, other formats for encoding the cryptographic message have been proposed to improve some particular aspect such as security, interoperability, etc. These formats are CMS, CAdES, XAdES and PDF signatures.

The Cryptographic Message Syntax (CMS) has been developed by IETF [2] on the basis of PKCS#7 to protect data by encapsulation. The syntax supports digital signatures and encryption, allowing nested encapsulation of digital envelopes, arbitrary attributes to be signed along with the message content (e.g., the signing time), and further attributes to be associated with a signature such as countersignatures.

The CMS Advanced Electronic Signatures CAdES [3] derives from both CMS and Enhanced Security Services for S/MIME (ESS) [4], where additional signed and un-signed attributes have been defined to describe information such as the MIME type of the data to be signed (by means of the Content-type attribute), the signing time, etc.

XML Advanced Electronic Signatures (XAdES) [5] is based on CAdES, but it uses the syntax of XML. XAdES provides the DataObjectFormat element to describe the encoding format of the signed data.

Finally, Adobe has introduced a proprietary format for digital signatures to be embedded in PDF documents [6], in such a way that the PDF format behaves as a container for both the PDF document to be signed and the information required by digital signatures, i.e., the user's certificate, the encrypted digest (both DSA [7]. and RSA are supported), etc. Besides the document, other data can be signed such as a time stamp obtained from a trusted server, a graphic signature and other information describing the user, the system and the software application. This kind of signature has some strong advantage in terms of resistance to ambiguous-presentation attacks [8].

3   The Italian Non-Qualified Electronic Signature

The Italian legal system has recently introduced a form of lightweight signature, called advanced electronic signature, with strong legal validity (under certain conditions) making this signature equivalent to handwritten signature.

The advanced electronic signature is defined by art. 1 , paragraph 1, lett . q -bis) of Legislative Decree 7 March 2005 n . 82 (the Digital Administration Code). It consists in "the set of data in electronic form attached to or associated with an electronic document that allow the identification of the signer of the document and provide the unique connection to the signer, created using means that the signer can maintain under exclusive control, connected to data to which that sign relates, such that they allow us to detect whether the data have been subsequently modified." The advanced electronic signature is a signature stronger than the simple electronic signature as defined by art. 1 , paragraph 1, lett . q of the Digital Administration Code. Indeed, (1) it allows the identification of the signer and the unique connection of her/him to the signed document, (2) such a connection is created using means that the signatory can maintain under her/his exclusive control, and (3) it allows us to detect if the data has been modified after the advanced electronic signature is applied.

Article . 21 , paragraph 2, of the Digital Administration Code provides that "the electronic document signed with an advanced E-signature, in compliance with technical rules able to ensure the identifiability of the author , the integrity and immutability of the document, is a complete legal proof of authenticity and integrity of the signed document, as established by the Civil Code. Therefore, the document signed by an advanced E-signature has legal value substantially equal to the qualified D-signature, provided that it has been generated and applied in accordance with the technical requirements of the Decree of the President of the Council of Ministers of February 22, 2013.

The advanced electronic signature is technology-neutral, so that it does not refer to the any technology. The most prevalent advanced electronic signature is the signature on the tablet, said also dynamic or graphometric signature. It is generated by using a particular tablet with a special pen and is suitable to store some biometric characteristics related to the handwritten signature such as speed of signing, pressure, acceleration. Obviously, the pure graphometric signature is not able to guarantee the required property of connection of the signature with the document. Thus, additional security measure appears necessary, even though a number of questionable commercial solutions exist without such additional mechanisms.

From a normative point of view the Italian definition of advanced E-signature corresponds exactly to the definition included in the EU Directive 93/1999. The inclusion into the Italian legal system of this type of E-signature was considered very important as it allows us to configure a variety of technical solutions, without coming to set up a proper qualified digital signature (i.e., based on a qualified certificate). However, it makes available to the user (and between citizens and the Public Sector) signature tools with a good level of security and reliability, which are presented as tools to simplify and thus encourage the use of new technologies and favoring e-participation.

4   Russian Digital Office Implementation

From the legal point of view, in Russia, the "reinforced" non-qualified digital signature can be used in case of electronic deals according to Federal "law" of April 6, 2011 N 63-FZ "About a digital signature". In addition to a digital signature the legislation allows us to use other tools analogs of the autographic signature. For example bank cards or electronic IDs.

The services classification based on information security risks and level of authentication appropriate to that risks is the following:

- Information services – such as requests for any information (document forms requests, institutions working hours requests etc.). This kind of services operates public accessible information, so they do not carry risks of any kind. Hence no authentication required.

- Non-personally-identifying services – services that operate non-personally-identifying data (public e-mail services, social-networks etc.). This kind of services operate information that is considered by user to be public, so there is no need to specially protect it, and it's compromising do not carry sufficient risks – information is already public. But in some cases losing this information may be personally harmful for user – it is sometimes hard to move to alternative e-mail account for example, since all your contacts familiar with old one. Hence this kind of services require basic authentication to protect user from regular threats – password authentication is acceptable.

- Services operating personal data – such as e-invoicing, e-billing, post-paid e-commerce. This kind of services carry user personal data compromising risk – personal data may be disclosed to trespasser and further used for some criminal activities (taking fake credits, registering fake organizations etc.). User personal data must be protected, especially because this is presumed by international and Russian Law. Due to the fact, the type of services require stronger authentication – for example two-factor authentication scheme. It is sufficient to take into account that for services of this group it is hard to estimate total loss of information security risks because that risks may rise indirectly.

- Services with direct information security risks – services that have direct financial risks if some user information is compromised: e-banking, e-commerce, e-government etc. For example in e-banking Russian Law sets the limit for daily operations of 400000 rubles (about 10k $) – this is sufficient amount of money to be lost in case of user account is compromised. For that kind of services strong authentication is not enough – more complicated measures must be taken to avoid fraud activities. Common practice is to strengthen authentication with transaction authorization and Location-Based-Services (LBS). For example user want to transfer some amount of money using e-banking service – he is already authenticated with his password and OTP via SMS to his cellphone from some place: next step is to validate his cellphone location, and if it is different from place where he started transaction, this is signal to take some additional activities to validate user transaction, make a call to him or put transaction on hold.

4.1   Digital Office Concept

In case of electronic interaction with involvement of individuals (C2C and C2B) it is necessary to provide remote primary registration. For this purpose, it is possible to use different protocols. The choice of the most suitable one is defined by the specifics of the application.

For example the participant has been logged by other certified systems. In this case authentication of the user is made on attributes of the bank account from which the user transferred money to the broker score. After that all functions of his account are available [9].

The use of the procedure of remote registration allowed us to raise significantly a flow of clients due to starting operations without the preliminary visit to the broker office. For the primary registration of partners of C2C "the digital office" (see Fig. 1), which will check registration data of participants, has to be created as an independent entity.

In C2B and B2C systems the primary registration executes by the business partner or like in C2C systems by independent "digital office".

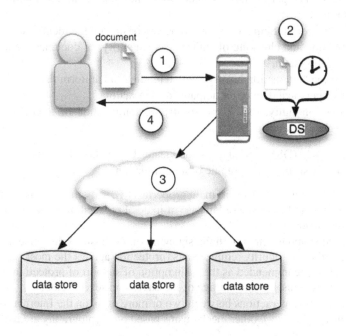

Fig. 1. Digital office in the Internet

1. Sending the document via the Internet to the site, where the DS (digital stamp) will be calculated.
2. Creation of the DS of the document (time of receiving and name of the sender);
3. Placement of copies of the DS in an independent data store
4. Transmission to the user of the copy of the DS.

The "Digital office" is the WEB TOOL to support of express document registration and transactions, created on the basis of the modern info-communication technologies and mathematical procedures according to the legislation of the Russian Federation [10,11].

In Digital office, it is carried out:

- Registration of the text, audio, video and other digital documents (time of registration, authors, authenticity);
- Setting the authorship and of the registration moment, of authenticity of documents and signatures on requests;
- Long-time storage of the registered documents;
- The issuing of notarial certificates and copies for administrative or judicial proceedings;
- Storage of the documents at the request of users with open access.

The operations provided at digital office are:

- Authentication of participants of interaction (individuals and legal entities) in case of registration,
- Authorization of participants in case of access basing on the identifier,
- Authentication and checking of authenticity (integrity) of documents and messages circulating in system,
- Storing of the "interaction history" with a binding to "uniform time",
- Security of personal data of participants of interactions,
- Interaction continuity, that is, possibility of continuation of interactions even in case of technical faults.

The digital stamp (DS) is used to authenticate documents. As usually, it is implemented on the basis of cryptographic hashing function.

- The digital stamp possesses all main properties to certify the document. Therefore it will be able to be considered in case of judicial proceedings (a warranty of the legal significance).
- The digital stamp together with the signature on the basis of the personal identifier provides all main security requirements (protection against the most security threats). It is recommended as the main option of support of protection of integrity in case of transmission and storage of messages and service data.
- In case of other interactions between two or more users on the Internet (electronic payments, ballot, etc.), other mechanisms based on cryptography are used.

The digital office is used during primary registration of participants and registration of each transaction between participants.

4.2 Primary Registration Procedure

Primary registration is aimed at associating the real identity of an individual to his digital identity, identified by an ID. Biometric data are: recognizable image of the person, prints of a hand or fingers, the genetic code, etc., which can be used for authentication in case of civil administrative or judicial processes.

After primary registration, the individual accepts the identifier which will be used in electronic interactions. Users conditions are contained in the agreement which is accepted by participants of interactions. This agreement is compliant to the requirements of the Legislation, otherwise, it can be recognized as negligibility in judicial or administrative processes in which it will be demanded. Identifier can be used for all the following operations where the registered participants take part.

Individuals, as a rule, are participants of different legally significant interactions outside the relations in which they are going to participate. Absence of legal restrictions allows us to implement possibility of distant primary registration without corporal appearance of the natural person in special office. For this purpose, there shall be an opportunity based on certain technological actions with sufficient reliability to identify the personality of the registered participant.

Technological process of electronic interaction shall be such that it was possible to provide evidential requirements of the Legislation for observance of the state interests and protection of interests of participants.

If primary registration is carried out in case of a corporal appearance of the user, after receiving the identifier he gets access to all regulated services.

In case of remote registration, the user can get access only to those services in which the risk of big losses lies on the user. User gets access to remaining services after procedure of additional check. This procedure is based on authentication of the identity of the user while he participates in legally significant procedure (judicial or administrative) or after a confirmation of his identity through payment banking systems.

To register the legal data of the users (clients of exchange transactions and payment services) all user keys, numbers of his cards, etc. bind to his passport data. The personal mobile phone is accepted as the main identifier. That is why the phone number of the user has to be registered before. By the next step the phone number and additional identifiers, in particular, a plastic ID-card, register together.

In practice, without restrictions, the system of remote registration can be used only for those services where:

— all risks, including financial and legal ones, from provision of a priori false information, lay down on the user of the service;
— responsibility of the user who gave a priori false data is included in the contract signed by participants of interaction.

This protocol is inapplicable for the systems supposing risk only from one of the sides. For example, when this side emits the cash or SIM cards. In this case, additional activation of received identifier is used when the first appeal to receive money or to buy the goods by means of a card.

The above mentioned protocol can be successfully used in case of the inference of contracts of insurance, or on exchange broker services, and also in the case in which the client, due to provision of unreliable information, risks at least to leave money.

Technology and devices are used participants selected in agreement to each other and pointed them out in the framework agreement signed by them.

The selection of devices has been done to satisfy to requirements of security, of integrity and reliability of transferred documents so that in case of judicial or administrative proceedings they couldn't be in doubt.

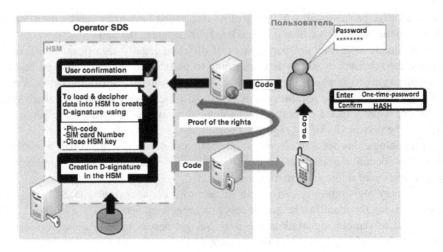

Fig. 2. Implementation of a digital signature on server side (SDS-technology)

Usability and user expenses are important factors in case of a choice of technical means. That is why it is necessary to take in consideration wide popularity of mobile communicators and pads (coming instead of personal computers) and use of cloudy technologies as more compatible.

In the selected solution the means of a D-signature are set on server side, instead of the tokens and smart cards. Such concept (let's name it SDS) of a D-signature is suitable for use in cloudy platforms and with any mobile communicator or a pad.

The SDS-technology is based on several basic principles (fig. 2).

— the key of a D-signature is stored on a remote server with use of special hardware to give access to a key only to the user to which this key belongs;
— the key never leaves the protected server in open form, all operations with key are executed in the hardware module and in the secure memory. Only the result of cryptography conversion with key can be used outside;
— access to a key is given only after authentication of the user. Authentication is based on the multiple-factor diagram with use of robust authentication mechanisms;
— each operation with a key is confirmed by the user;
— documents transmission for the signature and its confirmation are made via independent communication links.

4.3   Authentication

Authentication of documents and messages is needed to check their integrity (authenticity). It allows us to find with a high level of reliability against any random or premeditated changes in them.

Special case is authentication of the author(s) of the message. If in the message the user name (or the author) is not entered, there is a task of its determination (the task of identification of users).

It is necessary to accurately separate tasks of monitoring of authenticity (integrity) of an information message and authorship establishment from the encoding task. The last task is the most widespread in a discussed problem of providing access restriction to contents of the message (confidentiality of information).

Confidentiality support is the separate problem which is solved by well-known cryptography methods. The procedure of authentication can be applied to the ciphered and open document, depending on the rules of its use which is defined by the author (user) of the document.

Authentication of the author (user) of the document can be solved as cryptography methods (for example, on the basis of digital signature), and the methods used in control and management systems for access, by means of identifiers on the basis of logins and passwords. Both of these opportunities are used in the real-life operation.

The first of them, for a number of reasons, is recommended for legal entities (especially, for government structures). The second one is recommended for private entities. The technological decision is based on login restriction through a private digital office by means of the personal identifier.

When using the second option (without encoding), the problem of authentication of the message is solved by using so-called key-free resistant hash function (GOST 34.10-2012). The hashing function representing some numerical sequence, in this case, according to "the principle of analogy" (compliances), is considered as the analog of the "stamp" in paper documents. This option conforms to requirements of the new law about digital signature.

4.4   Extracts

Technological advantages of the above discussed conception (D-signature is executed on the server side) of non qualified digital signature (SDS) (for example, it is not needed to remember a large number of passwords and to have several hardware carriers) do this conception attractive for users. The decreasing of requiring to resources and getting new technological options is also positive for users, in particular:

— for average users – there is no need to buy expensive tokens and a software for them,   life time of the virtual token practically isn't limited, it is possible to use mobile phones and pads to receive   the digitally signed documents which conform to requirements of the legislation and the signature under them could be checked by standard means;
— for Business – SDS is an opportunity not to service own technology of a digital signature, but to get access to it on the basis of outsourcing. Today, to provide the staff of the organization DS, it is necessary to set additional software, to create instructions of use of DS, to care for life cycle of tokens and smart cards. In case of the SES, all these actions aren't necessary, the organization receives "turnkey" service from the outdoor supplier. Thus, it is possible to lower capital expenditure for

use of a digital signature inside the organization with full save of all opportunities which are given by DS use;

— for the State – the most important advantage of using SDS is opportunity to make much more wide the audience of users   (by attracting the 70 million Internet   and 150 million SIM cards users) to the G2C&C2G-communications where non qualified DS is enough.

SDS gives new options of use:

- in e-mail systems it's very popular now working with the thin client through a web browser where use of traditional means of DS is complicated.
- in new generations of e-mail where the client application is not used and the users watch the mail in a browser window, traditional means of support of integrity and confidentiality of messages, such as S-MIME, become not actual.   To build the means of ensuring of integrity and confidentiality in the server application the use of SDS   is prospectively .
- for electronic payment systems non qualified SDS can significantly simplify interaction of the client and service provider. The Client will be able to sign remotely contracts, to make the payments requiring his authentication, to receive different extracts and financial documents. Thus, the organization using such way of interaction with the client, already starts saving money only because instead of paper transactions cheaper electronic are used;
- for state electronic services where the number of users is commensurable with population of the country. It is possible to provide such number of users with means of DS without essential investments only using SDS when the cost of client part is minimum, and access of users to DS is most simplified.

5   Discussion

The study and practical case lead us to the following question:

1. How is the user key protected in the SDS technology?

In the technology of SDS the user can't influence safety of a key on the server. The information security is provided by Hard-ware Security Module (HSM). For example, a mobile communicator is used. All operations with keys of users in HSM are separated according to users ID. Thus, it is guaranteed that the user will get access only to his own key. Before use of the key the user shall be authenticated and only after that he will be able to get access to the corresponding functions. Keys of the user never leave HSM limits. Even loading of keys from outside isn't made, but keys are generated directly in HSM. Thus it is guaranteed that they will be never compromised.

2. The key is in the above discussed conception on server side. The token always with itself. Is it really safe system?

Signing key storage by the user has risks. In the contract signed during the procedure of the primary registration the transmission of the token to the third parties is a zone of responsibility of the user and is considered as the power of attorney for the next operations. In case of SDS the key is always in HSM (as the stamp in the safe), and access to it is guaranteed by well protected means received in case of primary identification and authentication. In case of loss of HSM procedure of the emergency lock is provided.

3. How is it guaranteed that only the user will be able to use the key?

To use the key, the user should become authorized by means of the identifier (for example, a mobile communicator). In SDS system each transaction is confirmed by means of the one-time password told to the user through the SMS that provides the additional operating control of use of a key.

6   Conclusion

The discussed approach to non qualified SDS has been used in different commercial and financial systems (the electronic exchange broker: www.dohod.ru (about 3400 users), electronic payment systems "Mobile card": http://card.ruru.ru/ (about 150 000 users) and "Money-Money": www.moneyps.ru (about 2 billion users). The positive result gives us possibility to recommend the solution as reliable, cheap and with high user ability for other applications.

Acknowledgements. This work was partially financially supported by Government of Russian Federation, Grant 074-U01.

This work was partially financially supported by research work №414648 "Development of monitoring system for socio-cultural processes in cyberspace".

This work has been partially supported by the Program "Programma Operativo Nazionale Ricerca e Competitivita'" 2007-2013, Distretto Tecnologico CyberSecurity funded by the Italian Ministry of Education, University and Research.

References

1. Kaliski, B.: PKCS# 7: Cryptographic Message Syntax Version 1.5. Lee, B., Kim, K.: Fair exchange of digital signatures using conditional signature. In: Symposium on Cryptography and Information Security, pp. 179–184 (1998)
2. Housley, R.: Cryptographic message syntax. RFC5652 (1999)
3. Pinkas, D., Pope, N., Ross, J.: CMS Advanced Electronic Signatures (CAdES). IETF Request for Comments, 5126 (2008)
4. Hoffman, P.: Enhanced Security Services for S/MIME. IETF RFC 2634 (1999)
5. Advanced Electronic Signatures (XAdES). ETSI TS, 101, 933 (1999)
6. Taft, E., Pravetz, J., Zilles, S., Masinter, L.: The application/pdf Media Type. Internet Proposed Standard RFC, 3778 (2004)

7. Locke, G., Gallagher, P.: FIPS PUB 186-3: Digital Signature Standard (DSS). Federal Information Processing Standards Publication (2009)

8. Buccafurri, F., Caminiti, G., Lax, G.: Fortifying the dalì attack on digital signature. In: SIN 2009, pp. 278–287 (2009)

9. Gorelik, S., Lyaper, V.: Technical Approaches for Relevant in Law Electronic Communications in Cloud Services. Information Systems for Research, 274-279 (2012)

10. Gorelik, S.: System of distant rapid documents registration. Patent's registration (May 14, 2012)

11. Gorelik, S., Lyaper, V.: Electronic Registration in Information and Communication Services with Personification. In: Proceeding of Joint Conference "Internet and Modern Society", IMA 2013 (2013)

Model of Digital Mediation to Support Communication between Teachers Unions and the Education Community

Artur Afonso Sousa[1], Pedro Agante[2], Carlos Quental[1], and Luís Borges Gouveia[3]

[1] Polytechnic Institute of Viseu, Viseu, Portugal
{ajas,quental}@di.estv.ipv.pt
[2] Libertrium, Viseu, Portugal
pedroagante@libertrium.com
[3] University Fernando Pessoa, Porto, Portugal
lmbg@ufp.edu.pt

Abstract. In the context of Portuguese teachers unions, the adoption of information and communication technologies is nowadays a reality. However, in our opinion, their internet portals still lack interaction, participation, and collaboration, as they are mostly concentrated on unidirectional information dissemination between union representatives and other education stakeholders. This paper aims at presenting a proposal of digital mediation based on a conceptual model and the corresponding proof of concept - a Web application - to support communication between teachers unions and other stakeholders. We strongly believe that this proposal can enrich web portals of teachers unions with innovative features and, as a result, contribute to strengthen the relationship between unions and the education community and to foster participation among all stakeholders in the education process. This paper also addresses an initiative carried out by the teachers union of the Centre region of Portugal, where the proposed platform was used to create sporadic participation events supporting bidirectional asynchronous communication.

Keywords: Conceptual modelling, Teachers unions, Digital mediation, Liberopinion, e-participation.

1 Introduction

Information and communication technologies (ICTs) have enabled creation of the so called 'electronic' dimension, resulting in paradigm shifts of already existing notions related to business, governance and education. In this context, the way people interact, participate and collaborate in the modern society was drastically modified. Uses of the Internet are becoming relatively more interactive and user-oriented. The Web 2.0 and more recently the rise of Social Media have not only created new playing fields for communication and self-expression but also new forms of social behavior. A key factor of both Web 2.0 and Social Media is participation.

Trade unions recognized the potential of ICTs too late and when they decided to adopt them, they limited their application to the storage, processing, and dissemination

A. Kő and E. Francesconi (Eds.): EGOVIS 2014, LNCS 8650, pp. 187–200, 2014.
© Springer International Publishing Switzerland 2014

of information through the Internet [1, 2]. In the Portuguese case, the major obstacle to their implementation lies essentially within the organizations either because of the required skills or, most importantly, because of the changes that they induce [3]. Recent studies show a predominance of one-way communication in most Portuguese trade unions websites [4, 5]. According to Quental and Gouveia the potential of ICTs in teacher unions will only be effective if the investment is framed within a strengthening strategy of the organization which implies the promotion of inclusion, participation and transparency [6].

From the observation of user participation in Portuguese teachers unions websites we realized that, in most cases, it is reduced to sending e-mails or to fill in contact forms, demonstrating lack of higher level e-participation initiatives. Moreover, when we analyzed the type of communication between unions and the education stakeholders, we also verified, as illustrated in Figure 1, that it is mostly concentrated in using unidirectional communication. These findings are aligned with the bibliographic research outcomes.

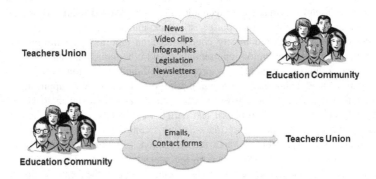

Fig. 1. Unidirectional communication between teachers unions and the education community

Hence, as a result of these findings, a preliminary important research question emerged: How to strengthen the relationship between teachers unions and the education community, and foster participation among all stakeholders in the education process, through digital mediation? Note that, in this paper, we adopt the definition of digital mediation proposed by Manuel Castells as the computer-mediated communication [7].

In order to address this question, we believe that it would be useful and desirable to develop a technological solution that promotes participation and structured and multidirectional (synchronous and asynchronous) communication between teachers union, its associated members and other education stakeholders, in a single, neutral and regulated place.

Such solution would take the form of an e-participation tool and take into account the requirements and needs of these actors. On the one hand it would enable teachers to become clarified on the most important education questions and problems and, on the other hand, enable unions to be aware of ideas and main concerns in different topics by the education community (e.g. teachers, students, fathers and enterprise representatives).

As a result, we propose a Web application, *Liberopinion*, designed to gather the main education stakeholders in a shared deliberative space. With this application it is intended to foster participation, narrow the identified communication gap and strengthen the relationship between these key actors.

The methodology used throughout this work was action research. In recent years, action research has become increasingly popular as a research method [8]. The following are some key features of action research, frequently described in literature [9, 10, 11]: it is appropriate for solving problems of a practical nature; it is suitable for implementing innovative initiatives; it promotes improvements through change; it is collaborative, that is, it provides possibilities of co-operative working; it uses a four stage cyclic self-reflection spiral process (planning, action, observation, reflection).

The research and development project outlined in this paper also presents some of these features: innovative, mostly practical in nature, in which change management had a leading role and where the demand for continuous improvement was a main priority. Therefore, these characteristics made action research an appropriate methodology for this project.

In this work we adopted a cyclical model of action research, based on the model proposed by Zuber-Skerritt [12], which consists of four stages: plan, act, observe and reflect. Move to a new cycle of the action research, which means re-planning, acting, observing and thinking, and so on. However, it is important to highlight the fact that the four stages were not completely independent and sequential. It was implemented an iterative process in which the phases sometimes overlapped, depending on the learning provided through experience and continuous reflection. Four cycles of action research were implemented in this project.

This paper is structured as follows: In section 2 a communication model for teachers unions Web portals is proposed. Section 3 describes the proof of concept of the model – a Web application. In Section 4 is addressed an initiative carried out by the teachers union of the Centre region of Portugal (in Portuguese SPRC – Sindicato dos Professores da Região Centro), where the proposed platform was used. Section 5 contains the conclusions and some topics for future research and development.

2   Communication Model for Teachers Unions Websites

Conceptual modeling is the activity of formally describing some aspects of the physical and social world for understanding and communication purposes [13]. It is an abstract representation of reality, highlighting the most important aspects in a specific context or under a particular viewpoint.

The first construction phase of the proposed model focused on the identification of key stakeholders and their roles in the education process. Thus, as a result of the research on teachers unions websites and the feedback gathered from personalities with expertise in this field, we considered the following actors for a communication model for teachers unions Web portals: teachers, teacher union and enterprise representatives, politicians, student and parent representatives.

Teachers are associated (and non-associated) members of the teachers union. Politicians, as decision makers, are also natural stakeholders. Student representatives include elected people by students (e. g. presidents of student and academic associations, leaders of student and academic federations, among others). Parent representatives are understood as people elected by students' parents. Examples include the parents associations at national, local and school level. Teacher union representatives are employees of the union that incorporates the (*Liberopinion*) participation Web platform. They can be, for example, directors, public relations, jurists, among others. Enterprise representatives encompass, for instance, elected members of national association of enterprises, entrepreneur and industry associations, among others. Figure 2 illustrates the proposed communication model for teachers unions websites.

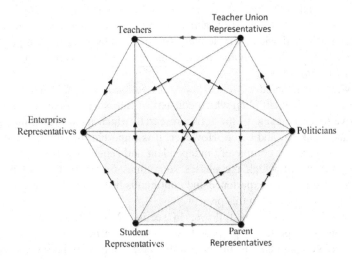

Fig. 2. Communication model for teachers unions websites

The arrows stand for the open channels of multidirectional communication between key actors. In the model above, technology is not explicitly depicted, since it is considered that the digital dimension is implicitly part of the model. Note that a Web application was implemented based on the proposed model.

Similarly, the editor is not explicitly represented, since, as well as technology, it is inherent to the model. It is a neutral element, whose main functions are to create, manage, boost and moderate the participation events, according to the terms of usage and to ensure the users management.

This role can be played by a team or by a single person that belongs to the staff of the teachers union which incorporates the *Liberopinion* platform in its web portal. What matters is that the editor has absolute neutrality and behaves as an authentic information curator of the participation platform [14].

3   Proof of Concept – The *Liberopinion* Platform

Liberopinion was designed and developed, based on the proposed model, to allow, through multiple participation events, a structured, mediated and multidirectional communication between all stakeholders. *Liberopinion* can be easily integrated (embed) into any teachers union website. Then it can be used as a participation area (of the site) that is continuously available. Alternatively, *Liberopinion* can be used as a separate tool to create sporadic participation events that can then be easily incorporated into the teachers union portal. Note that, this alternative way requires less editorial effort, since is not necessary to boost participation events 24 hours a day, 7 days a week, and 365 days a year.

In Figure 3 a simplified UML (Unified Modelling Language) class diagram is presented showing the actors, their roles and the different kinds of participation events which can be carried out on the *Liberopinion* platform.

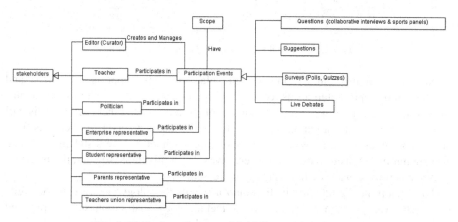

Fig. 3. UML class diagram of the *Liberopinion* platform

Succinctly, enterprises, students, parents and teachers union representatives, politicians, and teachers participate in events, which are created, managed, boosted and moderated by the editor (curator) of the platform. The participation events may consist of four different types, namely: (1) questions from the users and corresponding answers from the recipient; (2) suggestions and ideas from the user community; (3) surveys and (4) live debates.

The application is organized into five major areas: a personal user area and one area for each type of participation event. The management of users, editorial content, participation events and their moderation is made by the editor of the platform in a dedicated area, the back office. Next, in Figure 4, the main functional areas of the *Liberopinion* platform are presented.

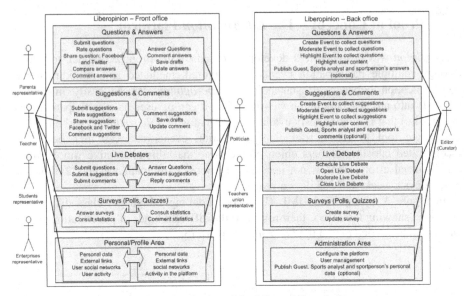

Fig. 4. Functional areas of the *Liberopinion* platform

Note that, in this initial approach, the platform only supports politicians and teachers union representatives as receivers of the remaining stakeholders submissions. However, in the future, we aim to assign the role of receiver to others actors. This will allow, for instance, for a parent representative to be also a receiver of questions from union representatives. Likewise, in this scenario, teachers or others stakeholders can also submit questions to parents representatives. With this improvement, the potential communication scenarios will be greatly increased.

To develop the digital participation platform, a methodology considering the Agile Manifesto was adopted [15], that is, a methodology that emphasizes rapid and continuous software development, embraces change, even in a late stage of the development cycle and that promotes teamwork [16].

In the following sections, the functional areas of the *Liberopinion* platform are described in more detail.

3.1   Questions from the User Community

The main purpose of this area is to conduct online collaborative interviews and discussion panels. If the context is an interview, in a first step, the editor of the platform challenges users to submit questions about a hot topic. Note that when creating a new event to collect questions, the editor defines whether the questions have an underlying theme or, on the contrary, have an open scope. The questions are then voted by the users on its relevance during a predetermined period of time, enabling this way to distinguish the best ones (that is, the most voted/rated) from the whole set of questions. In a second step, if *Liberopinion* is configured to be used without direct interaction of the interviewed person, the editor selects the (top) questions and sends them to the interviewee. In a last step, the interviewee's answers are inserted into the platform and published by the editor.

Note that in a more interactive mode, interviewees (in this initial release politician or teachers union representative) have an access account to *Liberopinion* and this area allows them to directly answer questions from users.

If the context is a discussion panel, the workflow is similar to the previous description. The main difference is that there are several persons to answer simultaneously the users' best questions. One interesting feature is the possibility to compare side by side the answers of different panel members to the same question. If *Liberopinion* is configured to be used with direct interaction of the panel members, these actors have a dedicated interface in the application where they can write the reply and automatically publish it. In order to help the interviewed or the panel member to draft a reasoned and thorough answer, it is possible to save the answer as a draft to be finished and published at a later stage.

Moreover, in order to foster communication, all interactions between users and interviewees or panel members are associated with a specific comments area. The comments section associated with every question and answers allows easy and intuitive follow up of discussion threads by implementation of a "reply to comment" mechanism.

Note that, in the future, it would be possible to support a scenario where the union representatives make questions to a panel comprising politicians, teachers and student, parents and enterprise representatives. This usage scenario allows union to be aware of education community ideas and main concerns in specific topics.

3.2   Suggestions and Ideas from the User Community

Whenever there is a wish to discuss and gather ideas and opinions about the hottest subjects and issues, the editor of the platform can open a new participation event to collect suggestions from the education community. The interaction model used in this area of the platform is similar to the questions area. Users are stimulated to provide their own ideas and encouraged to comment on and to vote on all the ideas submitted, enabling this way to highlight the best ones as seen by the overall community. One possible usage scenario is inviting users to expose what they would do if they were decision makers (e. g. politicians), or if they were the president of the teachers union, and highlight the best ideas. Then, in an interactive configuration mode, decision makers (in the role of politician or teachers union representative) are also given the chance to provide, in this area, feedback on the proposals by leaving comments on a text area designed for this purpose. To foster constant feedback and to provide means to ascertain the community reaction to the comments, all these entries are also subject to rating by the user community.

3.3   Community Surveys – Polls

In this section, several questions are presented to the education community members on the most up-to-date and controversial subjects. Through a simple and intuitive interface users are invited to give their opinion through voting. Each user can only vote once, but it is always possible change the vote. The main purpose of this platform section is to know the community opinion in relation to key education topics. Note that from the overall voting the statistics are gathered being therefore possible to ascertain the opinion of the community as a whole on the issues presented.

3.4   Live Debates

In this area of *Liberopinion*, users can read archived discussions, gather information about scheduled debates, and if there is a live debate ongoing, they can access and participate in this debate. Note that, the discussions in this area are moderated and will not require that users log in to submit questions and comments. One of the innovative features of *Liberopinion* consists in the use of the section dedicated to questions and suggestions for the creation of TOPs that can then be used during live debates. With the purpose of creating these TOPs, the community members are initially invited to submit questions and suggestions and vote on their relevance for a predetermined period of time. Then, along with the statistical information collected in the section dedicated to community surveys, the TOP questions and suggestions may be used to feed the live debates.

3.5   Personal Area

All registered users have a profile area where they can insert personal information, including contact details, links to their pages on social networks, blogs and their websites. Each user's public profile also presents its recent activity (questions, answers, suggestions and comments) in the *Liberopinion* platform. In this area, users can also set criteria for receiving notifications (e.g. when an interviewee or panel member answers a question or publishes a comment to the user submitted suggestion, when another user replies to a submitted comment, when initiates an participation event about the user's favorite themes, among others), and propose improvements to the *Liberopinion* platform.

4   *Liberopinion* Usage Experience in SPRC Website

In *http://fenprof.liberopinion.com/pergA.php?id=10&t=arc* is available, in Portuguese, an initiative carried out by the teachers union of the Centre region of Portugal (SPRC) that is member of the National Federation of Teachers (in Portuguese, FENPROF). Note that, the National Federation of Teachers is the largest Portuguese trade union organization and represents about 70% of the unionized teachers. According to Pordata (*http://www.pordata.pt/en/Home*), citing the Portuguese Ministry of Education, the total number of teachers in 2011 was 174 953, spread over 3632 schools.

In that sporadic event, the editor of the platform invited SPRC associated teachers to submit, during ten days (between 3 and 12 of December, 2013), questions and opinions about the possibility of performing an exam to entry into the profession, proposed by the Portuguese government. During the ten days SPRC representatives gave feedback to all 28 teachers' submissions. Thus, in that initiative, the *Liberopinion* platform was used to create a sporadic participation event, allowing a bidirectional asynchronous communication between SPRC and its associated teachers. Figure 5 illustrates the webpage for the initiative carried out by SPRC to discuss the possibility of performing an exam to entry into the profession.

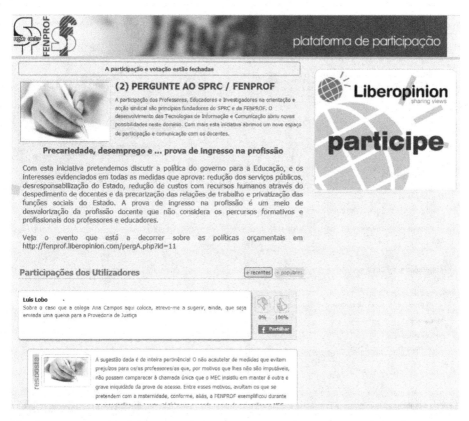

Fig. 5. Webpage for the initiative carried out by SPRC to discuss the possibility of performing an exam to entry into the profession

As illustrated, each answer from the union representative is displayed immediately below the corresponding teacher question. In this participation event, users could also vote and share to Facebook each published question.

In Figure 6 the back office page used to create, edit and configure the initiative carried out by SPRC is presented.

When editor choose the "create" option, in the questions area of the *Liberopinion* platform, is driven to the webpage presented in Figure 6. Here he can upload a picture and edit the text to appear in the front office (see Figure 5), set several configuration parameters, such as activate/deactivate voting, type of moderation (with or without), activate/deactivate user anonymity, limit the maximum number of characters allowed for each question, activate/deactivate the participation event state, among others.

When editor finishes the participation event creation process, the front office web page and the corresponding hyperlink are automatically generated. Then, editor can use this hyperlink to access the front office to see if everything is OK. If so, he can use the hyperlink to incorporate the participation event page into the teachers union portal. Note that, in this usage experience, *Liberopinion* was used by SPRC as a separate tool to create sporadic participation events that were then incorporated into the SPRC website.

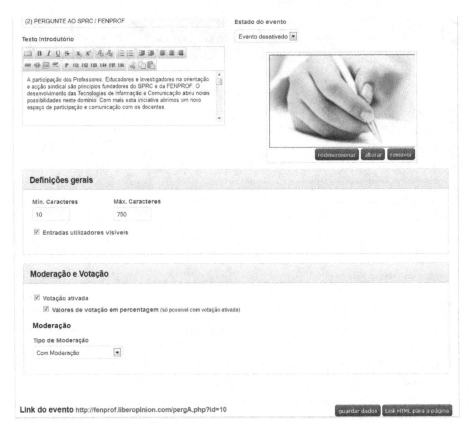

Fig. 6. Back office page used to create, edit and configure the initiative carried out by SPRC to discuss the possibility of performing an exam to entry into the profession

5   Conclusion and Future Work

Information and communication technologies can provide an important contribution to revitalizing teachers unions, since the Internet is faster and more far-reaching than traditional communication methods.

In this paper an approach based on digital mediation to support communication between teachers unions and other stakeholders is proposed. More precisely, the proposal is based on a conceptual model and the corresponding proof of concept - a Web application based on Social Media and e-participation principles, specifically designed to gather teachers union representatives and the education community in a shared deliberative space. The main objectives consist of contributing to strengthen the relationship between teachers unions and the education community, and to foster participation among all stakeholders in the education process, through open, multidirectional and regulated communication channels.

Taking into account the preliminary research question "How to strengthen the relationship between teachers unions and the education community, and foster participation among all stakeholders in the education process, through digital mediation?", we claim that preliminary SPRC experiences with the use of *Liberopinion* suggest that participation initiatives advertising (in a privileged location of the union website, in social networks, and through e-mails) can stimulate stakeholders participation. Furthermore, although we strongly believe that tools based on the Internet and Social Media, such as social networks and the application presented here will enrich teachers unions web portals with participation innovative features and, if properly used, have the potential to contribute significantly to foster participation and strengthen the relationship between unions and the education community, are not the only issues to consider. As so, we advocate that the main focus must be primarily on participation and the people (education stakeholders) rather than on technology. This position is also supported by other authors, in other participation contexts, arguing that the problem of e-participation is not just a matter of technology but also of an issue of social shift to a more open and collaborative culture [17, 18, 19].

We expect that teachers unions take advantage of Internet ubiquity and shift their main focus from traditional media in favor of Web 2.0 and Social Media for their communication strategies and spend more time and human resources to promote and participate in initiatives that bring them closer to the education community.

We may state that one contribution of this project is to allow multidirectional communication (horizontally, vertically, synchrony and asynchrony) between the different actors in the education process, solving the identified communication gap between unions and the others education stakeholders, who was essential unidirectional. As an additional contribution resulting from the lessons learned from this research and development work, we present a set of good practices. Therefore, we recommend: involve in conception and development of the technological solution the different actors in the participation initiative; define in a clear and concise way the usage terms for the digital platform. The best approach is to invite users to create such terms in a collaborative way; provide information to users in order that they can discuss and debate all the issues with the maximum knowledge possible and provide meaningful contributions; reduce to the maximum the necessary resources to participate (in this context, short timed events and live events are extremely proficient); promote recipients feedback for the education community members contributions; make a resume (info graphics, reports or news) with the most important contents and contributes of each participation event.

Tools as *Liberopinion* can also contribute from a pedagogic perspective because they allow the stimulus of a civic spirit, foster collaboration and sharing, and provide a channel to support an open and civilized dialog.

Considering future work in the *Liberopinion* platform, after a more detailed consultation of the stakeholders, the main functionalities needed are:

- Workflow and staff management (create the role of assistant). The implementation of these features is very important because it is expected to contribute to the division of labor and hence to decrease stakeholders' workload. Thus, we intended with these features to attract, or at least not "scare", the major players in this kind of participation initiatives;
- Develop new mechanisms for notifications. For example: notify an assistant who has pending work; notify the person in charge of an assistant that work has been

completed and needs approval before publication; notify the assistant's supervisor whenever the assistant publishes content on the platform;

- A documentation area associated with every participation event. It is very important to provide users with contextual information to foster better informed and knowledgeable discussions. Thus, in an early stage, the editor of the platform can use this area to provide a set of links and documents containing information related to the underlying theme of the event. At a later stage, it would be interesting to define a mechanism to allow users to suggest links and documents for publication in this area;

- Evaluate and, if necessary, rethink the comments component design. We consider deliberation a very important issue in the development and use of e-participation platforms. On the other hand, we realize the submission of comments and the response to comments as a mechanism that facilitates deliberation through dialogue;

- Add the ability to submit written content (questions, comments and suggestions) during a live debate transmitted via streaming video. For example, add a component for content submission underneath the area where the live debate is being broadcasted. The goal is to allow people who cannot be physically present in the debate to actively participate in the debate over the Internet;

- Check if there is a requirement for implementing a reputation mechanism based in the Gamification theories [20, 21]. We believe that, as in [22], reputation mechanisms can contribute to increase contribution quality and provide a user stimulus to participate and offer them some level of notoriety as a reward;

- Optimize the platform to be used on mobile devices (smartphones and tablets). According to a survey of the Pew Research Center (PRC), in May 2013, 56% of American adults owned a smartphone [23]. Other PRC survey highlights that in May 2013 a third (34%) of American adults ages 18 and older owned a tablet computer like an iPad, Samsung Galaxy Tab, Google Nexus, or Kindle Fire - almost twice as many as the 18% who owned a tablet a year ago [24]. A report from Gridley & Company states that, according to Goldman Sachs, by 2015, 81% of U.S. cell users will have smartphones [25]. The International Telecommunication Union (ITU) estimates that at the end of 2012 there were 6.8 billion mobile subscriptions worldwide [26]. Also according to the ITU, that is equivalent to 96 percent of the world population (7.1 billion) and is a huge increase from 6.0 billion mobile subscribers in 2011 and 5.4 billion in 2010. Moreover, the Portio Research Mobile Factbook 2013 predicts that mobile subscribers worldwide will reach 7.5 billion by the end of 2014 and 8.5 billion by the end of 2016 [27].

After using *Liberopinion* platform in organizations of professional nature, such as unions and professional associations, as a topic for further research, it would be interesting to conduct comparative studies to assess the quality and impact of participation compared to initiatives of a political nature [28]. For example, it would be useful to investigate whether it is more challenging for citizens to participate in initiatives of professional or political nature.

References

1. Pinnock, S.: Organizing virtual environments: national union deployment of the blog and new cyberstrategies. The Journal of Labor Society 8(4), 457–468 (2005)
2. Doucouliagos, H., Laroche, P.: Unions, Innovation, and Technology Adoption: New Insights from the Cross-Country Evidence. In: Proceedings of the 16th ILERA World Congress, Philadelphia, Pennsylvania, USA (2012)
3. Rego, R., Naumann, R., Alves, P.: Towards a typology of trade unions uses of the Internet: preliminary data on the Portuguese case. In: 9th Congress of the International Industrial Relations Association. FAOS, Copenhagen (2010)
4. Correia, M., Alves, P., Ulisses, G., Gonçalves, L., Fidalgo, F.: Sindicatos portugueses, utilização da internet e culturas digitais. In: VII Congresso Português De Sociologia (2012)
5. Rego, R., Alves, P., Naumann, R., Silva, J.: A typology of trade union websites with evidence from Portugal and Britain. European Journal of Industrial Relations (December 2013)
6. Quental, C., Gouveia, L.: Web platform for public e-participation management: a case study. International Journal of Civic Engagement and Social Change, IJESC (in press, 2014) ISSN: 2328-549
7. Castells, M.: he Rise of the Network Society. The Information Age: Economy, Society and Culture, 2nd edn., vol. 1. Wiley-Blackwell (2000)
8. Alber, S.M.: A Toolkit for Action Research. Rowman & Littlefield Publishers, Plymouth (2011)
9. Kemmis, K., McTaggart, R.: Participatory Action Research. In: Denzin, N., Lincoln, Y. (eds.) Handbook of Qualitative Research. Sage, London (2000)
10. O'Leary, Z.: The Essential Guide to Doing Research. Sage, London (2004)
11. Koshy, V.: Action Research for Improving Practice. SAGE, London (2005)
12. Zuber-Skerritt, O.: New Directions in Action Research. In: Zuber-Skerritt, O. (ed.), London, pp. 3–9 (1996)
13. Larman, C.: Applying UML and Patterns:: Patterns: An Introduction to Object-Oriented Analysis and Design and Iterative Development. Addison Wesley (2004)
14. Rosembaum, S.: Curation Nation: How to Win in a World Where Consumers are Creators. McGraw-Hill (2011)
15. Agile Manifesto. Manifesto for Agile Software Development, http://agilemanifesto.org/ (accessed September 2012)
16. Cockburn, A.: Agile Software Development. Cockburn - Highsmith Series Editors, 2nd edn. (2006)
17. Macintosh, A., Coleman, S., Schneeberger, A.: eParticipation: The Research Gaps. In: Macintosh, A., Tambouris, E. (eds.) ePart 2009. LNCS, vol. 5694, pp. 1–11. Springer, Heidelberg (2009)
18. Effing, R., van Hillegersberg, J., Huibers, T.: Social Media and Political Participation: Are Facebook, Twitter and YouTube Democratizing Our Political Systems? In: Tambouris, E., Macintosh, A., de Bruijn, H. (eds.) ePart 2011. LNCS, vol. 6847, pp. 25–35. Springer, Heidelberg (2011)
19. Susha, I., Gronlund, A.: eParticipation research: Systematizing the field. Government Information Quarterly 29(3), 373–382 (2012)
20. Pew Research Center. Gamification: Experts expect "game layers" to expand in the future, with positive and negative results. Pew Research Center's Internet & American Life Project (2012)
21. CubePoints. Ignite your users, http://cubepoints.com/ (retrieved October 2013)

22. Velikanov, C.: Requirements and Tools for an Efficient eParticipation. In: Proceedings of the 11th Annual International Conference on Digital Government Research, Puebla, Mexico, pp. 32–40. ACM (2010)
23. Smith, A.: Smartphone Ownership – 2013 Update, June 5. Pew Research Center (2013)
24. Zickuhr, K.: Tablet Ownership 2013, June 10. Pew Research Center (2013)
25. Gridley & Company. POS Goes Digital: Evolution of the In-Store Shopping Experience. Comprehensive Industry Overview (March 2012)
26. ITU. ICT Facts and Figures 2013. ICT Data and Statistics Division, Telecommunication Development Bureau, International Telecommunication Union, Genève (February 2013)
27. Portio Research. The Portio Research Mobile Factbook 2013. Portio Research Limited (February 2013)
28. Afonso Sousa, A., Agante, P., Borges Gouveia, L.: Model of Digital Mediation for Direct Public Participation in Electoral Periods - How important are the Media? In: Proceedings of ICEGOV 2013, Seoul, Republic of Korea, pp. 299–308. ACM (2013), doi:10.1145/2591888.2591942, ISBN: 978-1-4503-2456-4

Open Government and Electronic Government: Some Considerations

Roland Traunmüller

Johannes Kepler Universität Linz,
Altenbergerstraße 69,
4040 Linz, Österreich
traunm@ifs.uni-linz.ac.at

Abstract. Knowledge and innovation are hailed as an important advantage. The contribution considers two trends with promising innovation aspects, namely Open Government and Electronic Government. Both trends are interconnected caused by being based on fairly similar prospects. Although the standpoints are in some way similar the resulting views are diverging. The contribution deliberates mutually influences of both areas under discussion. In concrete, one locates sustaining and reinforcing impacts as well as disturbances and frictions. Finally, some links are considered, so participatory activities, social media and mobile communication.

Keywords: Open Government, Electronic Government, Digital Government, Electronic Governance, Open Source.

1   Knowledge and Innovation

Living in the Knowledge Society has significant implications on all fields, so the economic, social, cultural and political realm. The cardinal point is competition and the position in the race. Competition is growing among countries, companies and people and accordingly, knowledge is seen as advantage. So we all strive for a society that is imbued by knowledge. Yet, we seek not only knowledge in the broad, more we look for those quite specific pieces of knowledge which lead to favourable changes. Such profound changes have different names. In Religion one speaks about reformation, in Health the label used is total lifestyle change, while in Social Sciences and Business such changes are called innovation. Basically, we seek both, knowledge and innovation.

Innovation has become a vital driver, so in Commerce for heightening productivity or in Governing for sustenance and the ability to meet societal needs. In innovation discovery and development have to meet delivery and diffusion. The state goes into a knowledge supportive infrastructure. This includes building a digital infrastructure, establishing precompetitive consortia, building clusters and hubs, fostering public-private-partnerships and offering tax incentives. Further propitious points are a soft infrastructure exploiting tacit knowledge and group relationships as well as climate of

A. Kő and E. Francesconi (Eds.): EGOVIS 2014, LNCS 8650, pp. 201–207, 2014.

openness. The users play a growing role in innovation processes. Innovation guided by consumers and clients may result in creating features never asked before. Quite often not a single innovation alone but a synergy of several novelties brings "the innovation" which is seen as a decisive breakthrough.

2   Open Government and Electronic Government

The contribution considers two trends with promising innovation aspects, Open Government and Electronic Government. Between them various connections along with sustaining and reinforcing impacts are found; yet frictions appear as well. No wonder, because Open Government and Electronic Government have standpoints which are as well fairly similar and diverging. E-Government aims to better serving individual citizens, communities, enterprises as well as public authorities themselves. The entire range of relationships of public bodies to clients and partners is concerned. Although technology sets the pace and creates opportunities, e-Government denotes a socio-cultural and a socio-technical domain too. E-Government means a new service architecture relying on a division of labour between front offices and back offices. Then Government is perceived as seamless while the boundaries between organizations and their jurisdictions open up. For building E-Government a holistic view has to integrate several prospects. Such perspectives are users, technology, organisation, law, knowledge as well as culture, society and politics. Literature for E-Government is vast – we cite paradigmatically some recent proceedings [3, 4 and 7] and a widely used US Reader [2].

Open Government is a governing doctrine bestowing to citizens the right to access the documents and proceedings of the government. The origins of Open Government discussions can be dated back to the time of the European Enlightenment. It was proclaimed with the name "Freedom of Press" in the American and French Revolution. In general, Open Government provides a way to improve all parts of Government. So regarding the part about citizens their participation is improved. Citizen involvement has the goal of improving public responsiveness and reconnecting voters with politics. Also when turning to the the general administrative realm, Open Government has considerable impact. Anyway, the legal and administrative domain knowledge is widened by Public Information. Then internal improvements become enabled. As references to the topic of Open Government we give paradigmatically the following citations [1, 5 and 6].

3   Trends in Open Government

Open Government has a broad scope and encompasses diverse trends:

a)   Open Source governance stresses the application of the free software movement. Open Source governance is a political philosophy: Promoting decision-making methods that better cover public interest – as they are more open and less antagonistic. Thus Open Source software should enable any interested citizen to add to the creation of policy. Further, Open Source software is concerned with the ways under which computer programs can be distributed.

b) Another top issue is Open Government Data. Several public institutions provide data so creating an ample demand pull. The categories of data involved comprise geographical data, micro-census, regulations, traffic data etc. Applications are created in cooperation of agencies with private enterprises.

c) An important fact to mention is having public and private sector platforms. These provide a way for citizens to engagement. Areas concerned include citizen participation, budget spending, legislative tracking, etc. There is a ladder of involvement reaching from informing and consulting to involving and collaboration.

d) Public value is driving maxim and linked to several individual and societal interests. Anyway, there is already an intrinsic value in having Government itself. So a lot of public information is created in any case.

e) Additional value is generated by improving openness, transparency and accountability as well as efficiency and effectiveness. Some output of public value is quite tangible. So, as an example, efficiency is measured by higher outputs while more intense involvement rates may quantify the extent of participation.

4   Supportive Impacts

Open Government stresses openness and transparency and so promotes good governance. This will result in a more efficient and effective Government with higher user satisfaction and a lighter administrative burden. In praxis transparency means opening relevant information on budgets, plans, and events. This includes a long list, so data, documents, benchmarks, processes and meetings. The impact of Open Government can be measured. Assessing the general administrative realm, one finds an elevated feedback and an increased contact with the public. Also with regard to participation the improvements are tangible. So will Open Government lead to a better collaboration for policy formulation. Another impact is the implementation of policies; transparency and openness will accomplish a higher efficiency.

5   Conflicting Impacts

Open Government and Electronic Government have differing objectives and so occasionally tensions will occur. A potential conflict is rooted in the claim for using open source software. Under the flag of openness it is supposed to reach superior decision-making methods. Accordingly, open source software will be superior in covering public interest. It is assumed to make decision taking more open and less antagonistic. On the programme level this means using Open source computer programs. Open source as a development model promotes a universal access via free license to a product's design or blueprint. This means that the source code is available to the general public for use and/or modification from its original design.

Whether conflicts emerge depends strongly on the application. Concerning the planning level, coexistence is quite possible. Turning to running core administrative operations conflicts between Open Government and Electronic Government will happen. When it comes to administrative operations persons in charge dislike any external interference. They prefer to stick to dedicated systems and to preserve the long-lasting connections established with renowned software providers.

Further conflicting zones are rooted in the claim for having citizens involved in Government tasks. There are basic risks connected with any employment of Social Media. One is the fear of getting many low quality contributions which generates excessive "noise." It is also feared that a divide may occur by focussing participation to elitist groups. In addition there are worries that this may lead a loss of control for public authorities.

In addition, potential conflicting zones are created with the occurrence of destructive behaviour, either exerted by individuals or by groups. The list of possible infractions is long and comprises illegal content as well as false claims on wikis. Destructive behaviour of groups occurs as mobbing of users and as insults and harassment in chat-rooms. A quite common infringement is that groups try to systematically influence ratings.

6   Impulses for Public Governance

Improving Public Governance is high on the agenda. Reforming the public sector spurs the discussion on entirely new ways for Public Governance. The aspects diverge according to the point of view. Taking the standpoint of the state we have governance as an underlying principle guiding all activities. The activities of diverse branches of Government (legislature and the judiciary included) contribute to the balancing of societal interests and maintaining the stability of societal life. Seen from the citizen having good governance is the goal, which comprises features as citizen-centric, cooperative and seamless. Seen from outside the theme has been stimulated by the ongoing corporate governance discussion in Economy.

Public Governance can be divided in three zones, so an inner zone with Public Administration, a middle zone dealing with the "policy cycle" and an outer zone overlapping the fringe between the public and the private realm. On the whole, the term Public Governance encompasses the whole scope of governmental tasks in jurisdiction, legislation and execution. Consequently, the scope is exceedingly vast. Public Governance includes: a democratic and cooperative policy formulation; citizen and civil society involvement; an efficient implementation of policies; a continuous evaluation of results; an accountability of public decision makers.

One has to note an ongoing terminological discussion. Should we change the label from e-Government to e-Governance? There are some good reasons; however the request for renaming is not strong. It can be seen as the normative power of facts - after extended use the term e-Government has become a broadly acknowledged brand. Consequently, most authors have a split strategy. They prefer to use the term e-Government while having a broader scope in mind. This is the common linguistic feature called pars pro toto.

7   Social Media Exert Heavy Influence

Under the name of Social Media a new wave of web-based applications has emerged. Applications rely on the concept of the user as a producer of information. One may describe Social Media best as a set of features involving technologies, applications, and values. There are new maxims just as "users as producers" and "wisdom of the crowd". For new technologies stands XML; new applications are given with blogs, wikis and tagging. Blogs are online notes open to comment for other users, while wikis are built by collaborative edition of content. In addition there is tagging which means co-sharing of information. Enforcing democratic processes and institutions are a leading goal; consequently empowerment runs as a red thread associated with most activities. The idea of empowering means: giving someone the power that he was deficient before.

8   Participation is an Imperative Aim

Government is supposed to support the formation of a democratic culture. So Government spurs numerous activities which can be seen as innovative and participatory processes. The range of persons and institutions is wide so comprising citizens, public authorities, elected representatives. Accordingly E-Participation draws a lot of attention. The European Parliament sees three main issues for action: the perceived democratic deficit requiring new relationships between state and citizens; reconnecting citizens with politics; competing with the complexity of decision making and legislation.

Thus "Promoting participation and inclusion of citizens in policymaking and implementation" are points that are high on the political agenda. E-Participation should facilitate more direct and more numerous links between representatives and individual voters. Participation in planning processes will bring more input to the political system. Consequently, decisions become better and more sustainable. Somehow knowledge and expertise of citizens are being "tapped". As example here two instances:

    a) E-Campaigning means raising awareness about issues as well as engaging with people and encouraging people to engage with each other. Consequently, E-Campaining channels the power of public opinion to advance a progressive drive. Tools used are quite easy-usable and unsophisticated so blogging, forwarding campaign information via email or making fund raising sites.

    b) Monitoring is an important point and likely targets may include: events such as elections, groups such as political unions, persons such as politicians, modes such as proper fund spending and locations such as parking lots. In some cases it is an efficient form of law enforcement.

Initiatives are split: so in some participation projects Government have become initiative, often the civil society has organized participative actions. Occasionally facilitation of participation is organized and will improve procedure and outcome. The construction of a social environment is important for exerting e-Participation. For virtual communities tools are important. It is an advantage that most tools used are low-cost, so discussion forum, mailing list, mobile phone etc. From time to time advanced solutions are necessary such as collaborative platforms with multimedia support. Occasionally, E-Participation needs sophisticated tools, so spatial technology for visualization or mediation with the aid of an impartial third. A further point concerns smartphones allowing ad hoc documentation by making photos and sending them. This is a feature that may have a considerable impact, because photos from the location may be used by TV or in court trials.

9   Connection to Mobile Government

Mobile Business is defined as: "All activities related to a potential transaction conducted through communications network that interface with wireless or mobile devices". Mobile Commerce has already become an important factor and Mobile Government follows vigorously. Public Administrations need to adapt key applications to be run on mobile devices. For this aim service knowledge has to be combined with a good understanding of mobile technology, especially its restrictions and opportunities. Fundamentally, having a communication device at hand makes communication patterns change. Mobile activities can count on several benefits. First to list is staying in contact with one's tasks aided by instant access to computing and internet. This will speed up the decision process and offering a more responsive service to clients. For certain tasks an advantage is given by data capturing at the point of origin. Such a procedure heightens accuracy and reduces risky and costly errors.

Fundamentally, it means more than exerting a modern mobile lifestyle; there are concrete and substantial advantages. The demand "Keep in touch with your business" reflects a core component of client care. Managing client relationships has become crucial for agencies with an advantage for both sides. First of all, clients get a better and more individualised attention and treatment and agencies get more feedback. This gives input for administrations to improve exactness in and efficiency of their actions. In a greater view the exchange with citizens a valuable source of knowledge.

10   Conclusions

People want to live under "good governance" primarily comprising democratisation, openness and transparency. These ideals have to be mirrored in the way Government is built. Open Government and Electronic Government are both hailed, especially when contributing to such values. Seen from the citizen point of view both, Open Government and Electronic Government, produce obvious advantages which are tangible and clearly prevail over potential conflicts.

References

1. Deutsche Telekom Institut, Entdeckung, Erkundung und Entwicklung 2.0: Open Government, Open Government Data und Open Budget 2.0, Epublik GmbH, Berlin (2012)
2. Chen, H., Brandt, L., Gregg, V., Traunmüller, R., Dawes, S., Hovy, E., Macintosh, A., Larson, L. (eds.): Digital Government: E-government Research, Case Studies, and Implementation. Springer-Verlag, New York Inc. (2007) ISBN: 978-0387716107
3. Kő, A., Leitner, C., Leitold, H., Prosser, A. (eds.): EGOVIS/EDEM 2013. LNCS, vol. 8061. Springer, Heidelberg (2013)
4. Balthasar, A., Hansen, H., König, B., Müller-Török, R., Pichler, J. (eds.): CEEe-Gov Days 2014: eGovernment, Proceedings, Budapest, May 8-9. OCG, Wien (2014) ISBN: 978-3-854033004
5. Offene Daten Österreichs: http://data.gv.at
6. International Partnership, http://www.opengovpartnership.org
7. Schweighofer, E., Kummer, F., Hötzendorfer, W. (eds.): Transparenz IRIS 2014, Proceedings, Salzburg, February 20-22. OCG, Wien (2014) ISBN 978-3-854033028

Modeling, Fusion and Exploration of Regional Statistics and Indicators with Linked Data Tools

Valentina Janev, Vuk Mijović, Dejan Paunović, and Uroš Milošević

Mihajlo Pupin Institute, University of Belgrade, Serbia
{valentina.janev,vuk.mijovic,dejan.paunovic,
uros.milosevic}@pupin.rs

Abstract. This paper contributes to the understanding of challenges related to publishing and consuming public sector information using Linked Data tools. Linked Data paradigm has opened new possibilities and perspectives for the process of collecting and monitoring socio-economic indicators. Due to multi-dimensionality of the statistical data, in order to ensure efficient exploration and analysis, hierarchical data structures are needed for modeling the space and time dimensions. This paper presents several illustrative examples of modeling, analyzing and visualization of Linked Data from Serbian government bodies. The approach utilizes tools from the *Linked Data* stack, as well as the first prototype of the *Exploratory Spatio-Temporal Analysis* component that has been developed in the GeoKnow project framework.

Keywords: Linked Data, integration, modelling, statistics, transparency.

1   Introduction

In the last five years, the global Open Government Data (OGD) initiatives, such as the Open Government Partnership[1], have helped to open up governmental data for the public, by insisting on non-sensitive information, such as core public data on transport, education, infrastructure, health, environment, etc. Additionally, the European Commission (EC) has made considerable investments to improve efficiency in the provision of public services, increase transparency, define better strategies for delivering large amounts of trusted data to the public and improve interoperability. As part of alignment of national government activities with the EC 'Interoperability Solutions for European Public Administrations' (ISA) program[2] for the period from 2010-2015 [1], a lot of government portals have been established across Europe that allows different stakeholders to publish standards, guidelines and interoperability assets important at the national level. This openness, on one hand, will strengthen European democracy and promote efficiency and effectiveness in G2C, G2G, G2B services, while, on the other, it will expand creative use of data beyond its walls by encouraging application of innovative technologies such as semantic mash-ups and widgets.

---

[1] http://www.opengovpartnership.org/
[2] http://ec.europa.eu/isa/

A. Kő and E. Francesconi (Eds.): EGOVIS 2014, LNCS 8650, pp. 208–221, 2014.

This paper aims at discussing the challenges related to the possibilities of integrating open data for advanced analyses of socio-economic indicators in official government statistical systems. Furthermore, by using an illustrative case study of the Register of the Regional Development Measures and Incentives[3], maintained by the Serbian Business Registers Agency (SBRA), it demonstrates the adaption of the *Linked Data* stack for analysis and dissemination of official statistics.

The article is organized as follows. First, Section 2 introduces the main challenges of integration and analysis of open data. Sections 3 and 4 present the Linked Open Data (LOD) approach to modeling, fusion and analysis of spatial-temporal data and statistics. Some illustrative examples of visualization of statistics with the *Exploratory spatio-temporal analysis for Linked Data* (ESTA-LD)[4] component are given in Section 5. Finally, Section 6 concludes the paper and outlines the future work.

2   Sharing and Reusing Public Datasets Across Europe

2.1   Related Work

Linked Data paradigm [2] has been utilized recently in order to achieve linking of datasets together through references to common concepts. The standard for the representation of the information that describes those entities and concepts is RDF [3]. Several projects have been financed within the EU FP7 research program devoted to publishing and consuming data in Linked Data format. As a result, several repositories of open source toolkits, as well as platforms for building Linked Data applications have emerged recently, as presented in Table 1.

In the last three years, in the framework of the LOD2 and GeoKnow projects, the Institute Mihajlo Pupin (IMP) has been involved in maintaining the *Linked Data* stack[5], an integrated set of tools for managing the Linked Data life-cycle. All tools are RDF based and enable developers to build custom applications on the top of the public sector data. For instance, IMP was involved in development of a specific web interface (*Statistical Workbench*[6]) that aggregated several components of the stack organized in an intuitive way to support the specific business context of the statistical office. The *Workbench* contains several dedicated extensions for manipulating RDF data according to the Data Cube vocabulary: validation, merging and slicing of cubes.

In the GeoKnow framework, the *GeoKnow Generator*[7], an integrated solution for managing geospatial data, has been developed. Within the ESTA-LD development, IMP will further extend the capabilities of the *GeoKnow Generator* for managing spatio-temporal data.

---

[3] http://www.apr.gov.rs/eng/Registers/RegionalDevelopmentMeasur
esandIncentives.aspx

[4] *ESTA-LD* is an exploratory spatial-temporal analysis tool, see early prototype http://
fraunhofer2.imp.bg.ac.rs/esta-ld/

[5] http://stack.linkeddata.org/

[6] http://fraunhofer2.imp.bg.ac.rs/lod2statworkbench

[7] http://generator.geoknow.eu

The ESTA-LD development is driven by the GeoKnow requirements and by the features currently not supported by the GeoKnow components Facete [4] and Cube-Viz [5] such as visualization of statistics on a geographical map.

Topic	Project	Tool
Establishing and maintaining data and tool catalogues / repositories	LATC	LATC Data Publication & Consumption Tools Library, http://wifo5-03.informatik.uni-mannheim.de/latc/toollibrary/ and *LATC 24/7 Interlinking Platform*, see http://latc-project.eu/platform
	LOD2	PublicData.eu catalog Linked Data Stack
	PlanetData	PlanetData Tool Catalogue, see http://planet-data.eu/planetdata-tool-catalogue
	ENGAGE	ENGAGE Data, http://www.engagedata.eu/
Monitoring of Open Data Catalogues	OPENDATA-MONITOR	Harvesting framework, http://project.opendatamonitor.eu/
Harmonizing open data	HOMER	HOMER Federated Index, http://homerproject.eu/docs/Federation_technical_specific_CSI_V04.pdf
Managing Linked statistical data	LOD2	LOD2 Statistical Workbench
	OpenCube	http://opencube-project.eu/
	CEDAR	Census dataset, http://www.cedar-project.nl/
Managing Linked geo-spatial data	GeoKnow	GeoKnow Generator, http://geoknow.eu

2.2   Problem Statement

In order to share datasets between users and platforms, the datasets need to be accessible (regulated by licence), discoverable (described with metadata) and retrievable (modelled and stored in a recognizable format). According to the *World Bank Group* definition "Data is open if it is technically open (available in a machine-readable standard format, which means it can be retrieved and meaningfully processed by a computer application) and legally open (explicitly licensed in a way that permits commercial and non-commercial use and re-use without restrictions)."

As a part of OGD initiatives, a large number of data catalogues have been established across Europe that store descriptions of the public datasets. A *data catalogue* can be viewed as an electronic library index that structures descriptions (meta-data) about the actual data. An example of the data catalogues is the *PublicData.eu* (http://PublicData.eu), a Pan European data portal that provides access to open, freely reusable datasets from local, regional and national public bodies across Europe. Although OGD policies have spread fast (the number of the open data initiatives has grown from two to over 300)[6], the availability of truly open data remains low, with less than 7% of the dataset surveyed in the Open Data Barometer published both in bulk machine-readable forms, and under open licenses [7].

In order to illustrate the possibilities of sharing and re-using public datasets across Europe, in Figure 1, we have presented three types of the open data portals:

- Open Data Portal in Country X contains data and metadata descriptions, but does not provide DCAT[8] support for harmonization of portal/catalog with similar data portals/catalogues. Publishers can use the cross country portals for publishing data, e.g. the Engage portal[9],
- Open Data Portal in Country Y contains data and metadata descriptions, as well as a Linked Data SPARQL endpoint, but it is isolated , that is, it is not integrated at the international level
- Open Data Portal in Country Z is CKAN based, meaning that it can be easily harvested by other metadata catalogs at the international level.

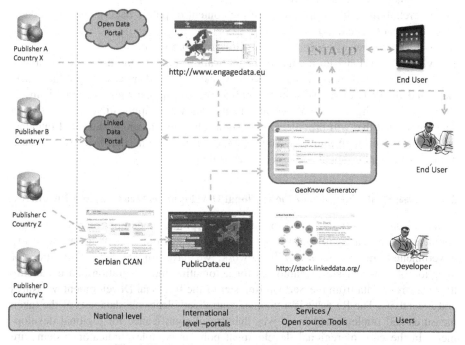

Fig. 1. Exploration and consumption of open data

The data can be exposed for exploration in different ways, e.g. via a SPARQL endpoint or downloadable dump file. Although there are best practices for publishing

---

[8] DCAT, `http://www.w3.org/TR/vocab-dcat/`, is an RDF vocabulary designed to facilitate interoperability between data catalogs published on the Web.

[9] `http://www.engagedata.eu/`

open (and linked) data[10], the metadata can be of low quality leading to the questions such as:

- Is the open data ready for exploration? Is the metadata complete? What about the granularity? Do we have enough information about the domain/region the data is describing?
- Is it possible to fuse heterogeneous data and formats from different publishers and what are the necessary steps? Are there standard services for querying government portals?

Our initial analyses have shown that automatic processing and consuming open data for building smart public service is hampered by many factors including
- lack of standard approaches for querying government portals;
- quality of metadata (e.g. incomplete description of the public datasets, changes on schema level);
- reliability and completeness of the content of public datasets (e.g. uptodateness of open data);
- heterogeneity of formats used by different publishers.

The vision for ICT-driven public sector innovation refers to the use of technologies for the creation and implementation of new and improved processes, products, services and methods of delivery in the public sector [8], see right side of Figure 1. However, in the light of the above statements, innovative application on top of open data are needed that will provide some insights about the meaningfulness of integrating data from different domains. Smart public services are needed that make the use of open data more efficient and less time-consuming.

2.3   Case Study: Register of the Regional Development Measures and Incentives

Statistical data are often used as foundations for policy prediction, planning and adjustments, having a significant impact on the society (from citizens to businesses to governments). In the GeoKnow framework, we have studied the possibilities for adoption of Linked Data technologies for automating the integration and enhancing the analysis of data from the Serbian Register of the Regional Development Measures and Incentives. The Register is a unique, centralized electronic database of the taken measures and implemented incentives that are of significance for regional development. In the case of regional development policies complex indicator systems are required due to the multiplicity of objectives, large number of projects (investments) in different domains and involvement of different level of government (local, regional, national, European) [9], [10]. Instead of the current way of collecting and visualizing data, innovative approaches could be applied that:

- extend the existing public service provided by SBRA and standardize the data collection process;

---

[10] http://www.w3.org/TR/ld-bp/

- ensure interoperability (e.g. integration of data from the Register with data from the Dissemination database of the Statistical Office of the Republic of Serbia, SORS) and improve transparency of data on European level;
- allow advanced spatio-temporal analysis of available indicators;
- offer user-friendly services in a secure and flexible manner allowing personalisation for different types of users (public administration, businesses and citizens).

Table below compares the basic characteristics of several example datasets published in Linked Data format by SORS and SBRA. Datasets can be explored via the Statistical Workbench interface [11].

Table 1. Basic characteristics of spatio-temporal data published by two Serbian government agencies

Publisher	Domain	1st dimension: Space Granularity levels	2nd dimension: Time period, granularity	Other dimensions
SBRA	Regional development measures and incentives by purpose	Country-region-area-municipality	2010-2013, yearly	Purpose type
SBRA	Regional development measures and incentives by financial type	Country-region-area-municipality	2010-2013, yearly	Financial type
SORS	Demographic statistics, Population projections	Country-region	2009-2010, yearly	Sex, age
SORS	Labour market	Country-region	2008-2013, yearly-monthly	Sex, age, occupation, type of settlement
SORS	Structural business statistics	Country-region	2007-1011, yearly	Enterprise type, NACE activity
SORS	Tourism (overnight stay)	Country-region	2010-2013, yearly-monthly	Tourist type

All indicators mentioned in the examples above have attributes related to both space and time, thus imposing challenges for visualizing both dimensions on a geographical map. Moreover, these datasets are often multi-dimensional originally, meaning that the information can be represented on different granularity levels in space and time, as well as the type of information (different attributes, see last column). In Figure 2, for instance, the distribution of incentives in different geographical entities in Serbia on different granularity levels is presented.

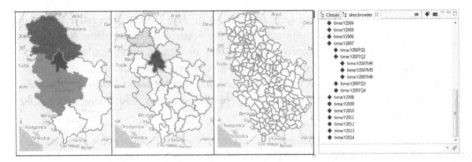

Fig. 2. Exploration and consumption of open data

3   Linked Data Approach to Modeling Spatio-Temporal Data

A statistical data set comprises a collection of observations made at some points across some logical space. The collection can be characterized by a set of dimensions that define what the observation applies to (e.g. time, country) along with metadata describing what was measured (e.g. economic activity, prices), how it was measured and how the observations were expressed (e.g. units, multipliers, status). We can think of the statistical data set as a multi-dimensional space, or hyper-cube, indexed by those dimensions. This space is commonly referred to as a *cube* for short; though the name shouldn't be taken literally, it is not meant to imply that there are exactly three dimensions (there can be more or fewer) nor that all the dimensions are somehow similar in size.

3.1   Modeling Statistical Data (Vocabulary RDF Data Cube)

In January 2014, W3C recommended the *RDFData Cube* vocabulary [12], a standard vocabulary for modeling statistical data, see http://www.w3.org/TR/vocab-data-cube/. The vocabulary focuses purely on the publication of multi-dimensional data on the Web. The model builds upon the core of the *SDMX 2.0 Information Model* [13]. In 2001, the Statistical Data and Metadata Exchange (SDMX[11]) Initiative was organised by seven international organizations (BIS, ECB, Eurostat, IMF, OECD, World Bank and the UN) to release greater efficiencies in statistical practice. An example how to use the vocabulary to represent one single observation is given in Figure 4. The observed socio-economic phenomenon is described using several dimensions modelled with the SKOS vocabulary.

In this example we have a *coarse-grained representation of the indicator* "Tourists arrivals" for the territory of the country of Serbia (geo:RS) and for year 2005 (time:Y2005). Additionally, the indicator represents the "Total" number of tourists including "Domestic" and "Foreign".

---

[11] http://www.sdmx.org/

```
http://elpo.stat.gov.rs/lod2/RS-DATA/Tourism/Tourists_arrivals/data/obs1>
    a qb:Observation ;
```

```
        rs:geo geo:RS ;
        rs:time time:Y2005 ;
        rs:dataType datatype:number ;                      SKOS Dimensions
        rs:obsIndicator "Tourists arrivals" ;
        rs:obsTurists "Total" ;
```

```
    qb:dataSet <http://elpo.stat.gov.rs/lod2/RS-DATA/Tourism/Tourists_arrivals/data> ;
```

```
sdmx-measure:obsValue "1988469" .
```

Fig. 3. Example of using the RDF Data Cube vocabulary

3.2   Modeling Spatial and Time Dimensions (Using SKOS Vocabulary)

In order to formalize the conceptualization of hierarchical dimensions (space, time), we can use the *Simple Knowledge Organization System* (SKOS), see http://www.w3.org/TR/2005/WD-swbp-skos-core-spec-20051102/. SKOS Core is a model and an RDF vocabulary for expressing the basic structure and content of concept schemes such as thesauri, classification schemes, subject heading lists, taxonomies, 'folksonomies', other types of controlled vocabulary, and also concept schemes embedded in glossaries and terminologies.

Concepts represented as skos:Concept are grouped in concept schemes (skos:ConceptScheme) that serve as code lists from which the dataset dimensions draw on their values. Semantic relation used to link a concept to a concept scheme is skos:hasTopConcept. Herein, we will present an example of coding the space and time dimension in RDF. SKOS properties skos:broader and skos:narrower can be used for relating concepts of the same type, in our case, geographical area (geo:Region). However, if the concepts are not of the same type (e.g. to regions and municipalities), the skos:related alignment can be applied.

```
geo:RS21
    rdf:typegeo:Region ;
    owl:sameAs
        <http://dbpedia.org/page/%C5%A0umadija_and_Western_Serbia
> ;
    skos:broadergeo:RS ;
    skos:narrower geo:RS212 , geo:RS216 , geo:RS211 , geo:RS215
, geo:RS213 ;
    skos:narrower geo:RS218 , geo:RS214 , geo:RS217 ;
    skos:notation "RS21"^^xsd:string ;
    skos:prefLabel "Region of Sumadija and Western Serbia"@en ,
"REGION ŠUMADIJE I ZAPADNE SRBIJE"@sr-rs .
```

The observed data can be described with time information using different formats (e.g. seconds from the begging of an event, day-time, day, month, year). One way to specify the data frequency (or time granularity) in a dataset is to use the SDMX Content-oriented guidelines[12]. A specific time period (e.g. January in year 1980) can be coded as following:

---

[12] http://sdmx.org/wp-content/uploads/2009/01/02_sdmx_cog_annex_2_cl_2009.pdf

```
time:Y1980M1
rdf:type time:P1M ;
skos:broader time:Y1980Q1 ;
skos:notation "Y1980M1"^^xsd:string ;
skos:prefLabel "1980/january"@en .
```

3.3   Fusing Statistical Data (RDF Data Cubes)

Data fusion is the process of integration of multiple data and knowledge representing the same/similar real-world object (e.g. socio-economic indicators for a region) into a consistent, accurate, and useful representation. Data fusion makes sense if the observations are on the same granularity level (described with the same number of dimensions), and are disjoint, meaning there are not two observations with the same values for all dimensions. However, if the tool for exploring statistical data integrates drill-down functionalities, datasets with different granularity levels can be used for merging.

Depending on the data sources and the alignment of concept schemes used in input datasets, different fusing algorithms are needed, e.g.:

- Same concept schemes are used in all input datasets.

    In this case the merging approach is rather straightforward: the user selects a reference DSD and the observations from all merged cubes are copied directly into the new cube. After the fusion step, check for validation of the integrity constraints can be run [14].

- Some input datasets do not use concept schemes.

    In this case, it is often necessary to perform additional harmonization of the concept schemes. One alignment approach is to compare the values of the properties that are used with identified concept schemes, and to consider that properties draw values from the existing concept schemes.

- Input datasets use different concept schemes.

    In this case, vocabulary matching algorithm for alignment of concept schemes is needed as a prerequisite for the fusion.

4   Linked Data Approach to Analysis of Spatial-Temporal Data

Exploratory data analysis (EDA) is an important first step in any data analysis that focuses on identifying general patterns in the data, and identifying outliers and features of the data that might not have been anticipated. The goal of the spatial-temporal analysis is to derive information from data using visualization techniques and standard EDA techniques including histogram, run chart, or scatter plot / scatter graph.

The selection of techniques for exploratory analysis of spatio-temporal Linked Data depends on the characteristics of data and the goals of analysis. Figure 4 presents a semi-automatic analysis process of socio-economic indicators that is currently supported by the Linked Data tools in the following way:

1. The user uploads a graph into the local RDF data store (Virtuoso);
2. The user checks for validation of the integrity constraints [14]. If errors are identified, automatic or semi-automatic repair of multidimensional model is available;
3. The user can proceed with the exploration using Facete, CubeViz or ESTA-LD. Facete provides faceted navigation of the model and visualization of points of interest (described with *WGS84*[13] vocabulary) on a geographical map. CubeViz is an *RDF Data Cube*[14] model exploration tool without possibilities to relate the indicators with geographical entities.
4. When launching the ESTA-LD component, the user specifies the SPARQL endpoint, and selects the graph that contains the data to be explored. The data is then retrieved from the specified SPARQL endpoint and visualized on the choropleth map. The choropleth map provides an easy way to visualize how measurement varies across a geographic area. It is an ideal way to communicate spatial information quickly and easily, since the data is aggregated or generalized into classes or categories that are represented on the map by grades of colour. The ranges of data values for different colors are recalculated every time a new set of data is retrieved from the SPARQL endpoint. After the data is retrieved, the user can utilize different filtering options that are currently implemented (see Fig. 5):

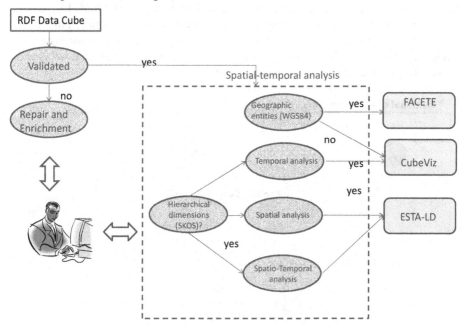

Fig. 4. Guided analysis of spatio-temporal data

---

[13] http://www.w3.org/2003/01/geo/

[14] http://www.w3.org/TR/vocab-data-cube/

- For selecting values from the time dimension,
- For selecting the indicator under study,
- For selecting the granularity level for the space dimension,
- Interactive selection of the area of interest on the geographical map (for the selected area a bar-chart or histogram (see Fig. 6) representation of the indicator is displayed).

5   ESTA-LD Implementation Details and Validation

ESTA-LD aims at overcoming the limitations of CubeViz and Facete and offering generic interface for exploring spatio-temporal data. In order to enable ease of integration with the *GeoKnow Generator*, ESTA-LD component was developed using HTML5 and JavaScript. Representation and interaction with geographic information was implemented using *Leaflet*, an open source JavaScript library for mobile-friendly interactive maps, see http://leafletjs.com/. The geographic data (such as region borders), originally created from shape files, is stored in GeoJSON format. It is brought in and programmed with JavaScript and added to maps to create interactive visualizations. On the other side, different statistical indicators, which are the subjects of the spatiotemporal analysis, are stored in the RDF Data Store. This data repository is accessed and queried using SPARQL query language. The actual retrieval of data from the SPARQL Endpoint is implemented using the jQuery library and its standard getJSON function. Finally, the results of the spatiotemporal analysis are visualized using *Highcharts*, a charting library written in pure HTML5/JavaScript, offering intuitive, interactive charts to a web site or web application see http://www.highcharts.com/.

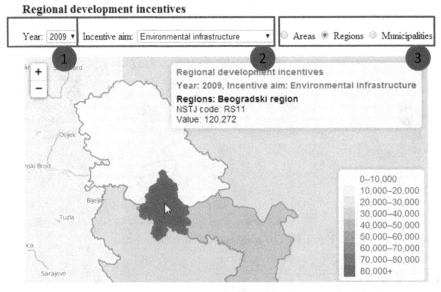

Fig. 5. Spatial-temporal filtering options

To validate our approach, we used data from two different institutions - the National Statistical Office and the Business Registers Agency of Serbia. Data (aggregated, interlinked with public datasets and fused) appear at different levels of granularity.

Our initial testing has shown that the first prototype of the ESTA-LD tool, although still under development, proved to be a valuable instrument for advanced spatio-temporal analysis of Linked Data. The whole geospatial information life cycle in the resulting first prototype for exploratory spatio-temporal analysis will be further tested with data from different countries and different statistical domains.

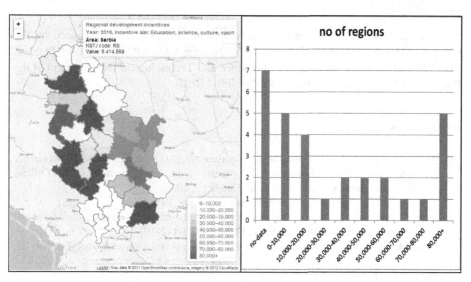

Fig. 6. Analysis of incentives (a. on a geographical map, b. histogram of a continuous variable)

6   Conclusions and Further Work

The EC ISA program envisions publishing of the public/private datasets in machine readable format, thus, making sharing, using and linking of information easy and efficient. The datasets will be offered through standardized data catalogues while standardized vocabularies (eGovernment core vocabularies, *WGS84, RDF Data Cube*) and ontologies will be used for data modelling. Taking into consideration the ISA recommendations, this paper discusses the challenges of integration and analysis of the open data and introduces the Linked Data approach to modeling and fusion of spatial-temporal data and statistics. To validate the approach, the 'Register of the Regional Development Measures and Incentives' case study has been elaborated and a new tool ESTA-LD has been developed.

Although, there are tools for visualization of Linked Data including geo-spatial data, this paper points to the need for guided analysis of the Linked Data retrieved from arbitrary SPARQL endpoint and proposes the ESTA-LD component as a generic interface for exploring spatio-temporal data. The ESTA-LD component contributes to further development and standardization of the Linked Data technologies. It shows the use of emerging W3C standards (RDF Data Cube vocabulary, SKOS vocabulary) in the field of statistical and temporal geospatial information management.

In future, a significant effort will be put into further generalization of the ESTA-LD filtering and exploration and integration of the component into the *GeoKnow Generator*. Challenges that will be addressed are generalization of the ESTA-LD filtering and exploration, so that the component supports different spatial and temporal SKOS based conceptual schemes. Finally, the tool will be further enhanced taking into consideration different aspects, such as scalability, flexibility and ease-of-use/friendliness.

Acknowledgements. The research presented in this paper is partly financed by the European Union (FP7 LOD2 project, Pr. No: 257943; FP7 GeoKnow, Pr. No: 318159), and partly by the Ministry of Science and Technological Development of the Republic of Serbia (SOFIA project, Pr. No: TR-32010).

References

1. Decision no 922/2009/EC of the European parliament and of the Council of 16 September 2009 on Interoperability Solutions for European Public Administrations (ISA). Official Journal of the European Union, L 260/20 (October 3, 2009), http://ec.europa.eu/isa/documents/isa_lexuriserv_en.pdf
2. Auer, S., Lehmann, J.: Making the web a data washing machine - creating knowledge out of interlinked data. Semantic Web Journal 1(12), 97–104 (2010)
3. Cyganiak, R., Wood, D., Lanthaler, M.: RDF 1.1 Concepts and Abstract Syntax (February 25, 2014), http://www.w3.org/TR/2014/REC-rdf11-concepts-20140225/Overview.html
4. Stadler, C., Martin, M., Auer, S.: Exploring the Web of Spatial Data with Facete. In: Companion Proceedings of 23rd International World Wide Web Conference, WWW, pp. 175–178 (2014)
5. Salas, P.E., Maia Da Mota, F., Breitman, K., Casanova, M.A., Martin, M., Auer, S.: Publishing Statistical Data on the Web. International Journal of Semantic Computing 06(04), 373–388 (2012)
6. Alonso, J.M.: Announcing the Global Open Data Initiative (GODI). World Wide Web Foundation (June 11, 2013), http://www.webfoundation.org/2013/06/announcing-the-global-open-data-initiative-godi/
7. Open Data Barometer - 2013 Global Report (2013), http://www.opendataresearch.org/dl/odb2013/Open-Data-Barometer-2013-Global-Report.pdf
8. Orientation paper: research and innovation at EU level under Horizon 2020 in support of ICT-driven public sector. EC Digital Agenda news (May 22, 2013), http://ec.europa.eu/information_society/newsroom/cf/dae/document.cfm?doc_id=2588
9. Indicators and regional development policies. The Italian position and current practice. Ministry of Economic Development - ITALY (2008), http://www.dps.mef.gov.it/documentazione/docs/all/postion_paper_indicators%2029%2002%2008.pdf

10. Schönthale, K., von Andrian-Werburg, S.: Identification and Selection of Indicators, DIAMONT Work Package Report, http://www.uibk.ac.at/diamont/downloads/workpackages/WP7_finalreport_070514.pdf
11. Janev, V., et al.: Supporting the Linked Data publication process with the LOD2 Statistical Workbench. Semantic Web Journal (under review), http://www.semantic-web-journal.net/content/supporting-linked-data-publication-process-lod2-statistical-workbench
12. Cyganiak, R., Reynolds, D.: The RDF Data Cube vocabulary (January 16, 2014), http://www.w3.org/TR/vocab-data-cube/
13. SDMX Information model: UML Conceptual Design (version 2.0) (November 2005), http://sdmx.org/docs/2_0/SDMX_2_0%20SECTION_02_InformationModel.pdf
14. Janev, V., Mijović, V., Vraneš, S.: LOD2 Tool for Validating RDF Data Cube Models. In: Trajkovik, V., Mishev, A. (eds.) Web Proceedings of the 5th ICT Innovations Conference, Ohrid, Macedonia, September 12-15 (2013), http://ict-act.org/proceedings/2013/htmls/papers/icti2013_submission_01.pdf

Environmental Thesauri under the Lens of Reusability

Riccardo Albertoni, Monica De Martino, and Paola Podestà

Istituto di Matematica Applicata e Tecnologie Informatiche
Consiglio Nazionale delle Ricerche,
Via De Marini, 6, 16149 Genova, Italy
{albertoni,demartino,podesta}@ge.imati.cnr.it

Abstract. The development of a Spatial Data Infrastructure (SDI) at European level is strategic to answer the needs of environmental management requested by the European, national and local policies. Several European projects and initiatives aim to share, integrate and make accessible large amount of environmental data in order to overcome cross-border/language/cultural barriers. To this purpose, environmental thesauri are used as shared nomenclatures in metadata compilation and information discovery, and they are increasingly made available on the web. This paper provides a methodological approach for creating a catalogue of the environmental thesauri available on the web and assessing their reusability with respect to domain independent criteria. It highlights critical issues providing some recommendations for improving thesauri reusability.

Keywords: Environmental thesauri, Linked Data, Spatial Data Infrastructure, Open Government, metadata.

1 Introduction

In recent years, different directives (e.g., INSPIRE[1]) and policy communications (e.g., SEIS[2]) have been launched at European-scale with the objective of improving the management of heterogeneous environmental data sources, nevertheless, an effective sharing of these resources is still an open issue due to the intrinsic multicultural and multilingual nature of the environmental domain. Thus, the development of a Spatial Data Infrastructure (SDI) at European level requires to deploy geographic data in a standardized way and with common nomenclatures. Different communities having a large spectrum of competencies are involved in the treatment and the management of geographical information, consequently SDI deals with several thesauri in order to deeply cover such a variety of competencies. Currently several thesauri for the Environment are shared in the web embodying different points of view and different ways of conceptualization. These thesauri are precious and their exploitation within a SDI for metadata compilation and data discovery is critical.

---

[1] http://inspire.ec.europa.eu/

[2] http://ec.europa.eu/environment/seis/

A. Kő and E. Francesconi (Eds.): EGOVIS 2014, LNCS 8650, pp. 222–236, 2014.

Our experience in the management of Environment-related thesauri started in the European project NatureSDIplus[3] aimed at supporting the implementation of INSPIRE. The goal of this project has been the harmonization and the integration, at European level, of the datasets on nature conservation, available on the web, to better exploit and access them. This has been a challenging task due to the several existing Knowledge Organization Systems (KOS), such as taxonomies, thesauri, code lists, gazetteers, etc... Moreover, the development of new resources might result in a huge waste of effort attempting to reinvent the wheel, and in a possible increasing of the information redundancy. Thus, the approach in the NatureSDIplus has been the creation of a framework for the integration of existing KOS, using Linked Data best practices, in order to harmonize the data (and metadata) entry and to support the information retrieval using metadata in a Metadata Information System. Following the agreement and the interest for the thesaurus framework shown inside the EU Community, a further activity, in the new ongoing EU project eENVplus[4], has been planned to enrich the thesaurus framework adding further environmental thesauri in order to improve the existing services to overcome cross-border and language barriers.

In recent years, several organizations have provided their KOS on the web using the Simple Knowledge Organization Systems (SKOS) [11] as common data model and they have published some of these SKOS as Linked Data. Considering the perspective of the integration of existing KOS in an SDI, the activity concerning the identification of the reusable KOS, is critical.

Some recent papers also contributes in addressing the reusability of environmental thesauri of considering different points of view. The paper [10] presents a survey for understanding the modelling style in terms of shape, size and depth of the vocabulary structured as SKOS vocabulary on the web. It mainly focuses on the usage of SKOS constructs, SKOS semantic relations and lexical labels. In [15] a framework for the automated assessment and correction of common potential quality issues in SKOS vocabularies is proposed. The quality measures defined in the framework consider not only structural issues, but also labelling and documentation issues such as missing or overlapping labels, and also Linked Data specific issues, such as broken links, missing inlinks, invalid URIs. Instead, [12] presents an analysis of the KOS available on the web which is independent from their SKOS structures. The considered KOS are identified using journal and scientific sources. Then, they are classified considering the type (thesaurus, ontology and glossary), the covered science domain, the continent of origins and the date on which they are made available on-line.

In this paper we present an approach to identify a set of environmental thesauri available on the web and to assess their reusability, in terms of easiness to access and to exploit their content. To this purpose, first of all, we consider the best practices for publishing Linked Data (see [7]), based on the 5 Star Linked Data principles (5 star LD [2]), that sets out a series of best practices designed to facilitate development and delivery of government data as Linked Data. Moreover

---

[3] http://www.nature-sdi.eu/

[4] http://www.eenvplus.eu

we refer also to the papers [5,14] stating respectively that the adoption of Linked Data best practices jointly with SKOS and the type of licence are essential in the deployment of a resource in the web. Thus, we address the assessment of reusability considering the openness of licence and the compliance to the 5 star LD, stressing on, for the latter, the deployment of *dereferenceable* HTTP URIs as identifiers for resources. Licence and HTTP *dereferenceability* are central prerequisites for every scenario of reuse and they are crucial for interlinking among structured data, but they are not considered at all in [10], [12] and [15].

The contributions of the papers are the following:

— the definition of a methodological approach which includes the employment of different investigation strategies to collect a set of possibly well known terminological resources for the Environment among those available in the web;
— the synthesis and explication of a set of reusability criteria which, although quite settled in the Linked Data community, are not yet fully received by environmental thesauri producers and publisher;
— a "reference" catalogue of thesauri which can be exploited by data users and applications in the Environment domain;
— the reusability assessment of the thesauri in the catalogue and the discussion of issues arising from the reusability analysis and some recommendations, which might result interesting for thesauri users and publishers for screening the thesauri they want to adopt or for improving the reusability of their own thesauri.

2   Introduction to the Methodological Approach

This section outlines the main steps and the characteristics of the methodology adopted aimed at identifying the environmental thesauri to be evaluated in the reusability perspective. The methodology is defined by a multi-task process as represented in the workflow in Fig. 1. It is characterized by three main phases:

— *Phase I. Resource identification and cataloguing:* identification of the available thesauri for the Environment and creation of the thesaurus catalogue.
— *Phase II. Identification of reusability criteria:* identification and formalization of technological criteria able to evaluate the reusability.
— *Phase III. Evaluation of thesauri:* assessment of the reusability of the thesauri according to the criteria previously identified.

It is important to highlight that different communities connected with the environmental domain have been involved in a continuous interaction in order to set up the initial set of thesauri and to sort out doubts and issues arising during all the three phases of the process. In the following we describe the three phases in detail.

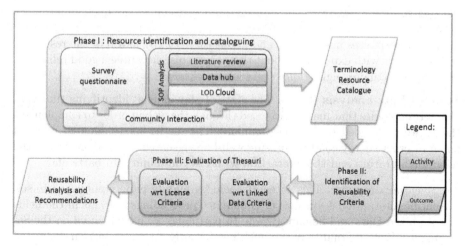

Fig. 1. Workflow of the methodological approach

3   Resource Identification and Cataloguing

This activity aims at identifying and collecting as many different environmental thesauri as possible in order to perform on them some representative analysis concerning reusability. The catalogue does not want to be exhaustive of all existing terminologies of the environmental domain. However the multi-strategy process adopted for identifying the thesauri entails the catalogue as a good "reference" catalogue, representative of the well- and quite-known environmental thesauri available on the web and possibly in Linked Data.

3.1   Resource Identification

In order to identify the available terminologies a multi-strategy process of investigations has been adopted, considering and combining different types of information sources. The strategies adopted are: (i) an on-line questionnaire, (ii) a State of Play analysis (SoP), and, (iii) the direct interaction with different environmental communities.

On-line questionnaire. An on-line questionnaire entitled *Thesaurus survey* has been created in order to identify a preliminary set of terminologies. It has been distributed among several environmental communities, such as National and European environmental agencies and terminological experts in the community of Networked Knowledge Organization (NKOS). The questionnaire has totally 85 questions divided in five sections. The information requested can be summarized into three main groups:

- general evaluation of the user's skills in thesauri;
- identification of new terminological resources;
- collection of technical details about the suggested terminological resources (e.g., licence, available format).

In order to give a weight to the information suggested in the questionnaire, we have evaluated also the users skills and experience in using thesauri. The total number of responses has been 54 and about the 70% (37 units) of the responses are from users with experience about thesaurus, this guarantee a good reliability of the questionnaire suggestions.

State of Play analysis (SoP). The state of play aims at identifying the available terminologies that may be accessed through the web in order to complement the answers provided by the questionnaire. The methodology adopted is based on an Internet survey conducted using well-known search engines/platforms, the scientific literature and the interaction with the community. In particular:

- *Scientific literature.* This category includes mainly papers published in scientific international journals or conference proceedings relevant in the fields of Linked Data and Semantic Web. In particular we have focused on the Semantic Web Journal (SWJ), which has recently started a section dedicated to the descriptions of impacting Linked Data Datasets. Terminological resources included in this section of the SWJ are usually of high quality and technically validated by the community of Linked Data. We have also considered a previous survey on environmental terminologies presented in [12].
- *The datahub.* The datahub is a platform developed to share open datasets through a specific section for Linked Data. We have searched in the datahub all the terminolgies associated to the keywords *thesaurus* and *skos*. Among them we have considered those thematically related to environmental domain and also those interlinked to one of the main thesaurus players in the Environment (e.g., GEMET, AGROVOC, EARTh).
- *LOD Cloud.* This category includes terminological resources shared in the datahub and included in the LOD Cloud. The LOD Cloud diagram represents datasets published by the Linking Open Data project from 2007-2011. Terminological resources have been marked as included in the LOD Cloud according to the analysis available in http://validator.lod-cloud.net/.

Community Interaction. Different communities related to the environmental sciences have been involved in compiling the on-line questionnaire and in sorting out issues arising during the SoP investigation. In particular, the involved communities are:

- Public and private environmental stakeholders;
- Members of National Environment Agency of several European country as well as the European Environment Agency (EEA) and the Joint Research Centre (JRC - European Commission);
- Terminological thesauri experts from the mailing list Ecoterm and community of experts on Networked Knowledge Organization (NKOS).

The coverage of these multi-strategy process seems to be quite adequate, since it stresses and combines quite all the available type of information sources: (i) the web; (ii) the literature, focusing in particular on previous survey on environmental thesauri [12] and on the Semantic Web Journal; and (iii) the community, through the on-line questionnaire and the continuous interaction with the environmental domain experts.

3.2 Reference Catalogue of Thesauri

The multi-strategy investigation has resulted in a collection of different types of terminological resources. In fact, even if our research has been focused only on thesauri, indications returned by the multi-strategy process has also included codelists, ontologies, taxonomic datasets, datasets, gazetteers, schema/rdf vocabularies, glossary, vocabularies for a total of 62 resources. This is probably due to an inappropriate use of the term "thesaurus" among the communities.

In this paper, we decide to consider the thesauri, that is a controlled vocabulary of terms where semantic relations (hierarchical, associative, equivalence) between terms are explicitly declared. The total number of collected thesauri is 24. Table 1 shows the catalogue of thesauri providing: (i) the resource acronym; (ii) the resource description presenting the name of the thesaurus and some descriptive information (URL, datahub ID, scientific reference, licence); (iii) the provenance indicating the sources from which the thesauri has been collected, i.e., the questionnaire (Q), the LOD Cloud (LC), the SWJ dataset section (L), the datahub (DH) and the community suggestions (C).

Let's note that the adoption of a multi-strategy investigation allows to detect the presence of the same thesaurus in different sources provide a thumb rule of its "popularity" in environmental and Linked Data communities.

Table 1. Reference Catalogue of 24 Thesauri

Resource acronym	Resource description	Provenance
ADL FTT	**Alexandria Digital Library Feature Type Thesaurus** URL:http://www.alexandria.ucsb.edu/ lhill/FeatureTypes/ver070302/ Licence:http://www.alexandria.ucsb.edu/gazetteer/#licensing	C
AGROVOC	**AGROVOC** URL: http://aims.fao.org/standards/agrovoc **Bibliographic Reference:** [3] **Datahub ID:** agrovoc-skos Licence:http://creativecommons.org/licenses/by/3.0	Q, DH, L, LC, C
EARTh	**Environmental Applications Reference Thesaurus** URL: http://linkeddata.ge.imati.cnr.it:2020/ **Bibliographic Reference:** [1] **Datahub ID:** environmental-applications-reference-thesaurus Licence:http://creativecommons.org/licenses/by-nc-nd/3.0/	DH, L, LC
EcoLexicon	**EcoLexicon** URL: http://ecolexicon.ugr.es/visual/index_ en.html **Bibliographic Reference:** [6] Licence: Not found	Q
EnvThes	**EnvThes - Environmental Thesaurus** URL: http://vocabs.lter-europe.net/ EnvThes3.html Licence:In progress	Q
EOSterm	**Earth Observation Systems Thesaurus** URL: http://thesaurusonline.iia.cnr.it/ tematres/eosterm **Reference:** [8] Licence:http://creativecommons.org/licenses/by-nc-nd/3.0/	Q
EuroVoc	**EuroVoc Multilingual Thesaurus of the European Union** URL:http://eurovoc.europa.eu/ drupal/ **Datahub ID:** eurovoc-in-skos Licence:http://eurovoc.europa.eu/drupal/?q=legalnotice&cl=en	DH, C

Table 1. (*Continued*)

GEMET	**GEneral Multilingual Environmental Thesaurus** URL: http://www.eionet.europa.eu/ gemet/ Datahub ID: gemet Licence:http://creativecommons.org/licenses/by/2.5/dk/	Q DH, LC
GBA	**Geological Survey of Austria (GBA)- thesaurus** URL:http://resource.geolba.ac.a Datahub ID:geological-survey-of-austria-thesaurus Licence:http://opendefinition.org/licenses/cc-by-sa	DH, LC
ICAN	**ICAN demonstrator thesaurus** URL:http://mmisw.org/ont/ican/thesaurus Licence:Not found	C
Inter WATER	**InterWATER Thesaurus** URL:http://thesaurus.ircwash.net/ Licence:http://creativecommons.org/licenses/by-nc-sa/3.0/nl/deed.en	C
IUGS-CGI	**IUGS-CGI Multi-Lingual Thesaurus of Geosciences** URL:http://www.cgi-iugs.org/tech_ collaboration/ thesaurus.html Licence:In progress	C
NALT	**The U.S. National Agricultural Library Thesaurus** URL: http://agclass.nal.usda.gov/ Datahub ID: nalt Licence: http://www.nal.usda.gov/web-policies-and-important-links#NAL%20Agricultural%20Thesaurus%20and%20Glossary	Q, DH, LC
NERC NVS2.0	**NERC Vocabulary Server version 2.0** URL: http://vocab.nerc.ac.uk Datahub ID: nvs Licence:http://www.nationalarchives.gov.uk/doc/open-government-license/version/2/	Q, DH
SEMIDE	**SEMIDE Thesaurus** URL: http://www.emwis.net/portal_ thesaurus Licence:http://www.emwis.net/about/copyright_html	C
SnowTerm	**SnowTerm** URL: http://192.167.230.177/tematres/snowterm/ Bibliographic Reference: [13] Licence:http://creativecommons.org/licenses/by-nc-nd/3.0/	Q
SoilThes	**SoilThes** URL: https://secure.umweltbundesamt.at/soil/en/ collections/SoilCore_0.htm Licence: http://creativecommons.org/publicdomain/zero/1.0/	Q
STW	**STW Thesaurus for Economics** URL:http://zbw.eu/stw/versions/latest/ Datahub ID: stw-thesaurus-for-economics Licence:http://creativecommons.org/licenses/by-nc/2.0/	DH, LC
TheSoz	**TheSoz (Thesaurus for the Social Sciences)** URL: http://lod.gesis.org/thesoz/ Bibliographic Reference: [16] Datahub ID: gesis-thesoz Licence:http://creativecommons.org/licenses/by-nc-nd/3.0/de/	DH; L
ThIST	**Italian Thesaurus of Sciences of the Earth** URL:http://sgi.isprambiente.it/OnThist/servlet/onthist Bibliographic Reference: [4] Licence:In progress	Q
UMTHES	**UMweltTHESaurus** URL:http://data.uba.de/umt/de.html Datahub ID:umthes Licence: http://opendefinition.org/licenses/cc-by/	DH
UNESCO	**UNESCO Thesaurus** URL: http://databases.unesco.org/thesaurus Datahub ID: unescothes Licence:http://creativecommons.org/licenses/by-nc/2.0/	DH
U.S.G.S.	**United States Geological survey (Science,Themes and Subject)** URL: http://www.usgs.gov/science/about/ Licence:Not found	C
WQPB	**WQPB (Water Quality Library Thesaurus)** URL: http://svc.mt.gov/deq/wqlibrarysearch/Thesaurus.pdf Licence:Not found	C

4 Identification of Reusability Criteria

This section presents the formalization of the criteria adopted for the evaluation of thesaurus reusability. We consider two different criteria, one based on the 5 star LD principles defined by Tim Berners-Lee in [2] and the other based on the type of licence under which the thesaurus is released. They are explained in detail in the following.

4.1 5 Star LD Principles

In this section we present the formalization of the criteria for assessing the thesaurus compliance with 5 star LD classification (see [2]).

In our analysis special attention is paid to dereferenceability of the URI associated to concepts in the thesaurus. Dereferenceable URIs are the mandatory prerequisite for Linked Data, in fact, without them, it is not possible to check what is attached to the URI, and thus the identifiers are not truly reusable. In particular, the provision of thesaurus concepts without dereferenceable URIs restricts the third-parties possibility (i) to check authoritativeness of information associated to thesaurus concepts; (ii) to exploit mappings among thesauri concepts in order to discover further information in a follow-your-nose fashion. Coherently with the importance of HTTP dereferenceable URI in the Linked Data design issues, we have assigned 4 stars only to thesauri whose identifiers are HTTP dereferenceable and return RDF/XML encoding. Thus, we have detailed the 5 star LD classification proposed in [2] adding the values 3.5 and 3.9 between 3 and 4 stars, as follows:

- *1 star:* resources available on the web (whatever format);
- *2 stars:* resources available as machine-readable structured data (e.g., Excel instead of image scan of a table);
- *3 stars:* as 2 stars plus non-proprietary format (e.g., CSV instead of Excel);
- *3.5 stars:* resources available as RDF dump without dereferenceable HTTP URI;
- *3.9 stars:* resources provided as RDFa (RDF embedded in XHTML) or SPARQL end point which are very close to be Linked Data ready but still without dereferenceable HTTP URI.
- *4 stars:* all the above plus, use open standards from W3C (RDF and SPARQL) and HTTP dereferenceable URI to identify things, so that people can point at published resources;
- *5 stars:* all the above, plus links to other people's data to provide context.

In order to correctly evaluate the HTTP dereferenceability, concept URIs have been tested following the standard procedure detailed in the second section of Heath's book [9]. This procedure relies on the basics of the HTTP protocol: it sends a HTTP GET request for the URI indicating RDF/XML as preferred representation, and then it interprets the server response following any 303 `redirects` till a 200 `OK` is reached. If the 200 `OK` is reached and a RDF returned then the URI is considered HTTP dereferenceable. Otherwise, it isn't.

4.2   Licence Criteria

This section presents the licence criteria considering the categories presented in [14] that are based on some existing and well-known type of licences, such as the framework defined by Creative Commons. We decide to consider this framework since it provides an exhaustive coverage, the licences are identifiable by URIs and they are intended for general intellectual works. In the following we explain the formalization presented in Table 2.

- **Licence (acronym)/Characteristics.** We have slightly changed the categories defined in [14]. In fact we have divided the category *Not specified* distinguishing the subcases *Not found* and *In progress* in order to capture all the cases we have faced during the search of licence information. The category considered in the evaluation are detailed in the following.
  - *Public Domain Licences (CC0)*. They waive all the possible intellectual property and neighboring rights of the resources.
  - *Attribution Licences (CC-BY)*. They waive all the possible rights, requiring only the mere attribution.
  - *Share-alike Licences (CC-SA)*. The rights are also waived requiring that derived or adapted resources keep the same licence.
  - *With restrictions (CC-NC, CC-ND, CC-NC-ND)*. These licences present some restrictions in particular: (i) non-commercial (NC) means that the exploitation of a resource and its derived work must be non-commercial; (ii) non derivative (ND) allows for redistribution, commercial and non-commercial exploitation, as long as it is passed along unchanged and in whole, with credit to creators/right-holders.
  - *In progress (Pr)*. In this case, there is an explicit indication on the web site that the licence is under construction or we have a direct knowledge that thesaurus licence is going to be defined soon. *In progress* is a quite common situation: often a thesaurus is a result of the integration of work of different actors, thus it is not easy to choose a licence model which fits for all the contributors.
  - *Not found (NF)*. No licence has been found in the website or elsewhere.
- **Licence reusability evaluation.** We have assigned to each type of licence a value meaning the level of reusability of the resource allowed by the licence (1=low reusability, 5= high reusability). As shown in the Table 2 the most important categories are those referring to open licences without severe restrictions (CC0, CC-BY, CC-SA), since they allow the complete reuse, transformation and the publication of a resource.

5   Evaluation of Reusability

The thesauri collected in the reference catalogue have been analysed and evaluated with respect to the reusability criteria. In the following we present the evaluation of the thesauri considering the 5 star LD priciples, the licence criteria and the overall results of the analysis highlighting critical issues.

Table 2. Definition of the adopted categories of licence and the levels of reusability of the resource allowed by the licence

Licence (acronym)	Characteristics	Licence reusability evaluation
Public Domain (CC0)	All the rights have been waived	5
Attribution (CC-BY)	Attribution is required	4.5
Share alike (CC-SA)	Copyleft licence	4
With restrictions (CC-NC , CC-ND, CC-NC-ND)	More severe restrictions	3.5
Closed (CR)	Closed licence	3
In progress (Pr)	Licence is going to be defined soon	2
Not found (NF)	No licence has been found in the website	1

5.1   Evaluation wrt 5 Star LD Priciples

The evaluation of the thesaurus compliance with respect to the 5 star LD principles is presented in Table 3. The following groups of thesauri can be outlined:

– *Linked Data ready thesauri (LD ready).* This group contains thesauri published according to the Linked Data best practices and exposing dereference-able concept URIs returning the proper RDF/XML fragments (i.e., LD stars $>=4$).
– *RDF ready thesauri (RDF ready).* It considers thesauri for which some sort of RDF document is provided but without exposing HTTP dereferenceable URI for their concepts (i.e., $3<$ LD stars <4).
– *Other format thesauri (Other).* It includes thesauri made available in other format than RDF (i.e., LD stars$<=3$).

Moreover, about 45% of the considered thesauri (11 out of 24) falls in the first category *Linked Data ready thesauri*. In particular, we find that all the thesauri in this category deploy SKOS as RDF vocabulary. Some of them deploy ad hoc RDF vocabularies or ontologies together with SKOS, for example AGROVOC exploits AGRONTOLOGY, an ontology that basically extends `skos:related` properties with domain dependent relations such as `afflicts` /affect, `controls` /isControlledBy. Six thesauri in this category are already interlinked with third parties thesauri (i.e., LD stars $>=5$). Then, about the 33% of the thesauri (8 out of 24) falls in the second category. These thesauri already provide some sort of RDF document for their concepts so their exposition as Linked Data is probably under consideration or in progress. All the thesauri in the second category, but ADL FTT, deploy SKOS as RDF vocabulary. ADL FTT deploys an experimental RDF version that is dated back to 2002 and is based on undocumented ESRI vocabulary, probably one of the first attempts to define a RDF vocabulary for thesauri which has been eventually superseded by SKOS. ThIST, EOSTerm, and SnowTerm are classified as 3.5 stars because already available as SKOS-RDF but without HTTP dereferenceability. Moreover, ThIST, EOSTerm, and SnowTerm do not provide a complete SKOS/RDF dump

Table 3. Analysis of the thesauri in the catalogue according with 5 star LD principles

5 star evaluation	Thesaurus acronym
5	SoilThes, GEMET, AGROVOC, NERC NVS2.0 ,GBA, TheSoz, EARTh, EnvThes
4	NALT, UNESCO, ICAN
3.9	STW
3.5	EuroVoc, UMTHES, SnowTerm, EOSterm, ThIST, ADL FTT, U.S.G.S.
2	IUGS-CGI
1	SEMIDE, InterWATER, EcoLexicon, WQPB

of their overall set of concepts. They provide only a RDF fragment for each concept which is downloadable from HTML concept page or via in-house web application. Similarly, UMTHES provides RDF fragments accessible from the HTML concept page, but it also implements HTTP 303 redirection to adhere to the Linked Data best practices. Unfortunately, when UMTHES concept URIs are dereferenced asking for RDF/XML document, the URIs redirect to HTML pages and not to the proper RDF fragments. Another interesting example is STW Thesaurus for Economics evaluated with 3.9 stars since its set of concepts is complete available as RDFa but without any HTTP dereferenceable concept URIs. Finally, there is the group of thesauri that are not yet available as RDF (5 out of 24). In this group we can distinguish between thesauri accessible on a machine-readable format such as IUG-CGI Thes. of Geoscience, that is available as Excel, and thesauri like SEMIDE, EcoLexicon, IUGS-CGI which are available only embedded in a web portal or as PDF.

5.2 Evaluation wrt Licence Criteria

The licence evaluation requires first of all a careful analysis of each thesaurus licence in order to match it with the main characteristics of the Creative Common categories explained in Table 2.

In Table 4 the sign X in a column implies that the licence of thesaurus has such specific characteristic. Beside X, in parentheses, we provide further details:

- (1.0)/(2.5)/(2.0)/(3.0): it is the number of the version of the licence;
- (dh): it indicates that the URL of the licence has been found on datahub platform. For example for the thesauri GBA and UMTHES the following situations arise:
  - the URL points to an HTML pages with links to different versions of the same licence (e.g., http://opendefinition.org/licenses/cc-by-sa/). Thus, it is not possible to identify the correct version (GBA, UMTHES);
  - on the official website of the thesaurus no licence is found. In this case we are not sure that the licence on datahub is correct, since in the past

Table 4. Licence analysis of thesauri in the reference catalogue

Licence evaluation	Thesaurus acronym	CC-BY	CC-NC	CC-SA	CC-ND	CC0	CR	NF	Pr
5	SoilThes					X(1.0)			
4.5	GEMET	X (2.5)							
	AGROVOC	X(3.0)							
	NERC NVS2.0	X(nstd)							
	NALT	X(nstd)							
	EuroVoc	X							
	UMTHES	X(dh)							
4	GBA	X(dh)		X(dh)					
3.5	TheSoz	X(3.0)	X(3.0)		X(3.0)				
	EARTh	X(3.0)	X(3.0)		X(3.0)				
	UNESCO	X(2.0)	X(2.0)						
	EOSterm	X (2.5)	X (2.5)		X (2.5)				
	SnowTerm	X(3.0)	X(3.0)		X(3.0)				
	SEMIDE	X(nstd)			X(nstd)				
	Inter WATER	X (3.0)	X (3.0)	X (3.0)					
	STW	X(2.0)	X(2.0)						
2	EnvThes								X
	IUGS-CGI								X
	ADL FTT								X
	ThIST								X
1	ICAN							X	
	U.S.G.S.							X	
	EcoLexicon							X	
	WQPB							X	

the datahub was a collaborative platform where everyone could modify the information associated to the shared resources;
- (nstd): it indicates that the licence does not refer to a standard framework, thus, it may be difficult to identify all the characteristics of the licence itself. In particular, for the SEMIDE thesaurus the sentence "Reproduction is authorized, provided the source is acknowledged, except where otherwise stated" is ambiguous since it is no immediately clear if derivative works (remix, transformation ect) are authorized. On the other side, for NALT and NERC NVS2.0 it is more simple to categorize the main characteristics, even if it necessary a careful examination of the licences content.

Among the thesauri included in the category *In progress*, we distinguish two cases. In one case the legal notice on the website of the considered resource declares explicitly that the licence is under definition (ADL FTT). In the other case we know that the licence will be defined soon because we are in contact with the developers of the thesaurus (e.g., for EnvThes, ThIST, IUGS-CGI). Then, we have assigned to each thesaurus licence a reusability value according with Table 2. Notice that, if the thesaurus licence matches more than one characteristics we have considered the minimum of the different reusability values associated to the considered characteristics. For example, the licence of the thesaurus *TheSoz* includes the clauses CC-BY (its reusability value is 4.5), CC-ND and CC-NC (their reusability value is 3.5 for both), thus we assign to *TheSoz* the value 3.5.

Using the information in Table 4, we can group the thesauri in three categories:

- *Open Licenced Thesauri.* It includes highly reusable thesauri that are released under public domain, attribution or share-alike licences. They can

Table 5. Analysis of the thesauri with the macro-categories identified for LD stars and licence

	LD ready	RDF ready	Other
Open Licenced	SoilThes, GEMET, AGROVOC, NERC NVS2.0, GBA, NALT	EuroVoc, UMTHES	
Partially Open Licenced	TheSoz, EARTh, UN-ESCO	STW, SnowTerm, EOSterm	SEMIDE, InterWATER
Closed Licenced	EnvThes, ICAN	ThIST, U.S.G.S., ADL FTT	IUGS-CGI , EcoLexicon, WQPB

be modified and extended as needed and deployed in commercial and non-commercial context (licence evaluation>=4).

- *Partially Open Licenced Thesauri.* This group contains thesauri licenced with some further restrictions in reusability (licence evaluation=3.5).
- *Closed Licenced Thesauri.* It considers thesauri in which licence forbids the free reuse or for which a licence is not provided yet (licence evaluation<3.5).

The thesauri in the catalogue are equally distributed among these three categories, that means that only the 33% of thesauri considered are truly open licenced. Within the Partially Open Licence Thesauri, non-commercial use is the most common restriction (7 out of 8 thesauri). Moreover, ND restriction is often combined with NC restrictions (4 out of 5 thesauri forbid both).

5.3   Overall Discussion and Recommendations

The overall results of the reusability analysis is summarized in Table 5, whose columns refer to the three categories concerning 5 star LD evaluation while the rows refer to those identified for licence evaluation. We can observe that most of the thesauri with higher values (>= 4) for both 5 star LD principles and licence, (e.g., GEMET, AGROVOC, NERC NVS2.0, GBA, NALT and UNESCO) have been detected in more than one source of provenance in Table 1; this could imply that there is a direct relation between the "popularity" of a thesaurus and its "reusability". Moreover, the analysis performed on the thesauri in the catalogue shows an average good level of reusability. In fact, about the 58% of thesauri considered are Linked Data ready or RDF ready and are licenced with open or partially open licences. However, some recommendations to improve their reusability can be outlined:

- More attentions should be paid to HTTP dereferenceability of concepts URIs. Currently, Linked Data best practices seem quite popular among thesaurus providers in the environmental domain: about the 46% of the thesauri considered are already in Linked Data. However, the 54% of thesauri fails in a complete adoption of HTTP dereferenceable URI showing that HTTP dereferenceability is not yet received in the environmental thesauri community of providers. This shortcoming prevents the discovery and the integration of concepts from distinct thesauri in a follow-your-nose fashion hampering the jointly use of existing thesauri which is a requirement when managing geographical information at the European scale.

– Licence should be more carefully stated. More than 50% of the thesauri in the catalogue are released with licences from standard framework such as Creative Commons or equivalent. However, determining under which licence a dataset is released is still a time consuming activity. Depending on the thesaurus, the licence can be stated in different sources, e.g., the web site of the thesaurus, the web site of the institution owning the thesaurus, the related datahub page or related publications. Many thesauri are available in more than one of the aforementioned sources, but, rarely the licence is stated in all the sources available. In some cases, an explicit web link at the licence page is missing or it is not possible to find which version of the licence is adopted. As far as we have tested, generally no licence is included in the RDF returned by HTTP dereferencing.

6   Conclusion and Future Work

This paper provides a "reference catalogue" of thesauri available in the web for the environmental domain, in the perspective of the integration and the sharing of a large amount of existing environmental data provided by the National/Regional Environmental Agencies and other public and private environmental stakeholders. This is an emergent issue since several recent European directives address a more global management of environmental information in order to overcome cross-border/language and cultural barriers and to improve the cooperation between nations at European level. To this purpose, we present a methodology to identify terminological resources available on the web, possibly in Linked Data, a definition of domain independent criteria for the reusability based on two characteristics: the licence openness and the compliance to HTTP dereferenceability of URIs. Critical issues arising during the evaluation process are also detailed in the analysis. The future works will be twofold. On one side, we will complement the analysis presented considering notions of quality that have been recently proposed. In particular, multilingual support and SKOS-compliance of Linked Data and RDF ready thesauri can be analysed by using quality measures proposed in [15]. On the other side we will improve the dissemination of our results among the environmental communities developing a web portal to expose the whole catalogue and the reusability evaluation performed on each thesaurus.

Acknowledgements. The paper activity has been carried out within the EU funded project eENVplus (CIP-ICT-PSP grant No. 325232). The authors would like to thank all partners and, in particular, Paolo Plini (IIA-CNR) and Carlo Cipolloni (ISPRA) for their important collaboration. The authors would also like to thank the team of the European Commission's Joint Research Centre (Italy) for the valuable contribution.

References

1. Albertoni, R., De Martino, M., Di Franco, S., De Santis, V., Plini, P.: EARTh: An Environmental Application Reference Thesaurus in the Linked Open Data cloud. SWJ 5(2), 165–171 (2014)
2. Berners-Lee, T.: Linked data (2009), http://www.w3.org/DesignIssues/LinkedData.html (accessed: March 20, 2014)
3. Caracciolo, C., Stellato, A., Morshed, A., Johannsen, G., Rajbhandari, S., Jaques, Y., Keizer, J.: The AGROVOC linked datasetaset. SWJ 4(2), 341–348 (2012)
4. Carusone, A., Olivetta, L.: Italian Thesaurus of Earth Sciences (ThIST). APAT (2006)
5. De Martino, M., Albertoni, R.: A multilingual/multicultural semantic-based approach to improve data sharing in an SDI for nature conservation. Int. J. of Spatial Data Infrastructures Research 6, 206–233 (2011)
6. Faber, P.: A Cognitive Linguistics View of Terminology and Specialized Language. Walter de Gruyter (2012)
7. Government Linked Data Working Group: W3C Working Group Note: Best Practices for Publishing Linked Data (2014), http://www.w3.org/TR/ld-bp/ (accessed: March 24, 2014)
8. Grignetti, A., Plini, P., Mazzocchi, F., De Santis, V.: A thesaurus for remote sensing and gis: preliminary version and future plans. In: 19th Int. Conf. Informatics for Environmental Protection, pp. 783–787 (2005)
9. Heath, T., Bizer, C.: Linked Data: Evolving the Web into a Global Data Space. Morgan & Claypool (2011)
10. Abdul Manaf, N.A., Bechhofer, S., Stevens, R.: The current state of SKOS vocabularies on the web. In: Simperl, E., Cimiano, P., Polleres, A., Corcho, O., Presutti, V. (eds.) ESWC 2012. LNCS, vol. 7295, pp. 270–284. Springer, Heidelberg (2012)
11. Miles, A., Bechhofer, S.: W3C Recommendation: Simple Knowledge Organization System Reference (2009), http://www.w3.org/TR/skos-reference (accessed: March 20, 2014)
12. Palavitsinis, N., Manouselis, N.: A Survey of Knowledge Organization Systems in Environmental Sciences. In: Athanasiadis, I.N., Rizzoli, A.E., Mitkas, P.A., Gómez, J.M. (eds.) Information Technologies in Environmental Engineering, pp. 505–517 (2009)
13. Plini, P., Salvatori, R., Valt, M., De Santis, V.: SnowTerm: a terminology database on snow and ice. In: 21st Polar Libraries Colloquy, pp. 82–89 (2006)
14. Rodríguez-Doncel, V., Gómez-Pérez, A., Mihindukulasooriya, N.: Rights declaration in linked data. In: 4th Int. Work. on Consuming Linked Data (2013)
15. Suominen, O., Mader, C.: Assessing and improving the quality of SKOS vocabularies. J. on Data Semantics 3(1), 47–73 (2014)
16. Zapilko, B., Schaible, J., Mayr, P., Mathiak, B.: TheSoz: A SKOS representation of the thesaurus for the social sciences. SWJ 4(3), 257–263 (2013)

Empowering Users to Specify and Manage Their Privacy Preferences in e-Government Environments

Prokopios Drogkaris[1], Aristomenis Gritzalis[2], and Costas Lambrinoudakis[2]

[1] Laboratory of Information and Communication Systems Security,
Department of Information and Communication Systems Engineering,
University of the Aegean, Samos, GR-83200, Greece
pdrogk@aegean.gr
[2] Systems Security Laboratory,
Department of Digital Systems,
University of Piraeus, GR-18534, Greece
agritz@ssl-unipi.gr, clam@unipi.gr

Abstract. The provision of advanced e-Government services has raised users' concerns on personal data disclosure and privacy violation threats as more and more information is released to various governmental service providers. Towards this direction, the employment of Privacy Policies and Preferences has been proposed in an attempt to simplify the provision of electronic services while preserving users' personal data and information privacy. This paper addresses the users' need to create, manage and fine-tune their privacy preferences in a user friendly, yet efficient way. It presents a Graphical User Interface (GUI) that empowers them to articulate their preferences in machine readable format and resolve possible conflicts with Service Provider's (SP) Privacy Policy, without being obliged to go through complex and nuanced XML documents or being familiar with privacy terminology. Users can now be confident that their personal data will be accessed, processed and transmitted according to their actual preferences. At the same time they will be aware of their privacy-related consequences, as a result of their selections.

Keywords: e-Government, Privacy Policy, Privacy Preferences, GUI.

1 Introduction

The notion of privacy is a complex and challenging concept, especially since the evolution and spread of Information and Communications Technologies (ICT). Most widely accepted definitions, revolve around the idea that privacy is the right to protect personal information or to limit and control access to them. The advanced provision of electronic services has not only braced users' demand for online privacy but has also raised their privacy awareness [1]. Equivalently, from the provider's perspective, the need to protect users' privacy and to comply with privacy legislation is also a growing concern, let alone obligation. The increased number of e-Government services, offered by Central Government, entails a continuously increasing amount of data

A. Kő and E. Francesconi (Eds.): EGOVIS 2014, LNCS 8650, pp. 237–245, 2014.

collected, processed and retained by Governmental Service Providers without the users being aware to whom, for what purpose and for how long their personal data is released to.

This situation has raised users' concerns regarding data privacy, data disclosure and emerging privacy violation threats, thus affecting their trust level to the service and, in turn, their willingness to accept and use therm. As a result, the formalization of providers' commitments regarding privacy practices and privacy requirements is an indispensable task since users will be able to review these requirements and practices and preserve their personal data privacy [2], [3] & [4]. A privacy policy can be regarded as a statement or document describing what information is collected by an electronic service and how this information will be used [5]. Most commonly, a privacy policy states explicitly what personal information (such as email addresses and users' names) is collected, whether shared or sold to third parties and for how long it will be retained. On the other side, users should also be able to formally express acceptable privacy practices and requirements. Such formal statements comprise the so called privacy preferences. Usually they affirm which personal information can be collected, for what purpose, whether they can be transmitted to third parties and for how long they can be retained.

This paper addresses the need of users to create, manage and fine-tune their privacy preferences in a user friendly, yet efficient way. It presents a Graphical User Interface (GUI) that empowers them to articulate their preferences in machine readable format, identify situations where their data privacy might be at risk and resolve possible conflicts with Service Provider's (SP) policy, without being obliged to go through complex and nuanced XML documents or being familiar with privacy terminology[1]. Users can now be confident that their personal data will be accessed, processed and transmitted according to their actual preferences. At the same time they will be aware of their privacy-related consequences, as a result of their selections. The rest of the paper has been structured as follows: Section 2 presents an architecture for incorporating Privacy Policy and Privacy Preferences in e-Government environments and Section 3 presents the proposed Graphical User Interface. Section 4 discusses existing research work on user interfaces for privacy preferences selection while Section 5 concludes the paper providing directions for future work.

2   Privacy Policy and Preferences Embodiment in e-Government Environments

The concept of embodying Privacy Policy and Privacy Preference documents in modern e-Government environments has been explored in [6], in an attempt to simplify the provision of advanced electronic services while preserving user's privacy. Through Privacy Policy documents, Service Providers deliver a formal commitment

[1] This work has been supported by the national project "Secure and Privacy-Aware eGovernment Sevices – SPAGOS" (Grant Agreement 11SYN_9_2059), under "SYNERGAGIA 2011" programme, of the Operational programme "Competitiveness and Entrepreneurship".

of the data required, the purpose of this request as well as of how data will be processed and to whom it will be disclosed. Data subject consents to the use of her personal data by specifying, for each data item or group of items, fine-grained privacy preferences defining how these data items should be used. This approach has the advantage of coping with situations where the data subject decides to revoke the right that has previously granted to the data collector. By properly updating the preferences stored, the data subject can constitute certain personal data be no longer validly accessible. Architecture's design has been based on modern – government environments structure which involves a central portal that operates as a one-stop shop being the front end for every service provider [7], [8] & [9]. Typically this portal implements the authentication and registration procedures or incorporates the federated identity management infrastructure for every Service Provider. Alongside to these entities, the Privacy Controller Agent (PCA) was introduced, being in charge of storing and comparing Service Providers' privacy policies and user privacy preferences. An overview of the architecture is presented in Fig. 1 below.

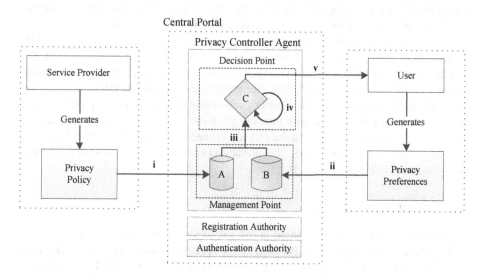

Fig. 1. Privacy Controller Agent Architecture [6]

The Privacy Controller Agent consists of two main units: the Management Point and the Decision Point. The Management Point features two storage repositories which are in charge of retaining the privacy policy of each service (A) and the privacy preferences of each user (B). When a service provider (SP) enrolls an electronic service to the central portal (CP), apart from the remaining information required, it is necessary to submit the corresponding Privacy Policy. The policy states explicitly the data required for the provision of the service, the purpose for which the data are required, how they will be processed, if they will be stored, for how long they will be retained and if they will be communicated to another service provider. The privacy preferences, defined by the user, apply to the entire set of her personal data irrespective of the specific service that utilizes them. Therefore the user needs to submit only one document (privacy preferences) that applies to all electronic services. User will have to specify what type of data will be included in the privacy preferences document, for what purpose these data can be used and by which service provider. After submission, the Privacy Controller Agent validates preference's origin and stores them at the Preferences Repository (action ii). Additionally, a simple XML schema has been proposed, in [6], to create the aforementioned documents. This schema consists of simple elements along with specific attributes, in an attempt to describe a strict privacy policy in a structured yet easy way.

3   Proposed Interface

This paper proposes the enhancement of e-Government environments with a privacy-enhancing mechanism that supports users to create, manage and fine-tune their privacy preferences in a user friendly, yet efficient way. The proposed mechanism pertains a Graphical User Interface (GUI) which enables users them to articulate their preferences in machine readable format and resolve possible conflicts with Service Provider's (SP) policy, without being obliged to go through complex and nuanced XML documents or being familiar with privacy terminology [6]. As discussed in [10], designing a user interface for specifying privacy preferences is challenging for several reasons: privacy policies are complex, user privacy preferences are often complex and nuanced, users tend to have little experience articulating their privacy preferences, users are generally unfamiliar with much of the terminology used by privacy experts, and users often do not understand the privacy-related consequences of their behavior. Consequently, in such interfaces, the privacy concepts must be presented through easily understood illustrations [11].

3.1   Specification Taxonomy

Based on the XML schema proposed in [6], two discrete categories have been identified; Personal Identifiers and Personal Data. For each one, the XML elements `Process`, `Process Type`, `Storage`, `Service Provider` and `Retention Period` must be specified. An overview of the taxonomy is presented in Fig. 2 below.

It is apparent that the specification of Personal Identifiers and Personal Data for each Service Provider would increase the amount of information and time required from users while creating their preferences. Moreover, a detailed description of each electronic service would be difficult for a user to administer and solelythe inclusion of SPs could not imprint actual user's preferences. To overcome this impediment, the establishment of sets and supersets has been adopted. Each Service Provider will constitute a superset that will contain all the electronic services that he offers; when a user allows his data to be processed or stored by this SP then this permission is transferred to each service. Similarly, a Ministerial Department will comprise a superset that will contain all applicable Service Providers. On the contrary, an acceptance

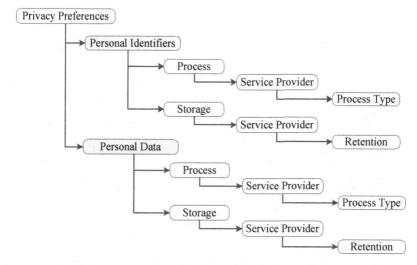

Fig. 2. Taxonomy of Specifications in User's Privacy Preferences

of a specific service does not imply approval of all SP's services. In addition to this principle, the lack of a SP or an electronic service shall be interpreted as a denial of data provision. Based on the approach of sets and supersets, the inclusion of attributes, relating to how data will treated by SP's, into specific supersets is also proposed. For instance, the Public attribute will also contain the Confidential one.

3.2 Graphical User Interface (GUI)

The Graphical User Interface (GUI) has been developed using Xcode[2], a development framework based on an Integrated Development Environment (IDE) which runs GNU Compiler Collection (GCC). The selection of Xcode allows for the exploitation of the proposed GUI by both mobile and desktop applications. Even though, at this point, they will not be directly connected to an e-Government Information System, the multi-platform functionality will allow for broader end-user engagement and participation during the foreseen e-acceptance use cases and trials. The overall interface's design has adopted principles discussed in [12], [13] and [14]. Furthermore it is expected to be improved based on the feedback received by participants during simulation trials. The main screen of the interface comprises of 4 distinct parts and is presented in Fig. 3 below.

Through the search function (Part I), the user is able to look for specific Personal Identifiers (e.g. National Identity Card Number (IdN), National Taxation Identifier (AFM), Social Security Number (AMKA) and Personal Data (e.g. First and Last Name, Address). The selected Identifier or Personal Data for which the user will specify her preferences are separately presented below. In Part II, the user can add or remove Ministerial Departments and Service Providers, specify how the selected data

---

[2] Xcode – Apple Developer: https://developer.apple.com/xcode/

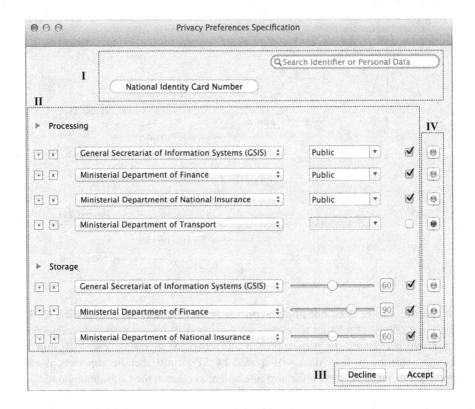

Fig. 3. Graphical User Interface (GUI) for Privacy Preferences Specification

will be processed and the maximum permissible retention period. Through the available check boxes, a Service Provider or Ministerial Department can be easily selected or deselected, without being obliged to completely remove it. Finally, in Part III, the user can accept to submit all her preferences to the Privacy Controller Agent or to cancel the procedure. Following the submission, the GUI creates the corresponding XML document, which is actually submitted to the Privacy Controller Agent. Based on the schema discussed in Section 2, the XML document generated from the interface selections is presented in Fig. 4 below.

When the user decides to invoke an electronic service, the comparison procedure is being invoked and her preferences are checked against service's privacy policy. If the user's preferences assent on the usage of data through the operations and for the purpose described in the policy, the agent informs the user, through the portal, of the concurrence and forwards service's request to the applicable Service Provider. Through this comparison and notification process, the user is now confident that her personal data will be accessed, processed and transmitted according to her preferences. In the case where these preferences don't match the policy of the SP, the PCA informs the user of the conflict. In part IV of the developed GUI, the deployment of visual notifications enable the user to quickly identify the conflict and review her preferences.

```
D.1  <Privacy_Preferences>
D.2   <Preferences_ID="[number assigned by Central Portal]">
D.3      </Preferences_ID>
D.4   <Data>
D.5    <Personal_Identifiers>
D.6     <Identifier_ID="="[number assigned by Central Portal]">National
D.7        Identity Card Number(IdN)
D.8        <Processed="Public">General Secretary of Information Systems
D.9                (GSIS)</Processed>
D.10        <Storage="Yes" Conserve="60">General Secretary of
D.11                Information Systems (GSIS)</Storage>
D.12        <Processed="Public">Ministerial Department of
D.13                Finance</Processed>
D.14        <Storage="Yes" Conserve="90">Ministerial Department of
D.15                Finance</Storage>
D.16        <Processed="Public">Ministerial Department of National
D.17                Insurance</Processed>
D.18        <Storage="Yes" Conserve="60">Ministerial Department of
D.19                National Insurance</Storage>
D.20     </Identifier_ID>
D.21    </Personal_Identifiers>
D.22   </Data>
D.23  </Privacy_Preferences>
```

Fig. 4. Generated XML Document

3.3   Security Evaluation

Even if Privacy Preferences documents do not contain personal or sensitive user data, it could be argued that they comprehend predilections on them and should thus not be made available to unauthorized entities. Furthermore, the integrity and availability of these documents should also be preserved so that the user is confident and assured that they are not modified or made unavailable. The incorporation of the Privacy Controller Agent and the provision of Privacy Preferences Specification service by the Central Portal, as described in Section 2, can indeed ensure these characteristics. Utilizing the underlying Public Key Infrastructure (PKI) of e-Government Information Systems, the user is able to digital sign her preferences document, after each creation, prior to submitting it to the PCA. After submission, the PCA validates preference's origin and stores them at the Preferences Repository, after encrypting them with the PCA's public encryption key [6].

4   Related Work

Several research projects funded by the E.C., including PRISE: Privacy enhancing shaping of security research and technology[3], PACT: Public perception of security and privacy: Assessing knowledge, Collecting evidence, Translating research into action[4], PRISMS: The PRIvacy and Security MirrorS: Towards a European

---

[3] PRISE Project: www.prise.oeaw.ac.at
[4] PACT Project: www.projectpact.eu

framework for integrated decision making[5] have conducted analysis and assessment on existing knowledge and technologies about the trade-off model between privacy and security and trust and concern. Additionally, they have proposed methodologies and frameworks for reconciling privacy, security, trust and concern that could assist end users and policy makers to consider privacy and fundamental rights when they evaluate security and privacy preserving technologies. A significant aspect of these proposals pertains users being able to hide and reveal personal information based on a particular usage context, user controlled information flows, where user can manage her privacy on different levels of detail and finally promoting guidance and awareness through advisory procedures.

As acknowledged in [15], "privacy poses a very difficult HCI problem"; GUI's not only represent an extremely complex decision space, depending on the context and the commitment of the user, in a simplified way but should also highlight context significant information and provide feedback and suggestions. The creation of Graphical User Interfaces for specifying Privacy Preferences has been initially explored at [16] and [17] where a user agent was developed for Internet Explorer 5.01, 5.5, and 6.0, as a browser helper object. The design approach focused on a subset of the P3P vocabulary, which could be easily realized by users, along to privacy options that used combinations of P3P data elements. During the development, authors attempted to avoid setting defaults for the main privacy settings as they wanted to compel users in selecting the actual settings themselves. Finally, they also developed appropriate agents that provide feedback, through icons and messages, about whether a privacy policy matched a user's preferences and make privacy suggestions as a more direct and appropriate mean to inform the user.

5   Conclusions

Privacy Enhancing Technologies (PET) pertaining Privacy Policies and Preferences have been largely accepted as suitable mechanisms to overcome user concerns regarding data disclosure and emerging privacy violation threats. The complexity however of SP's Privacy Policies pose significant difficulties on the automated development of personalized and fine graded Privacy Preferences since it inevitably requires intense interaction with the user. Towards this direction, a Graphical User Interface (GUI) was developed and proposed, as an addition to Privacy Controller Agent, enabling users to create, manage and fine-tune their preferences in machine readable format, taking also into account possible conflicts with Service Provider's privacy policy. The work, which is currently underway, is to create a sufficient number of Privacy Policies and exploit them during GUI validation use cases and trails, based on different types of users.

References

1. Chellappa, R., Pavlou, P.: Perceived Information Security, Financial Liability and Consumer Trust in Electronic Commerce Transactions. Logistics Information Management 15(5), 358–368 (2002)

---

[5] PRISMS Project: www.prismsproject.eu

2. McDonald, A.M., Reeder, R.W., Kelley, P.G., Cranor, L.F.: A Comparative Study of On-line Privacy Policies and Formats. In: Goldberg, I., Atallah, M.J. (eds.) PETS 2009. LNCS, vol. 5672, pp. 37–55. Springer, Heidelberg (2009)

3. Proctor, R.W., Vu, K.-P.L., Ali, M.A.: Usability of user agents for privacy-preference specification. In: Smith, M.J., Salvendy, G. (eds.) Human Interface, Part II, HCII 2007. LNCS, vol. 4558, pp. 766–776. Springer, Heidelberg (2007)

4. Bodorik, P., Jutla, D., Wang, M.: Consistent privacy preferences (CPP): model, semantics, and properties. In: 2008 ACM Symposium on Applied Computing, SAC 2008, Ceara, Brazil, pp. 2368–2375 (2008)

5. Salas, P.P., Krishnan, P.: Testing Privacy Policies Using Models. In: Sixth IEEE International Conference on Software Engineering and Formal Methods, Cape Town, pp. 117–126 (2008)

6. Drogkaris, P., Gritzalis, S., Lambrinoudakis, C.: Employing Privacy Policies and Preferences in Modern e-Government Environments. International Journal of Electronic Governance 6(2), 101–116 (2013)

7. Charalabidis, Y., Lampathaki, F., Sarantis, D., Sourouni, A.-M., Mouzakitis, S., Gionis, G., Koussouris, S., Ntanos, C., Tsiakaliaris, C., Tountopoulos, V., Askounis, D.: The Greek Electronic Government Interoperability Framework: Standards and Infrastructures for One-Stop Service Provision. In: 12th Panhellenic Conference on Informatics (PCI 2008), Samos. Greece, pp. 66–70 (2008)

8. Pei, Y., Jiao, G.: Researching and Designing the Architecture of E-government Based on SOA. In: International Conference on E-Business and E-Government (ICEE 2010), Guangzhou, pp. 512–515 (2010)

9. Drogkaris, P., Geneiatakis, D., Gritzalis, S., Lambrinoudakis, C., Mitrou, L.: Towards an Enhanced Authentication Framework for eGovernment Services: The Greek case. In: Ferro, E., Scholl, J., Wimmer, M. (eds.) 7th International Conference on Electronic Government, EGOV 2008, Torino, Italy, vol. 1, pp. 189–196. Trauner Verlag (2008)

10. Cranor, L., Guduru, P., Arjula, M.: User Interfaces for Privacy Agents, pp. 135–178 (2006)

11. Kolter, J., Pernul, G.: Generating User-Understandable Privacy Preferences. In: Barolli, L., Jakoubi, S., Tjoa, S. (eds.) International Conference on Availability, Reliability and Security (ARES 2009), Fukuoka, vol. 1, pp. 299–306 (2009)

12. McNamara, N., Kirakowski, J.: Defining usability: quality of use or quality of experience? In: Professional Communication Conference, IPCC 2005 (2005)

13. Nillson, E.: Design patterns for user interface for mobile applications. Advances in Engineering Software: Designing, Modelling and Implementing Interactive Systems 40(12), 1318–1328 (2009)

14. Lee, G., Eastman, C., Taunk, T., Ho, C.: Usability principles and best practices for the user interface design of complex 3D architectural design and engineering tools. International Journal of Human-Computer Studies 68(1-2), 90–104 (2010)

15. Ackerman, M., Cranor, L.: Privacy Critics: UI Components to Safeguard Users' Privacy. In: Altom, M., Williams, M. (eds.) Conference on Human Factors in Computing Systems (CHI 1999), Pittsburgh, vol. 1, pp. 258–259 (1999)

16. Cranor, L.: Designing a Privacy Preference Specification Interface: A Case Study. In: Patrick, A., Long, A., Flinn, S. (eds.) Workshop on HCI and Security Systems (CHI 2003), Tampa, vol. 1, pp. 38–47 (2003)

17. Ackerman, M., Cranor, L., Reagle, J.: Privacy in e-commerce: Examining User Scenarios and Privacy Preferences. In: Feldman, S., Wellma, S. (eds.) 1st ACM Conference on Electronic Commerce (EC 1999), New York, vol. 1, pp. 1–8 (1999)

Helios Verification: To Alleviate, or to Nominate: Is That the Question, or Shall we Have Both?

Stephan Neumann[1], M. Maina Olembo[1],
Karen Renaud[2], and Melanie Volkamer[1]

[1] Security, Usability and Society, CASED, TU Darmstadt, Germany
[2] School of Computing Science, University of Glasgow, Scotland
firstname.lastname@cased.de, firstname.lastname@glasgow.ac.uk

Abstract. Helios is an end-to-end verifiable remote electronic voting system which has been used for elections in academic contexts. It allows voters to verify that their vote was cast, and included in the final tally, as intended. User studies have shown that voters are unlikely to perform this verification, probably due to the effortful and cumbersome manual steps that are required by the system. To address this challenge, we propose, in this paper, two improvements: the first is to ameliorate the cumbersome nature of the verification process as much as possible. We offer two suggestions for doing this. To accommodate voters who have no interest in verifying, we propose a further improvement: delegation. This will allow voters to nominate a trusted third party to perform the verification on their behalf *as and when they cast their vote*. Hence no extra effort is required, and we can exploit existing trust in public institutions to provide voters with the assurance that the voting process is indeed honest and above board. In addition to providing end-to-end verifiability in a less effortful manner, we provide *stored as cast* and *tallied as stored* verifiability as well, for voters who do not wish to verify their own votes.

1 Introduction

Electronic voting, a hot topic that continues to attract interest in real world elections and in academic research, is generally separated into vote casting machines (e.g. [29]), vote-tallying machines (e.g. [23]), and Internet-based voting systems (e.g. [3]). Helios is one Internet-based voting system that has been thoroughly studied in the literature (e.g. [18]), and has been used in a variety of elections, primarily in academic contexts. For example, it was used to elect the university president at the Université catholique de Louvain [4], and since 2010, to elect the Board of Directors of the International Association for Cryptologic Research (IACR), to conduct the Princeton undergraduate student election [24], and for the Board Election of the Institute of Public Works Engineering Australia (IP-WEA).

Vote integrity in Helios implicitly relies on two assumptions. The first is that voters *will act* to verify that their vote was indeed "cast as intended" and "stored as cast". This requires them to take deliberate action subsequent to casting their

A. Kő and E. Francesconi (Eds.): EGOVIS 2014, LNCS 8650, pp. 246–260, 2014.

vote. The second assumption is that the voting environment (i.e. the device, such as the smartphone or laptop, used to cast the vote) or the voting client and the *ballot verifier system* (BVS) are trustworthy and have not been compromised. The latter assumption ensures that vote integrity and secrecy are assured. The first assumption can only hold if all voters are motivated to verify, and able to do so. Helios verification requires voters to write down a set of characters computed by the voting device and then to compare them manually to another set of characters computed by a verifier. Findings from user studies on verification in Helios suggest that voters tend not to verify their votes [30,17,16]. This applies to "cast as intended" verification ("stored as cast" verification has yet to be evaluated). Participants in these studies found the process cumbersome, especially since they were asked to repeat it several times. Such repetition is considered necessary to achieve adequate security levels.

Since verification is considered a valuable feature in guaranteeing the integrity of the election process, we suggest two improvements. The first is to attempt to ease the process so that voters no longer find it so arduous. We address this issue by proposing two means for simplifying the "cast as intended" verifiability process: (1) copy, web browser search and paste; and (2) a verification smartphone App (which weakens the second assumption that Helios relies on with respect to vote integrity). Moreover, we also propose a simple way to conduct the "stored as cast" verification process which currently is similarly cumbersome (although it differs from cast as intended verification as it only needs to be conducted once). For both verification options, we have taken an exploratory human-centered design approach following the guidelines given by [15] in designing and integrating these proposals into Helios.

The second is to accept that the interface might never be able to make it trivial enough and that there will still be many voters who will not verify. We therefore further tailor the voting process to acknowledge this reality by allowing voters to nominate one of a number of trusted institutes to verify on their behalf. We hope to achieve more effective security for future elections that use Helios.

2 Helios Voting System

Helios is an Internet-based, open source, end-to-end verifiable voting system [3]. It provides *cast as intended* verifiability, since voters can check that their actual votes are correctly encrypted. It also supports *stored as cast* verifiability, where voters can check that the encrypted votes are received by, and stored at the voting server, for tallying purposes without modification. Finally *tallied as stored* verifiability is supported, where any interested parties (including voters) can check that all stored votes have been tallied correctly. If it is confirmed that all stored votes were properly tallied, voters can be assured that their votes were properly tallied if they acted previously to conduct the other two verifiability steps. Note that in Helios vote integrity, as well as vote secrecy, is only assured under the assumption that the voting environment (the device, the browser and the network connection) is trustworthy. As such, the ability to verify only enables voters or observers to detect Helios system malfunction.

In order to provide "cast as intended" verifiability, Helios uses the Benaloh Challenge [6]. "Stored as cast" verifiability is achieved using a public web bulletin board that acts as a voting server to store votes [3,4]. Either verifiable homomorphic tallying [4] or a verifiable mix net and verifiable decryption [8] are used to provide "tallied as stored" verifiability. The focus of our research is on the first two verification steps as these have to be conducted by the voters themselves (if not, vote secrecy would be violated) while "tallied as stored" verification steps can be conducted by any interested party. Correspondingly, we also only explain these two steps in more detail. We will start our discussion with the original Helios version and then explain the relevant modifications proposed in [16] which we use as a basis for the research proposed in this paper.

Voters use the Helios interface, referred to as a *ballot preparation system* (BPS), to select the candidate(s) of their choice. The BPS encrypts this selection (i.e. the vote) and displays a hash value of the encrypted vote. Voters are supposed to record the displayed hash value in order to carry out both verification steps. Since the SHA256 hash algorithm and Base64 encoding are used, voters currently have to record 43 characters.[1]

Voters can then decide to cast the encrypted votes or to verify whether the genuine vote was indeed encrypted (which is referred to as the Benaloh Challenge). If voters decide to verify that their vote was "cast as intended", they interact with the independent and trustworthy *ballot verifier system* (BVS). BPS confirms the candidate(s) and the randomness used for encryption by displaying this information, which voters are supposed to select and copy to the clipboard in order to paste it into the BVS. The BVS then encrypts the corresponding vote and generates the hash value of this encryption. This hash value is displayed together with the provided candidate(s). In order to complete the "cast as intended" verification process voters need to visually compare both values to ensure that they are correct (the 43 characters of the hash value and the candidate/s). Note that since both hash values are displayed on the same device it is crucial that this device be trustworthy — if not, it would always display the expected hash value, independent from what BVS computes.

Voters can repeat the "cast as intended" verification step as many times as required and this should actually be repeated to ensure integrity. Votes that have been verified i.e. votes for which the randomness used for encryption has been revealed, can no longer be cast since voters could then prove how they voted if this vote could be cast directly. Therefore, depending on the Helios version, voters are re-issued with an empty ballot, or the vote is automatically re-encrypted. As the BVS is given the content of the encryption, it is recommended that voters verify test votes (that is, not necessarily the same as the one that will

---

[1] It should be emphasized that SHA256 provides overwhelming integrity assurance at the current point in time. According to Lenstra's revised recommendations for key length [19], a shorter hash value can be justified for this context. Assuming an election phase of 30 days and the adversary's financial limitations of 3 million dollars, a hash size length of 155 bits is sufficient to provide adequate security. According to the PGP word list [31], 155 bits could be presented by 20 words.

be cast) to avoid BVS being able to derive intermediate outcomes. To support this, it helps to use the Helios version in which voters need to start with the empty ballot once they have verified. While Helios provides verifiability, it does not provide accountability; i.e. if people or the verification tools falsely claim that the "cast as intended" or "stored as cast" step could not be completed, there is no way to distinguish between the two cases: dishonest voters/tools or Helios being untrustworthy. If voters choose to cast the vote, either directly or after vote encryption, they are prompted to authenticate themselves, and their encrypted votes are then posted to the public web bulletin board together with the hash value of the encrypted vote. To verify that the vote is "stored as cast", voters need to check whether the correct hash value appears on the public web bulletin board next to the voter's name [3], or pseudonym [4] depending on the Helios version used. It is only necessary to check this once as the Helios security model assumes that observers or other trusted institutes continuously make copies of the bulletin board and would detect malicious behaviour on the part of the bulletin board with respect to integrity. For example, detecting removal or replacement of single votes should be trivial.

Various aspects of "cast as intended" verification were improved in [17]. This included instructions and simplifications (in particular reducing the number of required steps from 15 to 7). For this paper it is relevant to point out that (1) the information necessary for the BVS is automatically transferred from the BPS and (2) several BVS systems are provided by different trusted institutes. Voters now only need to trust one particular institute and not rely on only one BVS. In [17], the authors show that this approach is as secure as the original Helios version. Note, both versions rely on the assumption that voters check that they are on the proper voting and verification web pages. The simplified verification procedure is depicted in Figure 1.

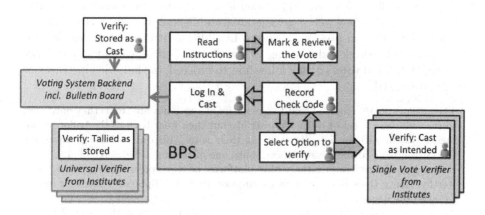

Fig. 1. Improved ballot casting and verification procedure according to [17]

These simplified steps and improved interfaces were tested in a lab user study with 34 participants [16]. The outcome was that most of the participants were able to verify[2] (after receiving instructions to do so). However, they still complained about the required steps being too cumbersome.

Therefore we propose less cumbersome alternatives to verify that the vote is "cast as intended" but also propose mechanisms to verify that the vote is "stored as cast". We focus on simple elections (n out of m candidate(s) to be selected in one race) to simplify the explanations in the following sections.

3   Alleviation Option 1: Copy, Search, Paste

In this section we discuss the processes that voters would carry out to verify their vote using the first alternative, namely the 'copy, search and paste' approach.

3.1   "Cast as Intended" Verification

Using this scheme to verify whether a vote is cast as intended, voters have to:

1. **COPY:** copy the check-code (using Ctrl + C) to the clipboard[3] which is displayed after the vote has been encrypted (see Figure 2, step 2)[4]. Note, on clicking the icon i for more information, voters would see the following instruction: 'Highlight the check-code with the mouse. Simultaneously press the Control and C keys to copy it to the clipboard.'
2. **SEARCH:** Voters can then decide to check the encrypted vote and select a verifiability institute, to which they will be re-directed. The interface provides several options to verify (see Figure 3): Six institutes are represented by their corresponding logos. An option to check using the QR checker App (outlined in the following section), and the Manual Check option, which refers to that provided by the original Helios interfaces also appear. The institutes[5] listed here were identified in a user study for Germany, detailed in [21]. On this new web page, the institute displays the check-code and the candidate(s) as in previous versions. In addition, it displays instructions to compare the check-codes (using Ctrl + F and Ctrl + V) and to check the candidate(s). If voters do not know how to proceed, the following instructions are displayed:

---

[2] The authors of [16] reported that two participants were not able to as they only went to the web page to select a trusted institute but then went back to the ballot preparation system without actually verifying their vote. This can be fixed by disabling the button back to the voting process until one of the institutes is selected.

[3] Remember, Helios assumes the voting platform, i.e. the voters' device, to be trustworthy. Hence there is an implicit assumption that the clipboard content is indeed equal to the displayed text.

[4] The steps and shortcuts outlined here are suitable for use on a Microsoft Windows platform. This differs from the instructions for other operating systems and platforms, such as Linux, Mac OS X, iOS, and Android. The idea is that the server detects the browser being used and displays the corresponding instructions.

[5] Note that we are not implying that the any of these institutes have agreed to provide such a service.

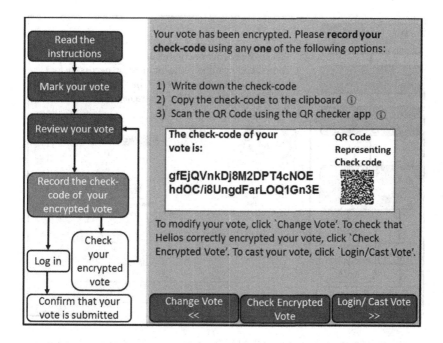

Fig. 2. Options to record the hash value (referred to as 'check-code')

(a) To open the web browser search bar, simultaneously press the Control and F keys on the keyboard.
(b) To paste the copied check-code from the clipboard to the search bar, simultaneously press the Control and V keys. Press the Enter button if necessary to compare the value in the clipboard to the value displayed below.

3. **PASTE:** Voters use Ctrl-V to paste. If the displayed check-code is highlighted and the candidate(s) is/are the one(s) selected before, voters can be sure that the vote was properly encrypted.

This proposed amelioration approach removes the need for manual recording and should thus ease the verification process.

3.2   "Stored as Cast" Verification

In order to confirm that the check-code has been stored correctly on the public web bulletin board, voters have to visit the corresponding web page and check this using the same copy, search and paste approach. They have to confirm whether the check-code appearing next to their voter ID or pseudonym is highlighted. Note that access to the public web bulletin board is provided once voters have been successfully authenticated, and their vote has been stored. Since the check-code is already in the clipboard it is possible for voters to carry out the second action independent of the first verification step. Again, as compared to

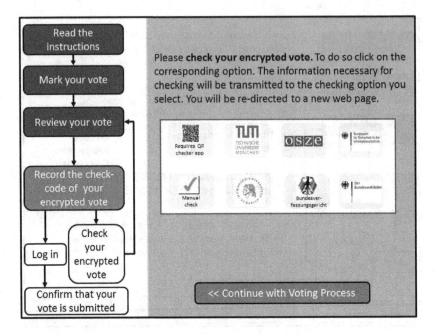

Fig. 3. Checking options available to voters - voters select the QR logo

previous versions, no manual comparison of the original hash value and the one displayed next to the voters' ID or pseudonym is necessary.

3.3   Reflection and User Testing

While it is obvious that this approach is less cumbersome, we wanted to determine whether voters would actually be able to conduct the necessary steps. We conducted a small user study including only participants who indicated that they would cast their vote over the Internet to ensure that we had a representative sample in the context of Internet voting. Prior to beginning the study, participants were briefly given context information, explaining how the system operated, and how to verify their votes. Twenty-eight female and 16 male participants took part in the study, with an estimated average age of 26 years. We asked all participants to use the copy, search and paste technique.

Thirty-seven out of the 44 participants were able to copy the hash value into the clipboard on their computer without further instructions. Thirty-five of these also correctly identified the hash value from the list without further instructions. After further instructions 86.4% of participants were able to carry out the copy, search and paste actions on the web browser. However, the results are admittedly less than perfect and show that we cannot rely solely on this approach. Extra support has to be provided for voters who can then revert to the manual process. Hence we still have to retain and facilitate a manual verification process (see Figure 2, step 1). To assist voters, several fields designed to hold these check-codes can be provided with the election material that is sent to voters, along with their voting credentials.

4 Alleviation Option 2: QR Codes and Smartphone App

In this section, we describe the processes that voters would engage in to verify that their votes were cast as intended and stored as cast by using a smartphone App[6]. A corresponding App would be developed by several trusted institutes. Voters decide which institute to trust and then download the App from that institute. The very sceptical could download Apps from several institutes, and use all of them to verify. Note, voters with a background in Computer Science can optionally develop their own App. The App approach, similar to the copy, search and paste approach, also avoids manual recording and visual comparison, making verification less cumbersome.

4.1 "Cast as Intended" Verification

To provide cast as intended verifiability, the ballot preparation system will display a QR code representing the check-code in addition to the human readable value (see Figure 2). Voters will scan the QR code using the App. The App's interface will display the scanned check-code (see Figure 4 for the corresponding App interface). Voters, on deciding to verify their votes, select the option 'Check Encrypted Vote' on the Helios interface (see Figure 2). Voters then select the QR checker App option (see Figure 3 for a corresponding interface). A second QR code is displayed. Note that while this QR code could be displayed on the same web page as the checking options (Figure 3), we required users to deliberately choose the option. The problem with allowing direct casting was uncovered by [16] who reported that some voters did not know how to proceed when they were on the web page providing the options. Some thought that they had already verified and did not proceed to do so. We thus opted to disable the 'Continue with Voting' button until at least one of the options on the web page had been chosen by voters and a separate window opened. When voters return to this first page, the 'Continue with Voting' button is enabled.

Using the App interface, voters elect to check that their votes are correctly encrypted. They then select the 'Scan' button to scan this second QR code. To avoid confusion, the App also instructs voters on the required steps to be carried out on the Helios interface. The App then displays the result (see Figure 5): either informing voters of a mismatch or a match in comparing the check-codes. In case of a match, it displays the candidate(s) and prompts voters to confirm whether this is what they marked earlier on the ballot. If voters confirm that the vote is correct, they will be reassured that the Helios voting system acted with integrity. The message will also recommend that they check the vote several

---

[6] Note that this obviously means that voters use one device to cast their votes and another to verify: perhaps a laptop and smartphone or two different smartphones.

times before submitting a final vote. If voters indicate that there is an error they will be directed to contact the election commission for more information on how to proceed.

Two prominent reasons why the check-codes might not match are that either the voter has made a mistake, such as scanning non-matching QR codes, or the Helios system could be untrustworthy. To address the first eventuality, the App would first instruct voters to make sure that they had scanned the correct QR code. If voters are certain of the mismatch, they can vote from another device, or contact the election authorities.

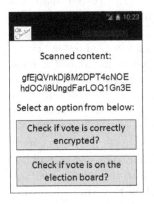 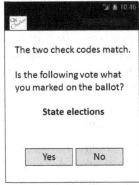 

Fig. 4. Scanned check-code and options for the voter

Fig. 5. Results of the verification process

Fig. 6. Positive result that vote is stored on the public web bulletin board

4.2 "Stored as Cast" Verification

In order to verify that votes are stored as cast, after scanning the first QR code (shown in Figure 2), voters can opt to check the public web bulletin board. Voters select the option 'Check if vote is on the election board' (see Figure 4). To prevent voters from proceeding in error, they are prompted to indicate whether they have submitted their vote or not. If they indicate that they have not yet done so, they are instructed to do so before proceeding. Once voters have submitted their vote, (or if they indicate that they have done so), the App checks the public web bulletin board by sending a query containing the received check-code. It then displays a message confirming whether the check-code was successfully stored on the public web bulletin board (see Figure 6). Given that Helios assumes that the public web bulletin board is continuously monitored by multiple parties, voters only have to check once.

4.3 Reflection

We anticipate that this solution will be acceptable to voters. Smartphones had a 51% penetration rate in Germany[7] in December 2012 [2] and during 2012 over

---

[7] Where this research was carried out.

1.7 million smartphone Apps were downloaded in Germany [1]. These numbers suggest that this verification solution is likely to be accepted by smartphone owners. Initial research suggests that smartphone owners who would be willing to vote over the Internet would verify their votes given an appropriate motivating message [20]. We did not carry out a user study to test the usability of the QR code based App since it is very simple and we already know that people are able to scan and use QR codes very successfully, as reported in various contexts including travel information [9], libraries [5] and consumer communication [12]. Hence we expect this application not to present users with any particular challenges. This will be increasingly true as the younger technically adept generation ages and reaches voting age.

Finally, the App weakens the need for the assumptions that Helios and the previous amelioration option rely on with respect to integrity. As opposed to Helios and the previous amelioration option, the second amelioration requires that either the smartphone or the App, and either the voting client or the voting platform do not collaborate. The multiple Apps, developed by different trusted institutes, will be bound to reveal any deception that would have been harder to detect using the previous mechanism. We acknowledge that not all voters own smartphones therefore, to ensure inclusivity, other verification mechanisms that do not require extra devices will have to be retained.

5   Delegating Verification to a Nominated Party

The arduous nature of the "write down and manually compare" process in Helios is addressed by the amelioration proposals we presented in the previous two sections. If the first two proposed options are integrated in future elections, it should make the "cast as intended" and the "stored as cast" verification process in Helios more efficient. Yet the element of effort undoubtedly remains, and humans are, unfortunately, effort misers.

5.1   Proposal to Extend the Process

It is difficult to propose further simplifications while retaining the existing process of (1) selecting the candidates, (2) verifying with one or more smartphone Apps or web services from trustworthy institutes, (3) casting a vote and (4) verifying with one or several smartphone Apps or trustworthy web services. Given that a significant number of voters will not make the effort to verify, we propose re-thinking the vote casting/verification process.

In the following, we focus on voters who would not verify their votes, while verification measures of the previous sections remain unchanged. We propose changing the voting protocol in the following way: The various institutes will provide web clients to allow voters to cast their votes directly. Hence, voters are provided with several voting URLs in the election invitation letter — one for each of the trustworthy institutes participating in the election. After deciding whom to trust, voters use the vote casting web client provided by that trusted institute. Voters cast a vote over the trusted web client and the institute takes care of the remaining verifiability steps. Throughout the vote casting process, the verification part would be less prominent as indicated in Figure 7. The institutes would verify that all votes cast using their own web service are stored correctly, i.e., they are "stored as cast". In addition, they would still — as in the original Helios as well as in our improved versions — be able to verify that all stored votes were properly tallied. We thus promote the idea of nomination, or indeed delegation. Note that delegation is a well-known and widely-used process [13]. An overview of the Helios variation, with nomination, is shown in Figure 8.

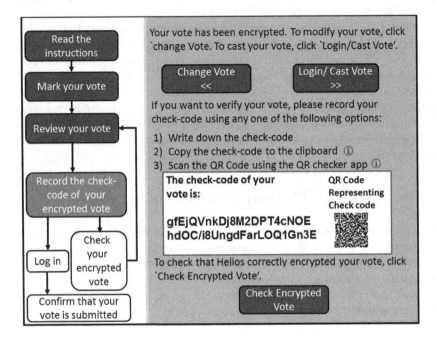

Fig. 7. Revised vote casting interface

5.2   Reflection

For voters benefiting from the amelioration, the fact that someone else is also verifying does not reduce security based on the vote casting / verification processes from [17]. For those voters *not* verifying their votes, integrity assurance is improved with the delegation approach because it is not possible for all votes to be manipulated by a single web client. Rather, one "bad" web client could manipulate only a subset of all the votes. On the other hand, distributing trust among several institutes does not address the issue of malicious voting environments. If the voting environment is compromised, integrity violations cannot be detected by any trusted institute.

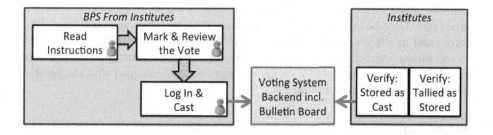

Fig. 8. Helios voting with nomination

6   Related Work

We will review two types of related work: (1) research aiming to improve Helios from a technical perspective and (2) human-centered research on verification.

Since Helios was introduced, a number of technical improvements have been proposed. Only two are of interest as they go on to propose implementations of their work. Cortier *et al.* [11] present an open-source variant of Helios providing distributed key generation. The authors do not focus on improvements regarding voter interaction with the system. Tsoukalas *et al.* [28] present Zeus, a verifiable voting and counting system based on Helios. The verifying process is modified such that the voter can decide how the vote should be handled once it leaves the voting platform. If voters submit so-called audit codes, generated by the voting server and sent to them via a secondary channel, they indicate that these submitted votes should be audited and not counted. The authors however point out that no voters in the elections run with Zeus used the audit feature. In our work we additionally propose a solution for voters who may not take up the verification opportunity.

Verifiability has been studied in various contexts from a human perspective while mostly in the context of (plain text) voter verifiable paper audit trails (VV-PATs) in poll site election settings; e.g. Cohen [10] and later on Selker *et al.* Selker et al. [26] showed that people are unlikely to detect manipulations in the paper audit trails. Similar conclusions were drawn by Herrnson *et al.* [14] based on the times participants spend examining the printouts. Recently, Budurushi *et al.* [7] found that the number of voters verifying plain text VV-PATs increases significantly, if voters are confronted with pre-printed "just-in-time" verification instructions. Besides plain text VV-PATs, verification has also been studied from a human perspective in the context of cryptographic verifiability. More precisely, it has been studied in the context of the Prêt à Voter [25] and Scantegrity [27] electronic voting systems. Both groups show that voters are not very likely to understand the concepts behind cryptographic verifiability. In [25], participants stated that they would be unlikely to verify their votes in an election. These results are not too surprising given the fact that, according to [22], most voters have a trust model rather than a verification model in mind when it comes to elections. Driven by these findings, Olembo *et al.* [20] studied how voters could be motivated to verify by different messages and instructions in different situations. Olembo *et al.* tested the impact of three messages based on risk, norms and analogies on intention to verify. The authors explain that there was no significant impact on intention to verify. This warrants further investigation into the nomination option as it seems much more closely aligned with the voter's electronic voting mental models.

7   Conclusion

This paper presents a number of proposals to improve the usability of the verification process in the Helios voting system. While the first two proposals actually improve the usability of the verification process by advancing two new options to verify, namely the *copy, search, and paste* approach and the *QR code checking*, the third option adds the opportunity to nominate trusted institutions to verify on voters' behalf. This third option is a departure from earlier research on verification. It is motivated by the realization that security researchers and voters have different mental models with respect to the verifiability of electronic voting systems. Researchers consider verifiability of electronic voting systems essential, because, in contrast to traditional voting, electronic voting builds upon insecure technology such as computers and the Internet. In some countries verifiability is required by law, which justifies the attention being paid to this aspect by electronic voting researchers. Voters, however, seem to have a different perspective. According to [22], most voters have a trust model rather than a verification model in mind when it comes to elections. Moreover, verifiability may make very little sense to voters in economic terms: it carries a cost but delivers very little personal benefit. Indeed, if the voters uncover fraud it will cost them even more effort to report it and to follow up to ensure that the case is investigated. At the end of the day voters may conclude that they would rather not know, than have to expend effort based on certain knowledge of fraud. We thus concluded that it was worth integrating all three options into Helios. As such, the answer to the question posed in the title *"Helios Verification: To Alleviate, or to Nominate: Is That The Question, Or Shall We Have Both?"* is: *We need both.*

Acknowledgments. This work was developed within the project *ComVote*, which is funded by the Center for Advanced Security Research Darmstadt (CASED), Germany. Further support was provided by Micromata (www.micromata.de).

References

1. Anzahl der Downloads mobiler Apps in Deutschland in den Jahren 2009 bis 2012 (in Millionen) (November 2012), http://de.statista.com/statistik/daten/ studie/168038/umfrage/anzahl-der-downloads-mobiler-apps-in-deutschland- seit-2009/ (accessed June 5, 2014)

2. 2013 Future in Focus - Digitales Deutschland (2013),
   `http://www.comscore.com/Insights/Presentations_and_Whitepapers/2013/`
   `2013_Future_in_Focus_Digitales_Deutschland`
3. Adida, B.: Helios: Web-based Open-Audit Voting. In: Proceedings of the 17th Symposium on Security, pp. 335–348. Usenix Association, Berkeley (2008)
4. Adida, B., De Marneffe, O., Pereira, O., Quisquater, J.J.: Electing A University President using Open-audit Voting: Analysis of Real-world Use of Helios. In: Proceedings of the 2009 Conference on Electronic Voting Technology/Workshop on Trustworthy Elections. USENIX Association (2009)
5. Ashford, R.: QR Codes and Academic Libraries Reaching Mobile Users. College & Research Libraries News 71(10), 526–530 (2010)
6. Benaloh, J.: Simple verifiable elections. In: Proceedings of the USENIX/Accurate Electronic Voting Technology Workshop 2006 on Electronic Voting Technology Workshop - EVT 2006, p. 5 (2006)
7. Budurushi, J., Woide, M., Volkamer, M.: Introducing Precautionary Behavior by Temporal Diversion of Voter Attention from Casting to Verifying their Vote. In: Workshop on Usable Security, USEC 2014 (2014)
8. Bulens, P., Giry, D., Pereira, O.: Running Mixnet-based Elections with Helios. In: Proceedings of the 2011 Conference on Electronic Voting Technology/Workshop on Trustworthy Elections, EVT/WOTE 2011, p. 6. USENIX Association, Berkeley (2011)
9. Canadi, M., Höpken, W., Fuchs, M.: Application Of QR Codes in Online Travel Distribution. In: Information and Communication Technologies in Tourism 2010, pp. 137–148. Springer (2010)
10. Cohen, S.B.: Auditing Technology for Electronic Voting Machines, Master Thesis. MIT, Media Lab (2005)
11. Cortier, V., Galindo, D., Glondu, S., Izabachène, M.: Distributed ElGamal á La Pedersen: Application to Helios. In: Proceedings of the 12th ACM Workshop on Privacy in the Electronic Society, WPES 2013, pp. 131–142. ACM (2013)
12. Dou, X., Li, H.: Creative Use of QR Codes in Consumer Communication. International Journal of Mobile Marketing 3(2) (2008)
13. Hawkins, D.G.: Delegation and Agency in International Organizations. Cambridge University Press (2006)
14. Herrnson, P.S., Niemi, R.G., Hanmer, M.J., Francia, P.L., Bederson, B.B., Conrad, F., Traugott, M.: The Promise and Pitfalls of Electronic Voting: Results from a Usability Field Test, `http://www.capc.umd.edu/rpts/Promise_and_Pitfalls_of_Electronic_Voting.pdf`
15. International Committee for Information Technology Standards, ISO: Ergonomics of Human-system Interaction – Part 210: Human-centred Design for Interactive Systems (2011)
16. Karayumak, F., Kauer, M., Olembo, M.M., Volk, T., Volkamer, M.: User Study of the Improved Helios Voting System Interface. In: Proceedings of STAST 2011 (2011)
17. Karayumak, F., Kauer, M., Olembo, M.M., Volkamer, M.: Usability Analysis of Helios - An Open Source Verifiable Remote Electronic Voting System. In: Proceedings of EVT/WOTE 2011 (2011)
18. Langer, L., Schmidt, A., Buchmann, J., Volkamer, M.: A Taxonomy Refining the Security Requirements for Electronic Voting: Analyzing Helios as a Proof of Concept. In: International Conference on Availability, Reliability, and Security, ARES 2010, pp. 475–480 (February 2010)

19. Lenstra, A.K.: Key lengths. In: Handbook of Information Security, ch. 114 (2004)
20. Olembo, M.M., Renaud, K., Bartsch, S., Volkamer, M.: Voter, What Message Will Motivate You to Verify Your Vote? In: Workshop on Usable Security, USEC 2014 (2014)
21. Olembo, M.M., Volkamer, M.: A Study to Identify Trusted Verifying Institutes in Germany, TU Darmstadt. Technical Report (2014)
22. Olembo, M.M., Bartsch, S., Volkamer, M.: Mental Models of Verifiability in Voting. In: Heather, J., Schneider, S., Teague, V. (eds.) Vote-ID 2013. LNCS, vol. 7985, pp. 142–155. Springer, Heidelberg (2013)
23. Popoveniuc, S., Clark, J., Carback, R., Essex, A., Chaum, D.: Securing Optical-Scan Voting. In: Chaum, D., Jakobsson, M., Rivest, R.L., Ryan, P.Y.A., Benaloh, J., Kutylowski, M., Adida, B. (eds.) Towards Trustworthy Elections. LNCS, vol. 6000, pp. 357–369. Springer, Heidelberg (2010), http://dblp.uni-trier.de/db/conf/wote/lncs6000.html#PopoveniucCCEC10
24. Princeton Undergraduate Student Government: The Elections Handbook, http://princetonusg.com/?page_id=975
25. Schneider, S., Llewellyn, M., Culnane, C., Heather, J., Srinivasan, S., Xia, Z.: Focus Group Views on Prêt à Voter 1.0. In: International Workshop on Requirements Engineering for Electronic Voting Systems, REVOTE 2011 (2011)
26. Selker, T., Pandolfo, A.: A Methodology for Testing Voting Systems. Journal of Usability Studies 2(1), 7–21 (2006)
27. Sherman, A.T., Carback, R., Chaum, D., Clark, J., Essex, A., Herrnson, P.S., Mayberry, T., Stefan, P., Rivest, R.L., Shen, E., Sinha, B., Vora, P.: Scantegrity Mock Election at Takoma Park. In: Electronic Voting 2010 (EVOTE 2010), pp. 45–61 (2010)
28. Tsoukalas, G., Papadimitriou, K., Louridas, P., Tsanakas, P.: From Helios to Zeus. USENIX Journal of Election Technology and Systems (JETS) and Electronic Voting Technology Workshop/Workshop on Trustworthy Elections, EVT/WOTE 2013 pp. 1–17 (2013)
29. Volkamer, M., Vogt, R.: New Generation of Voting Machines in Germany The Hamburg Way to Verify Correctness. In: Frontiers in Electronic Elections - FEE 2006 (2006)
30. Weber, J., Hengartner, U.: Usability Study of the Open Audit Voting System Helios (2009), http://www.jannaweber.com/wp-content/uploads/2009/09/858Helios.pdf (accessed June 5, 2014)
31. Zimmermann, P.R.: PGPfone: Pretty Good Privacy Phone Owner's Manual (1995), http://web.mit.edu/network/pgpfone/manual

Certification of SME Online: A Web-Based Service, of Universal Use, for SME Qualification

Miguel Cruz[1], Rita Serrano[1], and João Gonçalves[2]

[1] IAPMEI, Lisbon, Portugal
{miguel.cruz,rita.serrano}@iapmei.pt
[2] Binomial, Lisbon, Portugal
jrg@binomial.pt

Abstract. SME certification is an electronic service that certifies SME condition according to criteria defined in Portuguese legislation which, in turn, follows the EU recommendation. The process of certification occurs exclusively online. If the enterprise meets all necessary requests an electronic certificate is immediately generated, certifying it as micro, small or a medium-sized enterprise. The certificate may be accessed online by any entity, public or private, that is obliged to request the SME proof. The service reduces administrative burden, reduces contextual costs and promotes harmonization of SME classification.

This service is, up to the moment, the only structured, of general use, information-system based, online implementation of SME recommendation. Also, it is the first formal approach to SME dimension constraints modeling.

This paper presents the SME certification service, discusses its major implementation issues and evaluates exploitation results. Also points out possible future work from a national and European Union perspective.

1 Introduction

It is assessed in the Commission Recommendation of May, 6th, 2003, concerning the definition of micro, small and medium-sized enterprises (2003/361/EC), the following[1]: "In a report submitted to the Council in 1992 (...) the Commission had proposed limiting the proliferation of definitions of small and medium-sized enterprises in use at Community level. Commission Recommendation 96/280/EC of 3 April 1996 concerning the definition of small and medium-sized enterprises was based on the idea that the existence of different definitions at Community level and at national level could create inconsistencies."

"Following the logic of a single market without internal frontiers, the treatment of enterprises should be based on a set of common rules. The pursuit of such an approach is all the more necessary in view of the extensive interaction between national and Community measures assisting micro, small and medium-sized enterprises (SME), for example in connection with Structural Funds or research. It means that situations in which the Community focuses its action on a given category of SMEs and the Member States on another must be avoided."

A. Kő and E. Francesconi (Eds.): EGOVIS 2014, LNCS 8650, pp. 261–274, 2014.
© Springer International Publishing Switzerland 2014

"In addition, it was considered that the application of the same definition by the Commission, the Member States, the European Investment Bank (EIB) and the European Investment Fund (EIF) would improve the consistency and effectiveness of policies targeting SMEs and would, therefore, limit the risk of distortion of competition."

Furthermore, it is stated that "in order to ease the administrative burden for enterprises, and to simplify and speed up the administrative handling of cases for which SME status is required, it is appropriate to allow enterprises to use solemn declarations to certify certain of their characteristics."

SME play a central role in the Portuguese economy, as well as in the European Union. They represent 99.9% of the non-financial business structure, being responsible for more than 78% of employment, for almost 58% of turnover and for near 60% of gross value added.

Given the relevance of SME in the Portuguese economy, and having in mind the two basilar principles quoted from the Commission Recommendation, IAPMEI, the Portuguese Agency for Competitiveness and Innovation, decided to develop a tool combining them. That tool is the Certification of SME online.

The certification of SME online simplifies the process of SME proof in Portugal. Before service implementation the process was based on paper and conducted in isolation by each service.

The elimination of documents and the centralization of the process in a unique public organization – IAPMEI – was clearly advantageous either for enterprises, that no longer have to provide the same documents to several entities, if willing to apply to different support schemes or benefit from advantageous conditions for different purposes, and for Public Administration, that now have no obligations regarding documental verification and calculations in order to determine the dimension status of each enterprise. And the same applies to private entities engaged in administrative procedures targeting SME.

Furthermore, before the creation of the electronic service, enterprise dimension evaluation was usually based simply on the analysis of the enterprise, of its shareholders and of the enterprises where it held a participation in capital. Indirect relationships, voting rights or other control forms were frequently disregarded. Such approach is inaccurate, and may easily conduct to wrong results and incorrect evaluation of the enterprise dimension.

Various references point out that e-government services generally contribute to public services transparency and fairness [4]. The certification of SME online clearly contributed to the transparency of the classification process of SME in Portugal, ensuring equal treatment for enterprises concerning access to benefits targeted to SME.

The use of electronic forms and procedures to classify enterprise types and enterprise dimension also fastened the evaluation process, promoted accuracy and facilitated treatment of more intricate cases analysis, which is particularly relevant when considering indirect relationships in complex enterprise groups.

To the best of our knowledge, there is no other similar approach implemented in other EU country, nor literature considering the modeling or implementation of SME dimension concept. Recently, on behalf of Horizon 2020 (H2020) a SME self-assessment online tool has become available, but only of specific use for R&D programs at EU level. Therefore, the implementation of this service is a first experience in SME certification, as well as a relevant experience in the implementation of e-government services directed to administrative simplification and enterprise contextual cost reduction. Furthermore, this is a first formal approach to the question of modeling SME concept as stated in the recommendation.

The remainder of this paper is structured as follows: Section 2 describes the service from the standpoint of administrative simplification. Section 3 describes the internal models that support implementation. Section 4 reports service impact up to the moment. Conclusions, in section 5, evaluate service achievements and propose possible evolution of SME certification issue, both at national and EU levels.

2   The Principles of the Service

The service was defined in 2007 on behalf of an administrative simplification program. It aims at the reduction of the administrative burden inherent to the relation between SME and the public services responsible for the conduction of the public policies whose target is SME – on what SME proof is concerned – as well as the nationwide harmonization of the classification of SME.

An option was made by the Portuguese legislation to make the service mandatory to all entities that are obliged to request the SME proof on behalf of administrative procedures targeting these enterprises. This strategy surely enforces service impact [3] but also puts special constraints on acceptance by actors involved. Studies demonstrate that factors like simplicity and immediate results are key points for service acceptance [2]. The principles of process simplicity and of immediate generation of a usable electronic certificate were adopted from the start.

Also, it was embraced the idea of a trust based service. The trade-off between trust and the validation rules surely is a key point on e-government service design strategy [4]. The adoption of the trusting principle, combined with latter auditing, allowed the instantaneousness of certification, yet preserving legal cautions.

All the process of certification occurs exclusively online and it is completely paper-free. In order to obtain a certificate of SME, the enterprises have only to fill an electronic form with the information needed to calculate their size class dimension, accept a declaration stating that all the information is accurate, and submit it. If the enterprise meets all the requirements, an electronic certificate is automatically generated, certifying that it is a micro, small or a medium-sized enterprise. This certificate can be immediately visualized by the SME. And can also be immediately accessed online by any entity that is obliged to request the SME proof on behalf of administrative procedures targeting SME.

A major principle of simplification is requesting the minimum data necessary to calculate dimension, properly balanced with data reliability. The enterprise provides information about its direct relationships and indirect relationships, when they exist. The subsequent levels of relationships are requested only if they identify additional, relevant, partners or linked enterprises.

Data regarding staff headcount and financial amounts is collected only for the enterprise itself and for the enterprises automatically classified as partner or linked enterprises. Historical data is collected only when needed to determine the dimension.

A SME certified enterprise may remain permanently certified. The first certification refers to an exact date, corresponding to the date of the submission of the first certification form. This certificate is valid until a new accounting period is closed and tax declarations are submitted to tax authorities, regarding that no changes occur in the enterprise relationships before that.

If changes occur in the enterprise relationships, the enterprise must (it is legally obliged to) obtain a new certificate, in order to allow the reevaluation of its dimension. With this procedure it is guaranteed that in each moment each enterprise has a certificated dimension that really corresponds to its effective situation.

The electronic platform of each registered enterprise is personalized. In each moment it contains only the suitable certification forms and shows specific preventive alerts, reminding legal deadlines (as the alert for certificate renewing). It also stores all the certificates already obtained by the SME and presents complete certification chronograms.

Furthermore, it keeps records of all online accesses by authorized third parties to the specific certification process, allowing each enterprise to know at each moment which entities, and when, have verified its certificate of SME.

As referred above, the certification is given in accordance to the data declared by the enterprise. The information presented by the enterprise is not manually verified at this stage.

However, to guarantee the maximum security of data, the certification forms have strict validation rules that inhibit "blanks" and inconsistencies. This means that enterprises are always aware of the data they have to provide and are conducted to give minimal but sufficient data for operation.

Additionally, each enterprise is aware that at any moment of time could be invited to present proof of everything that has declared in the certification forms submitted (e.g. through register documents and tax declarations). That possibility and the obligation of the enterprise to comply with it are, also, legally defined. If false information is detected, the certification may be revoked, retroactively. If any benefit was granted to the enterprise, it may be lost. Depending on the falsities detected, the enterprise may be inhibited from obtaining a new certificate of SME for one year. In consequence, cannot apply for any benefits targeted to micro, small or medium-sized enterprises during that period. To note that the absence of cooperation of the enterprise in an auditing procedure (no delivery of the documentation requested) may also determine the revocation of the certification.

Data entered online by companies is audited through samples. These audit procedures occurs permanently. Certification processes may be randomly selected in order to be verified, but there also is a targeted control, based on suspicions.

There is a kind of network, including all the entities involved in administrative procedures targeting SME that are users of the electronic service, that are ready to alert IAPMEI to possible irregularities in certification processes. This is an informal, but a proven effective process. Through the electronic platforms of the certification service, these entities have access, not only to the certificate, but also to the reports with the summary of the data declared by each enterprise in order to obtain that certificate of micro, small or medium-sized enterprise. They frequently verify the report and if they detect contradictory information between it and the application forms they received form the enterprise, or between it and the general file they have about the enterprise, they simply alert IAPMEI or formally ask for an inspection to the certification process of the enterprise.

Similarly, IAPMEI's information services, that provide technical assistance to enterprises that request it in the process of filling the certification forms, are prepared to detect suspicious behaviors, and in that cases may suggest to the certification unit that those specific certification processes should be submitted to auditing procedures.

3   Implementation Issues

3.1   Dimension Ceilings

The dimension of an autonomous enterprise depends on three figures: staff headcount, annual turnover and annual balance sheet, also known as "activity data".

The category of SME is made up of enterprises which employ fewer than 250 persons and which have an annual turnover not exceeding 50 million €, and/or an annual balance sheet total not exceeding 43 million €. Within the SME category, a small enterprise is defined as an enterprise which employs fewer than 50 persons and whose annual turnover and/or annual balance sheet total does not exceed 10 million € and a microenterprise is defined as an enterprise which employs fewer than 10 persons and whose annual turnover and/or annual balance sheet total does not exceed EUR 2 million.

If the enterprise has partners or linked enterprises, its dimension is calculated considering its activity data, but also the activity data of its partner and linked enterprises. So, in order to calculate its actual dimension, one needs to inspect the enterprise relationships.

3.2   Relationship Model

The dimension calculations are based on a *relationship net* that models enterprise relationships. Fig. 1 represents a simple, one level, *relationship net*.

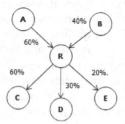

Fig. 1. *Relationships net* example

Within this model enterprises are represented as nodes of a graph and relationships are represented by directed labeled arcs. A directed arc from A to R, labeled with percentage P, represents an *individual relationship*, meaning enterprise A owns the referred percentage P of the capital of enterprise R.

The *relationship net* is centered across the requiring enterprise, that is, the one whose SME condition is under appreciation. The model starts at direct relationships (that is, enterprises that directly own participations or are owned by the requiring one). Then, as explained later, may evolve to include other layers of relationships.

If two enterprises, say R and C, are related with a percentage above 50% that means R "controls" C (R and C are said to be *linked*). Linked enterprises constitute a *group* meaning that they must be considered as a whole for all purposes concerning dimension calculation. For the purpose of dimension calculation the original *relationship net* is, then, transformed into a *calculation net* where individual *linked* enterprises are substituted by a *group*. The *relationships net* of Fig. 1 example is transformed into the *calculation net* of Fig. 2.

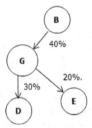

Fig. 2. *Calculation net* correspondent to *relationships net* of Fig. 1

Based on percentage P of participation on capital, each individual relationship is qualified as *autonomous* (P< 25%), *partner* (25%<=P<=50%) or *linked* (P>50%).

There are, however, circumstances that override this classification. For once, there are circumstances where an enterprise "controls" another one, even if it does not own the majority of its capital. This may be done, for instance, through a specific contract or special voting rights. This kind of situations classify as *linked,* the same way ownership of more than 50% does.

On the other hand, there are situations where ownership above 25% may still be qualified as *autonomous,* so being equivalent of ownership under 25% ([1]).

The certification system starts by considering quantitative ownerships. Then, given the specific nature of involved enterprises, it poses a set of additional qualitative questions in order to identify situations that overrule these quantitative relationships. Specific questions include detection of qualitative situations of control (e.g. "A contract between the enterprises enables one to exercise a dominant influence over the other"), *exceptions* included in the recommendation, like Universities or Institutional investors, or other entities with special treatments, like public bodies.

The net result of this process is always the qualification of individual relationships as *autonomous, partner* or *linked*. An *autonomous* relationship between A and B means that activity data of B does not contribute to that of A. A *linked* relationship between A and B means that activity data of A must be added to that of B. A *partner* relationship is additionally parameterized with a percentage P and means that the activity of B should be added to that of A in P percentage.

---

[1] Full discussion of this point is beyond the scope of this paper. Refer to [13].

The example of Fig. 1 is calculated as depicted in Fig. 3:

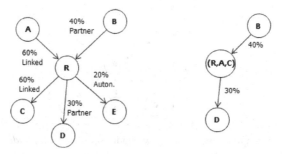

Fig. 3. Dimension of R results from sum of (R, A, C) plus 40% of B activity data and 30% of D activity data

A delicate point of the recommendation is that of "adjacent markets". It states that if an individual person (or a group of individual persons) owns relevant part of different enterprises and those enterprises operate in adjacent markets then those enterprises should be considered as *linked*.

Fig. 4 represents a *relationship net* where individual person P owns major participations in enterprises A and B. In this situation a question is popped asking if A and B operate in adjacent markets. If so, they are connect with an additional superimposed *linked* relationship.

Fig. 4. Enterprises A, B owned by individual person P and operating in adjacent markets are connected by a *linked* type relationship

One of the SME Certification service requirements is "minimum data necessary to decision" (see section 2). This leads to a specific order of data collection: at each step the system collects data related to an enterprise; if the collected data is enough for the calculation of dimension then data collection must stop there.

This order of data collection induces the *relationships net* to be constructed by layers, starting from the certifying enterprise. First layer includes enterprises directly related with the certifying enterprise. Those are named *direct relationships*. Then each one of *direct relationships* enterprise is asked for. This makes a second level layer, named *first indirect level*. Then this *first indirect level* is acquired forming a *second indirect level*, and so on.

Fig. 5 represents a net after acquisition of *direct relationships* and in course or acquisition of *first indirect relationship level*.

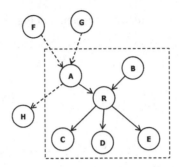

Fig. 5. Example of Fig. 1 with new relationships of A (*first indirect level*)

The order of relationships net construction puts severe constraints on calculation, because acquisition of new relationships may compromise previous *calculation net* by changing groups and individual relationships.

Consider, as an example, the net of Fig. 1. First level direct relationships originate group G (A,R,C) as indicated in Fig. 2, leaving B as partner of this group. Later acquired (B,E) and (C,E) second level relationships significantly alters the *calculation net* for E and B are now included in group G (R,A,C,B,E), as represented in Fig. 6.

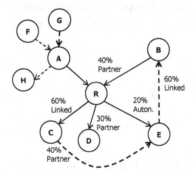

Fig. 6. Level 2 (B, E) and (C,E) relationships alters level 1 group formation

Another example: if the relationship (C,E) alters to "20% – Autonomous" then the original group G (R,A,C) remains and a new group G (B,E) is formed with a partner relationship of 40% with the G (R,A,C) group.

So, calculation net must be re-constructed after each new data relationship acquisition. The main algorithm of calculation goes like this:

> Repeat
>> acquire next enterprise relationships, extending *relationship net*
>> construct *calculation net* from current relationship net
>> calculate dimension form *relationship net*
> until no more relevant relationships exists or dimension is final

The algorithm for construction of *calculation net* uses a "depth first" recursive traverse of the relationship net, grouping linked enterprises and aggregating group participations.

Once a final calculation net is available dimension calculation is straightforward. In each group activity data is calculated as:

$$D(G) = sum(D(Gi))$$

where D(G) stands for the three activity data indicators (staff headcount, annual turnover and annual balance sheet[1]) and D(Gi) are the same indicators for each enterprise of group G.

The dimension of the requiring enterprise is, then

$$D = D(R) + sum(Pi*D(P))$$

where D(R) is the dimension of the group where the requiring enterprise is included, D(P) represents each *partner* group of that on and Pi represents the correspondent partnership percentage.

3.3   Certification Timeline

Previous section indicates the method for calculation of dimension based on a year activity data. This is called *year dimension*. The *actual dimension* (that is, the SME dimension assigned by the certification service) depends not only on *year dimension* but also on historic trend.

Recommendation states that an enterprise doesn't lose its status of micro, small or medium-sized enterprise unless the staff headcount or financial ceilings are exceeded or fallen over two consecutive accounting periods. Application of this principle leads to the following rule:

Consider the set of last three years dimensions (D0, D1, D2). If this set is sorted (this is, if the enterprise within the last three years exhibits a consistent growing or decreasing pattern) it constitutes a trend. In this situation actual dimension is D1. If the set is not ordered (that is, if the enterprise, within the last three years, exhibits both growing and decreasing dimensions) actual dimension is the one calculated for year D2). For example, all three sequences (Small, Small, Medium), (Medium, Small, Micro) and (Small, Medium, Small) determines a Small dimension, the first two being a consistent trend.

In some circumstances this historic trend ceases to apply. That is the case when the enterprise relationships change, originating a new group of linked and partner related enterprises. In those cases, the *year dimension* equals the *actual dimension*.

Dimension calculations are renewed on annual basis. At a certain scheduled date (depending on the tax calendar) the enterprise must renew its SME certificate based on the activity of the most recent year.

The timeline of SME certification goes along as suggested in the diagram of Fig. 7.

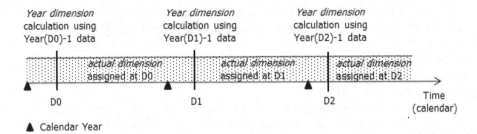

▲ Calendar Year

Fig. 7. Timeline of certification process

At date D1 SME certification is renewed using activity data from YEAR (D1)-1 (that is, activity data of the year before date D1). The assigned actual dimension remains valid up to the year after, say at date D2, when activity data of the YEAR (D2)-1 is reported. The actual assigned dimension depends on historic trend, as indicated in previous section. Fig. 8 shows an example.

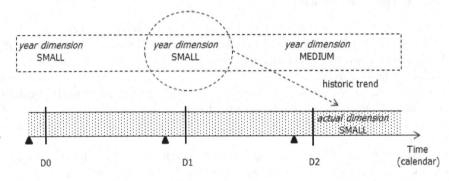

Fig. 8. Application of historic trend

The regular certification timeline is interrupted whenever some relevant enterprise condition changes, for instance when relationships change, thus potentially originating a different dimension. In that situation the enterprise must report that situation, originating an upgrade of SME certification at the date of the originating events.

Is it important to notice that SME certification is valid at instant time, and keeps valid until a new event generates the need for a certification upgrade.

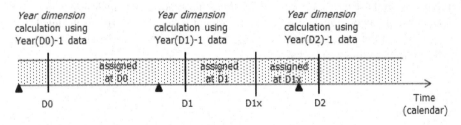

Fig. 9. Event at date D1x induces an intercalary upgrade of SME certification, still using Year (D1)-1 activity data

Data activity must always refer to full complete years. When such data is not available "good faith" estimates may be used instead. This makes SME certification somehow "reversible" in time.

If an enterprise starts its economic activity in a certain date D0 – say in the middle of YEAR (D) – the first complete year of activity is YEAR (D)+1. That way, the moment for accurate calculation of dimension is located somewhere in YEAR (D)+2, after official report of YEAR (D)+1 activity data to Tax Authority. The timeline is suggested in Fig. 10.

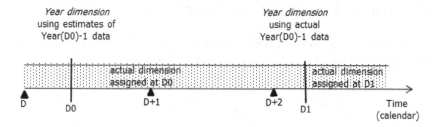

Fig. 10. Estimated timeline

However, the enterprise has the right to obtain a SME certificate starting at the time of the beginning of its activity. The service strategy to handle this question is the one stated at the recommendation, that is, in this circumstances use a "good faith" estimate of forthcoming activity. The estimated data must be confirmed when effective data is available, leading to recalculation of previous assigned dimension, eventually with a different result.

In this circumstances one might have two timeline SME certification paths, one based on estimated data, the other based on actual data. The situation is illustrated in the diagram of Fig. 11.

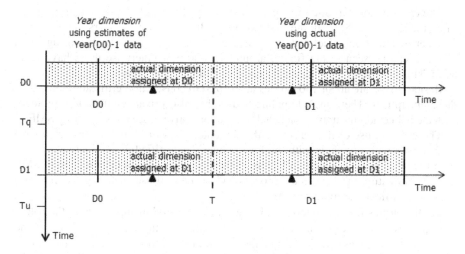

Fig. 11. Between D0 and D1 the actual dimension on date T is the one assigned at D0. After date D1 the actual dimension at T is the one reversely assigned at D1

That way, SME certification depends on two dates: the date of querying ("it might depend of when you ask") and that of instant validity. Reporting to Fig. 11 example, certification at Dimension (T, Tq), that is, on date T queried in date Tq, may be different from Dimension (T,Tu), that is, dimension in same date queried at date Tu.

It should be pointed out that the entitlement of SME certification based on "good faith" estimates is valid during that period D0 to D1. So, enterprise may legally use SME condition assigned at D0 for the period [D0, D1[until date D1.

4   Service Stand Point and Results

Until today, more than 120 000 enterprises have already obtained a certificate of SME. This represents a significant quota of national enterprises.

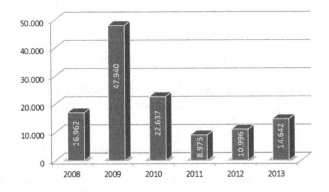

Fig. 12. Number of enterprises with a first certificate, by year

The certification evolution is represented in Fig. 12. Nearly 65 000 enterprises certified themselves as SME in the first two years. In the following years the number of first certifications has declined, but since 2011 that has been increasing again. In 2013, as can be seen in the figure, around 15 000 new enterprise users have registered. This represents a 33% increase regarding the previous year.

Besides, there are about 150 entities authorized to consult the certification process of those enterprises. These include public bodies, but also private entities with protocols with the public administration, on behalf of administrative procedures targeting SME.

The growing use of the service, either by enterprises or by public entities (or private entities with protocols with the former ones), is justified by the increasing number of legal documents specifically considering the obligation of certification of SME. The simplification inherent to the process and the ease of use encourages compliance with the certification online service.

Public entities managing structural funds were the first mainly users in the role of third parties entities, as estimated, but steadily other entities also adhered to this mechanism. Among these we find financial institutions (protocolled with public bodies), tax authorities, other public bodies in the sphere of the Ministry of Economics, but also of other governmental fields.

The large majority of certified SME are enterprises - more than 90%, being companies and around 8% sole proprietors. "Associations" engaged in an economic activity and entities alike constitute the other certified SME. The dimension distribution is represented in Fig. 13. In line with the Portuguese business structure, the majority of certified SME entities (about 2/3) are microenterprises; 27% are small enterprises and 7% medium-sized enterprises.

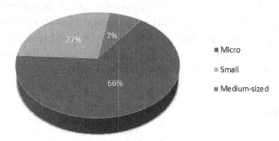

Fig. 13. Size dimension of the certified SME

5   Conclusions

The development, by IAPMEI, of an exclusively online and entirely paper-free mechanism to certify micro, small and medium-sized enterprises – the Certification of SME online – completely reformed the process of SME proof in Portugal.

The e-government solution adopted, where the classification of enterprise types and all the calculations of the enterprise dimension are automatically made by a computer, fastens the evaluation process, promotes greater accuracy and facilitates more intricate analysis.

Besides, it turns the procedures much easier and cheaper to the enterprises, since SME only have to fill and submit online an electronic form to obtain a certificate of micro, small or medium-sized enterprise from one entity, which is valid for any matters regarding SME proof. It terminates with the multiplication of dimension classification procedures amongst Public Administration, merely reducing them to one action: an online access to a certificate.

Additionally, it endorses transparency to the classification process of SME in Portugal, assuring equal procedures and equal results for "equal" enterprises.

SME qualification is one of the few areas where there seems to be a European wide consensus, based on a common accepted recommendation.

Certification of SME online certainly proved to be a valuable e-government solution in Portugal. It the author's opinion, in face of the Portuguese experience, it would be advantageous to promote the idea of automation on what concerns the classification of SME. Furthermore, it would also be pertinent the boosting of interaction amongst Member States in this field, sharing experiences or even, at a higher level, sharing data.

A major and feasible advance for that purpose should be working on a common semantic that facilitates future interoperability [8, 9, 10].

The authors also want to draw attention to the fact that the design and development of such an automated tool brought to light some insufficiencies of the Recommendation, namely the absence of more detailed orientations in some issues or articles. At a very detailed level this becomes perceptible. In consequence, several interpretations of the complete extent of the rules had to be done, which constitutes a potential risk of incorrect understandings. It also means that different understandings can be made, so that the same rules can be differently applied by different national authorities.

The conclusions of the last study conducted on behalf of European Commission in order to evaluate the definition of SME underpin this, highlighting the need of clarification of some rules and suggesting the improvement of the user guide on the definition. A collective work in this field should be beneficial.

References

1. Commission Recommendation 2003/361/EC, Official Journal of the European Union L 124/36 (2003)
2. Venkatesh, V., Chan, F.K.Y., Thong, J.Y.L.: Designing e-government services: Key service attributes and citizens' preference structures. Journal of Operations Management 30 (2012)
3. Arendsen, R., van Engers, T.M., Schurink, W.: Adoption of High Impact Governmental eServices: Seduce or Enforce? In: Wimmer, M.A., Scholl, H.J., Ferro, E. (eds.) EGOV 2008. LNCS, vol. 5184, pp. 73–84. Springer, Heidelberg (2008)
4. Elbahnasawy, N.G.: E-Government, Internet Adoption, and Corruption: An Empirical Investigation. World Development, vol. 57. Elsevier (2013)
5. Khadraoui, A., Turki, S., Aidonidis, C., Leonard, M.: Framework for e-Government Information Systems Engineering: Describing the Organizational Layers. IEEE (2006)
6. Sabucedo, L.Á., Rifón, L.A.: A Proposal for a Semantic-Driven eGovernment Service Architecture. In: Wimmer, M.A., Traunmüller, R., Grönlund, Å., Andersen, K.V. (eds.) EGOV 2005. LNCS, vol. 3591, pp. 237–248. Springer, Heidelberg (2005)
7. Berce, J., Bianchi, A., Centeno, C., Osimo, D., Millard, J., Shahin, J.: The Organisation and Coordination of European e-Government Research for the EU in 2010. In: Wimmer, M.A., Scholl, H.J., Grönlund, Å., Andersen, K.V. (eds.) EGOV 2006. LNCS, vol. 4084, pp. 37–46. Springer, Heidelberg (2006)
8. Shukair, G., Loutas, N., Peristeras, V., Sklarß, S.: Towards semantically interoperable metadata repositories: The Asset Description Metadata Schema. Computers in Industry 64 (2013)
9. Álvarez Sabucedo, L.M., Anido Rifón, L.E., Pérez, R.M., Santos Gago, J.M.: Providing standard-oriented data models and interfaces to eGovernment services: a semantic-driven approach. Computer Standards & Interfaces 31 (2013)
10. Miah, S.J.: A New Semantic Knowledge Sharing Approach for e-Government Systems. In: 4th IEEE International Conference on Digital Ecosystems and Technologies (2010)
11. Venkatesh, V., Chan, F.K.Y., Thong, J.Y.L.: Designing e-government services: Key service attributes and citizens' preference structures. Journal of Operations Management 30 (2012)
12. IAPMEI: As empresas utilizadoras do serviço de Certificação PME (internal report) (2013)
13. Decree n.^{er} 372/2007, Diário da República, 1st serie, n.^{er} 213 (November 6, 2007)
14. Decree n.^{er} 143/2009, Diário da República, 1st serie, n.^{er} 114 (June 16, 2009)

Open Government Data
Beyond Transparency

Monica Palmirani[1], Michele Martoni[1], and Dino Girardi[2]

[1] University of Bologna, CIRSFID
Via Galliera 3, 40121 Bologna, IT
{monica.palmirani,michele.martoni}@unibo.it
[2] University of Lapland, Lapin Yliopisto
dino.girardi@ulapland.fi

Abstract. This paper aims to present and analyse the Open Government Data (OGD) legislation framework in force in the current Italian legal system. The previous legislation has been compared with the recently enacted Legislative Decree about transparency (the so called Transparency Act d.lgs. 33/2013). After discussing the normative contest, this paper completes the theoretical analysis with an empirical research conducted on the Italian Municipalities' web sites (35 portals) in order to deeply understand the connection between the Open Government Data legislation and the new Transparency Act. The aim of this comparison is to test and prove our theory about the fact that the Transparency Act doesn't enable and reinforce the OGD – as FOIAs do – but it subtracts resources, human capital, skills, funds and motivations. The Transparency Act, in fact, implements an old-style model of web site oriented to a "Public Administration centered" paradigm instead of an "ODG centered" one. The authors, finally, wants to identify a method to combine the two different approaches, having a unique production workflow of data and documents in Open Data format, with a semantic web metadata classification that qualify the information.

Keywords: Transparency, Openness, FOIA, Open Government, E-Government, Public Sector Information, Open Government Data, Open Data Format, Right to Access, Transparency Portal.

1   Introduction: OGA Beyond Transparency

The Open Government Data (hereinafter OGD) has started in 2009 in U.S. and U.K.[1] as movement for improving participation, transparency and cooperation[2]. Open Government Data[3] is used for releasing and disclosing data coming from the Public Entities in favour of citizens, companies, other Public Entities. This movement aims to reduce the lobby powers by enhancing transparency through the participation of

---

[1] September 2009 the portal data.gov.uk was opened.
[2] http://www.whitehouse.gov/sites/default/files/omb/assets/
memoranda_2010/m10-06.pdf -
http://www.whitehouse.gov/sites/default/files/omb/memoranda/20
13/m-13-13.pdf http://www.w3.org/2009/Talks/0204-ted-tbl/
[3] http://okfn.org/opendata/

A. Kő and E. Francesconi (Eds.): EGOVIS 2014, LNCS 8650, pp. 275–291, 2014.
© Springer International Publishing Switzerland 2014

citizens, free availability and access to data and their reuse and redistribution aims also for driving the creation of innovative business and services that deliver social and commercial value. In Italy this movement has been so far really effective to fight corruption in Public Bodies, to counter criminal behaviours inside of the Public Administration, to combat mafia, to prevent unnecessary spending of public money and misusage the public resources[4] The E.U. already before the beginning of the OGD movement in 2003 adopted the Directive 2003/98/EC on Re-use of Public Sector Information (hereinafter PSI) introducing the concepts and the principles for the re-use of public sector information and establishing a minimum set of rules governing the re-use and the practical means of facilitating reuse of existing documents held by public Sector bodies of the Member States. The above-mentioned Directive has recently been amended by the Directive 2013/37/EU of 26 of June 2013. This new act has introduced in the recitals the concept of *Open Data* as to

> *"Open data policies which that encourage the wide availability and re-use of public sector information for private or commercial purposes, with minimal or no legal, technical or financial constraints, and which promote the circulation of information not only for economic operators but also for the public, can play an important role in kick-starting the development of new services based on novel ways to combine and make use of such information, stimulate economic growth and promote social engagement.*
>
> *At meantime the new Directive at Art. 6 has introduced the possibility to sell the Open Government dataset under some special conditions that are " marginal costs incurred for their reproduction, provision and dissemination" "together with a reasonable return on investment".*

This new provision opens an unexpected scenario for a business model[5] based not on the free circulation of the knowledge as to the OD movement concept, but on a "reasonable return on investment" that put definitely the Open Government Data beyond the principle of transparency as above illustrated. Different scholars dealing with the debate about OGD have stressed the idea that the OGD should go beyond the pure rhetoric of transparency[6] [1, 2, 3] or the spasmodic return of cash money as the result of an investment. The OGD is a new ecosystem capable to produce innovation, not only limited to transparency or revenue streams. The recent G8 Charter of Open Data introduces the concept of *free-release* of open data[7] retracting the principles of the

---

[4] http://www.opencoesione.gov.it/ -
http://www.openricostruzione.it/ - http://www.openpompei.it/
[5] The business models for balancing private and public sectors in the open data domain will be investigated by the authors in another research.
[6] http://beyondtransparency.org/
[7] "Principle 1: Open Data by Default. 11. We recognise that free access to, and subsequent re-use of, open data are of significant value to society and the economy." and "Principle 3: Usable by All. 20. We recognise that open data should be available free of charge in order to encourage their most widespread use." and moreover "Principle 5: Releasing Data for Innovation: 26. Recognising the importance of diversity in stimulating creativity and innovation, we agree that the more people and organisations that use our data, the greater the social and economic benefits that will be generated. This is true for both commercial and non-commercial uses."

new EU Directive on PSI where charging above *marginal cost* for the *return of investment* is also provided. So it seems that the transparency is not so longer the main reason that is leading the OGD strategy (see also the European Digital Agenda). A recent UNPAN [15] report remarks the areas where OGD should act: in government policy, social benefits and economical growth. We believe that the only transparency is a too limited goal for justifying a such world-wide phenomena, especially with the increasing of the private open dataset that should be integrated with the OGD dataset for making them usable and effective for substantial applications.

On the other hand the *Freedom of information act* (FOIA) [9] is for sure a pre-requirement in several countries where OGD has had so far a great improvement and success beyond the transparency concept (e.g. UK, Italy, Germany, Finland). The eGovernment survey 2012 by UNPAN[8] report remarks this relationship between FOIA and OGD. Also the OECD[9] report 2013 stresses the fact that PSI and FOIA are legislation enabling and favoring the OGD and so to reduce the resistances from the Public Administrations.

In this contest the Italian Government has introduced the so called *Transparency Act* with the aim to reinforce the *open by default* principle (see also the G8 Charter of Open Data [10]) with the intention of providing for Italy a FOIA Act. Actually, despite of the fact that the main principles declared in the first part, the above mentioned act doesn't follow this roadmap, the real goal of the *Transparency Act* is to supervise and keep watch on the public administration strategy, to monitor the performance of the public administration employees, to release information about the public administration plans and activities, to fight corruption and public employees absenteeism, to control the administration financial accountability and finally to compel the Public Entities to the publication of documents, that are already under the obligation of legal publicity, in open data format.

The Transparency Act has introduced in the Italian legal framework the principles of transparency; accessibility to the public administration public acts and documents. The Act has also introduced some good principles for reinforcing the Open Government Data application. However this Act has a different aim compared to the Open Data Paradigm as widely accepted within the OGD movement. The Transparency Act is target to monitor the performance of the public administration and to provide public documents to the citizens in Open Data technical format. The Act introduces a special section within the already existing public administration web sites, called "Transparent Public Administration" with a predetermined tree and typology of acts. In this respect Public Entities (in particular Municipalities that are enacting every day lots of different Acts) goes into confusion following the obligations settled in the d.lgs. 33/2013 and the Open Government Data legislations already existing.

This paper would like to present the current situation in Italy dealing with OGD legislation in comparison with the mentioned *Transparency Act* that is affecting the

---

[8] See [8], Figure 6.8 FOI laws in countries around the world: Global view.
[9] http://www.oecd-ilibrary.org/docserver/download/5k46bj4f03s7.
pdf?expires=1396804834&id=id&accname=guest&checksum=896E69C113
0F06422BE63EBA218452F8

Open Data Paradigm in favor of a very bureaucratic approach (§ 2). Secondly the paper completes the theoretical analysis with an empirical research conducted on the Italian municipalities web sites (35 portals) in order to understand the connection between the Open Government Data and the *Transparency Act* (§ 3). We would like to test and prove our theory that the *Transparency Act* doesn't enable and reinforce the OGD as other already existing FOIA in the World, but it is subtracting resources, human capital, engagements, motivations for implementing a parallel an old-style fashion web site more oriented to a *public-administration* center paradigm concept instead of a OGD centered concept (§ 4).

2   Italian Open Data Legislation

The Italian Open Government Data Legislation nowadays permits to the Public Administrations to have a reasonable legal framework for releasing open dataset at national, regional and local levels. The legal framework of the OGD is composed by several different Acts. Above all the fundamental important pillars are: the legislative decree n. 82/2005 and modifications, the implementation of the Directive 2003/98/EU with the legislative decree n. 69/2009 and the recent legislative decree n. 33/2013, the Transparency Act. The d.lgs. n. 82/2005 defines the Open Government Data modality, but there is no distinction between data and document in open data form. The d.lgs. n. 69/2009 provides the definition of document and the modality and practical means for the public administration that permit the release of documents in open format. In d.lgs. n. 33/2013 we can read a long list of public documents that should be published in digital format in a specific part of the official web site of the public administration as above referred but not mandatory in Open Data. We would like to investigate the contradictions and the ambiguities arising from cited legislation and especially to point put the norms that constitute an obstacles or a barriers for the OGA nowadays Italy.

2.1   Code for the Digital Public Administration

The d.lgs. n. 82/2005 the so called Code for Digital Public Administration (hereinafter CAD [18]) includes two important articles that defines the modalities and the format for the Open Government Data: see art. 52 and art. 68. Art. 52 in the paragraph 2, defines the *open data by default*. All the data and the documents owned by the public administrations and published in the web in any forms without license, are automatically released with an open data license. Art 52 refers to art. 68 where are defined two different concepts: open data format and Open Data Approach. The first definition is limited to the technical features such as neutrality from a specific technology. The second definition includes the characteristics of the Open Data phenomena: dataset in open format, with license that permits the reuse also for commercial purposes, free-release of data set or at charge at marginal costs.

2.2   Italian Implementation of PSI Directive

Italy implemented the PSI directive with the legislative decree n. 36, at 24 January 2006, after the adoption by Italian Government of the CAD Act. The harmonization of the definitions among the two mentioned acts sometime are not always perfectly aligned. In particular is that emerges referring to the definition of document, licenses, owner of the documents or data. Also the multiple citation to both are creating clashing interpretations. The implementation of PSI Directive is more nebulous respect the CAD, at the same time the PSI Directive is more oriented to the document rather than to dataset. This distinction between data and document is relevant. Data are objective atomic measurement of a phenomena (e.g. wi-fi access, environment data, sensor values, traffic mobility data). Documents, better administrative documents, represent some step in the administrative process, a function with legal validity, and authenticable interpretation from the Public Administration. This is the reason why it is important to preserve the integrity of the administrative documents even if public. From the document, especially if they are modeled in XML, it is always possible to extract dataset to publish in open data.

2.3   Transparency Act: d.lgs. 33/2013

The Law 241/90 on the Administrative Procedure introduced in the legislative Italian framework the right to access to the administrative process for the subjects with a lawful and justified interest. The law represented real revolution in the Italian legislation for disclosing the public administration information in favor of a more transparent and ethic behavior of officers. This act produced a substantial change in the cultural management in favor of a unprejudiced and impartial public service for fighting favoritism, subjectivity and unfair bad practices including corruption crimes.

Despite to the Law 241/90, the missing point in Italy was to adopt a real FOIA. For this reason at end of 2013 the government released a d.lgs. (legislative decree) 33/2013 called, in very demagogic way, *Transparency Act*. This law created in the OGD community a great expectation and several associations asked to the government to foster this occasion for filling the gap about the freedom of information. The expectations have not so far been met and to despite to the statements of principle, the substantial of the norms are different.

For understanding the real goals of this act we need to consider that it is the coordination of several previous actions included in a larger strategy for fighting against the corruption in the Public Sector. The previous actions where: i) act n. 69, 18 June 2009 that introduced provisions for economic development, simplification, competitiveness; ii) legislative decree n. 150, at 27 October 2009 that introduced measures for the optimization of productivity of public work and the efficiency and transparency of public administrations; iii) act 6 November 2012, n. 190 that introduced provisions for the prevention and repression of corruption and illegality in the public service.

Following this roadmap the Transparency Act can't be considered a FOIA because the purposes and the basis are completely different.

Art. 1 of *Transparency Act* defines the General principle of transparency concept:

"Transparency is understandable as total accessibility to information about the organization and the activities of public administrations, in order to encourage widespread forms of control on the pursuit of official duties and the use of public resources."

Reading this definition we can understand the real goal of this act as to the Government purposes.

Continuing the analysis of the Transparency Decree there are also other key articles that has an important implications and impact on the OGD.

Art. 2 defines the structure of the web site dedicated to the transparency as designed in the annex A. This structure is obligatory but is set up on an old-style, public administration oriented aimed to the internal organization and not based on the "event of life". The structure is very difficult to navigate.

Art. 3 statues the freely right to access to the public documents with the possibility to use and re-use them.

Art. 4 defines limits to the application of the free access to the digital documents that are in contrast with the OGD. In particular a large of number of information and documents are excluded by this Transparency Act included databases and the document collections that are managed as databases. On the other hand the norm imposes that the information should be indexable from any search engine.

Art. 5 can be considered he main provision of the *Transparency Act* The articles defines the right for everybody, without providing a justification, to access to those information. In case the administration has not yet published the information, any citizen can make a formal request and the public administration should disclose the document within 30 days, is the so called "Civic Access"

Art. 7 defines the format for the publication of document . The article statues that the information should be published in open format not in Open Data modality. The difference is substantial. The open data format is limited to the technical digital form and the citation is done exactly to the CAD Act in the part (art. 68, parg. 3, point a) where it is defined only the technical aspects. This means that is not required and obligatory to define a license, the metadata, the provenience and the persistency of the dataset. At the moment in Italy 80% of the published data are in PDF, only and some time there is also the Excel format, without any license and certainness about them persistency over time. Art. 7 of the Transparency Decree reinforces also the *open data by default* but with a citation of the CAD and of the implementation of the PSI . "The license should be without any restriction except the attribution and the integrity". This provision opens different interpretations about the concept of attribution and integrity of document. Theoretically a cc0 license is not eligible because it excludes the attribution. Also any other license that permits the manipulation of the document is not eligible because it changes the integrity of the document. So the perfect license, following art. 7 of the Decree statement, is *cc-by-sa-nd*, but this licence is contrary to the principle of free reuse. On the other hand the above explained transparency portal aims to comply with the legal publicity obligation and the document should guarantee the integrity and the conformity respect the original administrative act (art. 6).

Therefore art. 8, art. 14 and 15 define the limitation of time for the publication of the documents (from 3 to 5 years). This is another relevant difference with open dataset that not have limitation of time.

Thus for the explained reasons we can consider the Transparency portal a kind of old fashion web site dedicated to the publishing function for implementing the already existing right of access to public documents as to the Law 241/90. Publication of documents should be in open data format, but the license could be a non open license (e.g. *cc-by-nc-nd*[10]). There is a limitation of time for the publication and no metadata are mandatory.

The *Transparency Act*, enacted the 14 March 2013 and entered in force at 20 April 2013, has been already implemented by the majority of Italian the public administrations thanks also to the penalties provided by the act:

> *"within 6 months from the enter in force for any violation of the tree there is a disciplinary notice to the manager of the public administration responsible and also an monetary penalty"*.

The side effects of the Transparency Act is that all the public administration has now blocked or reduced the ongoing project of Open Data for concentrating the attention and the energy on the *Transparency Act* obligations.

Often because the transparency is a matter of the general secretary of the municipality it is not unusual to see different teams working on the same documents or datasets with two different perspectives: open data and transparency. This generates confusion in the end-user, duplication in different part of the portal of the same object, disorientation in the citizens that don't know which source is preeminent in case of clashing. A classical example is the balance-sheet: it is mandatory to publish the official balance-sheet of the Municipality in the Transparency area, usually it is published in PDF with the signature of the major. On the other hand a more machine-readable form is necessary for favouring the real reuse of the dataset inside of applications. This approach produces a duplication of documents, in the best scenario, or in the worst case the obligation to publishing in the transparency section, de facto, de-motivate the body to re-publish the same document in a different open format. Transparency Act becomes an excuse for publishing with a minor accuracy and attention to the Open Government Data Approach and in meantime it is an alibi for releasing PDF documents rather than to design a open data workflow.

3   Comparison Analysis between Open Government Data and "Transparency Portal"

3.1   Data.gov.it

Italy has an official government portal for collecting in a unique catalogue all the Open Government Data portals, at national, regional and local level. The current number of the official web sites dedicated to the open government data in Italy are 97[11] and 35 are municipality. The authors analyzed the OGD portals in comparison with the transparency portal starting from the official site.

---

[10] Creative commons with attribution, non commercial uses, no derivative works, http://creativecommons.org/licenses/by-nc-nd/4.0/

[11] http://www.dati.gov.it/content/infografica#Dove sono i data store italiani?
http://www.dati.gov.it/sites/default/files/dataset_infografica_27022014.zip

3.2   The Compass of Transparency

The Ministry of the Public Administration sets up a portal for helping the public administration to be compliance with the d.lgs. 33/2013 called "Compass of Transparency"[12] and so to implement the principles of transparency, access, accountability, participations, cooperation. This tool permits also to the citizens to monitor the implementation of the Transparency Act and so to directly participate to the improvement of the quality of the accessibility of the information. There is a session dedicated to collect comments, notices, and warning to send to the public administration entities. The system is based on a mathematical algorithm that calculates the compliance with the mandatory web site structure defined by law, the quality of the web sites dedicated to the transparency data, the presence of some type of data. There isn't a specific parameter dedicated to measure the form of open data (e.g. CSV, excel). For this reason we have conduced a separate research with the following goals:

1)   to know if all the municipality included in the data.gov.it have a session dedicated to the "transparency" as the law requires and in case which is the score calculated by "Compass of transparency" parameters;
2)   to verify the percentage of pdf document respect the other open format;
3)   to check the overlapping with open government data portal and in case if there is a strategy in the municipality for managing in coordinated way the publication of the information.

As to the research the average of the Compass of Transparency evaluation is 80,2%, the 86% of the public administration publish in PDF inside of the transparency portal without another corresponding open data format (usually xsl and csv), the 28,6% of the 35 municipalities has an overlapping in the area of tender and balance-sheets between transparency portal and open data. Only few administration has optimized the overlapping using links, avoiding redundancy. All the resources used for the Transparency portal could be invested also in the OGD and so producing more return of investment in the open data ecosystem. An interesting similar work that confirm our finding, even if with a different methodology and approach, is [13] conducted for measuring the quality of the "Transparency Portal" on the 20 Italian regions, 10 provinces out 105 and on 15 municipalities out 8100. The outcome is the same: the quality of the "Transparency Portal" of those public administration has an average index of completeness 0,577 out 1 for the Italian Regions, 0,622 out 1 for the Provinces and 0,543 out 1 for the Municipalities.

In our research we have tried also to analyze the relations between the quality of the Compass indicator (manually calculated) and the number of the open dataset released by the municipality. The goal is to see if the good practice in the open data paradigm can produce a better quality management of the "Transparency Portal". We have discovered that only three municipalities (Albano, Bologna and Florence) have a good relation between the two indicators (the number of the dataset is normalized with the *min-max* function in order to reduce the indicator in the range [0,1]. We have

---

[12] http://www.magellanopa.it/bussola/page/overview.html

used this formula $Xi-Xmin/Xmax-Xmin$. For the Compass indicator we have calculated how many parameters are passed out 74 and we have calculated the percentage). This means that the cultural and the human capacity of the open data staff are often isolated in a particular area of the public administration (usually ICT department) without a real integration in the whole policy of the institution, and so the add value of the open data is underused.

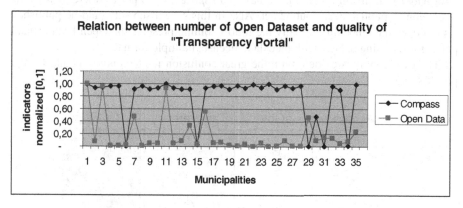

Fig. 1. Different characteristics of the four official web portals

4   New Strategy Beyond the Transparency

The OGD is entering the second generation era and the transparency principle is not so longer the main motivation for investing resources, human capital, time. The OGD is an ecosystem where at least three key areas should be involved: government policy improvement (transparency, participation, cooperation, accountability); social benefits (quality of services, quality of life, cohesion) and economical growth (new business models for the digital economy). The paradigm is not so longer *eGovernment* but *we-Government* [12] with a strong engagements of all the stakeholders: citizens, public sector, private companies, no-profit organizations, associations. In this scenario we need to have a real FOIA act for enabling a paradigm beyond the transparency and for permitting the real participation in the management of the public data and things (smart cities). Considering all the above mentioned and explained reasons the Italian *Transparency Act* in our opinion is not a FOIA. It disregards the expectations and affect the Open Data.

In the following figure 1 we show how complex is the relationships between the different web portals of the public administration. The first column represents the *right to access* to the documents that includes also not public documents but that could be access from everybody with a *eligible interest*. An example of type of information usually under the *right to access*, present in the eGov service but not in the OGD portal, is the administrative procedure for the building authorization (e.g. label *B*) presented by a physical person. Some documents could be public and so they are published in the *Transparency Act* portal, e.g. label *A* is present in all the three portals. An example could be the list of a tender selection. In the second column there are all the documents archived in the eGov services, usually they are the outcome of the interaction between the web services provided by the public administration and the citizens/companies. Some of them could be transformed in OGD (e.g. public financial funding released to beneficiaries for reimbursing damages caused by environment disasters or earthquakes. The label *L* and *M* could be those typology of information). In the third column we have *Transparency Act* portal where there is the obligation to publish every public act. Also in this case a sub-set could be published also in open data modality. Finally the fourth column presents the Open Data official portal for releasing dataset with metadata, license, multiple format.

The overlapping is evident with the great confusion for the end-users and for the public servants.

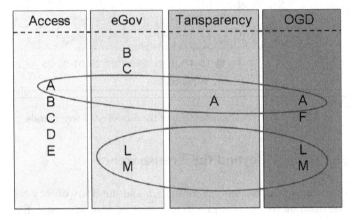

Fig. 2. Overlapping among different official web portals of the public administration

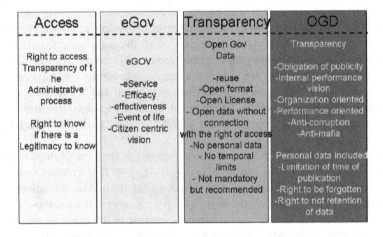

Fig. 3. Different characteristics of the four official web portals

The purposes of the four portals are different (see the figure 2) and we can see that there are strong overlapping (e.g. balance-sheets, employees data, tenders). The correct way, as to the opinion of the authors, is to design the web sites as output of an unique workflow of the data and document production oriented to the Open Data. If the OGA is a method of work and not only a method for publishing document and data, all the internal back-offices could be designed for producing output in Open Data.

5   Conclusions

Italy has a legal framework enabling and supporting OGD process in all the public administration and is a matter of fact that the web site data.gov.it has nowadays about 10.000 dataset. However the recent *Transparency Act* has affected the quality and the quantity of the dataset in the last six months. As referred *Transparency Act* is not FOIA and it is oriented to contrast bad practices in the public administration (corruption, mafia, nepotism, etc.) rather than helping and enabling the OGD, furthermore the solution proposed by the Transparency Decree is a web site old-style oriented. The theory of the authors, that *Transparency Act* affected the open data, was also tested using the "Compass of Transparency" for measuring the quality of the transparency area of the web site and we have also measured in the parallel open data portal how mach the two portals overlap (28,6% of overlapping). The solutions that some Municipality applies is to include inside of the open data portal a special session dedicated to the transparency act, but also this approach is not appropriate considering that some documents (e.g. contract, cv) should be removed according with the *right to be forgotten*. The authors maintain that should be appropriate and convenient to adopt a unique production workflow of data and document in open data format, with a semantic web metadata classification that could qualify the information and so to help the rendering in the correct portal and modality.

Secondly the author calculated also the relation between the quality of the "Compass of Transparency" indictor with the number of the dataset released by the administration in order to verify if it exists some positive correlation among the two phenomena. We have discovered that the open data paradigm rarely is adopted as a cultural opportunity to change the data quality management. This means that the open data staff is still isolated inside of the public administrations of Italy and it is remain a niche area, some time with marketing or political finalities. The real open data transformation, and so the real transparency, will be implemented when the open data principles are absorbed and digested by all the back-offices of the information systems working inside of the complex architecture of the intuitions and moreover by all the public servants as cultural behavior.

References

1. AA.VV.: Access Info Europe, the Open Knowledge Foundation, Beyond Access: Open Government Data and the Right to Re Use Public Information (January 7, 2011)
2. AA.VV., O'Reilly, T. Government as a platform, Open government: Collaboration, Transparency and Participation in Practice. O'Reilly Media, Inc. (2013)
3. AA.VV., UK Cabinet Office Open Data White Paper: Unleashing the Potential (June 2012)

4. Ashcroft, J.: The Freedom of Information Act. Office of the Attorney General, U.S. Department of Justice, http://www.gwu.edu/~nsarchiv/NSAEBB/NSAEBB84/Ashcroft%20Memorandum.pdf
5. Bertot, J.C., Jaeger, P.T., Grimes, K.M.: Using ICTs to create a culture of transparency: E-government and social media as openness and anti-corruption tools for societies. Government Information Quarterly 27(3), 264–271 (2010)
6. Darbishire, H.: Proactive transparency: The future of the right to information, World Bank Institute Governance Working Paper Series (2010)
7. Dawes, S.S., Helbig, N.: Information Strategies for Open Government: Challenges and Prospects for Deriving Public Value from Government Transparency. In: Wimmer, M.A., Chappelet, J.-L., Janssen, M., Scholl, H.J. (eds.) EGOV 2010. LNCS, vol. 6228, pp. 50–60. Springer, Heidelberg (2010)
8. E-Government, Survey 2012, E-Government for the People, eDepartment of Economic and Social Affairs, United Nations, New York (2012), http://unpan1.un.org/intradoc/groups/public/documents/un/unpan048065.pdf
9. Emanuel, R., Bauer, B.: The White House, Freedom of Information Act, http://www.whitehouse.gov/sites/default/files/rss_viewer/foia_memo_3-16-10.pdf
10. G8 Open Data Charter (June 18, 2013), https://www.gov.uk/government/publications/open-data-charter
11. Lathrop, D., Ruma, L.: Open Government: Collaboration, Transparency, and Participation in Practice. O'Reilly Media, Inc. (2010)
12. Linders, D.: From e-government to we-government: Defining a typology for citizen coproduction in the age of social media. Government Information Quarterly 29, 446–454 (2012)
13. Maurino, A., Spahiu, B., Viscusi, G., Batini, C.: Compliance with Open Government Data Policies: An Empirical Evaluation of Italian Local Public Administrations. Accepted for presentation at 2014 Pre-ECIS Workshop-Rethinking Information Systems in the Public Sector: Bridging Academia and Public service, Sponsored by AIS SIG eGovernment, Tel Aviv, Israel (June 8, 2014)
14. Ubaldi, B.: Open Government Data: Towards Empirical Analysis of Open Government Data Initiatives, OECD Working Papers on Public Governance, No. 22, OECD (2013), http://dx.doi.org/10.1787/5k46bj4f03s7-en
15. UNPAN Report, Department of Economic and Social Affairs, Division for Public Administration and Development Management, Guidelines on Open Government Data for Citizen Engagement, United Nations, New York (2013), http://workspace.unpan.org/sites/Internet/Documents/Guidelines%20on%20OGDCE%20May17%202013.pdf

Norms

16. Act of 7 August 1990, n. 241, Nuove norme in materia di procedimento amministrativo e di diritto di accesso ai documenti amministrativi, G.U. n. 192 (August 18, 1990), http://www.normattiva.it/uri-res/N2Ls?urn:nir:stato:legge:1990-08-07;241!vig=
17. Directive 2003/98/EC of the European Parliament and of the Council of 17 November 2003 on the re-use of public sector information, http://eur-lex.europa.eu/LexUriServ/LexUriServ.do?uri=CELEX:32003L0098:En:HTML

18. Legislative Decree of 7 March 2005, n. 82, Codice dell'Amministrazione Digitale, G.U. n. 112 (May 16, 2005), www.normattiva.it/uri-res/N2Ls?urn:nir:stato: decreto.legislativo:2005-03-07;82!vig=

19. Legislative Decree of 24 January 2006, n. 36, Attuazione della direttiva 2003/98/CE relativa al riutilizzo di documenti nel settore pubblico, G.U. n. 37 (March 14, 2006), www.normattiva.it/uri-res/N2Ls?urn:nir:stato:decreto. legislativo:2006-01-24;36!vig=

20. Legislative Decree of 27 January 2006, n. 69, Disposizioni sanzionatorie per la violazione del Regolamento (CE) n. 261/2004 che istituisce regole comuni in materia di compensazione ed assistenza ai passeggeri in caso di negato imbarco, di cancellazione del volo o di ritardo prolungato, G.U. n. 54 (March 6, 2006),
http://www.normattiva.it/uri-res/N2Ls?urn:nir:stato:decreto. legislativo:2006-01-27;69!vig=

21. Act of 18 June 2009, n. 69, Disposizioni per lo sviluppo economico, la semplificazione, la competitività nonché in materia di processo civile, G.U. n.140 (June 19, 2009), http://www.normattiva.it/uri- res/N2Ls?urn:nir:stato:legge:2009-06-18;69!vig=

22. Legislative Decree of 27 October 2009, n. 150, Attuazione della legge 4 marzo 2009, n. 15, in materia di ottimizzazione della produttività del lavoro pubblico e di efficienza e trasparenza delle pubbliche amministrazioni, G.U. n. 254 (October 31, 2009), http://www.normattiva.it/uri-res/N2Ls?urn:nir:stato:decreto. legislativo:2009-10-27;150!vig=

23. Directive 2013/37/EU of the European Parliament and of the Council of 26 June 2013 amending Directive 2003/98/EC on the re-use of public sector information, http://eur-lex.europa.eu/legal- content/EN/TXT/?uri=CELEX:32013L0037

24. Legislative Decree of 14 March 2013, n. 33, Riordino della disciplina riguardante gli obblighi di pubblicità, trasparenza e diffusione di informazioni da parte delle pubbliche amministrazioni, G.U. n. 80 (April 5, 2013), http://www.normattiva.it/uri- res/N2Ls?urn:nir:stato:decreto.legislativo:2013-03-14;33!vig=

Annex with Statistical Data

Data for creating the "Compass of Transparency" indicator

Municipality	Region of the municipality	Link to the open data portal	Link to the "PA transparent"	Num. datas et[13]	Percent age[14]
Comune di Albano	Lazio	http://dati.openda taground.it/comu nealbanolaziale	http://www.comune.albanolazial e.rm.it/flex/cm/pages/ServeBLO B.php/L/IT/IDPagina/170	557	98,6%
Comune di Bari	Puglia	http://opendata.c omune.bari.it/	http://www.comune.bari.it/portal /page/portal/bari/comune/ammi nistrazioneTrasparente	46	93,2%
Comune di Bologna	Emilia-Romagna	http://dati.comun e.bologna.it/	http://www.comune.bologna.it/tr asparenza/	533	94,6%

---

[13] Number of the dataset released by the municipality.

[14] Percentage of compliance calculated with the tool "Compass of Transparency"
http://www.magellanopa.it/bussola/page/overview.html

Comune di Borgomanero	Lombardia	http://www.comune.borgomanero.no.it/trasparenza/opendata.aspx	http://www.comune.borgomanero.no.it/trasparenza/trasparenza.aspx	7	95,9%
Comune di Busto Garolfo	Lombardia	http://www.comune.bustogarolfo.mi.it/index.php/opendata/	http://www.comune.bustogarolfo.mi.it/index.php/trasparente	6	95,9%
Comune di Cagliari	Sardegna	http://www.comune.cagliari.it/portale/it/opendata_info.page;jsessionid=6AC7856D951D3C7665E10CD06CFABA23		11	
Comune di Cesena	Emilia-Romagna	https://servizi.comune.cesena.fc.it/opendata/index.jsp	http://www.comune.cesena.fc.it/amministrazionetrasparente	265	91,9%
Comune di Cosenza	Calabria	http://www.comune.cosenza.it/pagina784_open-data.html	http://cosenza.etrasparenza.it/	9	95,9%
Comune di Faenza	Emilia-Romagna	http://www.comune.faenza.ra.it/Amministrazione/Bilancio/Open-data	http://www.comune.faenza.ra.it/Amministrazione/Amministrazione-trasparente	31	91,9%
Comune di Ferrara	Emilia-Romagna	http://www.comune.fe.it/index.phtml?id=3507	http://www.comune.fe.it/index.phtml?id=3590	28	93,2%
Comune di Firenze	Toscana	http://opendata.comune.fi.it/	http://www.comune.firenze.it/export/sites/retecivica/comune_firenze/comune/trasparenza/index.html	520	100,0%
Comune di La Spezia	Liguria	http://www.comune.laspezia.it/servizionline/open_data/	http://www.comune.laspezia.it/il comune/trasparenza	31	93,2%
Comune di Matera	Basilicata	http://dati.comune.matera.it	http://www.comune.matera.it/it/amministrazione-trasparente	49	91,9%
Comune di Milano	Lombardia	http://dati.comune.milano.it/	http://www.comune.milano.it/portale/wps/portal/CDM?WCM_GLOBAL_CONTEXT=/wps/wcm/connect/ContentLibrary/elenco+siti+tematici/elenco+siti+tematici/amministrazione+aperta/amministrazioneaperta_home	188	91,9%

Comune di Napoli	Campania	http://goo.gl/Mr658U	http://www.comune.napoli.it/flex/cm/pages/ServeBLOB.php/L/IT/IDPagina/21982	25	2,7%
Comune di Palermo	Sicilia	http://www.comune.palermo.it/opendata.php	http://www.comune.palermo.it/amministrazione_trasparente.php	316	93,2%
Comune di Pavia	Lombardia	http://goo.gl/bZBP9	http://www.comune.pv.it/site/home/il-comune/amministrazione-trasparente/home.html	35	95,9%
Comune di Piacenza	Emilia-Romagna	http://web2.comune.piacenza.it/comune/opendata	http://www.comune.piacenza.it/comune/trasparenza/amministrazionetrasparente	39	97,3%
Comune di Pioltello	Lombardia	http://goo.gl/6xRtR	http://www.comune.pioltello.mi.it/PortaleNet/portale/CadmoDriver_s_128378	12	91,9%
Comune di Pisa	Toscana	http://www.comune.pisa.it/it/progetto/8340/Open-data.html	http://www.comune.pisa.it/it/progetto/8867/Amministrazione-Trasparente.html	6	97,3%
Comune di Ravenna	Emilia-Romagna	http://opendata.comune.ra.it/	http://www.comune.ra.it/Amministrazione-Trasparente	23	93,2%
Comune di Reggio Calabria	Calabria	http://www.reggiocal.it/on-line/Home/AreeTematiche/OpenData.html	http://www.reggiocal.it/on-line/Home/AreeTematiche/AmministrazioneTrasparente.html	4	98,6%
Comune di Rimini	Emilia-Romagna	http://www.comune.rimini.it/filo_diretto/open_data/	http://www.comune.rimini.it/servizi/amministrazione_trasparente/	34	94,6%
Comune di Riva del Garda	Trentino-Alto Adige	http://goo.gl/gQ18Vz	http://www.comune.rivadelgarda.tn.it/Amministrazione-Trasparente	3	100,0%
Comune di Roncade	Veneto	http://goo.gl/fWlp7c	http://www.comune.roncade.tv.it/index.php?area=1&menu=327	9	91,9%
Comune di San Giuliano Milanese	Lombardia	http://www.opendata.sangiulianonline.it/	http://www.sangiulianonline.it/amministrazionetrasparente/atrasp/	54	97,3%
Comune di Sestu	Sardegna	http://www.comune.sestu.ca.it/open-data-sestu	http://www.comune.sestu.ca.it/amministrazione-trasparente	10	93,2%
Comune di Tolentino	Marche	http://www.comune.tolentino.mc.it/?page_id=37143	http://www.comune.tolentino.mc.it/?page_id=38146	10	97,3%

Comune di Torino	Piemonte	http://www.comune.torino.it/aperto/		256	
Comune di Trento	Trentino-Alto Adige	http://www.comu ne.trento.it/Comu nicazione/Traspa renza/Open-data	http://www.comune.trento.it/Co mune/Organizzazione-comunale/Amministrazione-trasparente	58	47,3%
Comune di Udine	Friluli-Venezia Giulia	http://goo.gl/pZtl o	http://www.comune.udine.it/ope ncms/opencms/release/Comun eUdine/comune/Nuovo_progett o_trasparenza/Disposizioni_ge nerali/Programma_per_traspare nza_e_integrita.html?style=1	84	0,0%
Comune di Venezia	Veneto	http://dati.venezi a.it/	http://www.comune.venezia.it/fl ex/cm/pages/ServeBLOB.php/L /IT/IDPagina/63887	75	95,9%
Comune di Verona	Veneto	http://www.comu ne.verona.it/nqco ntent.cfm?a_id=3 7264	http://portale.comune.verona.it/ nqcontent.cfm?a_id=37902	29	90,5%
Comune di Viadana	Lombardia	http://www.comune.viadana.mn.it/?q=content/infog en_altro_open-data		45	1,4%
Comune di Vicenza	Veneto	http://dati.comun e.vicenza.it/	http://www.comune.vicenza.it/a mministrazione/trasparente/	134	98,6%
			Total Dataset	3542	80,2%

Data for creating the figure 1.

Num.	Municipalities	Compass	Open Data
1	Comune di Albano	0,99	1,00
2	Comune di Bari	0,93	0,08
3	Comune di Bologna	0,95	0,96
4	Comune di Borgomanero	0,96	0,01
5	Comune di Busto Garolfo	0,96	0,01
6	Comune di Cagliari	-	0,01
7	Comune di Cesena	0,92	0,47
8	Comune di Cosenza	0,96	0,01
9	Comune di Faenza	0,92	0,05
10	Comune di Ferrara	0,93	0,05
11	Comune di Firenze	1,00	0,93
12	Comune di La Spezia	0,93	0,05
13	Comune di Matera	0,92	0,08
14	Comune di Milano	0,92	0,33
15	Comune di Napoli	0,03	0,04

16	Comune di Palermo	0,93	0,56
17	Comune di Pavia	0,96	0,06
18	Comune di Piacenza	0,97	0,06
19	Comune di Pioltello	0,92	0,02
20	Comune di Pisa	0,97	0,01
21	Comune di Ravenna	0,93	0,04
22	Comune di Reggio Calabria	0,99	0,00
23	Comune di Rimini	0,95	0,06
24	Comune di Riva del Garda	1,00	-
25	Comune di Roncade	0,92	0,01
26	Comune di San Giuliano Milanese	0,97	0,09
27	Comune di Sestu	0,93	0,01
28	Comune di Tolentino	0,97	0,01
29	Comune di Torino	-	0,46
30	Comune di Trento	0,47	0,10
31	Comune di Udine	-	0,15
32	Comune di Venezia	0,96	0,13
33	Comune di Verona	0,91	0,05
34	Comune di Viadana	0,01	0,08
35	Comune di Vicenza	0,99	0,24

Ahead in the G-clouds:
Policies, Deployment and Issues

Aliya Mukhametzhanova, Richard Harvey, and Dan Smith

University of East Anglia, Norwich, NR4 7TJ, UK
{a.mukhametzhanova,r.w.harvey,dan.smith}@uea.ac.uk
http://www.uea.ac.uk/computing

Abstract. Current governments are overhauling established administrative processes as they rapidly deploy e-government. In this paper we present examples of such development from two countries with well-developed e-government programmes: the United Kingdom and the Republic of Kazakhstan and provide a comparison of key aspects of e-government in each country. We observe that quite different policies often result in very similar outcomes. For example, in the area of g-cloud there are rather similar technologies, driven by completely different policies. We show how measures of e-government that focus on outputs may be missing a substantial part of the picture: why is this being done and what is the capacity of this technology to scale to social, economic and cultural environment of the country involved.

Keywords: e-government, cloud computing.

1 Introduction

E-government is rapidly becoming the default or only option to access many services, and rankings such as the UN e-government index [35] encourage the view that more e-government is a good thing. However, there are substantial capital investments needed to provide e-government at a time of cost pressures and also increasing concerns about privacy and data integrity. In this paper we show how these pressures have the potential to create a vicious circle of disenfranchised citizens who are mistrustful of e-government.

Our discussion starts with an overview of the background to e-government in our case study countries and the principal issues they face in developing comprehensive e-government services; our main focus is on government to citizen (G2C) interactions. We review these issues and the reasons why cloud-based services are a very popular solution to the cost problem. We then discuss reasons why G2C services may not be accessible by some people, including the newest concern which is electronic snooping. Next, we review measures of e-government effectiveness, focusing on the UN indices [35] and the eGEP [19] framework and the extent to which they reflect government priorities and citizens' perception of the quality of e-government services. Finally, we discuss the open issues and likely future developments.

A. Kő and E. Francesconi (Eds.): EGOVIS 2014, LNCS 8650, pp. 292–306, 2014.

The discussion is informed by case studies of the UK and Kazakhstan, based on interviews, survey and published information. Both countries have strong commitments to the development of e-government, but with very different motivations and backgrounds. The contrasts highlight a number of important common issues and differences, which we believe are not adequately reflected in e-government evaluation and development metrics.

2   E-government Context

In this section we briefly review a number of the key factors that help to determine the range and appropriateness of e-government strategies, as it is often easy to overlook the importance of physical, historical and cultural factors in constraining the range of feasible options available to individual governments.

2.1   Political and Economic Motivations

The UK has been at the forefront of the privatisation and outsourcing of government services over the last 30 years. Ministries are traditionally highly autonomous and are generally responsible for their own IT provision, with some central guidance. The overriding motivation for central government use of online services is to achieve greater efficiency and effectiveness, using cost savings as the primary success metric.

A major driver of e-government services for UK local government is the need for effective inter-agency working. The motivating use case is child protection, where numerous enquiries have found that a fundamental issue in most serious child abuse and neglect cases is a lack of coordination and sharing of data between agencies. This type of data sharing has been difficult because of concerns about privacy and translating the legal principles on data sharing – with and without prior consent – into operational procedures [1].

In the UK delivery of e-government services there seems to be a generally good awareness of the need to provide accessible services, but with little consideration of the needs of the digitally disenfranchised. What consideration there is of these groups' needs seems to be driven by service-specific, ad-hoc arrangements, often resulting from direct political intervention. Typically this results in the maintenance of existing channels, which may be at substantial cost, and with a less convenient service (e.g. less time to file paper-based returns).

The motivations for investment in e-government in Kazakhstan come from the desire to modernise the country's administrative systems, make the country attractive to external investors, and to connect a scattered population with a modern digital infrastructure. There is also a specific emphasis on e-government measures that improve its ranking in the UN e-government index.

E-government has a significant effect in reducing corruption [24], which has been widespread in Kazakhstan [13] and although substantial progress has been made [33], it is still 140th in the Corruption Perceptions Index[1]. An example of

---

[1] 2013 survey, http://www.transparency.org/country#KAZ

the benefits anticipated from e-government services is that in the early 2000s, to establish a construction company took an average of 156 days, and required applicants to produce 83 separate documents to obtain 12 different licences. Currently it takes less than a day to register a business, and under 70 days to obtain a construction licence. Making the process on-line and reducing its complexity has removed numerous opportunities for corruption.

2.2   Population Characteristics

The populations of economically developed regions such as the European Union are ageing, with 17.8% of the population over 65 and an average life expectancy of 76.4 for men and 82.4 for women. The largest recent change is in the increase of over 80s [20]. The population of emerging nations is generally much younger; for instance Kazakhstan has just 7.9% over 65, although this will increase substantially in the next decade [43]. Population density is an important consideration as many infrastructure costs are distance-based. The UK population is 63.7 million and the population density is 256 per km^2, making it one of the most densely populated countries in the world. Kazakhstan is the ninth largest country by surface area, with a population of 17.1 million^2 and a population density of 6.32 per km^2. These differences affect the feasibility of ICT infrastructure projects, in particular for cabling in less populated areas. In long-established major urban areas the density of activity and legacy pipes and cables can also increase costs considerably.

2.3   Administrative Culture

The differing economic histories of our case study countries affects their administrative cultures, and hence the feasible options for service development. Kazakhstan has a long history of highly centralised administration, with a very hierarchical structure, whereas the UK has a much mode devolved and informal structure. These differences are illustrated in the way outcomes from meetings are implemented. The UK model is that minutes are circulated and people act on those, but in Kazakhstan there is an expectation that specific written instructions will be issued, detailing the actions and timescales to all concerned.

There are also important differences between a mature telecommunications infrastructure where almost everybody can access broadband services in the UK, and Kazakhstan where in 2012 53% of the population were using the Internet [6] and there are are large sparsely populated areas with little telecommunications infrastructure. The growth in Internet use in Kazakhstan has been explosive, getting 40% of the population online in a three-year period from 2008–2011 (Fig. 2.3).

These differences in population, infrastructure, and administrative culture are reflected in the priorities for improving access to e-government services. The most frequently accessed services in our case study countries show a substantial

---

^{2} January 2014, http://www.stat.gov.kz

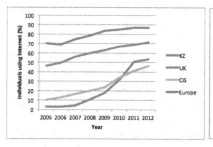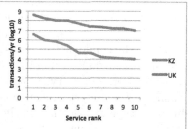

Fig. 1. (a) Individual Internet use [6] (b)E-government transaction volumes

difference of emphasis, between relatively infrequent transactions relating to real estate and life events in Kazakhstan[3], and tax-related transactions in the UK[4] (Table 1). The relative maturity of the two e-government systems can be seen

Table 1. Top 10 digital services

	UK	Kazakhstan
1	Share dealing tax	Certificate of residence
2	Payments made	Property ownership (title deed)
3	Customs	Certificate of pension contributions
4	Income Tax (PAYE)	Certificate that you are not a property owner
5	Tax payments received	Place a child on kindergarten waiting list
6	Check your own vehicle's details	Company registration
7	Tax a vehicle	Register a marriage
8	Notify Cattle Movements	Company information
9	VAT	Certificate of a company's registered activities
10	Income tax self assessment	Issue of certificate of convictions (if any)

in the fall-off of transaction volumes with rank (Fig. 2.3), where the UK rate of decrease is substantially less that of Kazakhstan. The number of e-government services in the UK is 766, but volume data is only available for 165 (2013 figures); in Kazakhstan there are 165 e-government services with a total of 20.7 million transactions (2012 figures) [37].

Many countries have very high formal literacy rates [18], but these can hide substantial numbers of people who are functionally illiterate, lacking the skills to deal with government documents and services – although reading skills are generally better than writing skills amongst those with low literacy. Definitions and estimates of functional illiteracy vary, but for example 16% of the UK population have literacy levels at or below those expected of an 11 year old [27].

---

[3] Data supplied by NITEC.

[4] https://www.gov.uk/performance/transactions-explorer/high-volume-services/by-transactions-per-year/descending

Classifications of e-government users and non-users in the UK and EU shows a core of mostly older people of lower socio-economic status, most of whom are likely to have had very limited exposure to computing technologies, who have neither the skills or the confidence to use e-government services, the "willing but unable". A second important group of non-users is those who additionally have no desire to use e-government services the "actively disengaged" [3], [42]. Other studies have shown that e-government non-users tend to be poorer, older and less well educated; they are also less likely to live in a household with children or to use internet search engines [12] [41]. These are not universal trends, as for example the government in Finland has closed many of its local offices, forcing service users to use online delivery channels: many of these (e.g. unemployed, pensioners) are lower income or older people [41].

3   G-clouds

Cloud computing [30] is frequently presented as an answer to rising demands for cost-control on government IT projects and to concerns about speed, scalability and accessibility of e-government. While there is strong evidence that cloud computing is more resilient, cheaper and more scalable than monolithic alternatives the questions on security, governance and accessibility remain only partly answered.

There is great interest in the adoption of cloud computing and a corresponding diversity of service offerings [47]. This interest is seen in governments who are attracted, not only to the cost savings, but also to the stated advantages of flexibility and elasticity. However, there are a number of long-standing challenges in cloud computing, principally related to service availability, security, and scalability [21] [45].

The proliferation of cloud services, offering a wide range of features, makes it difficult for inexperienced customers to choose suitable services [7]. For g-cloud purchasers, even if the pool of available services is restricted to approved suppliers, this can be daunting and is likely to influence new cloud customers towards monolithic contracts with large suppliers offering comprehensive solutions, support and training.

The UK has enthusiastically promoted g-clouds, using an Infrastructure as a Service (IaaS) model, primarily as a means of reducing government costs in four main areas.

First, by creating competition through multiple suppliers, many of whom are SMEs, providing commodity services. SMEs accounted for 56% by value and 61% by volume of UK g-cloud services by January 2014; the total spend on g-cloud contracts was GBP 92 million [8]. This reduces government's dependence on a small number of large suppliers who tend to have near-monopoly status. The estimated savings from UK g-cloud projects are GBP 100 million for the 2013-2014 year [8].

Second, IaaS allows government departments to buy additional capacity as needed and to share capacity. This achieves further savings, as the individual departments do not have to own infrastructure sufficient to meet their peak demands; this capacity would be unused for most of the time. The contract structure facilitates this, as all service provision and tendering is managed through a centralised portal[5], with six-monthly updates and short (renewable) contract durations for both service providers and g-cloud customers.

Third, by planning services to be digital by default and using the cost of transactions as an important metric for service planning. A major issue here is that many back-office processes are still paper-based (often for legal reasons), and migrating them is potentially expensive, disruptive and high risk.

Finally, g-cloud is a way of breaking down departmental information silos and providing integrated services, reducing coordination overheads and benefiting service users.

Many government activities require the analysis and summarisation of information from several sources, often with different departmental owners. In a cloud environment this can be much easier, but the choices between materialised and virtual approaches have significant impacts on security, privacy and data ownership issues. Virtualised approaches (mediator + wrapper) preserve data ownership and make it easier to control access to the underlying data, at the expense of additional query processing complexity. Materialised approaches (data warehouse) separate analysis and Business Intelligence processing from operational systems, but necessitate copying datasets to different locations. In many g-cloud applications, virtualised architectures have clear advantages [14].

Local government IT departments generally have less capacity and less experience with cloud-based solutions, and so are using large partnership contracts with major suppliers. For example, Norfolk County Council, which reckons itself to be a leader in local government IT provision[6], has a major contract with HP, Microsoft and Vodafone that covers all its planned cloud-based services. This approach is closer to Platform as a Service (PaaS) than IaaS, as it includes software and storage frameworks in addition to raw computation and storage services [47]. It is outside the UK g-cloud framework, which has only 37% of usage by local government.

The Kazakhstan government has taken a very different approach. The primary motivation, as in the UK, is to reduce software, hardware, infrastructure and support costs. The strategy of working with major multinational partners allows the Kazakhstan service providers to acquire expertise and start a g-cloud service; this is similar to the g-cloud strategy used by many UK local government authorities. The UK central government g-cloud model is not seen as viable as the local IT supply market is insufficiently developed and the underlying security model is different. A second major motivation is to increase the accessibility, transparency and openness of government information.

Most government IT services in Kazakhstan are provided through the National Information Technologies JSC (NITEC)[7]; although there are several other large

---

[5] http://ccs.cabinetoffice.gov.uk/

[6] http://www.computerweekly.com/news/2240212771/CIO-Interview-Norfolk-County-Councils-Tom-Baker-on-using-data-to-improve-public-services

[7] http://www.nitec.kz/index.php/en/pages/strategiya-i-missiya-kompanii

companies and consortia providing government IT services. Its g-cloud is being developed in partnership with Microsoft, using a Software as a Service (SaaS) model and private servers[8]. Work started in 2011 with a pilot implementation and requirements analysis of several ministries, with a programme of service development focusing on IaaS and SaaS services in the first phase, with a second stage planned to focus on SaaS and PaaS.

4   Privacy and Security

Trust in government, which varies widely between countries, has been shown to be a critical factor in citizens' willingness to use e-government services [34] [17]. Online privacy issues have recently become much more prominent, particularly in the USA, as a result of the disclosure of very large scale surveillance of electronic communications by security agencies, and documents suggesting that the US National Security Agency may have deliberately weakened an encryption algorithm used in a NIST-approved standard [32]. These have prompted widespread debate and public concern.

In the UK, g-cloud security levels are based on an assessment for each application of the impact on stakeholders of data being compromised. This is expressed as a business impact level (IL) [26], on a scale from IL0 (no impact) to IL6 (severe impact) for confidentiality, integrity and availability; the UK government also has a reputation dimension for internal use. The higher impact level applications are all managed in-house, so services from external providers are assessed from IL0 to IL3[9], based on ISO27001 assessments. In practice, this decentralised approach, coupled with the impact level classification, can mean that an IL0 project needing 100 email accounts could source them from a commodity supplier such as Google or Microsoft with no further risk assessment, but that a more sensitive IL2 project would need to carry out a detailed assessment before purchasing services.

Cloud computing has a number of security challenges that are particularly relevant to government services [36].

- Storage location. Many countries have data protection legislation that prohibits the processing of personal data in offshore locations unless it is done with explicit consent, or there are 'safe harbour' agreements in place (e.g. between the EU and USA) to ensure that data is processed in accordance with the origination country's legislation.
- Unauthorised access or disclosure of data to other cloud users or malicious third parties.

---

[8] http://mtc.gov.kz/index.php/en/o-ministerstve/mezhdunarodnoe-sotrudnichestvo/2367-memorandum-of-understanding-in-the-field-of-information-technologies-between-the-ministry-of-transport-and-communications-of-the-republic-of-kazakhstan-and-microsoft-kazakhstan-llp

[9] http://gcloud.civilservice.gov.uk/2012/08/23/accreditation-badges/

- Data leakage through logs and other records kept by cloud providers.
- Incompatible services and a lack of widely accepted standards to ensure interoperability.
- Robust audit trails to facilitate the tracking of security breaches.

The development of mobile computing brings some additional challenges for g-cloud services. Given the explosive growth in mobile broadband, rising from 18.5 (2007) to 74.8 (2013) active subscriptions per 100 inhabitants in the developed world [6], successful mobile services are increasingly essential for inclusive e-government. The principal additional issues are intermittent connections, communications channel vulnerabilities and the lack of security in smartphones [29] [23].

4.1 Authentication

A major issue in any large transactional system is the authentication of users: is this person who they claim to be?

In Kazakhstan, there is a strong administrative culture of signing, checking and counter-signing all administrative documents to establish chains of authentication and approval of content. This culture has been carried over to e-government processes, where the "wet ink" signature has been replaced by a public key infrastructure. This was initially rolled out to government employees and since 2008 has been extended to cover the whole population. In 2013 approximately 1.95 million individuals and 175,000 legal entities had been issued with digital keys, although less than half of them (930,000) were used during that year[10]. Citizens all have identity cards incorporating a digital signature, which are required for all interactions with government agencies. Kazakhstan was an early adopter of a national public key infrastructure (PKI) in 2006, using a locally developed standard, which has subsequently been migrated to an RSA-based system to allow integration with imported applications (e.g. MS Exchange Server). This provides a "ring of steel" around e-government activity.

The contrast with the UK is very sharp. There is no national identity card or unique national identifier for citizens; the strength of the opposition to a proposal to introduce identity cards in 2006 is a clear indication that this is politically impossible in the UK for the foreseeable future. The administrative culture tends to rely on memos and minutes of meetings as the basis for action, with the implicit assumption that communications from colleagues within the same department or other administrative unit are trustworthy. The "ring of steel" approach has been adopted by the UK National Health Service to connect its sites (approximately 11,000 in England); unfortunately it has been plagued by a history of data leaks and security issues (e.g. [11]).

UK e-government services are designed to require authentication only when there are risks in not doing so. For instance, no authentication is normally required for citizens paying money to government agencies. Central government

---

[10] http://pki.gov.kz/index.php/en/o-kompanii

is developing authentication mechanisms using the OAuth (IETF RFC 58490) framework and institutions such as banks as sources of credentials, since they already have well-trusted and reasonably secure online services. The department making the first authentication request for each user will pay the authenticator, but subsequent requests, by any department, will not be charged for.

These authentication issues are shared with local government, but with no common view of the solutions. For instance, Norfolk County Council is considering a two-factor identification system using keypads to generate single-use keys and a password, or a 'triangulated' approach, using multiple identifiers to authenticate users of its systems. The council plans to address the problem of not having a natural unique identifier for its citizens by linking records using a composite of National Insurance number[11], combined with name, date of birth, address and any other identifying information contained in existing records. Matches may be made manually, or probabilistically, with a high matching threshold for acceptance.

5   Indices and Evaluation Measures

E-government indices are widespread and measure a number of aspects. All the major indices have multiple dimensions, covering preparedness, e-government services, and e-governance issues (participation and transparency), which are conflated into a single measure; this can be problematic. Preparedness measures that are based on technological factors (e.g. number of TV sets, wired broadband connections) are susceptible to rapid change as new technologies and interaction modalities are adopted – particularly smartphones and mobile broadband. E-government service measures frequently do not distinguish between informational and transactional provision. Measures of participation typically cover a very wide range of activities, from the publication of ministerial speeches, through the public provision of analysable datasets, to the ability to email an elected representative.

The most widely used indices are the UN [5], EIU (see [22] for a discussion of its construction) and Accenture [9] indices; many evaluation frameworks have been proposed and there is a good comparative literature (e.g. [38] [40] [39] [28].

In the remainder of this section we discuss the UN index and the eGEP evaluation model in more detail, as they are influential and illustrative of the key issues for e-government indices and evaluation frameworks.

The UN measures on e-government development and e-government participation [5] are widely used and are often policy drivers. The results are based on biennial surveys conducted since 2002 and use the methods described in [2]. The e-government survey is essential a box-ticking exercise in which various features (such as the presence of a Chief Information Officer) are given scores. The scores are opinions based on a panel of researchers "...instructed and trained to assume the mind-set of an average citizen user in assessing each site". It combines things that would be very apparent to the average citizen (e.g. how easy it is

---

[11] Equivalent to a Social Security number elsewhere.

to use government websites) and things which are completely opaque (e.g. the existence of a national IT strategy). There are three scores, s_1, the online service index, s_2, the telecommunication infrastructure index and s_3, the human capital index. A factor analysis of the 11 component measures used to derive the UN e-government development index, shows that the index is unidimensional, and does not seem to distinguish between the online service, telecommunications infrastructure and human capital groups of measures [46].

The UN e-participation index is similar, with three components which measure the extent to which governments: share information with their citizens, allow interaction with stakeholders, and allow decisions to be made by citizens. Given the age of the survey (2002) it is not surprising that issues such as privacy and social cost are not addressed.

In Kazakhstan, corruption has been endemic in many areas and one of the motivations for adopting e-government has been to reduce petty corruption and bribe-taking. There is good evidence that e-government progress is linked to reductions in corruption. The use of e-government indices as predictors of corruption, measured by the Corruption Perceptions Index (CPI)[12], shows that the EIU index is the best predictor, closely followed by the UN index and the ITU ICT Development Index [4], with correlations of 0.95-0.85 [24]. The position of Kazakhstan in the UN index (38th in 2012) and its position in the CPI (140th in 2013) suggests that there may be a marked lag between the indices when countries are rapidly developing their e-government infrastructure.

As economic motivations are a major driver of e-government service development it is important to evaluate the economic impacts, both in terms of savings to government and benefits to citizens and businesses. The eGEP analytical model has been developed in an EU context, based on several different national evaluation methodologies from Denmark, France, Germany and the UK [19]. For benchmarking comparisons it identifies a set of 11 indicators in five groups (Table 5). These attempt to capture three dimensions of public value: the user as taxpayer, the user as citizen and voter, and the user as consumer. These measures are designed to be easily collectable, and indicative of the underlying dimensions ("signposts") of efficiency, effectiveness and democracy. Their grouping is intended to allow easy modification and the substitution of individual measures without compromising the index.

These dimensions are clearly relevant to the relatively mature economies of the EU, but do not capture the desire and need of emerging economies to demonstrate their progressive characteristics and hence attract inward investment. For these countries, the UN index is a more visible indicator of the modernisation of government.

6   Discussion

E-government is a priority area for many governments and the UN league tables appear to be interpreted by some as a sign of success (meaning a good rank in

---

[12] http://cpi.transparency.org/cpi2013/

Table 2. eGEP Indicators (after [19])

	Inclusion
1.1	Usage of eGovernment services by socially disadvantaged groups
1.2	Public websites' degree of compliance with accessibility standards
	Effectiveness and efficiency
2.1	Users satisfaction with eGovernment services
2.2	Amount of information requested from citizens and businesses
2.3	Number of transactions fully completed online
	Meeting customer needs
3.1	Proportion of public procurement available electronically
3.2	Proportion of public procurement carried out electronically
	Trusted services
4.1	Number of transactional public services with legally binding eID
4.2	Number of functioning online services
	Participation
5.1	eParticipation sophistication index
5.2	Number of unique users of online forums

the UN e-government list) or failure (a poor rank). However it is important to be clear what these league tables measure and what they do not measure (cloud adoption for example).

The measures of e-government tend to focus on the breadth and depth of online services rather than their cost or their accessibility. For example, the UN survey says nothing about the likelihood of a citizen's information being misused by their own government or another party. Nor does it cover the extent to which citizens can choose to opt out of e-government. This topic is certainly of interest to the UN Draft Resolution on the right to privacy in the digital age (A/C.3/68/L.45/Rev.1) so this is one of the rare cases in which the legislators are ahead of the statisticians.

A noteworthy trend is a reduction in e-participation scores among the countries with the best e-government practices [16]. Our informal suspicion is that many citizen to government channels and discussion forums – in common with almost all other open internet discussion channels – are hijacked by small numbers of highly opinionated participants, coordinated politically motivated campaigns and "sock puppets" (which may be controlled from another country[13]).

The provision of large-scale mission-critical services on cloud platforms is a recent development, and ensuring the management of the later stages (e.g. scale changes, termination) of these contracts is a challenge to cloud providers [31]. For large-scale and cross-border services an open issue is the coordination or aggregation of services from different providers [31]. This may be easier in g-clouds than in many other environments because the purchasing power and capacity of government to drive innovation can be used to facilitate the development and deployment of coordination mechanisms for cloud services. As government

---

[13] E.g., http://www.theguardian.com/technology/2011/mar/17/us-spy-operation-social-networks

agencies and authorities gain experience with cloud-based solutions it will be interesting to see if monolithic SaaS contracts with suppliers will remain optimal. The return of mainframe-like migration issues associated with changes of cloud provider is anticipated where cloud users have made extensive use of providers' proprietary software frameworks [44] or 'sticky services' [36]. Several commentators have suggested that open source collaborations to provide common functionality – especially for local government – should provide good quality cost-efficient services. This is more likely in countries (e.g. France) where there is already strong encouragement of inter-authority collaboration.

As services move online, they are increasingly attractive targets of criminal activity, making authentication of transactions critical to the continued effectiveness of e-government. Most countries have national identity cards which can be used as the vehicle for a national PKI; but the the X.509 [25] and EU passport [15] problems illustrate their vulnerability to security flaws. The federated approach, used in the UK, relies on third parties, which opens up a large number of potential weaknesses, but if the trust ecosystem is diverse, a single weakness is less likely to have a major impact. A significant aspect of any e-government policy must be to avoid perverse incentives which weaken security – Anderson's discussion is still pertinent [10].

7   Conclusions

The priorities and perceived benefits of developments in e-government vary greatly between countries and administrations. At a national level, we can see a clear and strong motivation for emerging economies to use progress in e-government as a surrogate to demonstrate their receptiveness to inward investment, and of the ease of doing business. Mature economies are less concerned with external perceptions of their e-government and tend to focus more on the effectiveness and efficiency of government services.

There are strong constraints imposed on e-government strategies by the telecommunications infrastructure, citizens' receptiveness to online services, trust in government agencies, and political and administrative traditions. These can lead to superficially very similar e-government programmes behind which lie very different sets of policies, motivations and priorities.

The major open issues we have identified are digital inclusiveness, service usability, trust and authentication.

There are powerful economic drivers for g-cloud adoption: first as cloud-based services reduce server and infrastructure costs and second as a means of facilitating data integration for analysis and service delivery. The strategies for developing g-cloud services are largely determined by the existing cloud computing expertise within government and by the maturity of the local IT sector.

The existing international measures for e-government capture some of these concerns, but do not look at the underlying technical infrastructures and – particularly the UN index – are easily susceptible to gaming by a country wishing to improve its ranking. It would be easy to underestimate the importance of these indices to emerging economies, as they are clearly seen as important external indicators of an advanced infrastructure, administrative modernisation and good governance. In contrast, the more developed economies seem to pay little attention to such measures, except as benchmarks for the efficiency and effectiveness of their own services.

Acknowledgments. This paper was written while Aliya Mukhametzhanova was a visiting scientist at the University of East Anglia under the Kazakh 'Bolashak' scholarship scheme. We wish to thank Nick Walsh and the Cabinet Office, Simon Smith and Norfolk County Council, Ruslan Ensebayev, Asem Jexembayeva, Kaiyr Shayakhmetov and NITEC for their inputs to this work.

References

1. Child protection – information sharing project (2009), http://systems.hscic.gov.uk/cpis
2. Statistical annexe (2010), http://www.unpan1.un.org/intradoc/groups/public/documents/un-dpadm/unpan038858.pdf
3. Digital landscape research (2012), https://www.gov.uk/government/publications/digital-landscape-research/digital-landscape-research
4. Measuring the information society 2012 (2012), http://www.itu.int/ITU-D/ict/publications/idi/
5. United Nations E-Government survey 2012 (2012), http://unpan3.un.org/egovkb/global_reports/12report.htm
6. ICT facts and figures 2013 (2013), http://www.itu.int/en/ITU-D/Statistics/Pages/stat/default.aspx
7. Cloud computing service composition: A systematic literature review. Expert Sys. with Applications 41(8), 3809–3824 (2014)
8. Sales information (2014), http://gcloud.civilservice.gov.uk/about/sales-information/
9. Accenture: From e-government to e-governance (2009), http://nstore.accenture.com/egovernance/main_egov3.html
10. Anderson, R.: Why information security is hard – an economic perspective. In: ACSAC 2001, pp. 358–365. IEEE (2001)
11. Anderson, R., Brown, I., Dowty, T., Inglesant, P., Heath, W., Sasse, A.: Database state. Joseph Rowntree Reform Trust, York (2009)
12. Bélanger, F., Carter, L.: The impact of the digital divide on e-government use. CACM 52(4), 132–135 (2009)
13. Bhuiyan, S.H.: Trajectories of e-government implementation for public sector service delivery in Kazakhstan. Int. J. Public Admin. 34(9), 604–615 (2011), http://www.tandfonline.com/doi/abs/10.1080/01900692.2011.586894
14. Breil, A., Hitzelberger, P., Da Silva Carvalho, P., Feltz, F.: Exploring data integration strategies for public sector cloud solutions. In: Kő, A., Leitner, C., Leitold, H., Prosser, A. (eds.) EGOVIS/EDEM 2012. LNCS, vol. 7452, pp. 271–278. Springer, Heidelberg (2012), http://dx.doi.org/10.1007/978-3-642-32701-8_24
15. Buchmann, N., Baier, H.: Towards a more secure and scalable verifying PKI of eMRTD. In: Katsikas, S., Agudo, I. (eds.) EuroPKI 2013. LNCS, vol. 8341, pp. 102–118. Springer, Heidelberg (2014)

16. Calista, D.J., Melitski, J., Holzer, M., Manoharan, A.: Digitized government in worldwide municipalities between 2003 and 2007. Int. J. Public Admin. 33(12-13), 588–600 (2013)
17. Carter, L., Weerakkody, V.: E-government adoption: A cultural comparison. Info. Systems Frontiers 10(4), 473–482 (2008)
18. CIA: World Factbook (2013), https://www.cia.gov/library/publications/the-world-factbook/fields/2103.html
19. Codagnone, C., Boccardelli, P., Leone, M.: egovernment economics project (eGEP): Measurement framework. Tech. rep., EC DG Info. Society & Media (2006)
20. DG Employment Social Affairs and Inclusion and Eurostat: Older, more numerous and diverse Europeans: Demographics report 2010. Tech. rep., European Commission (2011)
21. Dillon, T., Wu, C., Chang, E.: Cloud computing: issues and challenges. In: IEEE AINA, pp. 27–33. IEEE (2010)
22. Fathey, M., Othman, I.: Refining e-government readiness index by cloud computing. Jurnal Teknologi 65(1) (2013)
23. Fernando, N., Loke, S.W., Rahayu, W.: Mobile cloud computing: A survey. Future Generation Computer Systems 29(1), 84–106 (2013)
24. Grönlund, Å., Flygare, A.-M.: The effect of eGovernment on corruption: Measuring robustness of indexes. In: Andersen, K.N., Francesconi, E., Grönlund, Å., van Engers, T.M. (eds.) EGOVIS 2011. LNCS, vol. 6866, pp. 235–248. Springer, Heidelberg (2011)
25. Holz, R., Braun, L., Kammenhuber, N., Carle, G.: The SSL landscape: a thorough analysis of the x.509 PKI using active and passive measurements. In: Proc. ACM SIGCOMM Conf. on Internet Measurement, pp. 427–444. ACM (2011)
26. HMG IA: Technical risk assessment (2009), http://www.cesg.gov.uk/publications/Documents/is1_risk_management.pdf
27. Jama, D., Dugdale, G.: Literacy: State of the nation. Tech. rep. (2012), http://www.literacytrust.org.uk/research/nlt_research/2364_literacy_state_of_the_nation
28. Janssen, D., Rotthier, S., Snijkers, K.: If you measure it they will score: An assessment of international egovernment benchmarking. Info. Polity 9(3), 121–130 (2004)
29. Khan, A.N., Mat Kiah, M., Khan, S.U., Madani, S.A.: Towards secure mobile cloud computing: a survey. Future Generation Computer Systems 29(5), 1278–1299 (2013)
30. Mell, P., Grance, T.: The NIST definition of cloud computing. Tech. Rep. NIST Special Publication 800-145, National Institutes of Science and Technology (2011)
31. Moreno-Vozmediano, R., Montero, R.S., Llorente, I.M.: Key challenges in cloud computing: Enabling the future internet of services. IEEE Internet Computing 17(4), 18–25 (2013)
32. Newman, L.: Can you trust NIST? IEEE Spectrum (2013), http://spectrum.ieee.org/telecom/security/can-you-trust-nist
33. OECD Anti-Corruption Network for Eastern Europe and Central Asia: Kazakhstan monitoring report. Tech. rep., OECD (2011)
34. Plattfaut, R., Kohlborn, T., Hofmann, S., Beverungen, D., Niehaves, B., Rackers, M., Becker, J.: Unravelling (e-) government channel selection: A quantitative analysis of individual customer preferences in Germany and Australia. In: IEEE HICSS, pp. 1983–1991. IEEE (2013)
35. UN Public Administration Programme: UN E-Government development database (2012), http://unpan3.un.org/egovkb/

36. Rong, C., Nguyen, S.T., Jaatun, M.G.: Beyond lightning: A survey on security challenges in cloud computing. Computers & Elec. Eng. 39(1), 47–54 (2013)
37. Sarsenov, S.: Development by means of it innovations. Kazakhstan International Business Magazine 2013(4) (2013),
    http://www.investkz.com/en/journals/87/740.html
38. Seri, P., Bianchi, A., Matteucci, N.: Diffusion and usage of public e-services in Europe: An assessment of country level indicators and drivers (2013)
39. Stanimirovic, D., Jukic, T., Nograsek, J., Vintar, M.: Analysis of the methodologies for evaluation of E-government policies. In: Scholl, H.J., Janssen, M., Wimmer, M.A., Moe, C.E., Flak, L.S. (eds.) EGOV 2012. LNCS, vol. 7443, pp. 234–245. Springer, Heidelberg (2012)
40. Stanimirovic, D., Vintar, M.: A critical insight into the evaluation of e-government policies: Reflections on the concept of public interest. Int. J. Advances in Life Sciences 5(1 and 2), 52–65 (2013)
41. Taipale, S.: The use of e-government services and the internet: The role of socio-demographic, economic and geographical predictors. Telecommunications Policy 37(4), 413–422 (2013)
42. Tinholt, D., Colclough, G., Oudmaijer, S., Carrara, W., Tol, T., Schouten, M., van der Linden, N., Cattaneo, G., Aguzzi, S., Jacquet, L., Kerschot, H., van Gompel, R., Steyaert, J., Millard, J., Schindler, R.: Public services online: Digital by default or by detour (2013), doi:10.2759/13072
43. Tolesh, F.A.: The population history of Kazakhstan. In: European Population Conference (2012), http://epc2012.princeton.edu/papers/120586.pdf
44. Ward, J.S., Barker, A.: A cloud computing survey: Developments and future trends in infrastructure as a service computing. arXiv preprint arXiv:1306.1394 (2013)
45. Wei, Y., Blake, M.B.: Service-oriented computing and cloud computing: Challenges and opportunities. IEEE Internet Computing 14(6) (2010)
46. Whitmore, A.: A statistical analysis of the construction of the United Nations e-government development index. Government Info. Quarterly 29(1), 68–75 (2012)
47. Zhang, Q., Cheng, L., Boutaba, R.: Cloud computing: state-of-the-art and research challenges. J. Internet Services and Applications 1(1), 7–18 (2010)

Author Index